THE TYRANNY OF OPINION

THE TYRANNY OF OPINION

Honor in the Construction of the Mexican Public Sphere

Pablo Piccato

Duke University Press Durham and London

2010

© 2010 Duke University Press
All rights reserved
Printed in the United States of America on acid-free paper ∞
Designed by C. H. Westmoreland
Typeset in Warnock with Whitman display
by Keystone Typesetting, Inc.

Library of Congress Cataloging-in-Publication Data
Piccato, Pablo.
The tyranny of opinion : honor in the construction of
the Mexican public sphere / Pablo Piccato.
p. cm.
Includes bibliographical references and index.
ISBN 978-0-8223-4653-1 (cloth : alk. paper)
ISBN 978-0-8223-4645-6 (pbk. : alk. paper)
1. Honor—Political aspects—Mexico. 2. Mexico—Politics
and government—1861–1867. 3. Mexico—Politics and
government—1867–1910. 4. Mexico—Politics and
government—1910–1946. I. Title.
F 1233.P52 2010
972.08—dc22   2009039110

*para Xóchitl, Catalina,
Aída, Ana y Cecilia*

¡Cómo lucha la conciencia
con la virtud que se abate!
¡Qué gran campo de combate
el campo de la existencia!

(How conscience fights
against declining virtue!
What a great field of combat
is the field of existence)

"VELA," JUAN DE DIOS PEZA

En la estación del metro Balderas,
ahí quedó embarrada mi reputación.

(At the Balderas subway station,
where my reputation was stained.)

"METRO BALDERAS," EL TRI AND
ROCKDRIGO GONZÁLEZ

CONTENTS

ACKNOWLEDGMENTS

I incurred many debts writing this book. The main one I owe to my wife, Xóchitl, and my daughters, Catalina and Aída. I could not have done it without their patience, enthusiasm, and, when necessary, critical distance. Xóchitl read the manuscript multiple times and made it better. They are behind this book's attempt to understand gender inequality in Mexico. Also essential were the interest and encouragement of my family (my mother, Ana, brother Antonio and sister Cecilia, and the Medina family), and my friends. Theo Hernández conveyed some of the oral tradition about duels and fencing. My colleagues in the Department of History at Columbia University, with their high expectations and continuing support, made this book a reality. I name Ellen Baker, Elizabeth Blackmar, John Coatsworth, Victoria de Grazia, Alice Kessler-Harris, Adam Kosto, Claudio Lomnitz, Gregory Mann, Nara Milanich, Caterina Pizzigoni, but the community was broader. I had the privilege of working with students who contributed to this book in many ways: Victoria Basualdo, Ira Beltrán, Antonio Espinosa, Keith Hernández, Claudine Leysinger, Vania Markarian, Thomas Rath, and Pilar Zazueta. In Argentina, Mexico, and the United States fellow historians Claudia Agostoni, Paula Alonso, Silvia Arrom, Jacinto Barrera Bassols, Carlos Forment, Sandra Gayol, Renato González Mello, Paul Gootenberg, Luis Fernando Granados, Carlos Illades, Gilbert Joseph, Sandra Lauderdale-Graham, Elías José Palti, Erika Pani, David Parker, Ariel Rodríguez Kuri, Paul Ross, Cristina Sacristán, Elisa Speckman, Eric Van Young, and Richard Warren read and commented on chapters. I appreciate the great generosity of Elisa, David, Renato, and Rafael Barajas, El Fisgón. I would like this book to be a testimony to Charles A. Hale's integrity as a scholar and to his legacy as a Mexicanist. Two reading groups, in New York and New Haven, gave me detailed and deep comments: Amy Chazkel, Federico Finchelstein, Joanne Freeman, Seth Fein, Christopher Hill, Thomas Klubock, Nara and Caterina. Colleagues working on the history of women and gender in Mexico, Gabriela Cano, María Teresa Fernández Aceves, Ana Lau Jaivén, Víctor Macías González, Susie Porter, Carmen Ramos Escandón, and Mary Kay Vaughan, deserve special gratitude for their rigorous interest in the work of a newcomer. The participation of all of these persons is invaluable, and I wish I could describe the different ways in which each one made this book better. Robert Buffington read early versions and then the entire manuscript. Our conversations, his friendship and generosity, are essential to this book. Substantive research support came from Ana Rodríguez and Antonio Piccato, and from Laura Rojas and Lourdes Salgado, whose own promising careers as historians I might have delayed as much as I tried to help. All I can say is that their participation is more important than they imagine. I am thankful for the editorial work of Valerie Millholand, Miriam Angress, Mark Mastromarino, Lawrence Kenney, and an anonymous reader at Duke University Press.

Parts of chapter 7 were published in the *Journal of Social History*. In Mexico I presented papers related to this book at the Escuela Nacional de Antropología e Historia, the Instituto Nacional de Antropología e Historia, the Universidad Autónoma Metropolitana-Ixtapalapa, the Universidad Michoacana de San Nicolás Hidalgo, the Universidad Nacional Autónoma de México, and the Universidad Veracruzana; in Argentina, at the Universidad Nacional General Sarmiento and the Universidad de San Andrés; and in the United States, at Yale University, Georgia State University, the University of Iowa, the University of Chicago, the New School, Northwestern University, and many AHA and LASA conferences. Funding came from the University of Texas at Austin and Columbia University, in the United States; and from the Centro de Estudios Avanzados en Antropología Social and the Consejo Nacional para la Ciencia y la Tecnología, in Mexico. I am also grateful to the staffs of the Archivo General de la Nación, the Archivo Histórico del Distrito Federal, the Archivo Judicial de Michoacán, the libraries of the Universidad Iberoamericana, the Hemeroteca and Biblioteca Nacional, in Mexico; and to the libraries at the University of Texas at Austin, Columbia University, Yale University, the Library of Congress, and the New York Public Library.

Honor and the Public Sphere
in the Republican Era

In the eyes of Mexican public men who came of age after the triumph of the republic in 1867, the story of Santos Degollado contained a stark lesson about the power of public opinion. Justo Sierra, for example, wrote in 1900 that Degollado's honor was "transparent like the purest crystal." This reputation, more than military credentials, led President Benito Juárez to appoint Degollado in 1858 to coordinate the military effort against the conservatives. In 1860, however, as the war raged on and the liberal army became starved for funds, Degollado authorized the seizure of a private remittance of cash owned by foreign nationals on its way from Zacatecas to Europe. He explained to a subordinate the pragmatic reasons for his decision: "The blood of our soldiers is more precious than their dishonor."[1] Yet taking the money to rescue the Republic, Degollado later stated in a manifesto, meant the sacrifice of "my reputation, delivering it to mockery and slander." "I killed my name," he added, "destroyed my future," and sacrificed his family's patrimony—"a pure name to bequeath my children." Demoted and arrested by his own party, Degollado requested his release in order to avenge the death of Melchor Ocampo, another heroic leader of his generation. Congress, according to Sierra, granted the authorization, understanding the "death-wish" that soon thereafter pushed Degollado to succumb at the hands of conservative guerrilla forces.[2] His contemporaries recognized that his life had been a struggle against adversity, defamation, and, possibly, betrayal; his sacrifice spared the country international troubles and Juárez the embarrassment of the trial of a fellow liberal; his death, in sum, was meant to bring together "public men . . . so that their isolated sacrifices would not be unfruitful."[3]

Thirty-seven years his junior, Sierra described Degollado's "dilemma between staining the immaculate honor of his life and the need to save the revolution's life" as a sign of national crisis. It was a tragic moment that Mexicans, in both Degollado's and Sierra's generation, experienced in terms of honor—of someone's reputation and self-worth. Degollado (figure 1) could not escape his time: a bookish administrator, he had accepted his military post because it was "unseemly for a man of honor to turn his back on danger hoping to extend his life, when living in slavery means to die and to lose public esteem, something worse than all deaths." As he publicly recognized, however, he had committed theft—"Who can deceive his own *conciencia* [conscience]?" he asked. "Public esteem" was inevitably linked to "conscience."[4] In a parallel remembrance of that crisis, Jacinto Pallares, another member of Sierra's generation, equated honor and the self: the jurist Ignacio L. Vallarta had sacrificed for the liberal cause his "moral persona, that is, reputation . . . the essence of the self, everything that constitutes our moral and social individuality . . . our honor."[5]

This book is about the legacy of Degollado, Vallarta, Ocampo, and other heroes who, according to Sierra, "carried the pen, the word, and the sword" in the struggle against the enemies of the nation. It explores, in other words, how in their writings and in their lives Sierra and his contemporaries tried to untangle the links between public esteem and conscience. As civil war ceased to be the main mechanism to solve political disputes, Mexican public men sought to build a stable polity in the shadow of those elders' tragic combination of national and personal honor.[6] The material task was daunting: The state was bankrupt, infrastructure nonexistent, agriculture decimated, and foreign creditors reluctant to come back. Institutionally it was not easier: The country was still fragmented, with regional caciques and military caudillos constantly challenging the authority of the federal government and competing claims of ethnicity and religion still undermining modern citizenship. In order to tackle both aspects of reconstruction, the republican political

1. Santos
Degollado.
© 422389. CND.
SINAFO-Fototeca
Nacional del
INAH.

elite fashioned itself as a new group of *hombres de palabra*—men who
kept their word and answered to the obligations of credit and authority,
but whose political authority came from their ability to speak in the name
of public opinion rather than from their military accomplishments.[7]
   A diverse historiography has focused on the political aspects of the
restoration of republican order. The main narratives center on the careers of a few men or the expansion of the state under Juárez and Porfirio
Díaz.[8] There was always, however, another dimension to the process
of state building, one that has attracted no historiographical attention,
namely, the search for a generally accepted, stable notion of honor that
would legitimize the political elite's claim to embody the virtues of the
nation and to speak in its name. Thus, this book is not about nationalism,
always a collective proposition, but about its individual counterpart:
without honor there could be no patriotism. Setting the tone of politics
during the decisive decades of reconstruction, these hombres de palabra
imagined themselves as courageous representatives of public opinion
who argued about common matters in the public sphere, which they

conceived, without naming it, as a level field of reason and mutual respect. A masculine realm, too. Those who lacked the military credentials of the older generation tried to build their reputation by other means. As a young lawyer Sierra seized the opportunity to help quell a rebellion in the capital in 1871. As he passed by, carbine on his shoulder, he told a friend he was seeking, in reality, to "take lessons on epic vertigo."[9] Following words and deeds, this book posits that masculine honor was the keystone in the building of a modern public sphere in Mexico.

Mexico's political history offered Justo Sierra and his contemporaries contrasting examples of politicians' morality. The opposite of Santos Degollado and the moral baseline of national history was Antonio López de Santa Anna (1794–1876). Santa Anna earned a heroic reputation defending the integrity of the nation against the monarchical pretensions of Agustín de Iturbide's First Empire in 1824, the Spanish in 1829, the French in 1838 at Veracruz (at the cost of his left leg), and Texans and Americans, in 1836 and 1846–47, respectively. He capitalized on that reputation: On each of the eleven occasions he was president, Santa Anna seized power with the support of whatever sector of the political elite, conservative or liberal, happened to need him at the time. He was inevitable because he could quickly mobilize enough troops to unseat any government or prevent others from doing so. His reckless optimism as a commander, which most other officers wisely lacked, inspired the army's rank and file; but his failures against northern enemies exhibited the great cost of his leadership in terms of blood, money, and territory. According to the writer Heriberto Frías, he caused "so much shame" to the "desdichada patria" (unhappy motherland).[10] According to Sierra, Santa Anna had a "magnetic power" to attract support: his heroism, eloquence, trust in providence, and taste for cockfights, gambling, and women were dear to the plebes, yet their love was fickle: "After endless threats of divorce they returned to him, they hated him for a moment and adored him always." In a famous episode, a crowd in Mexico City disinterred his leg (which he had buried with honors) and dragged it through the streets of the capital. It was never a proper marriage: "The Republic was that seducer's lover; he left her stained."[11]

Santa Anna lived politics like a cockfight, in which the sheer thrill of winning and losing fed the urge to play. As fast as he was to earn political and social capital in the form of loans and honors, he was quicker to squander both through military or administrative ineptitude or in "deep seizures of melancholy and chronic sybaritism" during which he gambled away national and personal moneys.[12] Credit was indeed the main problem of a Mexican state that emerged from independence bankrupt: cash was urgently needed to pay for restless troops, interests were increasingly onerous, and forced loans were politically risky in a vicious cycle that made Santa Anna all the more necessary. By the time liberals rose against him, under the Plan de Ayutla in 1854, he had come to personify the old political vices, even the temptation of monarchism, that younger generations sought to eradicate.[13]

The best defense against Santannista turbulence was the law itself. Liberals formalized their institutional project in the Constitution of 1857, which established equality among citizens, a federal and representative political system, and an ambitious project of secularization and disentailment of corporative property—both the Church's and that of indigenous communities. In contrast to Santa Anna, Benito Juárez (1806–72) represented republican virtues (figure 2). In Sierra's admiring biography, Juárez's solemn image conveyed self-control and honesty and incarnated "the mysterious prestige of the law."[14] He rose from humble indigenous origins in the southern state of Oaxaca to the Supreme Court and the presidency, which he claimed in 1858 after President Ignacio Comonfort reneged on the Constitution. Juárez lead an itinerant government and the liberal army in a three-year war against the conservatives. After defeating them in early 1861, Juárez returned to Mexico City only to face French, Spanish, and English forces that had landed in Veracruz to claim payment of Mexico's foreign debt. When negotiations proved futile, the French army invaded most of the country, forcing Juárez to return to his peripatetic leadership. In 1864, the French and the conservatives installed Archduke Maximilian, an Austrian-born Hapsburg, on the throne of the so-called Second Empire. Maximilian (1832–67) wrapped his unsteady authority in the trappings of royalty but soon betrayed some modernizing leanings; his conservative supporters nevertheless maintained control of his regime. Facing constant military and guerrilla resistance in Mexico and mounting U.S. pressure after the end of the Civil War, Napoleon III withdrew his troops, and Maximilian was shortly thereafter defeated and executed—another famous example of Juárez's inflexible enforcement of the law. This "second independence," in which Juárez "saved the nation's honor," meant the definitive establishment of a republican system. He was elected president in 1867, reelected in 1870, and remained in the presidency until his death. His successor, Sebastián Lerdo de Tejada (1827–89), was a brilliant mind but an aloof politician unable to fill Juárez's shoes.[15]

During the period between 1867 and 1876, best known as the República Restaurada (Restored Republic), liberals set out to channel political conflict away from violence. Lawyers, writers, administrators, soldiers, and congressmen tried to replace social and political turbulence with modern republicanism. The "emancipation of thought" achieved by the liberal victory meant that public life felt the full impact of romanticism, followed shortly, as we will see in chapter 4, by positivism. A generation "glorious because of its civic virtues" was replaced by another one "anxious for the bloodless laurels that are conquered in times of peace." But the law alone was not enough to contain disagreements, and characters did not change as fast as institutions: conspiracies and rebellions continued, while political debates in the press and Congress reached unprecedented levels of virulence. These difficult but democratic times saw an expansion of the public realm and a politicization of everyday life that resembled, in the eyes of contemporaries, stories of the French Revolution. Such developments created a central role for the "political country," the small but growing number of educated men who had political clout, represented public opinion, and were willing to expose their reputation to criticism. As the following pages will show, these men's construction of their political authority was both a public and a personal enterprise.[16] We can measure the growth, both in size and maturity, of the political country in the 1860s by comparing the diverse and cantankerous federal congresses under Juárez and Lerdo de Tejada with Maximilian's submissive court and his *Libro secreto*, the rather short list of men whose names he needed to remember in order to assemble a loyal political elite.[17]

Porfirio Díaz, who overthrew Lerdo de Tejada in 1876 and went on to control national politics for three decades, was a liberal caudillo who promised to end caudillismo. A hero of the recent wars, also from Oaxaca, Díaz (1830–1915) lost in his electoral run against Juárez in 1867 (figure 3). From then on, he did not stop conspiring until he gained power. In one manifesto, he accused the government of refusing to reach out to "honorable officials" and promised to bring together "patriots of pure honesty." The decision to rebel, he claimed, had been difficult: He did not seek power and had retired to private life, yet felt compelled by an

2. Benito Juárez. © 18548. CND. SINAFO-Fototeca Nacional del INAH.

obligation "to my fellows in the armed service" who, like him, were not satisfied with the rewards earned through their sacrifice.[18] His regime combined an ostensible respect for the Constitution with a shrewd manipulation of clientelism and violence. Díaz used both to cement a pyramid of loyalties that, by the last decade of the century, consisted of a disciplined, nationwide political class. Against the contentious manner of the República Restaurada, this new political elite came to identify honor with bourgeois discipline and credit worthiness. Díaz's contradictory legacy, between the law and the personal guarantee of order, became evident when he resigned in 1911, forced by a revolution that espoused the same slogan he had used against Juárez and Lerdo de Tejada: "No reelection."

Why is this history of shame, integrity, and loyalty relevant? Modern historians generally explain the República Restaurada's precarious order and the Porfiriato's unprecedented stability as the result of the gradual consolidation of networks of patronage. These networks blended public

3. Porfirio Díaz.
© 34360. CND.
SINAFO-Fototeca
Nacional del INAH.

and private interests and allowed a minority to profit from the impressive, albeit unequally distributed, economic expansion that peace enabled. But that image of order and progress emerges clearly only in the last decades of the century.[19] If we look at the difficult transition between 1867 and the 1890s, the chronological focus of this book, growth and loyalty were not yet strong enough to explain the consolidation of republicanism. The cultural transformation examined in the following chapters is defined by the transition from a romantic notion of the self (which found in Degollado a paradigm and in Sierra an authorized if critical interpreter) to a new ethical model associated with positivism. Romanticism is a recurrent theme in the following pages, but less as a purely aesthetic style than as a moral paradigm that uneasily combined the cult of honor, the authenticity of subjective feelings, and the relentless need to engage publicity. Against views of romanticism as the precursor to twentieth-century antirational politics, this book will show the deep impact of romantic attitudes (like Bohemia, examined in chapters 2 and 3), literary genres (such as oratory, examined in chapter 4), and individualism (discussed in chapter 6) on the construction of a public sphere premised on a level field of reason.

This book, in other words, tries to describe a broad process shaped by multiple cultural crosscurrents. The standard chronology of the emergence and development of romanticism in Europe is of little help in understanding its Mexican counterpart. We lack studies that identify romanticism and establish a framework of its use in Mexico, particularly if we try to see beyond specific literary genres. Plays by Alexandre Dumas and others reached broad audiences in Mexico early on, as in Spain, but the impact of the romantic movement became clear there only in the second half of the century. Not until then did literary critics see the struggle against academic classicism as one of the "great combats" waged by Victor Hugo and those under his influence, mainly through poetry and the public figure of the poet but also in its association with emancipatory causes.[20] Jean-Jacques Rousseau was certainly read from the early years of the national period, and the poetry and example of George Gordon, Lord Byron, had a later impact, often associated with heroic individualism. In a parallel appropriation, midcentury authors in Mexico developed the moral and social implications of a romanticism inflected by spiritual values, the collectivist social thought of early European socialism, and a critical view of the dangers of passion.[21] Yet, although romantics generally engaged politics, there was no single ideological value for romanticism or common intellectual genealogy. In France it was identified with liberalism, although in other countries of Europe the associations could be as diverse as the political and social values associated with nationalism.

My book traces a strand of Mexican romanticism that is less tangible as a chapter of literary history but more broadly, if diffusely, spread as a set of dispositions and ethical ideas. Its periodization is equally blurry, yet it finds a mythical moment in the heroics of the Three-Year and Intervention wars and an apogee in the República Restaurada, precisely when it begins to be criticized by attitudes and moral ideas connected to positivist and more authoritarian persuasions. This ethical dimension of romanticism, albeit ignored by most studies of the movement, can be documented through the historical ideas of the early phases of romantic thought—the return to a world of chivalry portrayed by Walter Scott, but also the sense of a "spirit of the age" that determines the mission of individuals. In this strand, romanticism can be best comprehended as a series of cases rather than an explicit moral system. Through the stories of artists and poets, often retrieved in their own words, romanticism came to mean love of nature, rejection of the materialism of society, heroic individualism, and political commitment. Romanticism was a choice of destiny, the construction of a self defined in the struggle against the outside world and its contradictions, and, universally, as an expression of freedom and passion.[22]

Romanticism in Mexico came to be identified with individualism and revolutionary hopes, the influence of Hugo, and the engagement of writers on behalf of the liberal cause. But it was a late romanticism, one in which socioeconomic and political realities led to an emphasis on autonomous consciousness and agonic struggle. Poets especially were leaders of the people and "unacknowledged legislators of the world," in the words of Percy Bysshe Shelley, and their task was to couple literary emancipation with the democratic fight for social and political freedoms: in Mexico, as we will see, poets were legislators literally. It was a struggle, in other words, that pitched autonomous consciousness against the contradictions of the age.[23]

From this perspective, we can distinguish two phases of romanticism. The first is represented by poets-legislators whose lives were heroically intertwined with the nation's struggle for survival: "Your soil was my flesh," sang Guillermo Prieto to the beloved *patria*. They embraced public life as their mission. The liberal intellectual and sometime poet Francisco Zarco formulated the mission of the Mexican man of letters in 1851 as the romantic struggle against adversity: "We should not look at politics with disdain, nor think of it as an arid field, without flowers and fragrances. No: there is also beauty in it, there are also noble feelings, there is also the need [in politics] to dispel errors, uproot somber concerns, spread interesting truths, and overthrow the altars in which crime is adored and the human race is sacrificed."[24] Zarco's generation put the romantic embrace of emotions at the service of patriotism. Their poetry was superficial, but history demanded much from them, and they were followed by an era of prosaic politicians and rigorous poets.[25] In a second phase of Mexican romanticism as an ethical model, poets were still legislators, but their public role was fraught with tensions. Sincerity, over mission, became the paramount quality of poetry. For poets like Díaz Mirón and Sierra, however, public life was full of bitter personal dilemmas. The poet was no longer one with the patria, but an autonomous figure, sometimes an outcast, always, in any case, forced to deal with politics in the quest to achieve the romantic goal of "the internal made external."[26]

Public men of the times thus engaged with differing emphases the ethical aspects of romanticism to justify a republican regime. To do so, they built a theory of honor that placed it at the center of public life yet also addressed the dilemmas of conscience. The attempt may sound anachronistic or contradictory today, but it made clear sense to them because they knew exactly what they were talking about when they talked about honor, so much so that they made it the compass of their lives and of their sense of historical mission. In order to understand the casuistry behind this theory of honor (the examples that conveyed what I call the romantic ethos), we should focus less on stable ideals and concepts and more on the practical dimension of historically situated local and personal interactions.[27]

The category's very historical development, however, weaves social practices and normative meanings that cannot be reduced to the impact of romanticism. Honor, scholars agree, was the keystone of class relations in Latin America before independence. For Ramón A. Gutiérrez, "honor-status" ordered "along a single vertical continuum" people with or without honor. This external "hierarchical ethos" combined with religious belief and the baroque concern about status display to lessen the importance of the ethical prescriptions of "honor-virtue."[28] Colonial honor corresponded directly with race and class: rank was sanctioned by *honra* (the social acknowledgment of virtue), the privilege of a small group associated with the crown or belonging to patrician families. Sex was also integral to the ascription of *honores*: women were passive about honor because they could lose it but not gain it, as men did when they fought for their *pundonor* (point of honor). Control over the sexual behavior of women (their *honestidad*) was a key signifier of patriarchal honor, thus blurring the divide between the public and private realms. The Church sanctioned female virtue and male *honradez* (honesty) as integral to social difference.[29] Honor also articulated the interconnections between state power, patrician families, and personal careers.[30] Neatly organized *cuadros de casta* (casta paintings), in which each combination of racial components in a nuclear family had a specific offspring, posited that classifications based on miscegenation corresponded with those of morality. Nostalgia for colonial hierarchies survived independence through the memories of old families for whom wealth was less important than the chastity of women and the integrity of "honorable and honest" men (*hombres honorables y honrados*).[31]

Colonial historians dwelt on a version of honor, put forward by anthropologists of the Mediterranean since the 1960s, which focused on the relations between men and women in premodern societies. If we look back at that frame of reference, however, we can still find useful parallels with modern views of honor. In Julian Pitt-Rivers's classic definition, honor is someone's "estimation of his own worth, his *claim* to pride, but it is also the acknowledgment of that claim, his excellence recognized by society, his *right* to pride."[32] The definition encompasses the two dimensions of Santos Degollado's honor: one public, which he called public esteem, the other subjective, his conscience. Pitt-Rivers underlines "*claim*" and "*right*" and a few pages later notes the importance of public opinion in distributing honor. He echoes Degollado's vocabulary and the definition of *honor* in nineteenth-century Spanish dictionaries, which included the obligations imposed by opinion.[33] When applying the Mediterranean framework to colonial Latin America, however, historians have not considered the dialogical nature of opinion. By emphasizing its sexual dimension and top-down ascription of honor, they imply that negotiations in the public realm were less relevant.

This choice has made colonialists' use of honor liable to the same critique scholars have directed at the Mediterranean model. Objections center on the rigidity of the honor/shame, male/female, and public/private dichotomies that lie at the base of the analyses of Pitt-Rivers and others. Since the 1980s anthropologists have noted that honor/shame was not a schema that worked well in all Mediterranean societies, especially when urbanization changed the roles of women; evidence also challenged the rigid divide between the worlds of men and women and women's passivity, suggesting the need to go beyond chastity as the central value of femininity.[34] Michael Herzfeld took this critique further and argued that honor was a mistaken focus for research, a poor translation for local vocabularies, and a circular category that obscured more than it revealed. He proposed transcending questions about honor with questions about gender and masculinity in particular.[35] Another problem with the Mediterranean model is its historical definition. Talking about the Mediterranean as a homogeneous cultural area neglects many religious, economic, and political differences and implies a value-laden distinction between modern and primitive societies.[36] William B. Taylor has noticed the shortcomings of this framework in examining relations beyond small groups of equals; honor was an important element of political and social life in colonial cities—thus highlighting the role of public opinion.[37]

Contemporary ethnography of Latin American societies and recent explorations of gender in the colonial period show actors' ambivalent attitudes toward honor and shame, the limited role of the state in enforcing such ideas, and the frequency of sexual and violent practices that depart from normative views. Often based on studies centered on women, these works uncover subterranean challenges to patriarchal moral codes.[38] In colonial times, even the notion of purity of blood had locally specific meanings, while legalistic, less violent, and "highly public and ritualized" ways of pursuing honor predominated, giving a more active role to women than the one observed in mid-twentieth-century Mediterranean rural societies. Honor remains central, but it has multiple meanings according to time and place; it could hardly stay the same during three hundred years of colonialism: from conquistadors' forceful claim for royal rewards to wealthy families' acquisition of titles in the Bourbon era, much evolved in the cultural process of colonial domination over ethnically complex societies.[39] Thanks to recent colonial studies that use judicial sources to examine everyday life, it is possible now to combine the emphasis on local, "traditional," predominantly oral societies with a more explicit discussion of the political, thus "modern," problem of defining, distributing, and protecting citizens' honor.

After independence, the connection between social hierarchies and honor lost most of its legal force yet remained relevant. Honor as family patrimony was still a central political consideration. The name that Degollado sacrificed represented social capital that could mobilize political resources—and not only among the upper strata of society.[40] Honra, for example, was important for newly equalized Afro-Mexican citizens. As the state no longer adjudicated disputes about status or provided a stable framework for social difference, citizens experienced a greater need to go public in the defense of reputation and a renewed susceptibility to gossip that often translated into political battles.[41] New research on notions and practices of citizenship in Mexico and Latin America is illuminating. As groups that had been marginalized by the colonial order saw new opportunities to exert their influence, they embraced their new identity as *ciudadanos* (citizens), while preserving the importance of their local status as *vecinos* (literally neighbors). Sara Chambers has shown how public debates around the question of who was a respectable citizen in Peru were articulated in the language of honor.[42] The increasing concern about citizenship reinforced rather than challenged the continuing exclusion of women from the public sphere. In the nineteenth-century political and literary world of men, women were relevant only insofar as they could damage a man's reputation through their sexual misbehavior or become the passionate point of reference in man-to-man relationships. The alleged natural exclusion of women has justified a lesser concern with women as historical actors in the political literature about modern Mexico—an attitude that recent studies are beginning to redress. While criticisms of the Mediterranean framework stress a gendered perspective, studies of contemporary society are replacing prevalent views of the hypermasculine, violent *macho* with more nuanced views of men's place in households, where women are becoming increasingly important as wage earners. Other studies probe homosociality and homoerotic desire in literary depictions of "the Mexican."[43]

Assessing the impact of modern notions of honor on politics means placing gender, particularly the construction of masculinities, at the heart of the analysis. Rather than posit a dualistic opposition of masculinity and femininity, however, a productive tack is to ask how manhood was gained and secured with the participation of men *and* women. Although *the public* in independent Latin America came to mean the modern realm of civil society, against the old corporative order, the implications of public opinion for personal honor remained strong and gendered. In the new tyrannical rule of opinion, reason and taste could judge public men's actions and words, and the impact of such judgment on their lives was often much more tangible than abstract debates about sovereignty. While women were normatively reduced to the private realm, public opinion was the territory on which men defended their reputation. It is not surprising that the praise of heroes became one of the first functions of journalism in postindependent Mexico.[44]

Republican masculinity, however, was only partly a symbolic construction. The crafting of manhood involved the training of masculine sensibilities and bodies. Most notably, violence was an obligation of men that further justified the absence of women from public debates.[45] Questions about manhood and its performance are useful if one is to move beyond a purely negative understanding of female exclusion: What makes a man good at being a man? What are the gendered characteristics that allow access to public discussions and spaces where honor is judged? To answer such questions it is not essential to give the same weight as object of research to men as to women. Mexican women during the modern period were capable of having much the same concern about honor as men, yet their presence in the public record is limited: seldom autonomous, they often appear as the point of reference, a shared affective focus, in triangles where two men thought of themselves as free agents— a favorite situation of Mexican romanticism.[46]

My book, therefore, addresses the uses of honor that emerged along with citizenship and the national state's increasing willingness to regulate both. Such political transformation of honor was possible because the category, in its modern instantiation, became explicitly linked with that of public opinion. Even as he warned enemies in the battlefield of impending attack or punishment, Degollado used to appeal to "the irresistible weight of public opinion" in support of the Constitution of 1857.[47] In the following pages, the notion of public opinion will refer not to the sociological fact retrieved by contemporary opinion polls but to a historically contested category. In this, I follow historians of enlightened and revolutionary Europe who have looked at public opinion as a modern

Public opinion

cultural product, a term of political discourse that became prominent as men of letters sought to carve out and legitimate a space of influence under absolutism. Because it referred only to the reading public, yet was also a signifier of popular sovereignty, public opinion was fraught with contradictions and increasingly exposed to the authoritarian tendencies of the state.[48]

For Mexican ideologues of the national period, public opinion was a transparent expression of popular sovereignty, a clear marker of modernity. They described it as supreme, although lacking an institutional incarnation: it was alternatively claimed by the press, Congress, and parties. Public opinion ideally was unanimous and often discussed in opposition to the many, equally valid but often erroneous "opinions" of citizens and the amorphous masses.[49] The attributes of modern citizenship were not evenly distributed among the population. The solution to this paradox of equality was to redefine citizenship in order to stress education and the use of reason as virtues that made the vocal sectors of the population, the hombres de palabra, representatives of the silent people.[50] Recent scholarship has examined public opinion in elite political discourse rather than in the practices that constituted political life across class divides. The work of Elías José Palti offers a framework for the history of the uses of public opinion in nineteenth-century Latin America, from the "juridical" to the "proselytist" model.[51] Thinking of public opinion only as an abstraction or a rhetorical trope fails to address the implicit and explicit rules that justified its exclusive use by political elites and misses the changes undergone by the category during the nineteenth century. Works on artisan and peasant groups suggest that other groups could make an honorable claim to speak to and in the name of public opinion.[52] As the following chapters will show, the most interesting negotiation of these categories was engaged in largely by in-between groups with strong cultural, rather than economic, capital, such as students, journalists, and merchants.

Scholarly views of public opinion tend to miss a vital function contained in the original formulation of the idea: to judge the reputation of citizens and to shape mores. Rousseau spoke about public opinion when trying to account for the duplicity between the private and the public that civilization had imposed on men. In his view, others' opinion was a powerful agent of moralization that judged individuals and changed their habits like no law or government could; small cities were more democratic than territorial nations because in them "particulars are always under the eyes of the public." Theater, he believed, was the opposite of such democracy, as it constrained the gaze and movements of the public, fostering the duplicity of person and character. The best tool to preserve the coherence of morality and politics was not art but the free interaction of citizens expressed in public opinion.[53] For Rousseau, in sum, public opinion could not be divided into two separate functions—the expression of the common will versus the evaluation of reputations. Public opinion, he wrote in *The Social Contract*, is "engraved in the hearts of citizens. It is the true constitution of the state. I am speaking of mores, customs, and especially of opinion."[54]

Jürgen Habermas's theory of the historical development of the public sphere provides an organizing framework to integrate questions about public opinion and honor. In Habermas's words, "The bourgeois public sphere may be conceived above all as the sphere of private people come together as a public; . . . people's public use of their reason."[55] In his now-classic *The Structural Transformation of the Public Sphere* (1962), Habermas explored both the normative aspects of the public sphere and the structural conditions that brought about its emergence. Rather than considering the public sphere as a stable, well-defined product of the development of capitalism or as a normative ideal contained in inchoate form in modern politics, I use Habermas's ideas as a guide for an inclusive analysis of processes that encompassed social, economic, and cultural phenomena. His and other researchers' critical study of the uses of public opinion demonstrated the interactions, within that public sphere, of private interests, state policies, and social practices such as reading and conversation. Even the "reason" underlying public opinion, often used to exclude women from public debates, can be the object of historical examination.[56] Historical studies inspired by Habermas have stressed taking a close look at political and cultural discussions occurring in supposedly public spaces, usually restricted to the elite, such as newspapers, tea salons, market gossip, and the like.[57] Critical works have noted the exclusions that made possible a specifically bourgeois public sphere. Although the original formulation did not explore those negative aspects of the development of the public sphere, the model itself remains useful when enriched by perspectives that involve gender, ethnic, and colonial variables.[58]

This book tests the theory outlined above by hypothesizing that the link between honor and public opinion is the key to understanding the practices and attitudes of the men who shaped the public sphere in modern Mexico. Questions raised by this hypothesis include the basic sociological facts about the membership of an elite defined by education as well as political influence. Who were these men and, from a cultural point of view, what authorized them to speak in the name of the rest of society? While honor presided over the rules of the debates in which they engaged, honor also encoded the exclusion or subordinated inclusion of women and the poor and demarcated the public sphere in opposition to the private or intimate spheres. I will explore that opposition not as the stable premise of culture but as a continually changing product of public life. However, rather than a structural examination of the formation of elites, this will be a history of practices in the public sphere.

The following chapters, therefore, study diverse uses of honor as specific aspects of the development of the public sphere. Part I historicizes public opinion and places it in a social context. Chapter 1 follows legislation of the press from independence and shows that the protection of reputations was the principal concern in the evolution of institutional limits to freedom of speech. The specific version of honor discussed in this chapter pertains to the internal realm of privacy and its ambivalent relation with the court of public opinion. Press juries, the central institution in that story, revealed how urban citizenship implied neighbors' active involvement in judging the reputations of victims of press abuse. Press juries occupied a unique place between municipal and judicial authorities that reflected the urban dimension of the public sphere created by the modern press. The chapter also sets the scene for the rest of the book: cities, mostly Mexico City, and specific areas at that: downtown, certain streets and corners, restaurants. This urban space, however, also signified the national space, by nurturing public opinion through vecinos' protection of the press. Chapter 2 examines the ethics of journalists in the República Restaurada and early Porfiriato. Journalists cast themselves as representatives of public opinion, even while public opinion constantly judged their own reputations. The chapter analyzes honor as a good that represented public men's social capital and journalism's cultural prestige in the market of reputations that was publicity. Journalists bartered their honor and that of their peers, engaging in polemics, attacks, and duels that, as in the case of Justo Sierra's brother, Santiago, could have fatal consequences.

The second part of the book examines the expansion of such tyrannical public opinion, from institutional structures into less formal realms. It examines the wielding of honor and honra in the parliamentary and popular rebellion against the renegotiation of the nation's foreign debt in 1884. Exploring the premises of nationalism as an ideology, part II looks at the equation of the reputation and self-esteem of specific social actors and those of the nation. Chapter 3 focuses on congressmen and the increasing political value of rhetoric. Public men could speak in the name of society and the nation because they mastered the skills and rules of oratory. Romantic oratory, above all, articulated the combination of passion, intellect, and courage that hombres de palabra saw at the center of their self-definition. Representation, for them, was less about elections and regional origins than about character and the ability to wage dialectical battles at trials and in legislatures; debate, rather than party discipline, legitimized their decisions. Chapter 4 looks at students, the main factor in the popular mobilization that forced the government to withdraw the project of debt renegotiation. They occupied a special place in Mexican society: because bohemian life gave a favorable, albeit age-specific sanction to poverty, students could establish close relations with the city's lower classes and with women of all strata, while cultivating the social networks that would eventually allow them to become members of the elite. Memoirs of student life exhibit the role of sexual practices in building the masculinity of public men. The chapter also describes how the debates and demonstrations over the nation's honor created an opening in the public sphere through which popular groups, humbler vecinos and respectable ladies, engaged in more direct interaction with politicians. The urban space defined in the first part reveals itself to be permeable: the *populacho* (roughly, common folk) invaded the central city, expanded politics spatially, engaged directly with government officers, and broke implicit boundaries in their claim to participate in an expanding public sphere.

Part III describes the painstaking disassociation of honor and public opinion through state intervention—or how Mexican public men narrowed the public sphere by countering the tyranny of opinion with the opinion of a tyrant. Chapter 5 examines the enactment of a new legal framework to protect modern honor as an individual right, moving away from the agonic individualism of romantics. A central step in this process was the abolition of press juries and the Díaz regime's subsequent use of the protection of individual honor in penal legislation as a tool to harass independent journalists. Honor emerges as a pretext for censorship, yet the legal debates reveal a shift in perceptions of honor toward an increasingly stark delimitation of the political elite's public and private life. Reputation becomes an objective good of measurable economic value. Chapter 6 further documents this shift by analyzing cases of defamation in penal courts of Morelia, Michoacán, and Mexico City. The chapter shows the multiple ways in which citizens attacked and defended honor, its continuing social currency, and the growing formalization of the conflicts it generated. People of all classes but most frequently working women used the penal protection of reputations to defend their place in urban settings that uneasily combined anonymity and the gossipy life of work, home, and *barrio*.

The legacy of Santos Degollado was a symbol of the tyranny of opinion, but also much more. Fifteen years after his death, the son of Benito Juárez challenged Degollado's son, Mariano, to a duel because of an article Mariano had written about the real causes of his father's death. Mariano was acutely concerned about his father's good name but declined the challenge because dueling was against his principles. Were it not for the negotiation between their representatives, however, he would have exposed himself to a violent reaction from Juárez's son.[59] Chapter 7 examines the practice of dueling at the moment of its greatest popularity and the beginning of its decline. It analyzes the point of honor, the intersection of the judgment of public opinion and public men's intimate evaluation of their own worth. Dueling is the clearest demonstration of the linkage between masculinity and the exclusions of the Mexican public sphere. In its heyday during the last decades of the nineteenth century dueling channeled the role of violence in the disciplining of public men when war was decreasingly an option for acquiring prestige. Foreign and national codes of honor built a technology of disciplined bodies and respectable, even state-protected, rituals of courage. A few men died, if only to remind others, as Santos Degollado did, that it was "unseemly for a man of honor to turn his back on danger hoping to extend his life."

The deadly concern about reputation seems hardly the raw material for a history of the public sphere. Some aspects of this book would seem to undermine Habermas's emphasis on "people's public use of their reason" and to challenge a specifically Mexican claim of participation in that historical process. The following pages will indeed focus on conflict rather than on universal agreements, paying attention to violence, passion, gossip, challenges to the classic order, and even actors' inner doubts about their value as men. Yet, as I will try to prove, doubts and conflicts responded to rules that, even if in many cases implicit, upon reflection contemporaries saw as rational. By setting the conditions for communication among the broadest conceivable group of voices, those implicit rules were building, to use today's words, a "sphere of private people come together as a public," or, in the words of the actors in the following chapters, the rule of public opinion.

The conceivable universe of voices has changed since then. Exclusions were central to the continuity of dialogue in the nineteenth century, yet they have for a long time thereafter remained tacit. It seemed natural then to prevent the uneducated, including the poor but also women, from publicly using their reason. This book shows how that exclusion was not natural but historically contingent. The public sphere built during the Porfiriato relied on elite men's constant struggle to maintain a monopoly over honor and public opinion. This led to an increasingly authoritarian regime, one that eventually succumbed to democratic revolt and massive popular mobilization. The revolution of 1910 brought forth a new cohort of men with guns who were less worried than Degollado about the harmony between public esteem and conscience in the construction of sovereignty.

PART I

Travails of Opinion

Reading the daily press in nineteenth-century Mexico could be a turbulent activity. A caricature from *La Linterna* in 1877 shows Porfirio Díaz's political allies responding with alarm, eyes wide open and falling over backward, when confronted by a manifesto by Sebastián Lerdo de Tejada that Díaz is showing them (figure 4).[1] Other testimonies show men and women reacting to publications with anxiety, rage, or sadness. A character in a novel by Emilio Rabasa reads an article about his persona and says, "My head [was] about to explode, . . . rage, fear, shame and desperation drove me crazy . . . and a wave of blood reached my face."[2]

Passion, however, has been absent from the historiography on the Mexican press, which subsumed writers and readers under a narrative centered on political power; they may have been interesting characters, but they mattered only as supporters, speakers for, or adversaries of caudillos and bureaucrats. For these, in turn, the only quandary in their relation with the press was that between *pan o palo* (bread and stick), whether to feed it or repress it.[3] Freedom and censorship thus became the two poles of any history of the press. In the best study of journalists and politics during the República Restaurada and Porfiriato, the lengthy *Historia moderna de México*, Daniel Cosío Villegas transferred contemporaneous concerns about authoritarianism under the Cold War–era Partido Revolucionario Institucional (PRI) into a liberal narrative in

4. Response of the Tuxtepecanos to a manifesto by Lerdo. *La
Linterna*, 2 April 1877. Reproduced in Barajas Durán, *El País de
"el llorón."* Used by permission of the author.

which the struggle of nineteenth-century journalists against repressive
governments was a pivotal chapter in the history of democracy. "All of
Mexican liberal political writing," he claims, can be seen as the efforts of
"a small group of men" who were "the only road to the advancement of
Mexican democracy."[4] This liberal teleology made for a powerful narrative but circumvented the methodological problem of having journalists be the heroes of a struggle in which their own newspapers were
the privileged documentary record. Cosío Villegas claimed to have performed the first "modern," systematic reading of nineteenth-century
newspapers, yet he did not problematize the multiple roles of journalists
as judges, actors, victims, and witnesses of political life since, he argued,
they consistently wrote about important themes and never hid their
ideological and personal sympathies. Quoting and paraphrasing journalists as *pensadores* (lit. thinkers; men of action and literary merit), Cosío
Villegas wrote a history whose central tension was a tragic paradox: out

of the great freedom of the press fostered by the República Restaurada came the justification for the strong-arm politics and censorship of the Porfiriato's "constitutional relaxation."[5]

Revisionist and social historians in the last decades of the twentieth century began to see a problem in using newspapers as privileged historical sources and put political discourse under the light of a social context that Cosío Villegas had separated from the *Historia* volumes on politics. The result was a sounder image of the social foundations of the Mexican state, but also a neglect of public opinion as meaningful terrain of political struggle. In a highly stratified society, it was argued, readers were so few that the press could hardly impact the realities of class relations and political domination. In this perspective, the social background of journalists (often flattened under the sociological type "intellectuals") was a better predictor of the contents and influence of the press than ideology and politics. Often based on archives of the executive power, these accounts make the state and those who rebelled against it starring actors of political history.[6]

Recent studies of journalism have infused analysis of the press in nineteenth-century Mexico with new energy. Researchers are reading old newspapers more carefully and finding evidence of the modern construction of public opinion through print culture since the late eighteenth century. These studies do not try to contradict the revisionist theses about the social determinations of political discourse. The premise seems to be that it did not matter if few people read: modernity trickled down from the elites to the masses, and democracy was less important than other republican forms of representation, such as an enlightened public opinion. A teleology of modernity is the risk here: the inevitability of new forms of citizenship excuses the need to understand the details of their construction.[7]

This book concurs with revisionists' premise that, like any other cultural product, the press should be read in the social context of its producers and consumers. Yet this cannot be done at the expense of ignoring journalists' social and political function (brilliantly examined by the liberal narrative) and their effort to create a space of autonomy from the government. The existence of such independence has been established by works on the history of journalism produced by journalists themselves, works that depict the República Restaurada as an era of great diversity and quality in spite of newspapers' very limited income. With their attention to detail, these accounts make a point easily missed by other scholarly studies: journalists and newspapers survived because of their skill in meeting deadlines and filling pages with interesting copy, a socially necessary product even if poorly rewarded. In what follows I thus look at journalism both as a trade and as a sector of the intellectual elite.[8] This means removing the press from a teleological narrative of democracy or state formation and focusing on the texture of everyday life. In other words, who read matters, but so do how and what they read. The answer given in the next two chapters is not a quantification of readers and printed goods but a study of legislations and practices.

Part I specifically describes the ways in which Mexican public men sought to contain the power of the press to affect individuals' feelings, as they are affected, for example, in the portrayals of *La Linterna* and Rabasa cited above. In both chapters I follow the evolution of the idea of honor from a respectable, exclusive marker of status to a romantic, sometimes tragic feeling publicly judged and negotiated. Journalists recognized its power and used it with deliberation in order to build themselves a solid place in public life. Chapter 1 centers on press legislation since independence to lay out the institutional coordinates of the story. However unstable the country, governments never stopped drafting new laws concerning the press. The republican impulse of nineteenth-century press legislation was not only a doctrinal child of liberalism, but also a product of the strength of local institutions and interactions. The city, through its neighbors, its intense social networks, its gossip, shaped public opinion, making it a central aspect of political life. The press jury portrays the combination of ideological and practical conditions of free speech. Chapter 2 descends into more personal territory and examines the complex relationship between journalists and that vague yet powerful thing called public opinion. Public opinion, in Rousseau's comprehensive definition, seemed to grow stronger, faster than republican institutions themselves. Hombres de palabra oscillated between limiting free speech and openly negotiating reputations. They saw that ambivalence as a cost of a new era in which sovereignty was no longer external to the nation or imposed by arms.

CHAPTER 1

Setting the Rules of Freedom
The Trajectory of the Press Jury

According to Benjamin Constant, sovereignty needed a limitation, and establishing it was not just a matter of claiming abstract rights but of looking at what was possible. Such limitation, he argued, "will be ensured first by the same force which legitimates all acknowledged truths: by public opinion."[1] In early national Mexico, José María Luis Mora echoed this belief: "A true public opinion," he argued, was the only force that could stop tyranny and "the love of power, innate in man and always growing in the government."[2] In this chapter I look at what was possible by focusing on freedom of the press, an aspect of public life which (perhaps because historians have not considered it important in a largely illiterate country) has not been explored very deeply, in spite of its centrality for Constant and Mora. After Charles A. Hale's groundbreaking work on Mora, an expanding historiography has examined transforming notions of sovereignty after Mexican independence, focusing on themes first addressed by the illustrious liberal, such as federalism, representation, and citizenship. Yet few scholars have looked at the limitation of sovereignty that Constant proposed in the text from 1815 quoted above, and only recently a group has advanced the exploration of the impact of liberalism on actual political practices, especially among indigenous communities.[3]

I propose that freedom of the press should be studied not simply as an abstract right but, as Constant and Mora conceived of it, as practiced in public life. The result will be to displace the emphasis from unanimity and large national themes toward dialogues in a smaller, albeit still meaningful, scale of analysis. Rather than sovereignty, the research should focus on governance and the everyday interactions among citizens and between civil society and state. These interactions nurtured and transformed, often through personal decisions and conversations, the ideas that Mora and his contemporaries placed at the foundation of the national polis.[4] One advantage of taking such a close look at free speech and public opinion (understood as social practices rather than immanent values) is that, as we will see, it yields a more nuanced picture than the usual dichotomy of conservatives against liberals. Another result, perhaps more interesting from the methodological point of view, is that such an approach reveals the cultural and social texture of what we tend to call, rather vaguely, politics. The specificity of this texture is suggested by comparing Constant's views of freedom of the press with those developed by nineteenth-century Mexicans. Constant stressed that such freedom could be limited only if publications attacked authority and a strict (and, in his view, natural) division between public and private themes could be easily enforced.[5] The public men I examine in this chapter, by contrast, worried about the impossibility of establishing such a neat division and saw the difficulty in distinguishing attacks on authority from criticisms of public officers. Part of a constitutionalist tradition, they tried to legislate freedom of the press rather than allowing strongmen or precedents to decide what could be said. In doing so, they faced two practical problems that define the empirical substance of the following pages.

The first problem was that Mexican public opinion was made from the opinions of fallible citizens. Mora spoke about the importance of opinion and the multiplicity of opinions.[6] He identified the unity of public opinion with that of reason but noted that reason was only partially realized in individual citizens: different abilities distinguished them, although all men had the potential for autonomy and perfectibility. A product of the diverse polity that emerged from independence, public opinion could not come into being except through public discussion, yet the number and quality of interlocutors were themselves subject to debate. Early politicians recognized the need to allow public opinion to shape policy but warned against confusing "the popular voice with public opinion." Against the ignorance of the masses, they held that public opinion was "the general expression of the people convinced about the truth, which it has examined through discussion."[7] Mexicans were sorely aware, after all, that opinions may also hurt the public good by calling for insurrection, subverting Catholic doctrine, promoting debauchery, or offending private citizens. For Mora, reason and morality were essentially individual and free within a person's soul and thus difficult to regulate from the public realm.[8]

The second practical problem in legislating freedom of the press was tyranny itself, the tendency of Mexican politics to gravitate toward strongmen who were not prone to tolerate dissent. Mora warned that only open exchanges could validate opinion.[9] The problem was to create rules for discussion in the public sphere. The solution adopted by Mexican liberals was double-sided and not particularly original: while the state had to guarantee the freedom of opinions through the press, it also had to build effective institutions to contain the freedom of journalists.[10]

Honor was the most worrisome object of opinion because abuse could be damaging both at the individual and collective levels. After all, subversive writings could easily be explained as dangerous instruments of partisan or personal struggles for power, religious doctrine was no longer a matter of public debate, and stiff fines effectively countered "writings that are obscene and against proper customs." Instead, wrote Mora, "insults deserve the severest punishment" because libel made seditious writings more explosive and invaded "the secret asylum of private life."[11] Thus, the first rule to shape debate was that "private life should not be the object of public discussion."[12] Or, in other words, opinions took their first step toward public opinion and the nobility of reason by recognizing a realm of privacy. For Mora and most liberals through the first half century of independent life, the best way to move in that direction was by establishing a tribunal composed of politically and financially independent individuals who could punish the abuses of the press.

That institution was the press jury. This chapter will reconstruct the history and functioning of the press jury as a privileged terrain for the interactions between civil society and the state. Even though it shaped the contents of the press during the first six decades of national life, determining what could be expressed and how, the press jury has been neglected by historiography. First legislated in 1821, it found its moment of greatest influence between 1868 and its abolition in 1882, when it made possible unprecedented freedom of speech in spite of mounting political pressure. The institution was central to political life, I argue, because public opinion was not the pure rational distillation of popular sovereignty ideologues claimed, but the product of myriad, seemingly unimportant exchanges between individuals. This chapter begins to illustrate a thesis that is fully developed in the next one: that in nineteenth-century Mexico public opinion was more concerned with interpersonal relations than with the abstract purity of reason, and it worked as a judge of character as much as the expression of the general will.

Besides the discussions it channeled and the legislation that created it, the jury's membership is of central relevance: citizens' participation in press juries shaped the meaning of citizenship in nineteenth-century urban Mexico. The press jury's symbiotic relationship with the *ayuntamiento* (city council) and the social situation of the well-known *vecinos* (neighbors) who acted as jurors point to a republican tradition that can be traced back to colonial times. Rather than a democratic achievement of the República Restaurada, as the prevalent liberal narrative has it, the press jury was the product of a local tradition that subsisted through small political practices. This chapter, then, will not be a history of freedom against censorship but will stress the success of the press jury in protecting journalists and its key role in adjudicating honor in front of public opinion.[13]

Free Speech Through Jury Legislation

In the archives of the Ayuntamiento of Mexico City five volumes entitled "Jurados de imprenta" (press juries) contain a narrative of national life in which freedom of the press was the first outcome of independence and the principal path in the evolution of citizenship henceforth.[14] The volumes include trials conducted in the capital and most of their legal framework, constituting a corpus of texts that jurists like José María Gamboa, who studied press legislation in 1884, characterized as "the mirror of customs, the genuine expression of the peculiar character of each people." The first product of that narrative is the contrast between modern rules and old practices as recorded in the empire's legal compendium, the *Novísima recopilación*, which, in Gamboa's words, "seem today inconceivable, against nature . . . highly offensive and unfair . . . consequence . . . of an era that was completely different from ours."[15] Liberal jurists characterized preindependence legislation by its religious intol-erance and excessive zeal to punish libel. In the *Novísima recopilación*, believed Ignacio Ramírez, the "public writer, especially if he is a journal-ist, cannot take a step without insulting somebody, without venturing a profane look across the doors of private life."[16] The Inquisition, abolished in 1813, was the key point of reference, although other colonial authori-ties also had jurisdiction over the press.[17] Gamboa and Ramírez might have read those five volumes as testimony that the struggle between honor and free speech was the central drama during the most difficult period of national history.

Beginning with the establishment of provisional authorities against the French in Spain, legislation of the press made its way across the ocean. In November of 1810, the Spanish Cortes abolished prior censorship (*cen-sura previa*) with the purpose of bringing the nation "to the knowledge of true public opinion." The authorities of New Spain, however, believed the fight against the insurgency of Miguel Hidalgo subordinated any reforms emanating from the metropolis, and the viceroy did not publish the decree. Liberal legislation continued to arrive, notably with the Constitu-tion passed by the Cadiz Cortes in 1812. Its article 371 guaranteed citi-zens the "freedom to write, print and publish their political ideas." Au-thorities in Mexico City published the Constitution and a viceroyal edict establishing freedom of the press in October 1812.

Freedom came with penal responsibilities for authors of "defamatory libels and writings that are slanderous, subversive . . . and contrary to public decency." These three limits (slander, subversion, immorality) would become, with varying emphases, the basic structure of press re-strictions in the nineteenth century. Slander was defined in terms of a strict divide between, and different consequences for, statements of pub-lic and private character. A *Reglamento de la libertad de imprenta* ap-proved by the Cortes in 1813 established that printed accusations against public officers supported by evidence would not be punished, but every-thing that involved "private crimes, domestic defects and others that do not have immediate influence on the public good" would be prosecuted according to penal laws.[18]

The struggle for independence created a long-standing ambivalence among Mexican authorities regarding political news and debates. Creole writers had demanded greater freedom of expression as far back as 1805, and ideas about the role of the colony vis-à-vis Spain began to be printed in New Spain in 1808, testing a precarious middle ground of open discussion through the incipient periodical press. The edict of 1812 prompted the publication of new journals, but colonial authorities restricted news and discussions about the insurgency on moral and religious grounds. Viceroyal authorities responded to the Creole challenge expressed in the City Council elections of October 1812 by suspending the new press regulations in spite of the protests of Mexico City's neighbors and delegates to the Cortes. Ferdinand VII's coup against the 1812 Constitution in the peninsula returned things, in appearance, to the status quo.[19] But freedom of the press became an element of the insurgents' program, autonomist newspapers continued to appear in regions controlled by the rebels, and papers in loyalist Mexico City still reported on the advances of freedom of the press in Europe.[20] In 1814, the insurgent *Decreto Constitucional*, issued in Apatzingán, proclaimed "the freedom to speak, think and express opinions through the press," unless the writings attacked "dogma" or "the honor of citizens."[21] Although José María Morelos and the Apatzingán Congress were defeated, the liberal impulse did not stop completely. Multiple pamphlets published in Mexico City defended freedom of the press as one of the basic demands of the new political era.[22] The demand was all the stronger because it maintained the centrality of urban institutions in the process of reverting sovereignty to the people (*los pueblos*), both in Spain and in America, after the abdication of Charles IV in 1808.

The 1820s saw an expansion in the volume and intensity of political debate through the press. That year, a liberal Junta Provisional in Spain reestablished the Cadiz Constitution and freedom of the press in Spain and its colonies.[23] The new Cadiz Cortes approved further regulation that continued in the direction set by their predecessors, extending the character of *injurioso* (slanderous) to all writings that stained "the reputation or the honor of particulars, mentioning their private behavior." The Cadiz Reglamento of 1820 established a jury system to adjudicate on the transgressive character of writings and the penalties to be meted out to their authors—thus replacing the special judges and prosecutors set by previous regulations.[24] Even though Agustín de Iturbide's declaration of independence in September 1821 was to some extent a reaction against peninsular liberalism, the new Mexican authorities soon published the most recent press legislation coming from Cadiz. Two months later, Iturbide began what would become a long series of adjustments to the limits of freedom by issuing a *Reglamento Adicional del Imperio* that established new restrictions and penalties of up to six years of prison for subversive writings.[25]

The Mexican appropriation and design of press regulations since independence cannot be understood simply as a derivation of Cadiz liberalism. Press legislation, in Cadiz as much as in Mexico City, was the product of European, particularly French, examples that were never characterized by coherence and durability. Except for the English case (influential although difficult to apply in the Iberian world because of the primacy given to codes over precedents), there was an abundance of regulations whose duration was tied to that of the governments issuing them.[26] Even though the Cadiz laws were an example of openness, subsequent Spanish laws were characterized by expansive definitions of abuses of the press, including political, allegorical, and personal attacks, and increasing censorship. The central concern of most of these regulations was political control, rather than the protection of reputations. Thus, for example, they prescribed in detail the responsibilities of writers, editors, printers, and sellers who could be tried because of offensive texts.[27]

The press jury itself was introduced and dropped from European press legislations for multiple reasons. While in theory the mechanism offered the best procedural guarantee against abuses of power by giving the responsibility to private citizens, in practice legislators and prosecutors often saw jurors as benign protectors of abusive journalists. Thus, for example, Spanish regulations abolished it in 1823, but a restrictive law in 1837 reinstated the jury. In order to make it more responsive to state concerns, subsequent regulations limited its membership: a law of 1844 quadrupled the income required from potential jurors; a decree of 1852 limited the pool to the one hundred citizens with the highest income in Madrid and to thirty in other cities. A restoration of the jury by the conservative government of Antonio Cánovas del Castillo made possible a period without censorship between 1864 and 1874, but the general trend toward control remained, reflecting, according to Adrizan Shubert, the "contradictions and limitations of Spanish liberalism, and of European liberalism as a whole."[28]

This lack of coherence is also true for France, the country where the fate of the jury, regarding both journalistic and common offenses, seemed to measure the advance of modern institutions.[29] Following England, as advised by Constant, revolutionary France established the jury for common crimes as an organ of popular sovereignty. During the nineteenth century, the criminal jury was the object of criticism that also applied to the press jury: its members were not always honest, it protected the accused (particularly in cases involving honor), imposed antiquated remnants of the traditional Germanic and English accusatorial system (which gave greater weight in the process to the offended party, against the inquisitorial method, preferred by French jurists, in which magistrates had a more active role), and in general strengthened public opinion against the law. The French press jury established in 1819 was indeed less likely to convict than magistrates, while juries were commonly held to be defenders of freedom of the press.[30] Over the course of the nineteenth century, several laws and decrees alternatively placed press offenders under the jurisdiction either of criminal courts or of the press jury and, as in Spain, restricted the pool of jurors. A decree of April 1871 gave accused journalists the right to present supporting evidence for their assertions. Finally, a law passed in 1875, seven years before a similar reform in Mexico, required that all crimes committed by the press be tried in criminal courts, thus eliminating the press jury.[31]

Mexican press legislation since independence was built on the Cadiz foundation and the inspiration of European examples and developed its own peculiarities. Mexican laws and decrees reproduced many of the mechanisms devised in Spain and France to secure the penal responsibility of editors, printers, and authors, mandating, for example, the filing of signed original manuscripts for all texts published.[32] Like its European counterparts, the Mexican legislation expressed the tension between enlightened freedom and the demands of political control. Shifts in the use of the jury are examples of this ambivalence: although usually supported by liberal regimes and abrogated by more conservative governments, its fate ultimately depended on the perceived threat posed by the press to the government. Throughout the century, however, and as in Europe, attacks against citizens' and public officials' honor were the most important rationale for new restrictions. The concern about honor was particularly important in Mexico because of a significant feature of its press jury, to be examined in the following sections: the intimate connection between jurors, locally elected city councils, and, by extension, urban society.

The starting point in the evolution of Mexican regulations was the Spanish law of 1820, published in Mexico on 18 October 1821. It set a broad definition of writings offensive to reputation: the "news that may, as experience shows, upset spirits without any other goal than to make one class of citizens repulsive and contemptible in the eyes another." The *Reglamento* established a swift process. An initial jury, which decided whether a crime had been committed, had to meet no later than forty-eight hours after the complaint was lodged; a second sentencing jury had to meet twenty-four hours after the first one's resolution. Municipal authorities charged with convoking both juries were to pay fines if these deadlines were not met. Early regulations' definition of punishable behaviors and concern about timeliness framed subsequent regulations. Besieged by criticisms of his monarchical tendencies, Agustín de Iturbide decreed a *Reglamento adicional sobre libertad de imprenta* that increased penalties against journalists but maintained the jury; the federalist Constitution of 1824, however, which established Congress's duty to "protect and arrange the political freedom of the press," omitted mention of the defense of reputation as a limit of the press (common to previous legislation) and prohibited any additional restriction in the future.[33] Yet governments in the following decades felt a strong urge to pass further restrictions when political conflict created a sense of disorder.

That was the case of the reform in 1828 of the Cadiz law of 1820, decreed by President Guadalupe Victoria. In the months preceding the decree, *yorkinos* and *escoceses* (after the York and Scottish rites), early partisan divides centered on Masonic lodges, had openly campaigned for their candidates to succeed Victoria—Vicente Guerrero and Manuel Gómez Pedraza, respectively. The tone of the debates was surprisingly harsh: personal attacks reached private lives and eventually led to a military rebellion against the election of Gómez Pedraza. Yorkino positions against Church hierarchy and in favor of the expulsion of Spaniards added to the acrimony and played a part in instigating a riot that destroyed the Parián, a Spanish-dominated commercial building in downtown Mexico City, forcing Congress to name Guerrero president.[34]

The reform of 1828, decreed shortly before the riots, was the first Mexican redesign of the press jury and set basic rules that applied until 1882. Municipal authorities were to receive complaints against the press and present them before a nine-member jury drawn from a list of eligible citizens. The list, compiled every year by the City Council, had to include all citizens residing in the city who knew how to read and write and had capital of four thousand pesos or a trade that produced one thousand pesos a year; it excluded *jefes políticos* (centrally appointed district authorities), army commanders, and ecclesiastics with jurisdiction in the city. This initial jury (*jurado de hechos* or *de acusación*) decided the merits of the complaint, that is, whether the publication was indeed subversive, immoral, or slanderous. If that was the case, a lower-court criminal judge took over the process in order to suspend the sale of the publication and identify the person responsible for the article denounced. If the text was subversive, the judge had to arrest the suspect, and, in the case of an offense of private character, he had to prompt the victim and accused to reach a conciliation through a direct meeting. Once the intervention of the judge had concluded, and if the conciliation failed, a second, twelve-member jury (*jurado de sentencia*) met to sentence the accused; a minimum of eight votes were required to convict. Several provisions guaranteed the rights of the accused: he or she could post bail, speak at the jury audience, reject seven prospective jurors, and ask a judge to recuse the sentence. Although the reform of 1828 did not eliminate the *fiscales de imprenta*, prosecutors in charge of bringing up charges against authors when victims did not, they were henceforth subordinated to aldermen, juries, and judges.[35] Thus organized, the press jury came to occupy a position between journalists and their victims and between municipal and judicial authorities.

Political instability and external conflicts during the next forty years made use of the press jury intermittently at best. In September 1829, President Guerrero issued a decree against "press abuses," allowing state governments to punish, without a jury or any other judicial procedure, those writers who attacked the state, "protect[ed] the goals of any invader of the republic," or "favor[ed] any change to the federal system."[36] Guerrero was at the time besieged by a Spanish occupation of Tampico (defeated days later by Santa Anna) and by the same kind of urban unrest that had brought him to power in April. Seizing on the most divisive issue of the time, his adversaries in the press opposed the expulsion of Spaniards while casting doubts on the presence of invading forces on national soil—always a booster of government support. In 1831, the conservative government of Anastacio Bustamante published a law placing all crimes of the press, including "slanderous libels," under the rule of judges, thus eliminating juries. The law was part of an aggressive drive against opposition journalists and pamphleteers that included speeches made in Congress by the conservative ideologue Lúcas Alamán, attacks by official newspapers, fines, seizure of presses, arrests, and even beatings by the secret police and a paramilitary group ominously called *capo* [*sic*] *dei sbirri* (cops' boss).[37] Even though the liberal government of 1833–34 tried unsuccessfully to reestablish freedom of speech and the City Council continued to compile lists of potential jurors until 1835, restrictions mounted under conservative governments. In March 1834, the governor of the Federal District, José María Tornel, prohibited newspaper street sellers from reading the news aloud because, he claimed, the *voceo*, as the practice was called, attacked "the foundations of society and the honor of citizens."[38] A law issued in 1835 under President Santa Anna excluded vagrants, prisoners, the ill, and those whose address was unknown from claiming responsibility for publications—thus preempting editors' common device of avoiding prosecution against authors by buying the signature of people who did not mind a stay in jail.[39]

The centralist regime that prevailed in the succeeding years imposed unprecedented restrictions on freedom of the press. The first of the constitutional *Bases Orgánicas* of December 1836 recognized the protection of freedom of expression and the ban on previous censorship but also maintained the law from 1831 that eliminated juries. The defeat of Texan rebels in 1836 and the subsequent instability leading to the disastrous war against the United States justified further restrictions. A decree of 8 April 1839 by Interim President Santa Anna established harsh penalties against journalists, including prison sentences in the infamous fortresses of San Juan de Ulúa, in Veracruz, and San Diego, in Acapulco. The prologue to the decree justified the "strong hand" powers of search and arrest bestowed on the police after "the uncertain, precarious and ruinous state in which our society finds itself, as a result of the spirit of anarchy and immorality that prevails everywhere"—the main cause of this decadent state of affairs being "the continuous and scandalous abuse of freedom of the press." Thus, in a reasoning that would reappear in subsequent decades, both individual and collective morality authorized prosecution of subversive authors.[40]

Yet the premises of Cadiz were too firmly rooted to be easily eliminated by regimes that claimed republican legitimacy even as they favored undemocratic means. When Bustamante returned to the presidency in July of 1839, his government revoked the law of 8 April arguing that "it cannot allow freedom of writing, the first guarantee of the nations that have embraced a representative system, to remain suspended."[41] Besieged by newspapers that demanded a return to a federal system, however, Bustamante relapsed, proposing a law that forced editors to pay deposits, punished them for printing texts without a signature, and created special *procuradores* (prosecutors) to supervise all new publications —in other words, a return to colonial prior censorship. A statement by the Supreme Court against the project preempted approval of the initiative.[42] The tension between rule of law and military needs reached a high point in the subsequent years. A decree issued in 1842 by President Santa Anna, now in power in the name of federalism, denied congressional *fuero* (immunity) to public writers. The decree was specifically designed to prosecute the federal deputy and founder and editor of *El Siglo Diez y Nueve*, Ignacio Cumplido, who had criticized growing military spending and suggested prudence rather than intransigence in negotiations with Texas.[43] A decree by Santa Anna in 1843 tempered the penalties of the law of April 1839 but added a curb that would never again be stated in such blunt and broad terms, although it prefigured Porfirian legislation: "Under no circumstance will it be allowed to write about private life."[44]

Even in the midst of war, however, few challenged freedom of speech, and the protection of reputations continued to attract the energies of unstable governments. President José Mariano Salas, ruling in the name of the Constitution of 1824, decreed a press *reglamento* in 14 November 1846 that had been approved by Congress the previous year. The law lifted existing restrictions, reestablished the jury along the lines established in the 1820s, and increased the size of the jurado de hechos to eleven members and of the jurado de sentencia to seventeen, in order to reinforce the protection of writers. The decree nevertheless continued the trend of previous legislation in expanding the definition of abuses of the press and building a continuum of public and private transgressions that went from attacks against the form of government, religion, and morality to assaults against private life. The code did not allow authors of slanderous writings to present supporting evidence, as those who wrote about public issues could do, and gave the offended party in cases of libel the right to have the case tried by a common court instead of a jury.[45] Days after American troops left Mexico City in 1848, as if the nation's ruin was only a distraction from the need to protect individual honor, President José Joaquín de Herrera amended the law of 1846 to hold that all attacks against private life be tried by regular courts instead of a jury. The decree also expanded the definition of defamatory writings to include those "which attack the honor or reputation of any particular, corporation, or public officer, or offend them with satires, insults, or nicknames." The preamble portrayed the unresolved dilemma of nineteenth-century views of freedom of the press: on the one hand, it stated that "to express the thought through the press is one of the first rights of man," while, on the other, it warned that "writers can abuse the press, using it to vent debased passions."[46] The inclusion of public officials among those individuals to be protected set forth a connection that would in 1882 lead to the definitive elimination of the jury in the name of an individual's honor (see chapter 5).

As the confrontation between liberals and conservatives entered its final phases during the Reforma era and French intervention, the press jury turned into a clear marker of the distinction between radical *puro* liberals, on the one side, and conservatives and moderate liberals, on the other. A decree issued in 1852 by President Mariano Arista, a moderate liberal, placed seditious press offenses under the authority of military and government authorities. Voicing the political elite's concern about freedom of speech, the Supreme Court invited the president to withdraw the decree, which it deemed unconstitutional, and most governors refused to publish it. Arista backtracked twenty-two days later. But the following year Santa Anna returned to power, this time in fully authoritarian mode and with monarchical ideas—both strongly correlated in Mexico with the rejection of freedom of the press. Following the advice of the conservative Alamán, a stalwart enemy of free press since the first government of Bustamante, Santa Anna established greater restrictions, including monetary deposits by editors and empowerment of political authorities to suspend publications and arrest authors without the intervention of juries or municipal authorities.[47] The victory of the puro Plan de Ayutla rebellion against Santa Anna brought the reestablishment of the protection of journalists' rights. A decree in 18 December 1855 reinstated the law of 1846, but later that month President Ignacio Comonfort revealed his growing distance from the most radical liberals of Ayutla when he prohibited anonymous writings, suppressed the jury again, and channeled press offenses to correctional judges.[48]

An initial project at the Constitutional Congress of 1856–57 reinstated the press jury but placed its proceedings "under the jurisdiction of the corresponding justice court." For the puro deputies Guillermo Prieto and José María Mata this undermined the guarantees established by the regulations of 1828 and 1846 because it took the authority to convoke the jury out of the hands of city councils and placed it in those of a weak, politically subordinated judicial power. Their successful opposition contributed to the passing of articles 6 and 7 of the Constitution of 1857. The articles guaranteed the free expression of ideas as long as they did not infringe upon "the respect of private life, morality and public peace" and elevated the press jury into constitutional law.[49]

The new constitution also gave ample powers to Congress and sanctioned the Reforma's far-reaching social and legislative program. Soon, however, Comonfort staged a coup against it, sparking a three-year civil war. After the defeat of the conservatives and during the interlude before the French invasion, President Benito Juárez and Minister of Justice Francisco Zarco set the final legal framework for the press jury. Decreed by Juárez only days after his return to Mexico City, the law of 2 February 1861 regulating article 7 of the Constitution (commonly known as the Prieto Law after its main author, Guillermo Prieto) prescribed the jury in great detail and added mechanisms to protect journalists. Offenses were called *faltas* (misdemeanors) rather than *delitos* (crimes), as in previous regulations. The maximum sentence was set at twelve months in prison or exile from the state, and the number of jurors in the jurado de hechos was maintained at eleven but increased to nineteen for the jurado de sentencia. The law also defined in more precise terms the extent of offenses against private life: only those writings in which "a vice or crime is attributed to an individual, not being yet declared by courts."[50] All citizens able to read and write could be jurors; although no income requirements were included, the law mandated that jurors not be public officers and that they be laypeople and "have a profession or trade."[51]

The threat of foreign invasion and internal rebellion forced Juárez to follow the example of his predecessors and abrogate the law of 1861 through a decree in December of that year, reestablishing the Comonfort law of 1855 that had suppressed the jury.[52] After Juárez and his government left Mexico City and the French established military rule over the capital and most of the country, the restrictive trend continued. In June 1864, the commander of the French expeditionary corps, Marshal Élie Frédéric Forey, banned all publications while a new law was published and soon thereafter decreed a regulation that eliminated press offenses' special status and placed them under correctional judges. The Mexico City Ayuntamiento, which preserved some of its autonomy under

French occupation, opposed the new regulations and contended that the law of 1855 was still in force per Juárez's decree. Even though he departed from some of the most conservative stances of his Mexican supporters, Emperor Maximilian maintained the monarchical tradition against free press when he issued new regulations, without juries, in 1865 and 1867. The code of 1867 emphasized the respect owed the ruling dynasty and religion; it prohibited any criticism of public officials and did not allow writers to present proof of their statements as exculpatory evidence.[53] The defeat of the empire in 1867 brought a return to liberal institutions, which had been formally preserved by the itinerant Juárez government during the war. In January 1868 Juárez reestablished the law of 2 February 1861, and on 4 February 1868 Congress approved an identical text, thus lending its authority to Juárez's decree. The law governed the press jury until 1882, when the institution was definitively abolished through a reform of article 7 of the Constitution.[54]

The Press Law of 1861 made a strong jury the solution to the dilemma posed by the opposing forces of protection of freedom and restraint of press abuse. The law's definition of abuses continued to include writings against the reputation of citizens as well as those affecting public officials; it made no mention of the special press prosecutor (*fiscal de imprenta*) established by Cadiz and maintained in subsequent regulations. By giving the City Council the main role in organizing and carrying forward trials, the law moved beyond the Spanish antecedents and, like the reform of 1828, limited the role of the common judge to arresting seditious suspects and conciliating between the two parties; it maintained a speedy trial by mandating that verdicts be reached in a single, uninterrupted deliberation.

For all its democratic leanings, the law of 1861 was the last chapter in a long, dense history that began in 1812. The preceding account has noted that governments adjusted restrictions and liberties according to the urgency of political conjunctures. Implicit assumptions behind this narrative of free speech as the product of political alternatives are that the press was a key political battleground and that press legislation was nothing but a strategic device to maintain power. Testing such assumptions would require a revision of the entire political history of the country since 1812, although little in the literature suggests that the press was so influential in determining the outcomes of political conflict.[55] If the press was not a decisive political factor, however, why did liberal and conservative regimes spend such energy producing, reforming, and abrogating press codes? The notion that press legislation was a tool of power fails to account for the ideological and legal debates that accompanied that legislative process. If one is to have a full understanding of the chapter of Mexican legal history outlined above, it is necessary to go beyond the legislative process into the practice of the law.

The Press Jury in Practice

Debates about legislation concerning the press were based on a theoretical opposition between republican liberties and the preservation of order. It was not until the law of 1868 was in place, however, that the country enjoyed the institutional stability to develop a sounder understanding of the actual operation of the press jury. Jurists lost no time in faulting the institution for its procedural problems and jurisdictional hybridism. José María Gamboa, for example, argued that a single, uninterrupted jury meeting, as mandated by the law, was not practical because too many steps were required to establish who was responsible for the offensive writing or whether a crime denounced in print had been previously decided upon by penal courts.[56] The simplicity of the procedures in the Prieto law seemed to create undue safeguards for libelous journalists. According to Jacinto Pallares, the press jury created a serious problem, as it gave crimes committed through the press a double nature: they could be punished as press offenses, in which case the printed copy was the corpus delicti (the crime being publication itself), or they could be considered part of other crimes, such as sedition or slander, in which case the printed word was only evidence and the damage inflicted upon the victim or society had to be ascertained through regular inquisitorial procedures. Can the press jury be dismissed as part of that "generous liberal utopia," foreign to Mexican reality, that Justo Sierra and others saw in the Constitution of 1857?[57] The intermittent use of juries until 1868 would suggest so.

But Pallares's criticism, published in 1875, ignored the civic experience that had enabled liberals' embrace of the jury even while they continued to be concerned about libel. In the perspective of Prieto and others, the verbal, open, and local character of the jury allowed it to deal with the complex nature of offenses committed through the printed word. The jury, they believed, represented public opinion and was therefore able to evaluate the meaning of texts and the value of reputations—besides, of course, the political impact of seditious statements. The jury was sovereign in its ability to read and judge the written word, thus protecting both reputations and freedom of speech from long legalistic proceedings. Based on a deep-seated distrust of the judiciary and the executive branch expressed in the Constitutional Congress of 1856–57 by Prieto and Mata, the laws of 1861 and 1868 coupled the autonomous reason of jurors-citizens with the local, republican legitimacy of city councils. In a self-fulfilling prophecy, one practical consequence of such linking of literate citizens and local power was that the press jury became the representative but also the space for the emergence of public opinion.

Press juries in Mexico City met regularly and usually fulfilled the role intended by their designers, protecting journalists and reputations and associating, in a complex yet swift process, political, judicial, and municipal authorities. The description in the following pages is based mostly on the records of forty-three trials held in the capital between 1869 and 1877, extant at the Archivo Histórico de la Ciudad de México.[58] The image that emerges is one of consistent work in spite of the costs and difficulties involved in bringing jurors together, establishing the authorship of texts, and reaching across distances and jurisdictions.

The impact of the press jury can be measured, first, by journalists' success in avoiding persecution. As noted above, the last phases of conservative authoritarianism under Santa Anna and the French had been characterized by harsh restrictions of the press. Although he does not analyze the press jury in depth, the twentieth-century historian Daniel Cosío Villegas explained the respect for journalists' freedom during the República Restaurada as a self-defeating consequence of Juárez and Lerdo de Tejada's liberal beliefs. A look at available evidence, however, suggests that Juárez and Lerdo de Tejada nourished the same desire to control the threat of opposition newspapers of previous and subsequent presidents—as proved by Juárez's change of course regarding the jury in late 1861. After the defeat of the empire, the law of February 1861 was reinstated by congressional vote, not only by presidential decree, as a result of the continuing influence in Congress of surviving puro liberals like Prieto and Zarco. The strength and autonomy of Congress during these years prevented presidents of the República Restaurada from tinkering with article 7's mandate for the press jury. Although any statement about political motives is speculative, it is clear that the principal reason for the freedom of the press achieved during this period was the effective-

ness of the press jury itself: most accusations of sedition against newspapers found jurors predisposed against the government, and even cases
stemming from complaints of libel, thus seeking to protect individual
reputations, usually resulted in acquittals or the dismissal of charges.[59]

How did the press jury operate in the defense of freedom of speech?
Examination of the institution in practice demonstrates the connections
between liberal theory, republican traditions, and social networks. Trials
followed a tight schedule. The sequence of actions began with the president of the City Council receiving the complaint. In nine of the forty-
three cases examined here the complaint occurred on the same date as
the offending publication. In other cases it could be delayed because
publications printed in Mexico City took days to reach alleged victims
who lived elsewhere and were forced to travel to or to seek legal representation in the capital.[60] One or two days after the complaint the City
Council ordered the police to seize all copies of the publication from the
streets and the printing workshop and supervised the drawing of the
names of the first jury from the official list. The meeting of this jury took
place, an average of 3.6 days after the complaint, at the City Council
meeting room. The process could stop then if jurors found that the
accusation lacked merit because the suspect publication was not offensive or seditious or the victim was not properly represented. If the jury
found instead that the accusation was granted, the trial was turned over to
a correctional judge, who established who was responsible for the text. In
cases of libel, the judge then brought together the offended and the
accused and attempted a conciliation, which, if successful, ended the case.
If the accusation concerned a seditious writing, the judge limited himself
to arresting the suspect. After the arrest or failed conciliation, the City
Council drew the names for the jury in charge of sentencing. Following
the hearing and debate, in which both parties had the right to address the
jury and the audience, everyone left the room except for the jurors, who
discussed and voted anonymously. If the result was a condemnatory sentence, the City Council relayed the case to a correctional judge for execution. The process took place in the space of a few days: a median of seven
days between the first and second juries. Timing was essential if the jury
was to protect reputations, as any delay would suggest hesitation among
victims or complicity among authorities. Just as in duels, "dishonor does
not consist of receiving an insult, but of enduring it with patience."[61]

Throughout the process there were multiple ways for journalists to

TABLE 1. Results of First Press Jury, Jurado de Hechos,
Mexico City, 1869–1877

Result	Cases
Dismissed for lack of merits	20
Enough evidence to proceed	11
Accuser dropped the charges	3
Jury meeting did not take place	2
Acquittal	1
Jury lacked jurisdiction	1
No information	5
Total	43

Source: AHDFJ.

avoid punishment. As reflected in table 1, the most reliable protection
was the jurado de hechos. Of the thirty-six juries for which complete
information is available, only in eleven did the jury find grounds for the
accusation to proceed. In three, the trial ended when the complainant
dropped the charges, while in twenty-two the jury found that the accusation was not supported by the evidence, the accused was innocent, or it
was not within the jury's jurisdiction to decide the case.

Except for a few cases, processes against journalists and editors were
rather benign. Only those accused of sedition were imprisoned during
the trial. The seizing of copies was not effective for the most part: in ten
of the thirty-six cases for which information is available the representatives of the City Council were not able to find a single copy of the
denounced newspaper, and in another sixteen they seized fewer than ten
copies. Negotiations between the parties offered another avenue to avoid
punishment. The three cases in which the accusation was dropped by the
victim may be linked with informal negotiations, and in three of the
seven available cases where conciliation was attempted the meeting between victim and author was successful, thus concluding the trial. Agreements usually involved the publication of a text restoring the victim's
reputation in the same newspaper in which it had been attacked. Even if
all these options failed, the suspect had a good chance of escaping punishment: the second jury met in only seven of the eleven cases in which
the first jury had found favorably for the accusation and issued a prison
sentence in six of them. The accused had the right to appeal his indict-

ment or any aspect of the process before and after the second jury's sentence.[62]

The tone of the arguments exchanged during these trials exhibited writers' advantage in front of the jury. Newspapers presented their critical stance against the government as a patriotic duty, thus creating sympathy among jurors and an aura of heroism around certain editors: Vicente García Torres's newspaper, *El Monitor Republicano*, was accused in seventeen of the forty-three cases, followed by ten cases involving Cumplido's *El Siglo Diez y Nueve*—both editors took pride in their accusations. By contrast, complainants, including representatives of the government, tended to define offenses as apolitical attacks against private life. Official accusations, even before the República Restaurada, usually had a tentative tone or timidly referred to an "order from the supreme government."[63] A case from 1872 promoted by members of the City Council against *El Monitor Republicano* exemplifies the weakness of the state. One paragraph that alluded to *grangerías* (perks) that benefited aldermen prompted the complaint of one of them, Manuel López Mesqui. The accusation led to the seizing of a few copies, but the case did not succeed before the jury. The council then tried to pass a "vote of censure" against García Torres, who was also a member of the body—a harmless measure ridiculed by *El Monitor Republicano* and other publications.[64]

López Mesqui represented the City Council because complaints without an identifiable victim helped defendants. Official accusations talked vaguely about "humorous satire" that caused "the disrepute of authorities [and] provoke rebellion;"[65] while others mentioned obscene publications that offended public morality or vague insults against, for example, "the name of Spain."[66] Complaints against subversive writings were seldom effective. Of the forty-one cases for which we have information about the contents of the offensive articles, only in nine did the offending publications touch on purely political actions, and in nine others the text had to do with the use of public moneys by officials. Only in four of those eighteen cases did the jury find grounds to proceed against the author, and the reason was that those articles implicated specific individuals. As a consequence, most accusations referred to libel, even if there was a political backdrop to the case. In twenty-three cases (not including the nine cases concerning officials' use of public moneys), the offending publication touched personal reputations by discussing commercial practices (N=16), past political behavior (3), or private life (4). Nevertheless, only in six of these twenty-three cases did the first jury find that the accusation was supported by the evidence. In general, even if the private or political nature of the accusation did not have a great impact on the rather low chances of conviction, accusers against journalists found that their risk of suffering a resounding defeat in the court of public opinion was greater if they openly sided with the government by alleging sedition. Whether true or false, advantageous or not, the defense of reputation was the inevitable avenue to use press juries against abuse. As a result, the role of the government in these cases is less visible than that of its individual officials.

The most eloquent evidence of the jury's effective protection of authors is found in the trials against journalists brought up during Díaz's first presidency (1876–80) and González's government before 1882. Although neither caudillo was a lover of open debate and opposition press and both used extralegal means to keep the press under control, the jury was an obstacle for them. Famous was the accusation in 1877 brought against the French journalist and *lerdista* Alfredo Bablot, who wrote in *El Federalista* that President Díaz had paid three thousand pesos to have General Mariano Escobedo murdered. The complaint was introduced by Baltazar Téllez Girón, as representative of Díaz. Téllez Girón first accused Bablot of inciting rebellion, then changed the accusation to attacks against the private life of Díaz. The Secretaría de Gobernación tried to influence the composition of the jury, but the result was a poor show of political control. Well-known lawyers on both sides engaged in a heated and prolonged debate in front of jurors and a vociferous crowd. Even some jurors spoke. "Insulting references, injurious words, expressions of hate: that was all one could hear at the court of justice," reported *El Foro*. After the jury disbanded in chaos, an improvised jury formed of pro-government members of the audience found against the accused—but Bablot walked away. A district court soon gave him an *amparo* (injunction) against such an obviously illegitimate ruling. A second complaint by Díaz's representatives prompted a new trial. The jurado de hechos found merits in the case, but the proceedings were again interrupted during conciliation when Téllez Girón failed to prove his legal representation of the president, and Bablot introduced a second amparo.[67]

As both amparos suggest, the government could not easily manipulate or circumvent the jury. Appellate courts upheld article 7 in several cases, ordering Díaz and González to withdraw administrative punishments

against journalists or preventing correctional judges from arresting journalists.[68] Only indirect administrative penalties could be used: a month of
arrest or one-hundred-peso fines against editors who published unsigned
articles (which a decree of 1875 reforming the law of 1868 had prohibited
as an administrative misdemeanor, not a press offense to be tried in front
of a jury) or against seditious manuscripts that had not been published
yet and were therefore not protected by the Constitution. In 1881 the
Supreme Court unanimously upheld the right of public writers to be
tried by juries rather than common judges.[69]

The consistency and effectiveness of press juries' protection of journalists under the República Restaurada and early Porfiriato are all the more
remarkable in that several factors made it an onerous undertaking. Journalists, to begin with, knew the high cost of searches of their offices,
mistreatment by the police, and imprisonment among common criminals. Even if they were later acquitted, prison was a humiliating penalty
for educated men like Manuel María Romero, who until his imprisonment "had always kept my name pure; it had never been inscribed in a jail
book."[70] Successful editors like Cumplido and García Torres had to be
well versed on current press legislation and ready to face suits, arrests,
fines, beatings, and even personal scoldings from the president. Complainants, for their part, also faced costs. To denounce a publication, for
example, they had to pay for judicial stamped paper, from which some
tried to exempt themselves by claiming poverty.[71] When the outcome of
the trial was not favorable or remained uncertain, some victims felt
compelled to publish pamphlets in which they presented their case to
public opinion, often transcribing trial records or appeals. For both complainants and defendants the greatest expense was the honoraria of the
lawyers who addressed jurors and the judge and promoted appeals. Defense attorneys in particular were indispensable given their ability to
deliver speeches that would earn the sympathy of jurors and audiences.
Although lawyers sometimes worked out of friendship or solidarity, in
other cases they charged steep fees. Gustavo Gostkowsky, who had written an article critical of private pawnshops, had to borrow four hundred
pesos at 100 percent interest in order to pay part of the six-hundred-peso
fee charged by his attorney, Francisco Hernández—not an exaggerated
sum according to witnesses. Having won his case, Gostkowsky then sued
his accusers in civil court to recover the expenses.[72] Although these costs
may have deterred many from resorting to the press jury, it is not clear

that monetary costs normally favored either party—both, in any case, were moved by the inexorable demands of freedom and honor.

The direst practical problem for the work of press juries, however, was the selection of jury members. Occupying a unique place in the judicial system and municipal government, the press jury could be delayed at many points in its work. One problem was jurors' limited knowledge of the law and the lack of institutional advice to guide their operation. In April 1861 this became clear when a jury due to consider an accusation against a paragraph in *El Constitucional* disbanded because no members of the City Council were present to select eleven of the thirteen potential jurors who had showed up. Three days later they met again, and they had to argue for awhile before deciding whether the law allowed them to admit evidence in support of the article that had been challenged.[73] The limits of City Council support were clear in the process of summoning reluctant vecinos. Each year, representatives of each city block compiled a list of citizens eligible to be jurors. The lists were then received and verified by the council. Often, however, they were produced late or not at all—thus forcing the council to use old lists to draw the names of jurors. Lists had to be posted around the city so citizens could be apprised of their duty or, as they often did, request to be exempted because work or health prevented them from fulfilling their duty. Even after aldermen corrected and published new lists exemption requests continued to arrive in city hall. In order to establish the final group of jurors to hear a specific case, the City Council met in the presence of both parties, drew names from the list, and sent letters to the chosen ones. Some of them still did not show up when summoned, in spite of the threat of a five-hundred-peso fine. Absences forced the council to conduct a new drawing and send for substitutes.[74]

Citizens did not always avoid participation in press juries. This is indicated by the size of the lists of potential jurors, whose number varied from year to year according to changing regulations, City Council criteria, and citizens' willingness to participate (table 2). Although evidence is not evenly available for all years, the number of available jurors and the willingness to participate apparently increased. This may be in part a consequence of changing legislation and enforcement, as in the high numbers for 1847, one year after passage of the law of 1846, and 1871, the first year for which there is evidence after the laws of 1861 and 1868. Although the population of the city grew by 80 percent between 1822 and

TABLE 2. Citizens Summoned, Excused, and Appointed from
Press Juries, Mexico City, 1822–1882

Year	Summoned	Excused and Excluded	Appointed
1822		5	18
1823		33	72
1824		10	72
1825		9	72
1826		11	72
1827		9	72
1828		2	72
1829	322		97
1830	580	61	
1831	598	35	563
1832	730	57	1,110
1833	505	26	
1834	183		
1835	604	13	503
1847	2,491		
1856	101	3	98
1861	222		228
1871	1,095	5	110
1879			586
1880		1	908
1882	716		680
Average[a]	678.91	18.67	313.71

Source: AHDFJ.

[a]Average of years for which data is available.

1882, these numbers still suggest an increasing involvement of citizens in issues concerning the press.

Yet the number of potential jurors is small compared with that of the people who could read, and particularly those who read newspapers—although data on both accounts is less than perfect for the nineteenth century. According to the first general census, in 1895, 49.5 percent of the Federal District's population (476,413 in total, 339,935 of them in Mexico City) knew how to read—a high figure compared to 17 percent in the country as a whole. In terms of the number of publications the difference was clearer: Mexico City had 120 of the country's 285 periodicals in 1888—42.1 percent of them—when only a little over 3 percent of the national population lived in the city.[75] Those publications catered to workers, women, and educated readers, but the large number of periodicals did not necessarily mean many readers. Based on the number of copies actually printed, the number of newspaper readers has been estimated at below 10 percent of the population during the Porfiriato.[76] If one also considers the increasing number of copies of newspapers printed in the 1890s (around 100,000), then the size of newspaper audiences may have been larger than that.[77] More than a tenth of the population, for example, was involved in electoral politics. The ballots distributed by the City Council for municipal elections (38,570 in 1885 and 84,131 in 1911) indicate as much—although those numbers are lower than that of those who had the right to vote.[78] Reading pamphlets, edicts, and newspapers to those who could not do so was a common practice since the early national era, if not before.[79] The small number of potential jurors (see table 2), plus anecdotal evidence from the Ayuntamiento archive, suggests that council members never attempted to establish the actual universe of potential candidates, nor did they assume a large reading public: they just listed people they knew.

Besides the practical difficulties in their operation, press juries faced multiple obstacles in discovering the facts. The first jury's goal was to establish whether an offense had been committed—a fairly straightforward job since the defining trait of press offenses was their publicness and the ready availability of material evidence, the newspaper itself, a copy of which was usually provided by the victim. Things became complicated when the jury found there had been an offense and turned the case over to a correctional judge, who had to identify the offender. The judge had to reconstruct the process of printing, editing, reporting, and writing that preceded publication. In doing so, he faced subterfuges that journalists had developed during years of censorship. Ever since early regulations were instituted, printers had to keep a signed original of all texts published, and newspapers had to print the name of a legally responsible editor. But authors of "abusive writings," to quote Mora, hid behind false or hired signatures, thus not only delaying just punishment but also creating "cavilling and gossips" that subverted public life.[80]

Playing with signatures was more than a ruse. Modern ideas about the author in Europe were the result of the development of a lucrative market of readers. In nineteenth-century Mexico, by contrast, sales of newspapers and novels were rarely profitable. This made it rational to pay for someone else's signature or to use pseudonyms, as writers such as Guillermo Prieto and Federico Gamboa did.[81] Authorship was particularly evasive in the daily operation of newspapers, as it occupied a fuzzy place between the typesetter and the source of information. Scissors added to the ambiguity: entire columns were taken verbatim, sometimes without proper citation, from other newspapers. Many of the texts denounced in court were *gacetilla*—a mélange of paragraphs containing firsthand reports, quotations, letters, debates, and opinions, sometimes signed but often not. Gacetilla closely resembled the open structure and detailed texture of conversation and established a bridge between press and gossip. Responsibility, therefore, was diluted to the extent that accusations could shift from the editor or writer to the person who had provided the information.[82] Conversely, gossip, hearsay, and *fama pública* (public reputation) could be cited as objective evidence against writers. When the public prosecutor José Joaquín Segura denounced an anonymous paragraph published in *La Polémica* of Morelia, he stated, "I have strong suspicions, confirmed by public opinion" that the author was Jesús Cárdenas.[83]

A case from 1849 in the city of Colima demonstrates both the circuitous road that judges had to follow in order to reach a culprit and the ambiguous journalistic ethic engendered by censorship. Threatened with jail for printing a subversive manifesto, the printer Bruno García handed the judge a manuscript of the "Pronunciamiento de Colima" signed by Camilo Vidriales. Brought to court, Vidriales declared in turn that he was not the author but a scribe who had made a clean copy and signed it out of ignorance. Although Vidriales refused to state the real name of the author, other witnesses told the judge that the author was the justice of the peace Bartolomé Quintero, Vidriales's boss. One witness declared that Vidriales had said that Quintero forced him to sign the manuscript by arguing that no responsibility would fall on Vidriales because he was "just a clerk." But there was another trick. As the investigations continued, Agustín Ceballos confessed that Quintero had asked him to forge Vidriales's signature on the manuscript, eight days after the publication of the "Pronunciamiento"—although Ceballos frankly added that "he had not been a *pendejo* [a fool]" and had received money from Quintero.[84] All the actors in the Colima process, including Vidriales, knew about the legal responsibilities involved in publishing and all participated willingly in the deception. Paradoxically, such behavior was compatible with journalists' concern about honor. Many editors simply refused to reveal the identity of authors in the name of "chivalrousness," even if that caused them to land in jail, like pendejos.[85]

In this context, journalists shamelessly subordinated the dictates of the law to friendship and loyalty. The law, after all, was always subject to political pressure, while the tyranny of opinion was unmovable. Editors accepted a guilty verdict, as José María Elizondo did in Nuevo Laredo, when authors made themselves scarce.[86] And when an article threatened to provoke a duel, editors were also eager to come forward and face the consequences. The best-known example of this combination of chicanery and honor was the trial against the anonymous author of the novel *Tomochic*, an exposé of the army's brutal repression of a peasant rebellion published in episodes in *El Demócrata* in 1893. The editor Joaquín Clausell went to jail rather than reveal the name of the author of the novel, Heriberto Frías. A member of the military, Frías was liable to the death penalty in martial court. Although the secret survived officially for a few years, it came to be commonly known that the author was Frías.[87]

While complete anonymity was impossible to achieve in the face of *fama pública*, journalists had other means to evade judges and juries. Press laws established that accusations had to be brought up to the City Council of the town where the offensive article had been published, regardless of the place of residence of victim or suspect.[88] In some cases the authors simply skipped town and did not appear in audiences or published articles about their local politics in different cities to avoid the obligation to appear. Newspapers in Mexico City often published news and opinions about politics in other localities, thereby forcing victims to empower attorneys in the capital. These strategies undermined the action of the jury because the suspect's or the victim's absence could invalidate the trial on appeal and because juries could refuse to hear cases in which they deemed the victim to be improperly represented. That was the case for Gaspar Sanches Ochoa, who did not appear in the Mexico City audience. He was already in prison in Puebla for having criticized the governor.[89] Sanches Ochoa faced the double jeopardy of a press jury in the capital and extralegal punishment at home. But for other writers Mexico City was a haven. The case in 1869 in which Narciso Dávila, from Monterrey, Nuevo León, denounced Lucas González, who lived in Saltillo, Coahuila, is a good example. The article had been published in *El*

Monitor Republicano, in Mexico City. The first jury decided that the case could not be heard because it was not "legitimately constituted" since the representation of the victim was not established. Dávila insisted months later, now in person, after being elected federal deputy. A new jurado de hechos found in his favor, but González, the accused, did not show up for conciliation and requested a continuance. A date was set three months later, but he missed that appointment also. The second jury finally met in April of 1870 and sentenced González in absentia to six months in prison. A judge in Mexico City requested his arrest from a peer in Coahuila but nothing happened, in spite of Dávila's bitter complaints.[90]

Freedom of Speech as a Local Right

The local nature of the press jury in Mexico City was the main source of its strength. Since federal authorities had no intervention in press cases, except as complainants, juries came to represent the autonomy of the capital's City Council and its sometimes tense relationship with national authorities. In yet another case against him, also in 1877, Díaz's critic Bablot asked jurors to recuse themselves, invoking the intimate association between City Council and press jury: since the legitimacy of the City Council elected in the last days of 1876 was still in dispute, he argued, the list of eligible jurors compiled in 1877 had been published by an illegal "municipal commission" installed by President Díaz. "It would be a sarcasm," he added, "if the jury, whose origin and respectability come from the people, was formed by a City Council that is not the legitimate representative of the popular will."[91]

The contested Ayuntamiento election of 1876 was indeed a turning point in the relationship between municipal authorities and the presidency. The City Council remained strong after independence and by the mid-nineteenth century had become the main political venue for decisions concerning urban development. This raised a potential obstacle to the national political elites' plans to exercise greater political control and develop a profitable real estate market—two related goals, in their view. The Ayuntamiento was traditionally composed of upper-class neighbors, yet elections could generate turbulence in broader circles. In 1876, when Díaz had just seized national power, he decided to let local elections run their course. The result was an object lesson in the need for a strong hand. In the recollections of José Yves Limantour, a prominent member of the *científico* group, the rabble had elected a City Council that lacked respectability, a creature of "schemers and neighborhood caciques [who] reign over polls." Disorder and theft in the council's building characterized its first meeting in early 1877. On this pretext, Díaz withdrew his recognition of the elected body, appointed a municipal commission, and henceforth secured informal control over elections through "the usual procedures."[92] Subsequent *ayuntamientos* were mostly formed by men close to the president, many of whom were involved in the development of infrastructure and new residential areas. Díaz eventually took away much of the council's power through informal means and through statutory reforms in 1903. When postrevolutionary authorities abolished the City Council in 1929, they completed the dictator's project by transferring full powers to a presidentially appointed mayor and continuing with the lucrative development of residential areas.[93] Diane Davis has framed the political disputes over development and use of public spaces within a long-term confrontation between powerful economic interests and the state, on the one side, and petit bourgeois merchants and professionals, often residing downtown, on the other. That relationship, she convincingly argues, is a central theme in the history of the Mexican public sphere.[94]

Yet tensions between local actors and federal authorities were not only about business: in a city that even today sees itself as a sanctuary for writers, the press jury was the focal point of tensions between local elites and federal officials regarding freedom of speech. By referring to the elections for the City Council, Bablot pointed to the press jury's main institutional support. Even during the periods when the press jury was not part of press legislations, trials against journalists took place in City Council chambers.[95] This is not surprising: like the City Council, the press jury only interested a relatively small number of citizens; both represented public opinion, defined as an expression not of the majority of city neighbors but of a small yet authoritative group of vecinos.

The representative value of the press jury came from its roots in urban networks of friendship and prestige. Although early regulations established income requirements, the duty of being a press jury member was never defined purely in terms of class or even literacy. In other words, the key consideration was not externally defined but internal: the web of connections that held together a group tied "by a general treatment of friendship," similar to that held among "the neighbors of the same town."[96] It was not only through their reading of the press that they knew about those networks: Their knowledge of other vecinos came from personal interactions that the press only reflected ex post facto. Jurors' visible place in urban society demonstrated their membership in that web: They were people who could be easily recognized in public spaces. Thus, the small size of the pool of jurors did not undermine but reinforced the legitimacy of the press jury as an expression of opinion—jurors were expected to be fair and impervious to political pressure because their names and addresses, posted on lists around the city at the beginning of every year, bespoke independence and social standing. They had to live close to the Ayuntamiento building, downtown, a multiclass area of the city that, for most of the nineteenth century, was home for established families. Jurors had much to lose if they failed to attend a meeting. Besides fines, the City Council printed their names in another list, now as delinquents of "democratic principles."[97]

These attributes were on the minds of aldermen when they drafted lists that, albeit not exhaustive, responded both to the requirements of the law and to their assessment of neighbors' reputation. The Ayuntamiento of 1828 exhibited that attitude when it decided to nullify the list from the previous year because it contained names council members did not know and others with dubious "opinions about our system" or untested willingness to defend freedom of the press from "the enemies of the fatherland." In their stead, the council summoned citizens whose patriotism "they have demonstrated in so many ways." The governor of the Federal District, Juan de Dios Cañedo, objected to the procedure and had the decision reversed, correctly arguing that the City Council's role was not to vote on each person in the list but merely to eliminate those who did not fulfill the requirements of the law.[98] Although mistaken in its interpretation of the law, the Ayuntamiento was correct in assuming that press jurors had to belong to the urban social networks of friendship still visibly deployed in nineteenth-century urban spaces and comprised in the term *vecino*.[99] The City Council followed Cañedo's indication and recruited more jurors after 1828 (see table 2, above). The list produced that year was enhanced with new names added in council members' own handwriting, suggesting that personal knowledge was still an important part of the process. In subsequent years, city employees compiled names by district but the editorial intervention of aldermen continued.[100] The

TABLE 3. Press jury members summoned in 1832

Trade	Summoned
Merchants (*Comerciantes*)	290
Butchers (*Tosinerías*)	40
Bakers (*Panaderías*)	43
Property owners (*Propietarios*)	80
Lawyers (*Abogados*)	43
Artisans (*Artesanos*)	44
Ecclesiastics (*Eclesiásticos*)	96
Agriculturalists (*Labradores*)	94
Total	*730*

Source: AHDFJ, 2739, 19.

largest number of citizens summoned was in late 1846, after a new press law was passed, but also in the midst of the crumbling of federal institutions owing to the war against the United States—whose army would seize the capital in September of 1847 without interrupting the City Council's work. As was true of the press legislation examined above, war and politics could not overwhelm the basic functions of urban public life.

The increase in the number of jurors between 1822 and 1882 (see table 2) did not mean that press juries were made up of common people. The high number of merchants, lawyers, landowners, and ecclesiastics present on the list of 1832—totaling 509 out of 730 names—confirms that jurors belonged to the upper economic and social strata (table 3). Furthermore, "labrador" could include journeymen as well as ranchers, and artisans were a diverse group that included workshop owners with some capital. The presence of artisans and agriculturalists (*labradores*) might suggest that the group did not represent a closed social universe. "Comerciantes" included a wide range of activities, from street vendors on up.

The selection of jurors defined the public that read newspapers and that decided about reputations. In his book about Juárez, Justo Sierra defined such a population as the "thinking country" because of their literacy but, most important, because the group "has personality, is often in touch with local passions and needs, and sometimes with politics in general."[101] Status and independence were expected of press jurors because their defining role was the rational interpretation and discussion of a written text and the weighting of free speech against individuals' reputations. According to Prieto these operations involved intellectual abilities that judges' legalistic and politically motivated brains lacked. Only intelligent citizens could read a publication with the subtlety required "to know if there is injury in using italics, points of ellipsis, or interrogation marks after a compliment, and to know if these devises are used to attribute a vice or a crime to an individual."[102] Like many liberals of his time, Prieto saw literacy as a defining feature of citizenship, even though the Constitution did not require it of Mexicans for purposes of voting. Later, more conservative liberals drew the logical consequence: for Carlos Basave, illiteracy in Mexico excluded "four-fifths of its inhabitants, who . . . neither understand nor wish other rights than those pertaining to animal life in its more primary functions."[103]

In contemporaries' eyes, the surest test of a man's rightful membership in the "thinking country" was exposure to public opinion, his fama pública. The lists of potential jurors authorities posted on corners each January authorized other neighbors to judge those names not only by their social standing, but also from a political point of view, as the council did in 1828. In 1872, *El Monitor Republicano* accused municipal authorities of rigging a jury in order to help the governor of the Federal District. The secretary of the City Council, Ramón Fernández, responded with an argument that left no room for debate: the best proof of the jury's independence were the names of its members, who "are well known, fortunately." He listed them and added, "If I may descend to purely personal considerations, it would easily be known that if some of them have preconceived opinions, they are certainly not favorable to the Governor." Furthermore, concluded Fernández, during his experience on the City Council "it has never been the case that the sentence of the juries has been adverse to any public writer."[104] Defiance of authority was sometimes the only honorable option for jurors exposed to such public oversight. Perhaps the strongest example of that independence was a case in 1861 in which the Juárez government denounced a publication that had presented an unflattering description of the diplomatic representative of France—just as that country was preparing to invade Mexico. The jury, presided over by Gabino Barreda (later to become Juárez's main education reformer), decided that the accusation had no merit. The case may explain why, weeks later, Juárez abrogated the press law passed in February of that year.[105]

The closeness to "local passions" was additional evidence of press jurors' representativeness. Sentences reverberated throughout the city, as many people witnessed jury audiences and rapidly spread information. Juries were always mindful of the feelings of audiences, which did not shy away from expressing their views. Even though audience members had no formal role in the process, the presumption of jurors' independence extended to them. Many were offended, for example, when Arcadio Cabrera said that the spectators whose shouts and hissing drowned out his defense in front of a San Luis Potosí jury were a "claque" sent to support the complainant, Manuel Baranda.[106] The audience's views were relevant, if extralegal, because after the trial jurors had to face the personal consequences of their decisions. According to the law journal *El Foro*, jurors who neglectfully supported libelous writers could themselves be accused of attacking a victim's "reputation as an honest man."[107]

Jurors resided within a web of personal relations that included writers and victims and allowed them to gauge the seriousness of offenses in subtle ways. Words could be offensive because of their elocution and in reference to the persona of the speaker and the person alluded to. This, not simply literacy, made it possible to read texts with the nuance expected by Prieto—perceiving the tone that the text acquired when performed aloud or the irony of a silence. One example of such reading is the case in 1861 brought by Gabor Napheggi against the following two sentences, published in *El Amigo del Pueblo*: "Mr. Napheggi is the individual appointed to collect the money contributed by foreigners to the benefit show entitled 'For the victims.' We think it is convenient that this appointment be widely known."[108] The jury voted unanimously to sentence the author, Miguel Zomoza, to the maximum penalty of six months of prison. Where was the insult? We can understand the verdict only if we imagine this passage being read in the City Council room with a specific intonation and in the context of a rivalry that, although not given to print, was well known to the members of the jury.[109]

The spoken dimension of any text was not exclusive of gacetilla, of course. A poet's ode to a woman in a novel by Juan Antonio Mateos required some explanation for the cuckolded husband to understand its meaning. Those who read for audiences at cafes, colonnades, and salons put great effort into finding the right emphasis, intonation, and gestures, which explains the importance of rhetorical devices in early Mexican journalistic texts. Conversations about newspapers or simply the voices of young street sellers advertising their contents could be as powerful as the text itself. In 1834, Governor Tornel prohibited the voceo, as noted above, because it exercised "no small influence in the increase of political and personal hatred."[110]

The continuity between written and oral communication in press trials is illustrated by the case against the "Pronunciamiento de Colima," discussed above as an example of the difficulties of ascertaining authorship. José María Gutiérrez was strolling under the arcades of downtown Colima and stopped to talk to his friend Antonio Ochoa. Ochoa told him about the "Pronunciamiento," and both speculated about its contents. Bartolomé Quintero, the author of the manifesto, joined them and bragged that he would avoid penal responsibility. Jokingly, Ochoa advised Quintero not to trust other friends too much—and indeed both Ochoa and Gutiérrez testified against Quintero later in the trial.[111] The casual yet loaded exchange between three men under downtown colonnades could give more resonance to *pasquinades* glued at night on walls and posts. Although they usually came in a few copies and were mostly handwritten, pasquinades multiplied many times through verbal exchanges about their salacious contents. Such "disgusting banners" showed up on the walls of Orizaba in 1869 to attack the jefe político[112] and in "several public places of the city of Texcoco, the morning of August 13, 1853." The posting in Texcoco, which denounced ecclesiastic graft, prompted a civil suit against Cruz Balcázar. He was acquitted for lack of evidence of his authorship, but victims appealed, claiming that anonymous writings had been banned by a law of 1808 and were thus not protected by press laws.[113]

The allegation in that case touched on the thorny problem of defining a publication as such. As noted earlier, critics of the press jury, like Pallares, pointed to the dual nature of press crimes: they had their own legislation, but they also broke penal laws by constituting slander, libel, sedition. Paradoxically, for Pallares, while in common crimes the publicity of the insult aggravated the offense, in the case of press offenses publicity itself protected the offender.[114] Press jurors' sensibility to orality could drive them to expand the definition of what a published text was and potentially overlap with criminal courts' jurisdiction, that is, verbal insults and defamation.[115] Mindful of that, a press jury in San Luis Potosí decided in 1882 that the statements written by Arcado Cabrera about Manuel Baranda on blackboards were not publications but manuscripts and should thus be criminally prosecuted. Cabrera was a journalist who wrote news and advertisements on blackboards located in several places of the city— a line of business he had engaged in in the capital. *El Foro's* report of the incident noted that article 7 of the Constitution protected the freedom "to write and publish writings on any subject" and cited a decision by the Supreme Court protecting the owner of another blackboard who had been forced by administrative authorities to remove it.[116] Press codes were comprehensive in listing the media to be considered under their regulations, yet local authorities tended to use any opportunity to try writings according to penal law. Manuscripts that had not yet been typeset, for example, could be treated as evidence of a common crime. Antonio Vidal was arrested in Chalco in 1881 while in possession of some pages he intended to publish in newspapers in Mexico City.[117] Given the relative strength of the capital's City Council compared to the de facto power of political authorities in smaller cities, the above cases suggest that the line between journalism and gossip shifted according to local circumstances.

Conclusions

The history of the press jury demonstrates the need to think again about the interaction of local, urban politics and national history. The process reconstructed in this chapter cannot be characterized as a dialectical struggle between modernity and tradition, individualism against corporative ties, or the state against civil society. Between the diversity of opinions that worried Mora and the locally rooted "thinking country" of Sierra and Prieto, the press jury became central because of its ability to link social networks and republican protection of free speech. These practical connections shaped the meaning of public opinion in nineteenth-century Mexico and limited sovereignty to the realm of the possible. The press jury played a double role that is recognizable only in practice: (a) the protection of the press, in order to preserve the "true knowledge of public opinion" against attacks from power, and (b) the creation of an institutional frame for freely deliberating citizens to represent public opinion in all its diversity and propensity to personal conflict.[118]

Nineteenth-century Mexican political actors understood citizenship as something more specific than abstract rights, yet less determined than class status. As early as 1820 Spanish and Mexican authorities praised the republican wisdom of citizen-jurors and characterized their participation in juries as an act of "patriotism," "honor . . . virtue . . . and good sense."[119] As the press jury turned into the decisive point of reference of press debates between 1868 and 1882, it also came to incarnate the complexity of public opinion and its reach into "the secret asylum of private life," to quote Mora once again. For Ignacio Ramírez, the press jury's authority over alleged invasions of privacy embodied a central aspect of citizenship because it supported "the sovereign people as the original judge" of both reputations and governments. Ramírez cited as antecedents of the press jury the debates in the public square of the classical age, and "Lynch's law," which, he explained, "authorizes certain kinds of popular executions in the United States."[120] There was indeed a tumultuous side to press juries. But rather than violent exclusions or meticulous discussions about points of law, their debates often turned into celebrations of free speech in which the accused article was read aloud while the audience cheered and mocked the victim, her or his reputation thus ruined.[121] It would be hard to find an image that better portrayed the continuity between the written and oral dimensions of the public sphere and the trepidations of Mexican liberals' faith in the harmony of reason, open debate, and the sovereignty of popular will.

Jury audiences' fluctuations between emotion and reason and journalists' work at the edge of gossip and libel required that jurors be aware of vecinos' reputations. To be rational, public opinion had to be defined as the product of a small, educated sector of the people, the opposite of the mob alluded to by Ramírez—even if sometimes its deliberations were anything but civilized. The history of the public sphere during subsequent years is that of the building of the exclusions that derive from those ideas. It would be incorrect to synthesize that process, however, as the weakening of public opinion and debate. The public sphere was at the same time prestigious, locally rooted, and exclusive, as were the press jury and the City Council. These institutions, like all others, were made up of individuals with inner feelings and personal relationships.

CHAPTER 2

Representing Public Opinion
Combat Journalists and the Business of Honor

If public opinion was centrally concerned with honor, one must understand journalists in their double role as preeminent representatives of
public opinion and as men whose reputation was exposed to it. In 1888,
Emilio Rabasa put it in the ironic voice of a fictional journalist: "Imagine
yourself representing public opinion! . . . You will not open your mouth
except in the name of such a lady, who is a decent person even though
she is in everybody's hands."[1] Rabasa's allusion to the double morality of
public opinion expressed his belief that the lofty standards of journalists,
as men of honor, collided with the negotiations in which, as producers of
cultural and political goods, they engaged in order to advance their reputations and careers.

I want to address that contradiction by placing journalists in the context of an era of changing political and social demands on their trade. My
basic contention is that journalists bartered their reputation in the market of public life. That operation guided the content of their writings,
their everyday behavior, and their perception of themselves individually
and as a group. Through the press, particularly in the capital, they gave
voice to public opinion's judgments regarding not only matters of common interest but also the qualities of other public men. Those "anointed
by public opinion" in Mexico City had set up a "wholesale factory of
reputations," argued a critic from Guanajuato in 1888.[2]

Although public opinion operated as a "decent person" when it judged personal honor, the conflicting claims of its representatives made it seem as if she were "in everybody's hands." Were Mexican journalists any better than her? They were not entitled to honra because of inherited status (many of them were moving up socially), or because of their military achievements (they were mostly civilian). Their mastery of the written word allowed them to claim honor as a right, rather than a privilege received from the state or the family. To do this, they engaged in dangerous public and personal debates. Contemporaries defined this as *periodismo de combate*: writers' political engagement but also their disposition to conflict. I argue here that combat journalism made possible the accumulation of the social capital that honor signified, promoting several journalists to high places within the country's elite, but also causing the proud poverty of others. The symbolic and the material were never separated in the ethics of combat journalism, as it encompassed both romantic freedom and disinterest and the economic pressures of the business of publicity.

Pierre Bourdieu's sociology offers a systematic way to formulate the premises and implications of this chapter, although with some caveats for the case of Mexico. Journalists, as we will see, turned the symbolic capital generated by their writings and practices into social capital. They could work such a transformation because those forms of capital represented the accumulation of other people's labor—cashed in as friendship, loyalty, patronage, or money. Yet a purely economistic explanation does not suffice: They did not want only to be rich eventually. What they did (and what defines the importance of journalists in nineteenth-century Mexico) was to exercise their unrivaled ability to move between multiple fields (literary, political, bureaucratic) and come back strengthened by the trip. This was a practical virtue, not an ideological function: their influence was more a product of their relationship with public opinion, than a product of their role as mouthpieces of sovereignty. In other words, it was not a stable position in Mexican society that defined them, but the relations they engaged in, at multiple levels and political moments, with other actors.[3] I will consider honor here as something they produced, accumulated, and exchanged. In doing so, I will illustrate how it is one of the goods that, to quote Bourdieu, is "rare and worthy of being sought after in a particular social formation"; a good that is not simply material yet whose importance is not weakened by a monetary economy.[4]

The decades after the republican triumph over traitors and monarchists in 1867 saw the emergence of honor as a key commodity within a public life overshadowed by moral ambiguity. The Constitution of 1857 reigned at last, guaranteed by the irreproachable leadership of Benito Juárez; yet dissent was more open and acrimonious than at any time in memory. Porfirio Díaz, a hero of the republican struggle, seized power in 1876 after rebelling against legitimate presidents, first Juárez, then Sebastián Lerdo de Tejada. Throughout this period, newspapers, thanks to the protection of the press jury and, sometimes, of the money of *juaristas*, *lerdistas*, and *porfiristas*, oscillated between sedition and satire in their response to power.[5] Once in power, Díaz dealt with the highly litigious atmosphere by promising that his plan of Tuxtepec would be the rebellion to end all rebellions. The first, urgent step was to control the ambitions of the "civilian and military heroes" who had emerged from the war. Díaz was careful in his allocation of public resources and positions and in the display of his affections. He sent some men, like Ignacio Ramírez, to Europe on diplomatic posts, while others he formally recognized for their past merits with decorations and promotions. A second problem for his regime was the moral implications of a "policy of conciliation," which sought to integrate former conservatives into the new regime. The French intervention had established a clear divide between traitors and patriots, but, in the eyes of veteran liberals, Díaz seemed to be eroding it. In 1878, José María Vigil accused the Tuxtepec group of corruption because of its "illicit intercourse with traitors and *mochos* [defenders of the church]."[6]

Honor became the locus of public men's concern about their place in the new order. As exemplified dramatically by Santos Degollado in 1860, honor was conceived of as a stable norm of behavior rooted in one's intimate beliefs and thus invulnerable to the shifts of partisanship, but also as social status recognized publicly. In a pamphlet defending his reputation, published in Mazatlán in 1868, Francisco de Paula Vega formulated a doctrine to which all actors subscribed:

> There is nothing more sacred or of greater value in the eyes of cultivated and educated men than honor. Thus we see, in all times and in all countries, the sacrifice not only of well-being in the present, not only of material goods, but even of life itself; thus we see how, in order to preserve a pure name without stains, individuals, families, cities, nations, and the whole of humanity sacrifice themselves . . . because the conscience of good behavior produces the

most intimate and pure joy in our heart, and contributes most directly to a
real and truthful peace of the spirit. . . . I defend the only inheritance that I
seek for my children: a good name, the never-contradicted example of an
accredited behavior; I defend, finally, the only moral capital I own, the most
valuable jewel of my fortune.[7]

The doctrine expressed by de Paula Vega illustrates the tension between
the two aspects of honor: publicly recognized, it was part of a family's
legacy, but subjectively it was also an intimate feeling worth sacrificing
"life itself."[8]

Among public men, journalists were the most sensitive and vocal regarding honor. Three aspects of their trade determined their access to
that "moral capital" extolled by de Paula Vega. The first concerns the
political economy of journalism. In a country of few readers, newspapers
operated in a market in which sales, patronage, and public resources
were always intertwined. Frequent polemics increased sales but also expressed journalists' drive to multiply their offerings by producing contradictory opinions. As a result, they wrote about each other as much as
they did about "real" politics.

Concern about business did not necessarily translate into monetary
results. Most journalists during this period were poor, but were able to
accumulate social (or moral) capital. The example of three authors who
wrote about their experience in the trade (Rabasa, Federico Gamboa, and
Heriberto Frías) shows how material poverty was not an obstacle but a
necessary component in their drive to acquire the connections and prestige that would later allow the first two to advance through the ranks of
the Porfirian regime. Frías was different because his embrace of a bohemian lifestyle revealed the contradictions of the romantic ethos shared
with his contemporaries. In any case, the social capital accumulated by
journalists also translated into gendered rewards for them in their roles
as lovers and husbands.[9]

The third aspect of the trade that determined journalists' access to
moral capital was the role of polemics in their lives, as exemplified in the
famous confrontation in 1880 between Ireneo Paz and the brothers Justo
and Santiago Sierra. The dispute, which ended in a fatal duel, exposed the
personal ramifications of electoral politics, the tensions between two
generations of public men in the early years of the Porfiriato, and the
difficult separation between the intimate and the public spheres.

An ethnographic description of the life of a group is not easy when its members are educated men who had a taste for individualism and a proud contempt for materialism. Nineteenth-century Mexican journalists generated material goods (daily columns of prose) but were also authors: public personas with literary prestige and a penchant for independence. They saw their audience as abstract strangers but also as specific names, one of "us."[10] Like other forms of symbolic capital, the prestige of journalists was materially expensive, yet accrued well to young men like Gamboa and Rabasa who moved up in the world of government and diplomacy.

Political Economy of Journalism

Vicente García Torres (1811–94) was emblematic of nineteenth-century Mexican journalism (figure 5). His *Monitor Republicano* was a model of editorial quality and courage in its criticism of the government and a favorite target of press juries. At the same time, he was one of the most successful entrepreneurs in the business. Although lacking formal education, he possessed expertise, language proficiency, and the influence of utopian socialism from his travels in Europe. In Mexico, he rose quickly during the 1840s by acquiring several small presses in the capital and becoming one of the most prolific producers of pamphlets, books, and periodicals.[11] His success derived from the quality of his publications, his ability to vertically and horizontally integrate the business, combining typesetting and printing, distribution via subscriptions and voceo, the hiring of the best available writers, and, in at least one case, the unauthorized translation of foreign books. Receiving some official support was not beneath him, his adversaries claimed. All this did not result in great personal wealth but was enough to prompt charges like the one levied against him by *La Bala Roja* in 1869: "Speculator and not apostle, merchant and not priest of the noble vocation of the press."[12] The accusation referred both to García Torres's business acumen and to the combative style of *El Monitor Republicano*. When he decided to suspend publication of the newspaper in 1896, after a forty-six-year run, he cited both financial and political reasons: readers were abandoning him, while "for us only the prison had its doors open."[13]

García Torres was exceptional because he was one of the few journalists who maintained a viable business without constantly receiving official

5. Vicente García Torres.
© 644259. CND. SINAFO-
Fototeca Nacional del
INAH.

sponsorship or embracing powerful patrons.[14] Most other publishers had
to make such compromises because of the reduced number of copies sold
by newspapers of the era. By the early 1880s *El Monitor Republicano* sold
up to ten thousand copies on Sundays, while *El Siglo Diez y Nueve* had
dwindling sales of around six hundred copies. Until the foundation of *El
Imparcial* in 1896, no publication was able to reach the twenty-thousand-
copy mark. During those decades, newspapers and magazines printed
between a few hundreds and forty-five hundred copies, totaling between
thirty thousand and one hundred thousand copies. Printing data from
newspapers themselves were always suspect, but it was clear that only a
few publications broke even based on their sales.[15]

This does not mean that the market was weak. As suggested in chapter 1, the number of direct and indirect readers was probably more than
20 percent of Mexico City's population, which totaled approximately a
quarter of a million in 1880. The number of publications is a better index
of the vitality of the industry, and it shows that politics was the driving
force. While the traditional publications declined, new ones emerged.

The República Restaurada, particularly around election times, was a period that witnessed an extraordinary increase in the number of newspapers.[16] Díaz's first period saw a continuation of this boom, with as many as 48 newspapers in Mexico City in 1878. A decrease took place during Manuel González's presidency, but the numbers were still higher than in later years. In 1888, Mexico City was home to 120 of the country's 285 periodical publications, 14 of which were newspapers. During the rest of the Porfiriato, growth in the size of printings coincided with a consolidation in the number of titles.[17]

This "writing market" of politics (to use Angel Rama's term) could not be measured only by the number of readers, but also by their quality. Newspaper prices oscillated between three and five cents, and compared to twentieth-century dailies advertisements occupied a small part of their columns. To survive, Mexican editors had to look beyond sales for income and tap the demand of the political marketplace. In contrast with *El Monitor Republicano* and *El Siglo Diez y Nueve*, most newspapers appeared and survived thanks to subsidies from governments and individual politicians who wanted to advance their careers or respond to attacks from other publications. While the *Diario Oficial* was the government's stable voice, other newspapers would suddenly change sides or even stop publication after the election, promotion, or appointment of their sponsor. Editors could make one candidacy their central theme or simultaneously promote several candidates in different races. In all cases, shifts in reputations measured the impact of subsidies. Personal endorsements could be explicit or presented as a "program of ideas" but most frequently were expressed through attacks against political rivals or their hired writers. By deliberately making or destroying reputations, according to Emilio Rabasa's novel about the profession, *Moneda falsa* (Counterfeit money) (1888), the *periodista de combate* (combat journalist) became a "trafficker in reputations, honors, titles and military ranks."[18]

Yet editors and writers recognized that politics could not be the only focus and tried to add other values to their product, such as serialized novels by authors like Paz and Francisco Zarco and foreign authors. Newspapers also offered scientific, legal, technological, medical, and educational news, in addition to information on topics thought to be of special interest to female readers. Commercial information—from advertisements to opinions about products and merchants' behavior—appeared on the back pages.[19] Most important, perhaps, all these additional goods justified the paper's existence. A free paper, entirely paid for by sponsors, contradicted the idea of journalism as a valuable good in the market of everyday life.

Subsidies, always shamefully admitted to, came through the payment of multiple subscriptions rather than direct financing. This could work as a kind of forceful sales representation, as with the *Gaceta de Policía*, supported by the police chief of Mexico City, Félix Díaz, a nephew of the president. The *Gaceta* circulated among jefes políticos, governors, and mayors in other cities, all of whom were encouraged to pay via the political influence and aspirations of don Porfirio's relative.[20] Subscriptions did not mean readers. In another novel about journalism, *El cuarto poder* (The fourth estate), Rabasa described the simple arithmetic of the business: the fictional *La Columna* printed four hundred copies a day; one hundred were distributed among high-level employees of the government in the capital and the rest were sent to several governors, some of whom bought up to fifty subscriptions. Beyond a few bureaucrats, Rabasa added sarcastically, *La Columna* did not have actual readers. According to the novelistic chronicler Heriberto Frías, newspapers adjusted their praise or criticism according to the number of subscriptions bought by the beneficiary. A subtler way to funnel the money from the government to the press was to provide editors with a few no-show jobs in the administration that they would then distribute among their staff. The poet Manuel José Othón, for example, wrote in "ministerial newspapers" and received a government salary approved directly by the Secretaría de Gobernación.[21]

As Díaz consolidated power he strove to limit the seditious cacophony of the República Restaurada press. While lesser politicians continued to spend their money on individual publications, the central government began to distribute subsidies among multiple newspapers, regardless of their editorial line or immediate political goals—as long, of course, as they did not criticize the president. By 1888, the government spent almost forty thousand pesos a year on approximately thirty publications in Mexico City. This was the same amount, according to the rough calculations of *El Hijo del Ahuizote*, spent on the salaries of federal deputies and senators and state legislatures. After 1896, *El Imparcial* tended to receive most of the subsidy, although support of other publications and suspicions about their integrity did not disappear entirely.[22]

Historians and commentators have interpreted journalistic texts through the lens of ideology, conspiracy, and gossip. It would be a mistake, however, to read newspapers of the República Restaurada and early Porfirian period as mere mouthpieces of politicians and to search for hidden meanings in articles and bylines according to underlying *personalista* politicking.[23] Against a cynical or conspiratorial reading, I would argue that subsidies enriched the contents of the press by adding a layer of tension to every article and increasing the importance of newspapers in the building of public opinion. What modern readers analyze according to an instrumental rationality of interests and rhetoric, late nineteenth-century readers and writers saw as a demonstration that disputes over public matters were authentic precisely because they involved both common interests and personal reputations, giving each debate greater intensity and deeper meaning. The journalist Manuel Caballero expressed this predisposition when he told Victoriano Salado Alvarez that "in a town of one hundred inhabitants one can write a newspaper that would deserve to be read with interest by one hundred thousand people."[24]

Conflict was the key offering of combat journalists. The system of multiple competing subsidies determined a specific structure for the press business in which the key to survival was diversification. The variety of voices, all speaking in the name of public opinion, was a reason to spread the money around. From journalists' point of view, the best way to underline and publicize a diversity that was based only on ideological grounds was to engage in as many polemics as possible—even if the reasons for disagreement needed to be exaggerated or even invented—thus keeping their ability to "generate political events," to use Elías José Palti's words.[25] According to state prosecutors and witnesses, Trinidad Martínez, the editor of *El Correo del Lunes* and *El Valedor*, pushed his writers to write venomous articles in order to improve sales. Other journalists did not need monetary encouragement to spice things up. Juan Quiñones, a character in Rabasa's *El Cuarto Poder*, dreamed of engaging in polemics against other journalists, preferably someone "well known and respected in the world of letters." This would focus the attention of "literati and public men" on his writings and increase his salary and his reputation.[26] Quiñones's boss took the strategy to its extreme, engaging the anonymous writer of a rival newspaper in a ferocious debate. Only later, when the sales of both publications had increased, did it become known that the two adversaries were Quiñones himself. Although this may be a figment of Rabasa's bitter recollections of life as a journalist, it is

6. Federico Gamboa,
c. 1914. © 647408.
CND. SINAFO-Fototeca
Nacional del INAH.

clear that many shared the impression that some in the trade trafficked in insults and "profited from scandal," and that polemics were less dangerous than they appeared.[27] In 1884, *La Libertad* mocked the trivial disputes: "Today we journalists are used to the system of bloodless little duels. . . . We insult someone, appoint seconds, they decide that combat is not necessary, 'and honor is satisfied!' "[28] Frías described in *Miserias de México* (1916) this "bullying" kind of combat journalist as someone who exploited his "mordacity for personal injury . . . the easy talent to win journalistic polemics by personalizing them, replying with mockery to reason, and with sarcasm to truth."[29]

A consequence of this diversification of voices was the self-referential character of most journalistic prose. For journalists, adversaries' writings mattered more than objective reporting. In his memoirs of his youth, *Impresiones y recuerdos* (1893), Federico Gamboa (figure 6) recalled that the walls of the office of the first newspaper he worked at were covered with clippings from "every newspaper in Mexico City and a few from the most important states."[30] Along with pens, cigarettes, and a dictionary, the most important tool for writers was a pair of scissors. Many articles consisted of long quotations and comments on the praise or criticism received by authors from other newspapers.[31] Originality, in the market of opinions, was less important than combustibility.

The Material Poverty and Social Riches of Public Writers

Hard work and low salaries were rewarded with reputation and connections. As Quiñones's dreams suggest, conflict meant the possibility of increasing social capital. Journalists' reading, quoting, and fighting each other created a self-contained world in which public opinion was constantly married to personal honor. Independence of thought was represented as proud autonomy, and simple making of money and enjoyment of bourgeois comfort were not acceptable. Yet, as I observed, polemics were a direct or indirect consequence of the central role of subsidies in the operations of the business. The complex intertwining of symbolic and material rewards is evident in the economic troubles, social prestige, and ethical dilemmas faced by the members of "this most noble and ungrateful career."[32] The combination of intellectual prestige and gritty effort expected from tradesmen was accurately portrayed in doggerel published by *El Monitor* in 1886:

> Who would want to be a journalist?
> God help him! God assist him!
> He must be director,
> Writer, corrector,
> Administrator, editor, typesetter,
> Censor, collaborator,
> Correspondent, operator,
> He must replace the printer,
> And sometimes . . . even the reader.[33]

The category of *escritor público* (public writer), often used by journalists to describe themselves, encompassed a range of trades, from scribes to fiction writers. A similarly broad and quite evocative term, although less common, was "athletes of the word."[34] The broad definitions responded to the multiple skills exercised through texts. According to

Manuel Gutiérrez Nájera, a journalist "can divide himself into a thousand pieces and remain a whole. Yesterday he was an economist, today a theologian, tomorrow a Hebraist or a miller."[35] Federico Gamboa learned multiple abilities first in the judicial daily *El Foro*, then at the *Diario del Hogar*, both edited by one of the masters of the art, Filomeno Mata. Gamboa began translating articles from English, then copyediting and, for three years, practicing the basic skill of the trade: to quickly churn out texts of different lengths on diverse themes, texts based on almost no information but inflated with opinions and embellishments.

The format that best displayed the ability of good journalists was the *gacetilla*, that unstructured mix of short reports, opinion, and gossip. Salado Alvarez, remembering his beginnings as a *gacetillero* in *El Diario de Jalisco*, noted the influence of colleagues like Francisco Cosmes and Jesús Rábago, who "gave the newspaper interest, . . . grace, substance, and salt." They went beyond reporting the news and "added humor, intention, charm, and jokes that people understood and celebrated."[36] As mentioned above, gacetilla could be filled also with passages from other newspapers and sometimes, according to Rabasa, even fabricated stories. There was no risk in fabrication, he suggested, as competitors would validate such inventions by repeating them the following day.[37] Style was more important than the objective reporting positivists would later favor, at least in appearance, at *El Imparcial*.

The flexibility and spontaneity of this method of writing made sincerity, rather than objectivity, a key moral value for journalists. In true romantic form, they saw this personal style as an aesthetic choice that blended with personal commitment. Ironically, writers' integrity justified their shifting of opinions and partisan loyalties, keeping the realm of "conscience" as ultimate guarantor of their honor. Sincerity could not be based on formal education, which most journalists lacked anyway, but on spontaneity: Gamboa was told to write "whatever comes [to mind] first."[38] The graceful and casual choice of words and themes, however, concealed a systematic building of public writers' character. Rabasa described in *El cuarto poder* the training behind a budding journalist's spontaneity: first, he had to overcome fear and self-criticism, something that was easily achieved by considering the literary inferiority of most of his colleagues; second, a personal program of study was necessary, including grammar, geography, history ("to lose the fear of talking about Prussia and Turkey, or Philip II and John Lackland"), politics, law, and

7. Manuel Puga y Acal.
From Manuel Puga y Acal,
*Los poetas mexicanos con-
temporáneos: Ensayos críticos
de Brummel.* Mexico City:
Ireneo Paz, 1888.

"some nice and polished Rhetoric, the careful study of which teaches beauties to be writer, not just journalist."[39] This haphazard education prepared public writers to effortlessly produce paragraphs full of foreign and classical references and eloquent metaphors—a useful ability for a writer in the middle of polemics or the crunch to fill columns before a deadline but "with no time to open a book or check a dictionary."[40]

Building the disposition for sincerity went beyond writing and involved a bohemian model of behavior. According to James Green, journalism was a respectable professional option for bohemians in the belle époque in Brazil. Journalistic work erased youthful indiscretions and gave arriviste dandies a prestigious place within the elite: setting cultural trends, exploring urban life and sexual adventure, yet keeping a safe distance from popular mores.[41] The description applies very well to the Mexican writer and literary critic Manuel Puga y Acal, "Brummell," from Guadalajara. Salado Alvarez remembered Puga y Acal's public persona as being at one with his writing: "He had a gentle demeanor, he dressed elegantly ('he had been in Paris, after all!'), and was a social, erotic, and literary *lion*. . . . At fourteen he was writing with fluency and poise, at eighteen the government persecuted him for his criticisms, at nineteen he went to Europe, and at twenty-two he returned with an amazing literary erudition"[42] (figure 7). Puga y Acal was an exception, though, in his ability to

travel and dress well. Most Mexican journalists were closer to the penni-
less characters of Giacomo Puccini's *La Bohème* than to the refinement of
Beau Brummell. Young journalists like Paz, Sierra, Gamboa, Rabasa, and
Frías embraced a romantic view of *la vida bohemia* as an existential
model full of aesthetic meaning, while being at the same time socially
rebellious and self-centered.[43]

As noted in the introduction, Mexican romanticism must be understood not as a coherent cultural project but as a set of ethical and aesthetic dispositions. Nevertheless, combat journalists shared certain aesthetic emphases (particularly on the use of the metaphor) and a belief in
continuity between art and life. Both were exemplified in an exchange in
1888 in which Puga y Acal praised the poet Salvador Díaz Mirón's ode to
Lord Byron but disapproved of its abuse of metaphor; more seriously,
he doubted Díaz Mirón composed his verses with the spontaneity he
claimed. The observation was not just a matter of stylistic choices but
touched on the poet's sincerity, and the polemic almost ended in a duel.
Díaz Mirón, who was famously susceptible to any personal offense, re-
plied that metaphor was the most direct way to express his thought. This
was a moral as much as an aesthetic belief, grounded in Díaz Mirón's self-
perception as a visionary: "I follow no other path than my thinking nor
any other advice than that of my taste. The style is the man."[44] Puga y
Acal believed it was a mistake to confuse aesthetic critique with anything
"that could hurt the honor of those authors."[45] Three decades later, he
recognized that the subjects of his writings represented the impact of
romanticism, which, in Mexico, was a movement of "renewal, not only
literary but also philosophical, social, and political" characterized by an
"individualistic spirit of freedom and rebellion."[46] The connection between poetic images and sincerity that Díaz Mirón defended in 1888 was
emblematic of the vindication of autonomy through literature that characterized this strand of Mexican romanticism defined both by moral and
political commitment and by individualism.[47]

A close look at journalists and writers reveals the practical impact
of romanticism to be a specific combination of intellectual emphases
and material conditions. Besides the ideal of "absolute autonomy," a bohemian lifestyle was a requisite because it accounted for the poverty
that characterized the experience of journalism and literary endeavors in
general. For Gutiérrez Nájera, writing was "of all the roads leading to
poverty . . . the broadest and fastest."[48] Gamboa remembered how each

Saturday the staff of *Diario del Hogar* waited anxiously for Mata to arrive with the payroll. Often, however, there was not enough money to pay everyone. Not that salaries were high: Gamboa's first earnings were only thirty pesos a month.[49] By the end of his career as a journalist, before he took a low-level job in the federal bureaucracy, Gamboa was promoted to theater reviewer yet had to keep a morning job as court clerk in order to survive. An older colleague of his, Aurelio Garay, suffered more "because he had a little daughter who cost him tears and deprivations."[50] In *Miserias de México*, Frías described the misfortunes of his alter ego, Miguel Mercado: his wife's illnesses, his failed projects, and his trips to other cities in futile attempts to start afresh. Gamboa clerked to make ends meet, while others wrote serialized novels or religious texts or sold advertisements; but all knew that the path to financial stability lay in a government salary.[51]

To the domestic poverty that hurt Garay and Mercado, journalists had to add the high cost of social life. Long hours of nightly socializing were essential to maintain one's place among colleagues. The illustrator José María Villasana, for example, boasted about his social connections: "I know all of Mexico, its men and its things."[52] Yet good clothes, restaurants, and theater tickets seemed beyond the means of most journalists. Some, suggested Rabasa, required the subsidies just to pay for the high life. Others, like Gamboa, could keep up because they did not have to worry about maintaining a family. The intense social life of the members of the political and cultural elite usually started after work, at 1 p.m., included lunch at a restaurant, walks on 5 de Mayo or Plateros avenues, chocolate at cafeterias, theater, and dinner, and ended at midnight. *Cantinas*, where alcohol consumption was cheap, were important places for journalists. For all public men, bars were essential places of comradeship where "friendships got started, alliances were strengthened, businesses were aired, and problems were easily solved." When Mercado's moral and physical decay (suffered in real life by Frías) forced him to stop drinking, he lost the opportunity to learn the latest political gossip, and his colleagues mocked him whenever he dared show up in bars—which, in spite of his abstinence, financial troubles, and shame, he needed to frequent in order to reap the social rewards of the job. He thus soon acquired a reputation as a misanthrope.[53]

The first of journalism's rewards was social recognition. Gamboa remembered Garay as a disheveled, poor man who worked long hours in a grim office, yet was possessed of "an unlimited personal and literary pride." He had risen from typographer to staff writer thanks to his self-taught skills.[54] His trajectory, although predictable, was socially important because the "unlimited . . . pride" was based on his ability to write profusely but with eloquence and grace. The boundary between literary life and journalism was never precise: strictly literary polemics, such as the one between Puga y Acal and Díaz Mirón, could be as intense as those involving politics. Yet not all journalists were aspiring or failed writers. According to Salado Alvarez, Manuel Caballero was a journalist because of a "spiritual calling" different from that of poets and novelists.[55] Díaz Mirón is probably the best example of the ways in which journalism enjoyed literary prestige yet remained a discrete talent. His father had been a journalist, and Díaz wrote for local newspapers from the time he was fourteen years old. Although he came to be revered as a poet, he remained close to the trade throughout his life. Even though his editing of the counterrevolutionary *El Imparcial* in 1913 brought him exile, he maintained the same exacting linguistic standards there as in his poetry. Newspapers helped him feed his large family (thus his misadventure of 1913, he later claimed) and also allowed him to buttress his national reputation by engaging in well-publicized disputes. Angel de Campo disliked the personal attacks he endured as a result of practicing journalism but continued writing in newspapers to satisfy the same combination of financial needs and literary inspiration. In the end, however, it was only inspiration that counted. Remembering the ill-fated Manuel Acuña, Justo Sierra recalled the poet's ability to forget the readers of "our poor, idiotic society" and find solace in "the immortal Olympus of his contempt."[56]

In addition to literary merit, journalists' prestige grew when they took the risk of condemning social and political evils. As opposed to mere judicial accusations, public writers' censure of official malfeasance had "a seal of nobility" that placed them on high moral ground.[57] The foundation for that perception was the sacrifice of men, like Santos Degollado, who "carried the pen, the word, and the sword in the struggle" against dictators, conservatives, and invaders.[58] The late Porfirian regime offered journalists plenty of opportunities to echo this heroism, but most commonly the problem was that journalistic virtue did not allow for a protective separation between public and private life. The attorney Francisco Llamas Noriega defended a citizen of Zacatecas accused of libel by the staff of the local newspaper *El Constitucional*. He claimed that public writers could not appeal to the protection of privacy because "their acts, judgments and all their behavior fall under the public domain."[59] Civic courage and personal exposure to public opinion explain the individualist disposition of upwardly mobile journalists, while the domestic concerns of Garay and Mercado account for their inability to become selfish, famous, and well-to-do.

The masculine pleasures of homosociality and sexual adventure associated with individualism required the exclusion of respectable women from public life. The passage by Rabasa in the epigraph above allegorically presents public opinion as a woman of dubious virtue, yet one that could please whoever represented her.[60] Gamboa saw journalism as part of his seduction of another allegorical figure, literature—"feminine from the name and as such demanding, cruel, forgetful, but . . . passionate."[61] Respectable society was also an object of journalists' lust; as an anonymous writer of *La Patria* put it, "Society is a tres chic coquette who makes me happy."[62] Gamboa described Garay's theater reviews as "discreet and voluptuous caresses of [female] artists," and he admired Hilarión Frías y Soto's writings, like "arrows" in an "intellectual fencing [that] left painful marks," particularly his allusions to sexual adventures that dishonored his rivals.[63]

A consequence of such sexual construction of the profession was the need to exclude actual women from conversations about politics and literature. These conversations usually took place in homosocial public settings in which friendship was the strongest tie and in which women occupied only a socially subordinate position often identified with prostitution. The love of a woman was only the reference for two men's bonding: in Rabasa's *Moneda falsa*, Juan makes his peace with General Mateo Cabezudo, the uncle of his beloved Remedios, as both wait in vain at her bedside for her to recover from a serious illness. In a characteristically circular scheme, Juan and Cabezudo had come close to dueling because of articles Juan had published in a newspaper secretly subsidized by Cabezudo. After Remedios dies, the two men return together to the province they came from and live in friendship. In this paradoxical denouement, Rabasa restated his ironic view of journalists' obsession with honor—a hollow sentiment compared to love and friendship. Absent from most testimonies is any reflection about Mexican lettered culture's exclusion of female readers and writers. Although the number of publications for and by women increased in the República Restaurada and after, female writers did not cross from this niche into the editorial rooms of dailies or the higher echelons of the republic of letters.[64]

Bohemian poverty, literary and civic pride, and masculine pleasures were all part of journalists' accumulation of social capital. This accumulation was not discussed in contemporaneous accounts of journalism in the terms used here, yet its importance is quite clear if one considers the existential dilemmas journalists confronted in their careers. One presented itself to Frías's alter ego, Miguel Mercado, as he drank tequila and read Díaz Mirón's "iron stanzas" while traveling on a train toward a new professional destination: "Will he [Mercado] go to a government newspaper where he would be well paid and 'jobs' would be a possibility?" or will he veer instead toward the "beautiful field of Honor," to become "a combat writer who, if defeated, would die like a gentleman wrapped in his flag."[65] Frías had been in trouble after writing *Tomochic*; he left the army and became a full-time writer for newspapers and other editorial projects. Condemnation was easier with distance. After the Revolution, he expressed his "moral displeasure" with those "men of mud . . . capable of erasing in the abject desk of the bureaucrat all the beauties written on the table of the free journalist."[66] Gamboa wrote about the dilemma in an entry in his diary about a banquet in 1908 attended by old colleagues who had followed two separate routes: oppositionists like Paz and "gobiernistas." Gamboa was one of the *gobiernistas*. He left the *Diario del Hogar* in 1887, when Mata started "an all-out war against the administration." After a brief stint at *El Lunes*, paid for by General Sóstenes Rocha, Gamboa left the trade altogether and began an ultimately successful diplomatic and literary career.[67] Rabasa, in turn, became a prestigious politician and jurist, which may explain the caustic view of journalists found in his novels—although they do acknowledge the profession's ability to bring distinction to men of humble origins.[68]

Literary merit and courage in the face of polemic brought journalists' names to the attention of the powerful and, with luck, paved the way to better-paid governmental jobs. When required to do so by their careers, they could translate the symbolic and cultural capital of their trade, through the personal ties cemented in editorial rooms and cantinas, into social capital. But social capital was itself an unstable good in a society that was rapidly changing: the family was no longer the only receptacle of honor, and the uncertainties of business and politics often translated into lonely battles against adversity or the cruel judgment of public opinion.

Journalists not only spoke "in the name of such lady" but also had to defend the sincerity of their voices in front of the public eye. The best way to preserve and defend their prestige and influence was to organize them into a compelling biographical narrative.

The construction of a personal story was an essential step in the process of reaping the benefits of combat journalism. The tension between gobiernismo and combat journalism was starker in the retrospective narratives analyzed above than in reality, where the two paths could cross over. Frías, for example, swung back and forth between attacks against the government, intoxicated depression, and attempts to please powerful men with his writing. Others who early on chose opposition and ended up in jail—figures like Carlos Roumagnac and Joaquín Clausell—later became tamer and managed to pursue more profitable careers in public service.[69] The narratives of Gamboa, Rabasa, and Frías are highly relevant here because they framed the ethical dilemma in the transition from combat journalism to the domesticated press of the late Porfiriato. Their accounts also share a deliberate effort to produce an objective narrative of their own personal trajectory. Gamboa maintained a cautious distance from the extremes of opposition or abjection and thus never came very close to becoming a combat journalist. His memoirs are a deliberate attempt to consign journalism to a youthful and now-concluded phase of his life. Starting in 1888, Rabasa wrote ironic novels that his contemporaries had no difficulty interpreting as critiques of the romantic pretensions and moral frailties of journalists. Rabasa took special pleasure in exhibiting the contradictions of honorable (public) men who melted in the (private) presence of a loved woman. Obsessed with reputation, they speculated with their own honor and that of politicians; yet their currency was "counterfeit money" (*moneda falsa*) in contrast to the "pure gold" of a woman's love.[70] In novels of a darker tone, Frías portrayed the personal tragedy of men who succumbed to the impossibility of separating their dreams of public heroism from the personal troubles caused by poverty and alcoholism. In *Miserias de México* he wrote that honor was an equivocal term often invoked to justify wrongdoing: "There is no other word that lends itself more to multiple, opposite ideas, than the golden word, emblem of all heraldry: honor!"[71]

The three memoirists were critical of the ethos of journalism precisely because they saw it as being guided by an outdated notion of honor. Their common thesis in this regard was a stoic argument: all was *vanitas vanitatum*, honor was an empty framework that contained only the hollow promise of prestige, and the only true redemption was internal. But we can also read this thesis as a critique of the romantic ethical model of idealistic heroism. In this view, the three men proposed a more positivist notion of the individual, less dependent on public opinion and based on an irreducible realm of intimacy (see chapter 5): honor as an individual's right. The manner in which they presented this argument was a product of the literary conventions that the three authors were using to build, simultaneously, objective narratives of their own temptations, failures, and redemption and texts that would help them capitalize on the intangible merits of combat journalism.

They followed very different paths, however. Gamboa was explicitly autobiographic, yet discreet in alluding to his past sins. He published his remembrances after abandoning journalism for a respectable diplomatic job. Rabasa wrote, from the point of view of a provincial man recently arrived in the capital, novels that were more explicit about the contradictions of men of honor in the press yet indirect in their autobiographical dimension. Both of the authors' intended readers presumably knew the stories that lay behind what was on the page and thus could judge better the documentary value of the testimonies. Nemesio García Naranjo, writing about Gamboa, describes very well how this implicit knowledge of the author's youth made sense of his entire life: "Tempestuous youth of pleasure. . . . He sinned in the spring and with his youthful indiscretions prepared the sanctity of his autumn."[72] The condition under which one read these two testimonies of bohemian life was that their authors were no longer bohemians. They had established a strong distance, if not chronological (Gamboa published *Impresiones y recuerdos* at the age of twenty-nine, Rabasa *El cuarto poder* and *Moneda falsa* at thirty-two) at least existential: they were mature men when they produced their biographical narratives and had a new perspective on the arc of their lives. Frías, by contrast, had a more intimate knowledge of the dangers of bohemian life and could never claim a position in the literary or political establishment. His novels are brutal descriptions of decadence caused by poverty and dissipation. It was obvious to readers that Miguel Mercado was Frías's alter ego. Instead of distance, he offered dramatic confession of his struggles with addiction as proof of his veracity.

The three authors wrote testimonies about the reality of journalism because their goal was not purely aesthetic or disinterested, but to offer a truthful product that would benefit their careers as bureaucrats and authors—in the case of Frías, after the revolution. They were successful in that, as contemporary scholars recognize, their writings still shape the way their story is told.[73] Thus, however critical of honor, none of them was fully able to dismiss the allure of combat journalism.

Conflicts of Honor: La Patria versus La Libertad

Conflicts reveal with clarity the rules of everyday practice that memoirs and novels may hide under moral judgment. Actors understood these rules very well, yet did not have to make them explicit. Their choices in the context of a potentially violent dispute exhibit, better than any retrospective account, the options available to them. Since journalists traded their social capital in the currency of honor, any doubt about their integrity prompted strong rebuttals, often leading to verbal and printed insults or to the threat of violence through a duel. Given their self-referential quality, their accounts open a window on rules of honor that applied broadly. The best example of this is the polemic in 1880 that resulted in a meeting on the field of honor of Santiago Sierra, a writer for *La Libertad*, and Ireneo Paz, the editor of *La Patria*. The two duelists and their newspapers reflect paradigmatically the tradition and new directions of journalism and politics in the early Porfiriato.

Paz represented the attitudes and trajectory of the last pure generation of combat journalists (figure 8). Born in 1836, he was a veteran of many military campaigns, prisoner of the conservatives, later an adversary of Juárez. By the 1870s, he earned his living editing newspapers, writing satires and serial novels, and printing books and pamphlets for government and private customers. Yet he was unable to reap the benefits of his heroic youth and was briefly incarcerated in the latter years of the Porfirian regime because his newspaper upset President Díaz and members of his inner circle.[74] But that was a calculated risk. Paz and the writers at *La Patria* were predisposed to incite belligerent press debates. They claimed that passion dictated neither libel nor adulation in their pages, yet, in March 1880, for example, physical violence erupted during a dispute with *El Sufragio Libre* about impending presidential elections. The writers at *El Sufragio Libre* claimed they were ready to accept a challenge from those of *La Patria* but "without scandal." This meant a duel—a practice that the Penal Code punished but that members of the upper classes condoned. Manuel Caballero, of *La Patria*, offered to meet on the field of honor with any "gentleman without a stain" from *El Sufragio Libre*—thus implying that Cástulo Zenteno, who had called Caballero a coward, was not a real gentleman.

The dispute would have ended in a duel but for a scuffle between Zenteno, Caballero, and others that took place in Escalerillas Street. Blows and gunshots were exchanged, and Caballero and an employee of *El Socialista* were arrested. A duel could not take place because having a criminal charge disqualified one from the right to meet on the field of honor. *La Patria*, however, claimed that the disorganized violence of the episode was a result of the dirty ways of the supporters of Manuel González for the presidency.[75] *El Monitor Republicano* reported on the dispute and recommended moderation: contemporary journalism was sinking into an unprecedented "bastardy" in which political passion all too easily led to insult and defamation. "Nobody reasons," an editorial opined; "everybody screams excessively."[76] *La Patria* countered these criticisms by arguing that "intemperance" was necessary in the defense of political ideas. Sure enough, its pages during those days were largely occupied with ironic or threatening attacks against newspapers that supported Díaz and González.[77]

Santiago Sierra's newspaper, *La Libertad*, represented a different set of journalistic values than *La Patria*. Published since 1878 by Justo Sierra and Francisco Cosmes, *La Libertad* was the first systematic articulation of what Charles A. Hale has called the transformation of Mexican liberalism: a political program that appealed to the rule of science and supported Díaz's authoritarianism against the chaotic legacy of Jacobin liberalism.[78] Although these ideas became official doctrine in subsequent years, in the late 1870s and early 1880s the writers of *La Libertad* struggled to shed old political uses while retaining a romantic view of honor. Thus, they justified their ideological mission by holding a negative view of the existing press and by emphasizing the authenticity of youth. The newspaper's founding group was indeed precocious: Cosmes was twenty-seven years old, Justo Sierra twenty-nine, and his brother Santiago, a staff writer, was twenty-seven (figure 9).[79] In an editorial in which he presented the "liberal-conservative" project of *La Libertad*, Justo contrasted the dismal situation of the country with his generation's hopes for renewal through order and progress: "We are young and new to public life, still full of dreams."[80]

La Libertad's editors proposed a break with the past because science,

8. Ireneo Paz. © 643842.
CND. SINAFO-Fototeca
Nacional del INAH.

9. Santiago Sierra.
La Casera, 2 May 1880.
Reproduced in Barajas
Durán, *El País del Llorón*.
Used by permission of
the author.

not old habits, guided them toward political and social reform. Thus, they claimed they could replace "personalism," the single-minded promotion of a candidate, with fair opinions. The sense of mission came at the cost of self-criticism: they did not see a contradiction in acknowledging that they received a subsidy from Díaz because, they argued, that would not prevent them from criticizing his decisions. In an article of 1879, Justo proudly stated that "even if they prove that we wrote in a newspaper supported by government resources, they would never be able to prove that we have departed a single jot from the imperatives of our beliefs."[81] Proof, however, was not obvious: the subsidy was material, but conscience, being intimate, could not be observed. Sierra and his readers did not see a problem because the premise was that, among honorable men, internal beliefs and external behavior were indissolubly linked. It would have been an insult, by contrast, to doubt the sincerity of each line signed by Sierra.[82]

"The imperatives of our beliefs" were tested by the demands of the writing market. Sierra's positivist defense of authoritarian rule, for example, sounded suspicious to those who knew the classical liberal constitutionalism of his earlier pieces. In 1876, from the pages of *El Federalista*, Sierra had opposed a legislative project that would have given President Lerdo de Tejada extraordinary powers. In doing so, he invoked the need to maintain "absolute freedom," including freedom of the press. He argued then, using the same organicist vocabulary that would later justify Porfirian strong-arm tactics, that the press had to be free because it fulfilled "a function of great importance" and "curtailing it means closing the valves that drain the social mechanism."[83] By 1879, however, Sierra was defending presidential authority beyond the "verbal freedom" granted by the Constitution of 1857 and supported the abolition of the press jury.[84] In view of the "weakness" of the social body, the executive power had to be excused for its strong reaction against rebels and its "manly" disregard of constitutional guarantees.[85]

Sierra's support for manly rule implied a critical view of the Mexican press. He complained that "all the energy of journalists is spilled through the channels of small texts about personal disputes; but when serious matters need to be addressed, it is done with stupendous ignorance or a noticeable lack of virile backbone, the high civic value that is needed to tell the truth, the whole truth, to a poor people sick with vanity and anemia."[86] "Vanity," a feminine defect, could be remedied only through

the scientific realism embraced by *La Libertad*. Antonio Guerra y Alarcón described journalism's progress as an evolution from the pasquinades of ancient Rome, full of personal attacks, toward a new role as
"soldier of civilization in the defense of new ideas" against "theocracy."
Ultimately, this role implied removing the newspaper from the "over-
whelming" drudgery of politics and turning it into a less polemical "daily
volume offered to publicity" that contained "a universal exhibition of
products of all kinds."[87] Defining the press as a daily "universal exhibition" aimed at commercial, scientific, and literary values that undermined the political economy of combat journalism. In this, *La Libertad*
expressed the unfulfilled hope of public writers from older generations.
In an homage in 1874 to Francisco Zarco, Guillermo Prieto, who devoted
himself to the trade for six decades, stated that journalism "embraces all
literary genres, criticism, philosophy, science, customs . . . it is a reflection of the entire society . . . ideas, concerns, customs in their most
intimate details."[88]

In spite of these high-minded views, *La Libertad* was not able to avoid
the *personalismo* that dominated politics by the end of Díaz's first term.
The newspaper supported Diaz's designated successor, Manuel González. *La Patria* threw its lot in with the candidacy of the governor of
Zacatecas, Trinidad García de la Cadena.[89] The ensuing exchanges, fea-
turing open criticisms of the candidates in an increasingly aggressive
tone, rekindled earlier disputes between the two papers. In February
1880, *La Libertad* forgot its admonitions against politicking and personal
attacks and accused *La Patria* of receiving money from García de la
Cadena, branding its columnists "pamphleteers without common sense."
La Patria said the writers of *La Libertad* were pedantic, sarcastically
characterized them as "incorrupt youngsters of the evolutionist school"
who had never been in a battle, and countercharged that they took
money and orders directly from Díaz.[90]

Words grew harsher over a period of two months, gradually becoming
less about the candidates and more about a vaguely described "personal
issue" between two members of each staff. *La Patria* mocked an initial
offer to settle the issue on the field of honor, stating that they were not
ready to mount a puppet show—alluding to the fact that *La Libertad*'s
offices had been used for that purpose and to the youth of its writers.[91]
In April, two anonymous pieces, probably written by Agustín F. Cuenca,
cast the worst possible accusation against Paz: he was ungrateful because

he had abandoned Díaz after having supported him. The article mocked Paz's self-proclaimed titles of "patriot, liberal, constitutionalist, revolutionary, caudillo, apostle, martyr, poet, journalist, deputy."[92] Paz responded that it was Díaz who had been an ingrate in spite of the eleven years and many sacrifices the journalist had made for the general. Days later, in an editorial, Paz accused Santiago Sierra of writing an anonymous piece that insulted him personally and of avoiding the seconds he had sent to *La Libertad* to settle the issue. They were told that Cuenca had written the piece. But Cuenca, according to Paz, was just "a small man, whom I only know for his effeminate voice and manners," who avoided a duel by means of suberfuges. Paz added that Santiago had been spat upon and insulted recently and had not responded like a man. Given the unwillingness of the writers of *La Libertad* to arrange things according to "the rules that society has established," Paz warned them that he felt free now to "repress [them] in another fashion," that is, with informal use of force.[93]

The situation could no longer be solved through discussion: *La Patria* stated that henceforth it would not acknowledge the existence of *La Libertad* in its pages—no doubt the harshest slight between two Mexican newspapers of the time. Cuenca wrote inviting Paz to a duel, but Paz responded directly to Sierra. Santiago wrote on April 25 that he had not addressed Paz and had no interest in his person; nevertheless, he called him a "villain" and a coward in response to the "imaginary events" mentioned by Paz, and invited him to cross the street to prove his manhood— as both newspapers were located on opposite sides of Santa Inés Street.[94] From the balconies of their offices, a duel was arranged. Following the dictates of the code of honor, they met on April 27 in suburban Tlalnepantla. Santiago Sierra died as a consequence of a gunshot to the head.[95]

His brother Justo, who did not write extensive memoirs or autobiographical novels, left a brief annotation about the duel in his autobiographical "Apuntes": Santiago fell at 9:00 a.m. at the hands of the "murderer" Paz. Santiago's seconds had been Jorge Hammeken and Eduardo Garay, writers at *La Libertad*, while Ignacio Martínez, Colonel Bonifacio Topete, and Manuel Caballero had been on Paz's side. Justo (figure 10) blamed the outcome on the machinations of the "infamous" Caballero, who had attributed the anonymous piece to Santiago. Caballero also caused the fatal result of the duel—not the usual outcome in Mexican duels, as we will see in chapter 7—because, after a first round of shots had

10. Justo Sierra, c. 1868. ©
651533. CND. SINAFO-Fototeca
Nacional del INAH.

missed (perhaps deliberately), he exclaimed, "A duel is not a joke!," and
forced a second attempt. Standing at a shorter distance from each other,
the duelists fired again, and Paz's superior marksmanship had its deadly
effect. Instead of trying to find an honorable way out after the first round,
as contemplated in dueling codes, the witnesses had failed to attempt a
negotiation.[96]

The resigned tone of Justo's annotations hid an intimate drama surrounding Santiago's death. Justo's granddaughter, Margarita Urueta,
wrote a family account years later that placed Justo between domestic
and political obligations. Her aunt, Evangelina, then a child, remembered
that dawn in April: her mother cried and pleaded with her father, Santiago, not to leave, invoking the unborn child she was carrying. Santiago's
answer suggested it was a problem of family honor: "They have insulted
us, and you cannot insult a Sierra without being punished; you cannot
ask me to be coward. . . . I am stronger than Justo." Before leaving,
Santiago left a note for his brother, who lived next door, but did not wake
him up. In the note he asked Justo to join him in Tlalnepantla. As Justo
was hurriedly boarding a coach to leave for Tlalnepantla, their mother,
Doña Luz, warned him, "You are responsible for my youngest son!" But

Justo arrived too late: the witnesses were already fleeing, and Paz ran past him, saying, "Justo, forgive me, I just killed your brother!" When Justo returned home, his mother blamed him for Santiago's death and called him Cain.[97]

The Sierra family, particularly on Santiago's side, would suffer the consequences of the duel, falling into a difficult economic situation. His wife and mother believed he had been singled out because "they envy his intelligence, his youth. He is the favorite of the government."[98] Aggravating them even further, his corpse was treated in an undignified manner: the police picked it up from the field, where witnesses had abandoned it to avoid arrest; it was carried to the Tacuba police station and then to Toluca, where it waited for a night until it was returned to Mexico City, to be buried the morning of 28 April. Only two friends attended the funeral. While all the newspapers lamented his death, none dared print the reason because doing so would invite prosecution of those involved—not an honorable way to conclude the affair.[99]

The silence in Justo's "Apuntes" about the domestic drama conceals the depth of his reaction to the duel. Fate had placed him at a crossroads of private and public obligations that he was not able to reconcile. He felt responsible because, following his duty as a newspaper editor, he did not reveal that Cuenca had written the piece that led to the duel, yet, being weaker than Santiago, he had failed to engage Paz in writing and to fight the duel himself. After his brother's death, Justo wrapped himself in silence, and his hair turned white. He abandoned political journalism and quit *La Libertad*, which operated for only four years.[100] From then on, he devoted himself to his work as a congressman and official, to education, and to historical and literary writing. Nevertheless (or perhaps because of this self-imposed distance from the writing market) he became one of the central científico ideologues.

Faced with the dilemma between intimate conscience and outward behavior that was so onerous for Santos Degollado, Justo had gladly chosen the first. In a letter he wrote to a friend in 1884, he said he now avoided honors that would make him the object of public attention. He no longer read the newspapers, even if they mentioned him. His world, he declared, was circumscribed by the borders of friendship: "I seek the appreciation of some, the friendship of a few, I do not mind the indifference of most, and the enmity of certain people has given me some of those delightful moments in which we feel wholly in agreement with our conscience."[101] It was clear, however, that such haughty neglect was merely a failure to live up to the model of older men of the word and the sword. In a eulogy pronounced just a few months earlier, Justo had praised Ignacio Ramírez for fulfilling the duty of being "in the heart of his peaceful home, humble and good" but at the "rostrum of the tumultuous forum" a fearsome "angel emerged from the deep" to save the Republic.[102] Acting otherwise, as Justo did after the duel, came at a personal and social cost.

In withdrawing from journalism, Justo was also reneging on the rules that saved those responsible for Santiago's death from punishment. The police arrested Paz, Martínez, Garay, Hammeken, and Topete shortly after the duel but released the first three immediately because they were federal deputies. The Chamber of Deputies rejected a petition to strip them of their parliamentary immunity in order to allow judicial authorities to prosecute them. Authorities also released Hammeken and Topete a few days later and did not even arrest Caballero.[103] Dueling was widely recognized as a legitimate way for public men to solve disputes, in spite of being outlawed by the Penal Code of 1871. The absence of serious prosecution in this case did not indicate official protection for Paz or for *La Patria* so much as the state's acknowledgment of elite men's extra-official immunity when they followed the rules of the code of honor.

The duel and its consequences directly contradicted *La Libertad*'s scientific optimism about the future of Mexican journalism. Days after the duel, Francisco Cosmes described the situation in a tone of helplessness:

> Reasonable and courteous polemic has become impossible among us. In any discussion we must sustain, regardless of how peaceful and unlikely to cause irritation the subject matter, we find ourselves from the second or third article surrounded by a tempest of personal insult that forces us to depart from the limits of decorum and return affront with affront, or solve with weapons a matter in which only rationality and knowledge should prevail. Our existence is full of distress. We are always expecting a provocation, if not more, . . . forcing us to always take to the street with a gun under our belt, always full of disappointments that embitter the bread we make with our pens.[104]

Few duels actually took place during these years, but violence was always potentially present in the trade of journalism. In October 1884 Cosmes found himself entangled in a "personal matter" that demonstrated the impossibility, even for critics of belligerent polemics like himself, of avoiding the tyranny of opinion. He had written a comment on a speech by Guadalupe Castañares, a student at the Escuela Preparatoria, in which he compared her with the French socialist Louise Michel. The comparison was interpreted by other students of the *escuela* as an allusion to Castañares's private life, under the assumption that Michel was a prostitute. Cosmes was challenged to a duel, but his seconds and those of the defender of Castañares's honor reached an arrangement that averted it. Afterward, he stated in a public letter that he had not clarified the meaning of his comparison earlier because that would have been interpreted as cowardice. He concluded the incident with an assertion of journalism's right to judge public behavior: "I have the right to appraise whatever is in the public domain and, on the occasion I was discussing, both the students and the lady mentioned subjected their acts to the judgment of the press."[105]

Cosmes's longing for debates within "the limits of decorum" inspired his colleagues to establish formal procedures for arbitrating the disputes between journalists. Deferring to seniority was a common device. Alfredo Bablot, the publisher of *El Federalista* and a famous defendant at press juries, had a "difference" with Justo Sierra, then a writer for that journal, because Sierra complained that unauthorized changes had been made to a text he had written. After a "friendly" discussion, they submitted the problem to the veteran journalist Ignacio M. Altamirano, who issued a decision.[106] Disputes could also be solved through spontaneous "friendly negotiations": in 1884, Jacinto Rodríguez and Manuel Gutiérrez Nájera ran into each other on the street; they talked about the attacks exchanged between *La Libertad* and *Diario del Hogar* and decided that, since no actual offense had been proffered as yet, an informal solution was still possible, and the affair was solved before anybody issued a challenge.[107]

Ideally, a permanent system seemed necessary to secure the press's ability to judge all matters in the public domain (including the press itself), without fear of reprisal. Several attempts to formalize arbitration between journalists led to the organization of short-lived associations similar to those created in Europe to solve disputes inside the profession. In 1872, the founders of one such association promised, "by their word of honor, to eliminate the polemics that would emerge among them, every personally affronting word or insinuation, understanding as such attacks against private life, false reproaches about public life, and insulting assessments about the press."[108] A month after Santiago's death, *La Constitución*, *La Voz de México*, and *La Libertad* proposed the establishment of a Junta General de Periodistas, whose goal was preventing duels caused by press disputes. A *junta de honor* (honor tribunal) would mediate and arbitrate disputes, decide about "satisfactions that were due in case of affronts," and eventually determine whether a duel was unavoidable. The Junta General included among its members the old liberals Ignacio Manuel Altamirano and José María Vigil.[109] Paz, in turn, promoted the Asociación de la Prensa Unida, which he intended to defend freedom of the press by financing legal aid for imprisoned journalists. Other professional associations emerged during the Porfiriato, all of them combining mutual-aid goals, such as savings accounts and schools, with the desire to solve disputes over honor through arbitration. The preservation of the independence of the trade was the explicit focus of Paz's organization, but it also expressed a latent concern among those who agreed with Cosmes's views about the conflicts "that embitter the bread we make with our pens."[110]

Even if they addressed the material conditions of journalists, these organizations could not guarantee their autonomy from the writing market. *El Monitor Republicano* warned that the project in 1880 of a permanent Junta de Honor was not going to be effective as long as the government continued to subsidize the virulence of certain writers. The statute of the Prensa Unida made an explicit connection between matters of honor and journalists' sustenance, thus pointing to the thorny issue of the role of subsidies in the economy of the business and to the consequent ambivalence between survival and the honorable purity of opinions. As in Spain, France, and England, however, in Mexico such organizations did not have enough power to enforce their decisions because they lacked official character and depended on authorities' benign neglect to keep their disputes outside the judicial realm.[111] But it was money that ultimately contradicted the desire for autonomy. Justo Sierra had claimed that subsidies could not move his writing "a single jot from the imperatives of our beliefs"; but denial was presumptuous and, as revealed by the confrontation with *La Patria*, only fueled more conflict.

Conclusions

The men discussed in this chapter saw the contradiction inherent in being part of a chronically weak business, usually dependent on subsidies, while claiming sincerity and a strict obedience to their conscience as the central ethical norm. A result of this tension was that the pursuit of factual truth was rarely the goal of journalistic writing; journalists and their readers placed more value on opinion, style, and, above all, a polemic disposition. The truth that mattered was not the objective statement of facts, but the union between a man's conscience and his words and his willingness to prove that union with deeds—"the imperatives of our beliefs." Thus the constant need to debate reputations through the press, which often meant the obligation of taking, or at least trying to take, the conflict onto the field of honor. Combat journalism meant an attitude toward the trade, toward politics, and toward society in which honor measured gains and losses. Honor and public opinion, in this context, had an agonistic character: they were not inherent to a person or a social body, but the result of conflicts and exchanges. By revealing fractures in the union between conscience and words, those exchanges generated events, creating the reality behind the news: men's honor or lack thereof. This was a circular process, one in which a public writer's authority to judge others was based on others' judgment of him; yet it was a cycle from which it was almost impossible to escape. That shifting reality was also the basic referent for memoirs and novels that tried to cast a critical eye on the miseries of the trade and, by extension, on *Las miserias de México*—as in Frías's novel.

The self-referential production of news in the pages of Mexican newspapers made it possible for Rabasa's characters and others to talk about public opinion as a lady to be seduced and, at the same time, as a merciless tribunal that judged personal reputations. Journalists, like the broader category of *letrados*, possessed a skill (which they defined as style) and, however precarious, the material infrastructure that allowed them to be the voice of public opinion. But more important in giving authority to their voice was their integrity as men of honor—which could be validated only in the eyes of public opinion. Combat journalists were able to translate their symbolic and cultural capital into social capital because they had the ability to turn their words into real events. Thus loyalty and friendship were matters of life and death, vital in the success or failure of political and literary careers. The public culture examined in this chapter suggests that the divide between symbolic, cultural, and social capital might be artificial. It is analytically useful to define diverse axes in the fields where actors were situated: the men who had more prestige, education, or money were not always the same. But journalists were able to move from one scale to the other, turning their reputation as men of words and action into literary recognition and jobs. No other group or trade did that during these formatives years of modern Mexico.

But characterizing Mexican journalists and public men in general as a quarrelsome, exhibitionist bunch that spent its time in restaurants and cantinas gossiping, bragging, and occasionally fighting does not tell the whole story. The attempts to create associations and juntas de honor to negotiate and solve personal confrontations reveal an underlying effort to establish peaceful rules for public debate that would preserve the business's diversity. The effort failed not because violence became widespread (it never did) but because journalism lost its independence as the Porfirian regime systematized subsidies and replaced press juries (another tribunal of honor, after all) with repression (see chapter 5). Yet, if one places these efforts and the evidence discussed here in a longer chronological framework, one sees a broader effort among Mexican public men to consolidate a public sphere in which independent debate and disagreement would be preserved by setting clear rules for their exchanges.

PART II

Tumultuous Opinion

Chapters 3 and 4 narrow the focus onto a brief moment of revolt during the early Porfiriato, the last gasp of "emancipated freedom" inaugurated by the liberal triumph. In late 1884, approaching the end of his presidency, Manuel González tried to obtain diplomatic recognition from Great Britain and reopen European sources of credit lost during decades of instability and fiscal penury. Since the Chamber of Deputies had granted González extraordinary powers regarding fiscal matters, it also had to sign off on his negotiation with European bondholders. Congressional approval turned out to be harder to achieve than expected. Newspapers criticized, deputies gave rousing speeches against the onerous terms of the agreement, and rhetorical battles spilled into riots. After a few nights of violence in the streets of the capital that threatened even his personal integrity, González withdrew the project. By then, November 1884, he had lost much of his popularity.

Since the battle in Congress and the streets took place when Díaz was about to return to the presidency, historians have interpreted the episode of the *deuda inglesa* (English debt), as it came to be known, in terms of a narrowly defined notion of politics in which the relevant fact was Díaz's increasing strength as González emerged from the crisis too weak to be a contender for the presidency in 1888. What mattered, in this perspective, was not popular opposition but closed-door negotiations among the two generals and other members of the Tuxtepecano group. The historian Daniel Cosío Villegas and others have seen the episode as an illusory triumph of democratic groups against increasing presidential power. In the end, they argue, elite actors used popular participation and public opinion for their own ends.[1] Yet the specific connection between popular groups and elite conflicts remains vague in explanations that posit such top-down causality. In order to explain that connection, the following pages look at how public opinion and honor mobilized individual and collective actors. Honor, according to the opposition in 1884, referred simultaneously to the reputation of public speakers and to the national honestidad personified in the *patria*. The eventual success of authoritarian Porfirismo, as we will see, stemmed precisely from its ability to separate those two meanings of honor.

While previous chapters described the rules of public debate and conflict, the next two look at contingent events and practices. During November of 1884, citizens who judged the patriotism of others and were willing to risk their own reputation in defense of their ideas spoke in the name of public opinion. The conflict started as a press debate, moved to Congress, and came to involve urban popular actors. Chapter 3 shows how contemporaries saw the episode as a predominantly verbal battle among public men in which, after so many years in which military strength had been the ultimate arbiter of civil struggle, rhetoric was a key political weapon. Romantic orators like Salvador Díaz Mirón and the bohemian students who led the unruly crowds, examined in chapter 4, embodied politics in a literal and metaphorical sense: they defended the national honor with their bodies through duels and street fights, engaged caudillos in almost personal confrontations, and gave a tangible force to public opinion by bringing together private reputations, civil society, and the state. At the intersection of elite politics, popular revolt, and individual careers, the episode evinces the inextricable connections formed in the public sphere of nineteenth-century Mexico.

Both chapters advance an alternative interpretation to views of the deuda inglesa episode as an intra-elite dispute: the events of November 1884 were not a maneuver by Díaz to weaken González but a challenge to the authority of both men and in general to that of the executive power. It was a short-lived challenge, eclipsed by the inherent instability of the transition between two presidents, but nevertheless a dangerous attack on the authority of both. This interpretation is inspired by recent historical reappraisals of the construction of citizenship in Latin America. New research looks at contingent historical processes in which multiple actors negotiated the meaning of popular sovereignty and representation against the backdrop of a traditional "communitarian dimension" of citizenship—a thesis advanced in chapter 1 as the continuity of urban representativeness of vecinos through city councils. Simultaneously, historians now consider rhetoric part of the repertoire of political elites in the construction of hegemony. Studies of urban revolts, in turn, provide useful tools for moving beyond discourse analysis as they reveal the diversity of popular groups involved in riots and the specificity and rationality of their goals.[2]

Postindependence urban plebes in Mexico City were usually reluctant to join rebellions if they could instead bring to bear their closeness to the national government—always a local actor in the capital's politics. Recent studies suggest that the relationship between leaders and the populace was more complex than a coincidence of the manipulative cunning of the former with the naiveté or pragmatism of the latter.[3] Chapter 3 discusses the behavior and values of orators, as they personified public opinion. Rhetoric was not only a technical ability of persuasion, but also a demonstration of the inner virtue of public men: they could speak well because they were good. Some congressmen expressed this attitude by using the pejorative *populacho* (populace) to refer to the crowds that rose against the government and mocked authority. In order to understand both closeness and distance, the chapter emphasizes the importance of oratory in establishing connections between leaders and masses and in building a public sphere in which participants could bridge class distinctions according to certain rules. Chapter 4 looks at the behavior of students in establishing direct relationships between urban lower classes and educated elites. It returns to the ideas and practices of Bohemia to further explore the gender and age construction of public men under the sometimes permissive eye of public opinion.

CHAPTER 3

"The Word of My Conscience"

Eloquence and the Foreign Debt

The deuda inglesa began as an episode in nineteenth-century Mexico's difficult financial history. Secret negotiations between the French financier Edouard Noetzlin, representing the Mexican government, and British holders of Mexican bonds concluded with the signing of an agreement on 18 September 1884. The agreement converted debt contracted since independence into a new issuance of bonds worth one hundred million gold pesos. The cost of the operation was thirteen million pesos, and the loan was guaranteed by 10 percent of the country's customs income.[1] President Manuel González expected a smooth ride after that, but he lost control of the process of congressional approval when the press revealed the terms of the agreement, and the discussion of the financial negotiations went beyond the narrow circles of financial experts into the agitated public sphere. In December of 1883 González had faced similar violent popular opposition to monetary reform after his government introduced nickel coins. The nickel coins had provoked speculation, quickly lost value, and compounded the economic problems of low-income groups. Since the government distributed coins through private firms that received them at a discount, people believed that the wealthy were illegally benefiting from the operation. Protests exploded in the capital, and by some accounts a mob threw stones at González in front of the National Palace. He withdrew the coins from circulation, resulting in a loss for the already weak federal coffers.[2]

In 1884, parliamentary debates and popular protests forced González to withdraw the proposal to have the debt renegotiation approved by the Chamber of Deputies. This brought down the prices of Mexican bonds and drove the state into serious fiscal difficulties, as it had to contract onerous short-term loans and stop payments of some of its obligations. According to the historian Carlos Marichal, the crisis exhibited for the first time "the close interaction between the evolution of Mexican and international financial markets."[3] As in 1883, the decision and the riots that forced it were setbacks for the government's plan to establish financial stability and strong credit in the country. Since the first government of Porfirio Díaz, Finance Minister Matías Romero had set in motion a "financial revolution" by linking the issuance of paper money, the development of banks, and the recovery of international credit. The third item was particularly charged because it potentially involved recognizing the claims and debts incurred during Maximilian's empire, another step toward the reconciliation with conservatives and imperialists that alienated many liberals from Díaz's side.[4] Although their objectives were different, the episodes of the nickel coins and the deuda inglesa articulated popular resistance to a single process of financial consolidation that linked foreign credit and the introduction of paper money, or, in other words, the country's honra and the economic transactions of common people.

Rationalizing the monetary system and recognizing the foreign debt were, in hindsight, essential to achieve the stability and continued investment that made possible growth. Díaz and the experts who would eventually dominate policy believed that popular dissatisfaction could not stand in the way of modernization. In June of 1885, Díaz approved the renegotiation by presidential decree, obtained British recognition, and repressed those who had defied him and González. It took several years for his government to shift the center of budgetary deliberations away from parliamentary debates, as required by the Constitution of 1857, toward the presidency, but the episode of the deuda inglesa marked the beginning of an era of severe restrictions to public freedoms and mobilization. At the same time, in the view of Javier Pérez-Siller, the process consolidated a "national financial elite" that would exercise its own dictatorship within the dictatorship.[5]

That outcome, however, was not a given in 1884. Against the grain of the Porfirian teleology, one must understand Congress to have been not a body controlled by the president, as it would be later, but an institution in which individual deputies' decisions to take sides on the issue at hand responded to the capacity of oratory to shift the direction of public opinion.[6] These public men lacked the expertise of financiers yet, given the history of agitation of previous decades, seemed to be on solid ground. Thus, on November 12, 1884, the freshman deputy Salvador Díaz Mirón began the offensive against the project with a rousing speech. Within days other deputies, including the liberal patriarch Guillermo Prieto, attacked the project. Justo Sierra and Francisco Bulnes, científicos, defended the government by giving good speeches but achieving poor results. I examine here the parliamentary debates of 1884 as the epitome of oratory in Mexico's nineteenth-century political life. Díaz Mirón and Prieto, as poets, exemplified the power that romantic orators could muster when they found receptive audiences and favorable political circumstances. Yet 1884 was also the point at which the influence of oratory and of romantic attitudes generally began to be neutralized by a scientific critique of rhetoric (presented by Sierra, also a poet, and Bulnes) and a narrowing in the realm of government matters open to debate.

The opposition to the deuda inglesa brought together a brief but powerful alliance of journalists, deputies, students, and segments of the lower class against González. The manifest reason for such opposition was nationalism: the agreement had been secretly negotiated and signed by a Frenchman in the name of the Mexican people, its terms were unfavorable for a country in fiscal problems, and it compromised future state income. I look first at the spontaneous creation of that confluence of media and actors and then examine the art of oratory that made that confluence possible by giving the reputation of public men a larger meaning. A critique of the reign of rhetoric will be at the center of the third section. The chapter will conclude with a brief reflection on national honor.

From the Press to the Chamber of Deputies

The journalistic polemics, parliamentary debates, and urban riots that surrounded the deuda inglesa occurred in a space shared by members of the political elite and other inhabitants of the city. Three days into the parliamentary discussion, Deputy Eduardo Viñas illustrated this in his first speech on the topic: "Through newspaper reports I learned about what was going on here; through rumors in the streets I found out about the current state of the question; and through everybody's conversation I found out about the great struggle to defend national interests that had already started in this place. Then came to my mind the idea that it would be criminal if, neglecting my public duties, I did not intervene, and I ran to this Chamber."[7] *El Monitor Republicano* similarly reported that the English debt is "the subject of the day. . . . Nothing else can be heard around . . . in the press, at home, in the circle of friends, in the groups of dandies in Plateros Street." "Everyone has become a politician and a diplomat," commented the same newspaper days later.[8] Discourses and debates circulated via verbal and written channels that were already part of public life but that, for a few days in November 1884, found a new sense of urgency in "the current state of the question."

The first link in this chain was the press. Everyone knew that national and foreign newspapers could have a direct impact on the government's financial policies; a case in point was the failure of debt negotiations with European bondholders that Carlos Rivas, a personal friend of President González, conducted in 1883. Rivas had signed an agreement in London, but the Mexican government returned it with some corrections. The corrections resulted in, in the words of the Porfirian financier Joaquín D. Casasús, a "great scandal created by the British press," including "insults against our public men and the good faith of the nation." As a consequence of the scandal, bondholders lost the little confidence they had in Rivas, particularly after he left his counterparts in the negotiations waiting for him while he went on expensive trips throughout the Continent.[9] The Mexican government was not above protecting its image in the foreign press with subsidies and, in some cases, personal interventions by Mexican envoys. In a private letter to Casasús, the writer Ignacio Manuel Altamirano described four ways available to him, as a diplomat in Europe, to respond to *chantage* (blackmail) against the honor of Mexico and its representatives in the foreign press:

1st. Reply in the newspapers, in any style.

2nd. Bring my offender to court.

3rd. Bring him to the field of honor if he deserves it.

4th. Have him beaten in my name.[10]

Mexican newspapers could also have a negative impact on the prestige of the government, yet they lacked their English peers' influence on international financial circles. For opposition papers like *El Monitor Republicano* there was a fatal inevitability to Díaz's autocratic behavior. On 22 October 1884, the staff writer Francisco W. González denounced the existence of an agreement the government was trying to keep secret. Days later, he claimed that the "ruin of the republic" had been consummated, since "nothing can be expected from those who have decided to impose their will on public opinion and the country's interests."[11]

Sharing the *Monitor's* pessimism (and the self-referential disposition examined in the previous chapter), Mexican newspapers' coverage of the episode focused not on the agreement and its financial implications so much as on the journalistic debate itself and its echoes in Congress and the streets. Newspapers reproduced entire articles by friends and foes and weighed them according to their impact on public opinion. Only *La Libertad*, the most vocal in its support of the agreement, took a critical stance toward the role of public opinion and the press in policy making. The matter under consideration, argued *La Libertad*, was the concern of financial specialists, not of amateur journalists, and it was an issue of economic rationality, not of national dignity. Given the plebs' "multiple will" in the street, nothing useful could come of relying on public opinion.[12] Most newspapers, however, followed events in the street as a direct index of public opinion. *Diario del Hogar*, edited by Filomeno Mata, gave little information about the project as presented by the government to obtain approval of the negotiation in Congress, but was thorough in its coverage of the shifts in public opinion and of the events taking place since November 18. *La Patria* declared that "our mission as public writers" meant adapting to changes in the public mood. At the beginning of the debate, the newspaper supported the agreement because, in its view, it did not contradict the dictates of common sense and morality.[13] Its position began to change as a result of the poor quality of the speeches delivered by deputies who were on the government's side—some of them, for example, Bulnes, Sierra, and Manuel Gutiérrez Nájera, current and former writers at the rival *La Libertad*. Newspapers did not reproduce speeches but synthesized and commented on them in their "parliamentary reports." In light of the popular reaction against the project, *La Patria* tersely announced days later that its editor, Ireneo Paz, also a deputy, had voted according to the dictates of his conscience against the government and had vowed to continue to fight it.[14]

La Patria's concern about the quality of the speeches delivered in the Chamber of Deputies responded to the importance of rhetoric in Mexican politics and to Congress's role as its showcase. The chamber, the second link in the chain of verbal and written reactions against the deuda inglesa agreement, had been a central space of political debate ever since the República Restaurada, and it would take years for Díaz to discipline its members—although he never achieved the silent unanimity described by postrevolutionary critics. Legislatures in the República Restaurada included strong factions of civilians that were independent of Juárez and Lerdo de Tejada and proved their autonomy during discussions about the budget. Besides voting on legislation, speeches and audiences were intended to "create opinion,"[15] and thus have a larger political impact. Juárez sponsored the establishment of the Senate to counter the Chamber of Deputies, and by the end of Díaz's first tenancy presidential initiatives were usually passed without great difficulty thanks to the personal control he exerted over the appointment of candidates. This was no small power, since a seat in Congress was a desirable position for men like Justo Sierra in 1869, who saw in it the opportunity to move to Mexico City. For others, like José Y. Limantour, the job guaranteed a decent income even as he traveled around Europe.[16] The events of November 1884 demonstrated, however, that the discipline built by loyalty was not strong enough yet to prevent parliamentary rebellion. A strong speech could trump the weight of patronage.

The Renewed Power of Eloquence

How could rhetoric be such an important element of political process in Mexico, where the combined legacies of militarism and patronage seemed to relegate open discussion of public issues to ornamental status? The centrality of deputies' oratorical performance in newspapers' evaluations of the debates around 1884 shows that rhetoric in late nineteenth-century Mexico experienced a revival. It not only offered politicians powerful tools, but also shaped the expectations of audiences toward the men who could speak in the name of public opinion. Combining the beauty of words and the prestige of heroes, the art of eloquence transformed those men's perceptions of themselves.[17]

Following classical traditions, Mexican public men defined eloquence as the art which "convinces through the living word" and makes truth more persuasive. As an art, it sought to embody at once beauty and technical skill. Persuasion could be a dangerous weapon if not wielded in the name of truth. Mexican authors used the words *elocuencia* or *oratoria* more often than *retórica*, a choice that can be traced back to their reading of Cicero and Plato, in whom rhetoric as pure technique, devoid of ethical content, implied the political danger of manipulation of the masses.[18] To solve the old problem of the divorce of means and ends, they emphasized the unity of art and ethics in "the living word." "The oratorical unity," according to the jurist Jacinto Pallares, was the art of persuading of the truth through the unity of form and a deep knowledge that could be found only in good men. This meant that eloquence and philosophy, rhetoric and science were, as in the classical past, not foreign to each other but mutually supportive.[19] More important, such unity also referred to the intrinsic ties between eloquence and the honor of the speaker.

The alliance of eloquence and philosophy also alluded to religious oratory. Enlightenment had diminished the import of rhetoric in Mexican higher education even before independence, but lovers of the art in the late nineteenth century believed that eloquence was destined to recover the central place in public life it had enjoyed since colonial evangelization. For the oratory professor Francisco Elguero, Christian orators and theorists were as important as Greek and Roman ones and, if anything, were even superior because they held correct, eternal beliefs.[20] In sermons and theological debates held even in the most isolated towns, priests were the model for secular orators. After the war of independence, which involved priests on both sides, sermons became more political, using the Bible in defense of partisan arguments, and began to adopt the structure of civil orations. Although liberal politicians appropriated eloquence and secularized the contents of public speeches during the nineteenth century, they continued to quote the Bible as a source of inspiration, images, and motifs. This also helped impress audiences, as did the knowledge of Latin and the classics imparted in seminaries.[21] Not a believer himself, Díaz Mirón nevertheless embraced the religious legacy of oratory when he began his attack against the project of the deuda inglesa by defining his political duty as a "sacred" one and describing the parliamentary speaker as a "priest of reason and justice [who] must sacrifice his personal interests as propitiatory victims, if this sacrifice can bring forth the light of truth and justice, like a lustral blood that impregnates and purifies the public spirit."[22]

The "public spirit," however, was the secular child of national history. Civil oratory became a central feature of patriotic celebrations after independence. Secular orators became well known in such multiple venues as Congress, jury trial debates, funerals, events organized by literary and civil associations, local celebrations, and commemorations of the Grito de Dolores (Miguel Hidalgo's call to revolt in 1810) on September 15. New lay topoi—conventions about equality, fraternity, freedom, progress, the glories of pre-Hispanic civilizations, and the sacrifice of insurgent heroes—expanded their repertoire.[23] Francisco Zarco (1829–69) was the model of the new republican tribune who engaged every theme and every situation: "in the small gathering, in the club, at the lodge, at the rostrum, in the press and in epistolary correspondence"; he combined the "tempestuous language of the tribune" and "the simple manner in which the innocent peasant conveys his thoughts."[24]

Oratory built nationalism because it brought together the lower classes and the educated elites, young and old, in public and private spaces. The night of September 15, 1870, for example, Justo Sierra and a group of his fellow law students were returning home from the commemoration of the Grito when they saw Guillermo Prieto, the author of the above description of Zarco, standing on a bench and speaking to an enthusiastic gathering of people at the *plaza de armas*, or *zócalo*; the official celebration, probably conducted by President Juárez himself, had just finished, but patriotic spirits were still high. Prieto joined Sierra and his friends and walked to the Café de la Concordia, where they toasted the patria. The crowd followed them and forced them to return to the plaza, where Sierra gave a rousing speech that Ignacio Altamirano, another famous orator, praised in *El Siglo Diez y Nueve*. Prieto's and Sierra's success that September night suggests that oratory was a bridge between the classical education of elites and a popular culture that was still strongly oral. According to Sierra, the art of oratory provided a culturally valued outlet for public men who had a "bodily need" to talk expansively about many themes and to extend civic education to the humble people.[25] Prieto depicted public oratory as a genre "for the people on the people's day . . . a conversation with the masses about its antecedents and its future. . . . a family tradition, conveyed in the shadow of the laurels of Dolores, among the tombs of the heroes of Independence."[26]

Rhetoric was also an art of memory, and as such played the central role in the process of building a national history. Just as the classic models included mnemonic techniques based on the use of spaces and images, so nineteenth-century commemorative practices used public spaces like the plaza de armas to create narratives that rooted national identity in the triumph of liberalism over foreign invaders; in Mexico City, the history lesson narrated by statues and monuments along the Paseo de la Reforma is evidence of that impulse.[27]

Multiple oratorical genres allowed speakers during the nineteenth century to try a diversity of approaches beyond the traditional religious and legal frameworks. By the 1840s, Prieto distinguished himself in parliamentary discourses, which sought to convince through polemic, and in civic discourses, in which he used evocative resources to move and indoctrinate. In the expanded public sphere of republicanism, speeches could now target new listeners, like children, and limit the number of arcane references in order to reach wider audiences.[28] Funerary speeches for national figures became a staple of public and literary life, the perfect combination of artistic beauty and civic virtue. They were part of events that included poetry and music, targeted at an audience that was educated but still receptive to emotional effusions about the passing of great men. The genre allowed speakers flexibly to combine quasi-religious allegories—the nationalist cult of the patria—with secular narratives of personal heroism. The speaker and the illustrious dead were above partisan politics, on a higher ethical level that disdained rhetoric used as a "party weapon." Eloquence, in these speeches, was an art of memory fighting "bitter oblivion," an art that kept alive the heroism of an earlier generation who had shed blood on battlefields.[29] Pallares summed up the civic and ethical value of the genre: "The cult of great men is the religion of what is truthful and good, the most solemn revelation of a national conscience illuminated by the purest ideals."[30]

In 1884, opposition to the deuda inglesa owed much to this tradition, but it modified it by strengthening the ties between personal reputation and eloquence. As polemics in the press became heated in the discussion of the government's proposal, Congress and congressmen became the focus of everybody's attention in the capital. A rowdy crowd filled the galleries of the old Teatro Iturbide, seat of the Chamber of Deputies on the downtown corner of Canoa and El Factor streets, seeking to wake congressmen from what was regarded as their sopor and expecting, if not a defeat of the government, at least a strong debate before the chamber granted its approval. The speech by Díaz Mirón on 12 November, in

11. Salvador Díaz Mirón. From Manuel Puga y Acal, *Los poetas mexicanos contemporáneos: Ensayos críticos de Brummel.* Mexico City: Ireneo Paz, 1888.

SALVADOR DIAZ MIRON.

which personal integrity and oratorical civism were central to the argument, further encouraged popular participation and proved that this parliamentary debate, with its heroic resonance, was not going to be like any other in recent years.[31]

Díaz Mirón (figure 11) was not the typical careerist deputy of the Porfiriato. He was the son of a well-known liberal from Veracruz and had already forged his name in the politics of his home state. Before coming to Mexico City as a substitute deputy he had been a journalist, a local representative, and a participant in several duels and violent incidents. The best-known episode of his early career was his failed attempt to force the governor of Veracruz, Manuel Mier y Terán, to face him in a duel by writing that he had ordered the execution of nine alleged Lerdista conspirators in 1879.[32] In spite of the fact that his accusation was likely erroneous in that Mier y Terán had probably followed orders from Díaz in the execution episode, Díaz Mirón was elected in 1884 as a substitute representative for the tenth electoral district of Veracruz and the thirteenth of Oaxaca. He owed his election to the support of then-governor of Veracruz José de la Luz Enríquez, González's *compadre* (godfather) and former member of Díaz's military staff. Once the legislature was inaugurated in September, Díaz Mirón did not take long to occupy his seat in the chamber (as was the usual practice once the main elected representative began to receive his salary and returned home) and to seize the first opportunity to raise a dissident voice.[33]

Díaz Mirón's speech on 12 November set the subsequent debate on the deuda inglesa as a battle about public speech itself. Expectation in the crowded galleries had been fueled by the rumor that he was going to voice his indignation over the project and then present his resignation from Congress.[34] Turning the debate itself into the main event, the initial sentences of the speech posited rhetoric as the key to the upcoming battle and its potential political reverberations:

> A duty that I deem sacred has brought me to this rostrum, where I find myself truly bewildered by the magnitude of the goal I will pursue and the weakness of my means. And my bewilderment increases when I consider that, being new to the parliamentary tournaments, I speak for the first time and without preparation, in front of an Assembly that includes among its members distinguished orators and that is used to hearing eloquent harangues. As an excuse for this my audacity I offer the obligation in which I find myself, to speak the word of my conscience in this discussion which is so grave, that so deeply affects the honor and welfare of Mexico.[35]

Through additional references to "this discussion" and to Díaz Mirón's role as speaker for the opposition, the rest of the speech emphasized the importance of debate over analysis. Díaz Mirón and other opposition deputies as well as the press based their claims about the illegitimacy of the official proposal largely on the intensity of the indignation it provoked.

Díaz Mirón embraced the tradition of civic oratory through the deliberately orthodox construction of his speech. According to classical rules, an oration's exordium, or introduction, was the moment for the speaker to earn the sympathy of the audience. The assonance of "my bewilderment" (*perplejidad mía*) and "my audacity" (*audacia mía*) expressed Díaz Mirón's strategy: to present himself as a humble, young deputy willing to challenge the government's machinations, yet someone who, a poet after all, was not afraid to show off his mastery of the language. By speaking "the word of my conscience" (*la palabra de mi conciencia*), he framed the discussion in personal terms and made sincerity more valuable than science and age. He offered that "sincerity is honesty, . . . and I want to be honest here as everywhere else." He opposed that attitude to "what is exclusively arithmetic about the issue" of the debt, thus making integrity rather than technical knowledge the condition for an open, egalitarian debate. Instead of personal attacks, therefore, he demanded respect from the "representatives of an enlightened and free people."[36]

Claims of humble sincerity were effective in earning the audience's goodwill, but they also conveyed Díaz Mirón's deliberate blend of personal heroism and formal perfectionism. In this regard, his speech was all the more sensational because it put forward Mexican oratory's new synthesis of form and content. "The style is the man," he believed, and he was keenly aware that style itself was going to be a key element of his success. In fact, when he stated that he had climbed to the podium unprepared for the debate, he was lying. He had prepared the speech several days in advance, tested passages with friends at cafes, and rehearsed it multiple times in front of the mirror in his hotel room—always paying keen attention to the tone and gestures of his elocution, another central part of classical oratory.[37] The systematic, sometimes painful method was the same one he followed when writing poetry: multiple drafts, a close continuity between oral presentation and written text, and a strong recitation.

Like his other extant speeches, the one he gave on 12 November shows a rigorous concern with structure—the all-important disposition of classical models. The introduction was followed by the narration, in which he presented the main facts of the argument while maintaining the initial impetus through the use of frequent interjections and improvised passages that earned applause. He concluded with a peroration that summed up his arguments in a strong, emotional call for action in which he equated the preservation of congressmen's honor with the fulfillment of their duties to the nation. Díaz Mirón left a lasting impression on the audience: a man with piercing, big eyes and a deep voice, gesturing with his right hand while clutching a handkerchief in his left hand, which a bullet had years ago rendered useless. The image as much as the content of the speech summed up the unity of personal virtue and rhetorical skill that shaped the honor of modern public men. Deputies and spectators in the galleries loudly acclaimed him at the end of the speech. Reproduced and quoted many times the address became the foundation of Díaz Mirón's national reputation.[38]

Prieto's intervention later that afternoon was another triumph of the opposition, although one that represented a different approach to oratory. He began his speech by affirming the inexorable imperative of public duty over personal feelings: "I have to overcome my dearest affections and call myself reprehensible or ungrateful because I have never been able to subordinate my duties toward the patria to the feelings of my personal gratitude." The exordium was effective because it alluded to Prieto's heroic political career, which became the central argument of the speech as he presented himself as the very embodiment of honor and eloquence united.[39]

Prieto (figure 12) was a member of a prestigious generation of young intellectuals who sided with Juárez from the early moments of the Reforma movement; younger cohorts, like Sierra, dubbed that generation "the guerrilla war of the pen" and equated their eloquence to the military bravery of soldiers.[40] At the time, Prieto had been elected to Congress for the twentieth time, was at the peak of his fame as a poet, and was the official orator at the celebration of 15 September 1884. Everybody in the audience knew that his words had saved Juárez's life in Guadalajara in 1858, when Prieto stood in front of the guns of conservative soldiers who had been ordered to take the president's life. In his improvised harangue to the soldiers, he uttered a phrase that would become emblematic of the period's values: "You are brave, and the brave do not murder."[41]

Prieto's speech on 12 November was, by contrast with Díaz Mirón's formalism, an example of an early romantic oratory more concerned with pathos than with structure and substantive arguments. Moving audiences, rather than carefully adhering to the dictates of classical rhetoric, was Prieto's strength, as demonstrated in the popular speeches he gave on 15 September.[42] Yet both men represented the heroic persona of the opposition orator. Prieto's emotional impact on the audience was all the more powerful because his health deteriorated visibly as he spoke. He had to stop three times, until the president of the Chamber of Deputies told the assembly that physicians had decided Prieto could not continue.

12. Guillermo Prieto.
© 453559. CND. SINAFO-
Fototeca Nacional
del INAH.

Even though Prieto's intervention lacked the concision and solidity of Díaz Mirón's, he too earned applause and, according to newspaper reports, managed to further weaken the official project.[43]

While Díaz Mirón's dwelling on classic structure was an example of a continuing classicist taste among Mexican orators, Prieto's disdain for orthodoxy and his intimacy with "the people" (*el pueblo*) illustrated the strength of romantic sentiments and patriotism. The classical tradition, as interpreted in 1914 by Elguero in his class on eloquence at the Escuela Nacional de Jurisprudencia (School of law) in Mexico City, offered both an "Attic" style, elegant and discreet, preferred by lawyers, and an "Asian" style, characterized "by the luxury of metaphors, the sumptuosity of the expressions and sometimes vehemence." Elguero nevertheless voiced the widely shared critical view of rigid, schematic Ciceronian precepts.[44] The dichotomy between classic and romantic, however, is deceiving:

Díaz Mirón's exordium on 12 November, like his poetry, represented a new appropriation in Mexico of the romantic sensibility, both highly personal and concerned about form.[45] Here lies an indication of the phases of Mexican romanticism I proposed in the introduction: from the spontaneous, Byronic heroics embodied by Prieto, Díaz Mirón represented a subtle yet momentous change toward a more deliberate construction of the poet's self.

Public speaking offered the most transparent example of this change because of its explicit ethical and political dimensions. Political and literary figures of the Reforma generation like Prieto and Ignacio Manuel Altamirano had relied on an oratorical style that stressed the sincere expression of passion over the classicism of rhetorical structure—although never quite abandoning the admiration for Greek and Roman themes and examples. The young Justo Sierra saw from a new perspective the romantic hero/orator in Altamirano's fiery parliamentary speeches of 1861, when political events fed a "national fever throbbing in the nation's brain, and . . . the unique intensity of the capital's life." Altamirano was bringing together beauty, power, and intellect through "his gesture and his accent and . . . above all, the word, the image, the idea."[46]

To be this effective, romanticism could not be conceived as just a literary trend but had to stress sincerity and content. Sierra defined another veteran of that generation, General Jesús González Ortega, as a romantic because "he liked that sentimental politics that can be wonderfully tried in supreme crises"—such as that faced by the country during the 1860s.[47] The epic undertone of romanticism survived in later generations through, for example, Díaz Mirón's emulation of Victor Hugo and Lord Byron. But now, perhaps because of the lack of glorious episodes in the lives of these younger romantics, the ethical program is more explicit and derivative. For Díaz Mirón the key was to combine idealism and integrity; like Hugo, he believed that Mexicans had to "think highly" and "feel deeply."[48] The clearest symptom of Mexican public men's recycled embrace of romantic models was their admiration for the Spanish orator, journalist, and politician Emilio Castelar (1832–99). Mexican liberals revered Castelar for his support of the Mexican struggle against the French invasion and because many of his most famous speeches had been delivered in adverse political circumstances. He was the pride of "our race." Mexicans like Francisco Cosmes and Ignacio Manuel Altamirano met him in Spain and exchanged correspondence.[49] Sierra praised

Castelar's eloquence because it expanded the parliamentary genre and produced poetry, "oral music," with erudition that encompassed history, philosophy, science, and art. His "voice of gold," wrote Sierra, had the power to keep "assemblies magnetized." Mexican readers consumed Castelar's novels, poetry, and newspaper columns but valued them as by-products of his oratory.[50]

Castelar's main influence in Mexico—absent the possibility of listening directly to his speeches—was his ability to subtly alter orthodox architecture while conveying a romantic stress on sentiment. In a discourse in 1876 that may have served as a model for Díaz Mirón's speech in 1884, Castelar confessed that the importance of the matter at hand had forced him to improvise and neglect "perhaps what is most essential: the architectonic part of the speech." As in Díaz Mirón, the apology thinly disguised a clear command of technique. Castelar coyly acknowledged in the same speech that "no orator must reveal to his public the intimacy of his art."[51] While both Castelar and Díaz Mirón preserved the classical structure and took great care with their elocution, both also exploited the emotional possibilities of the exordium and the peroration (the beginning and the end of the speech), rather than the middle part (the narration, proposition, and confirmation), which could be dry and technical. While the beginning had to be dominated by humility and sincerity, the end of the speech had the highest emotional tone, in fact, creating a crescendo that concluded in resounding phrases. Closely examined, Castelar's speeches were divided into smaller units or periods that generated a pleasing rhythm, allowed for comfortable breathing after the exertions of elocution, and punctuated the crescendo with the applause of the audience. Dramatic antitheses and repetitions were features of Castelar's speeches that commentators saw as lying behind his ability to convey vividly ideas and emotions to the audience. They compared his soaring periods with flat and antiquated sermons—a contrast that was all too clear to Mexican audiences.[52]

To those who were able to observe Castelar in action (the only way to truly appreciate his art), he also demonstrated the physical beauty of the romantic orator's art. In an homage to Castelar celebrated in Mexico City shortly after his death, Sierra described the "physiological pleasure caused by the way in which the great poet spontaneously strings the images and connects the words."[53] The poet Juan de Dios Peza described admiringly Castelar's cheeks, "still red" after a speech he gave in Parliament, and conveyed the powerful impact of his voice on an audience who, ignoring certain defects in the rest of his body, adoringly set "all eyes" on his face.[54] While eliciting the fervent attraction of his mostly male audiences, Castelar's passion had nothing to do with the erotic appetites found in early romantic inspirations like Lord Byron: the Spanish orator's command of language produced pure beauty. Sierra reported that the Spanish tribune was never concerned about "sensual love" and always stayed at a distance from women; chastity made him a "priest of reason and justice," to use the words of Díaz Mirón in his speech of 12 November.[55]

Oratory nevertheless allowed Mexican publics to admire and praise the bodies of public men. An image from Mexico evokes the physical language of the orator: an index finger pointing upward, the body bent over the balustrade, the gesture of intensity drawn in the face (figure 13).[56] Sierra (whose own "noble beauty" when reciting was praised by his contemporaries) stressed this physicality when he described Prieto saving Juárez from the soldiers in Guadalajara: "The great voice . . . the imperative gesture . . . the hands extended toward the mouths of the rifles and covering the president with the body"; the soldiers lowered their arms because that "was the effect, almost physical, of that musical voice."[57]

As opposed to other artistic forms, oratory did not dwell on the representation of female bodies to convey beauty. As noted in chapter 2, literature could be feminized, while in theater and music hall shows foreign and national divas became objects of admiration and desire for audiences and reporters. Oratory, by contrast, while appropriating feminine ways, kept a masculine tenor. Men at the rostrum could express all their feelings, even cry and raise their voices in ways that in other contexts might be considered feminine. The almost complete exclusion of women from the practice of the art in this era was therefore a requirement of the art itself. How could a virile orator cry or agitate himself until his cheeks were red and then be followed by a woman engaging in the same kind of effusions? Appropriating the open expression of passion from women was a foundation of the monopoly over the public sphere by the hombres de palabra.[58]

Castelar's red cheeks, Prieto's fainting, and Díaz Mirón's weak hand clutching a handkerchief signified the strength of emotions overcoming the orator's control of his body and provided the most convincing mea-

13. Orator. Clipping, n.d.,
Lafragua Collection, CESU,
vol 1516, p. 23. Reproduced
by courtesy of the Uni-
versidad Nacional Autóno-
ma de México.

sure of authenticity, a key element of the romantic ethos. When they claimed to reject classical architecture, romantic orators implied that they gave priority to sincerity. Castelar declared in 1890 that he was speaking on a controversial topic (the dangers of demagoguery) "follow-ing the decisions of my heart and not those of understanding. . . . because the powerful feeling drags along with it the alienated will."[59] Passionate authenticity could seem like madness, Castelar and his followers argued, but they also believed that the unity of feelings and form ultimately led to beauty. The stress on passion, however, raised a dilemma: was the romantic energy of modern orators threatening the public use of rea-son? For Pallares, logic and eloquence simply had different rules. "Elo-quence lives off images," he claimed, "ratiocinates through feelings, ar-gues through facts that can be shaped like a sculpture, and its greatest perfection lies in its emancipation from the abstract fortunes of logic."[60] The debate of 1884 shows that reason and sentiment in Mexican roman-ticism interacted in a balance dictated by political circumstance. Reason, however, was also used by critics of romanticism when they tried to counter the popular success of Prieto and Díaz Mirón.

Didactic and Critique of Oratory

On 12 November Justo Sierra had the unenviable task of speaking after Díaz Mirón. Ostensibly dispensing with the weapons of rhetoric, Sierra framed the problem in political terms: those who opposed the project opposed President-elect Díaz—to whom he and many in the room owed their jobs. But the argument, which Sierra presented hesitantly, elicited the indignation and boos of the crowd in the galleries. He later was insulted and threatened by students of the Escuela Nacional Prepara-toria, where he taught and was at the time interim director, both in the chamber and at the school. Two days later Sierra returned to the podium to explain his opinion and declare that he had been "violated by the insulting pressure of the audience."[61] He evoked the same kind of per-sonal dilemma Díaz Mirón and Viñas described in their exordia: "Before entering this debate it was necessary to fight a struggle inside ourselves, a struggle that is inevitable for all men who have begun to emerge in public life, for those who have come to the rostrum or expect to come one day." The dilemma, however, was framed by Sierra in terms that sought to turn the impact of eloquence on its head: "whether to confront unpopularity or be disloyal."[62] Although sincere, such a confession, in the eyes of the audience, was self-defeating in that there could be no legitimate distinc-tion between private and public honor. Just as public opinion encom-passed different spaces (the street, the newspapers, Congress), it had the authority to judge the ethical integrity of individual public men—as, in this case, did the spectators who jeered Sierra every time he mentioned his conscience.[63]

Sierra's implicit criticism of his adversaries' populist oratory and his failure to defend the official project did not mean he was unfamiliar with the art of rhetoric. Quite the opposite, Sierra—notwithstanding his im-promptu speech to a crowd during his encounter with Prieto in 1870—came from a tradition of academic oratory that saw passion as a minor, malleable aspect of eloquence. This professional background explains Sierra's contrast with Díaz Mirón and Prieto. Classical rhetoric saw the counselor as paradigmatic orator: skillful in attack and defense, moved by an intimate conviction about the guilt or innocence of the suspect yet ready to use all the tools of his trade to obtain a just verdict. Judicial dialectic was the model for the battles engaged in by political speakers;

it defined the agonistic character of a democracy that contemporaries understood as the open debate of public issues rather than strict electoral representation.[64]

Higher education provided solid support for the continuity of forensic tradition. Rhetoric, broadly understood as rules for writing in different genres, had been at the center of literary education in the nineteenth century, but the discipline became increasingly identified with public speaking and higher education by the beginning of the twentieth century.[65] Official programs for the study of law in Mexico City established obligatory courses on forensic oratory in 1843 and eventually made oratory a required subject in law schools. Reforms in the curriculum of the Escuela Nacional de Jurisprudencia in 1889 and 1903 conflated the philosophy of law and forensic oratory in one course and moved it from the first to the last year of studies. The union of philosophy and rhetoric responded to Pallares's influential argument of 1883 about the unity of oratory as both form and knowledge (see above). During the last decades of the century, students in Mexico City could learn oratory from such luminaries as Pallares, Antonio Ramos Pedrueza, and José María Lozano.[66] A common way of training was mock trials and speeches on various topics that tested students' ability to quote prestigious authors and European and ancient history. Notes preserved in the archive of the revolutionary ideologue Antonio Díaz Soto y Gama, who trained at the San Luis Potosí Escuela de Jurisprudencia in the late 1890s, show that imitation of great models was a basic didactic tool. This meant strict adherence to classical structure, although the fictional situations discussed in the mock trials alluded to contemporary crimes of passion or politics.[67]

The teaching of eloquence was also associated with instruction in Latin. The Escuela Nacional Preparatoria included two years of Latin for prelaw students in its first plan of studies in 1867, until a reform in 1896 reduced it to one course in Greco-Latin etymology and added French and English. Revolutionary intellectuals like José Vasconcelos and other former students of Sierra's, reacting to what they regarded as the pragmatism of the positivist curriculum, revived the study of the classics and Latin for prelaw students in 1918. In doing so, however, they succeeded only in prolonging the tension between positivism and classicism that dated to the foundation of the Preparatoria in 1867.[68] In all probability few students mastered Latin, but for many an acquaintance with the language was a tool to impress jurors and judges and to invoke the Stoic lineage of an honorable "line of conduct."[69]

From the sublime to the ridiculous the distance was short. Orators came bearing diverse qualities, in terms of both skill and beauty (figures 14 and 15). The Preparatoria's program dropped oratory in 1907, but the art survived in the old Escuela de Jurisprudencia and became a feature of the prestigious new Escuela Libre de Derecho (Free School of Law), founded in 1912. Although by the 1920s the curriculum at Jurisprudencia, now part of the Universidad Nacional, still did not include a separate course in rhetoric, law students continued to be expected to acquire rhetorical competence. They developed it in extracurricular oratory contests, which became as popular as sporting events and involved students from outside Mexico City, including some who had participated in international events. Contestants improvised speeches on random topics, sometimes producing comic examples of the vacuity of the post-revolutionary regime's official language. A popular parody of forensic oratory is found in the trial scene of the movie *Ahí está el detalle* (There's the rub) (1940), in which Mario Moreno "Cantinflas" turns the judge's and prosecutor's pretentious speech on its head with a trademark spiel of meaningless interjections, gestures, and incomplete sentences.[70]

In 1884, Sierra's critique of the opposition's oratory derived from an academic tradition that valued rhetoric, but in specific institutional settings and in a moderate tone. Inevitably, the defense of the government's project became an argument for containing the role of eloquence in politics. Knowledgeable in classical forensic oratory yet identified with romantic aesthetics, Sierra was not successful because he could not distance himself from this combined legacy—particularly regarding ideas about the honor of public men. Francisco Bulnes, who spoke later during the debates, was more effective because he contrasted oratory, which could decay into empty speechifying, with a discourse that placed reason and pragmatism at the center. Bulnes, an engineer by training but also a formidable, although unorthodox, polemicist, presented a critique of rhetoric that was more radical than Sierra's. Although unable at the time to turn the tide of the parliamentary battle, this critique would eventually become an important theoretical aspect of the consolidation of Porfirian political control.

Bulnes's first intervention in the debate had taken place on 10 November, when, representing the committee that recommended its approval,

14. José Guadalupe Posada, "Orators. High style. Back cover." *La Patria Ilustrada*, 1889.

15. José Guadalupe Posada, "Orators. Third class. Turn-off-the-light-and-leave class." *La Patria Ilustrada*, 1889.

he read aloud the project to the plenary. The review in *El Monitor Republicano* described the chamber as being almost dark and Bulnes, who did not have good eyesight, using candles to read the project in a hesitant voice. According to the review, the exercise was a theatrical disaster: "All dramatic authors with a modicum of experience know which phrases in their work will make the audience laugh. The writer of the project found laughter where he least expected it."[71] The sentence passed by the press echoed that of other sectors of the city's population. In the days after the debate, Bulnes's students boycotted his class at the Colegio de Minería (School of Mines).[72] Knowing that the rhetorical advantage was on his rivals' side, on 12 November Bulnes reframed the debate in terms that challenged the heroic stance of his adversaries. To counter Prieto's intervention, he questioned the importance of history in the making of policy decisions with a double-sided argument: on the one hand, Bulnes invoked the positivist belief in progress ("If patriotism demands that the past be declared perfect," he asked ironically, "why discuss the present, why concern ourselves with the future?"); on the other, he cast doubt on the personal authority granted by participation in the national struggles of the past. Bulnes, who would gain notoriety as a revisionist historian years later, reminded Prieto that as a minister of finance in the 1850s he had recognized the country's obligation to pay the national debt. Prieto's ethical coherence was not so strong, then, if he acted one way "in the capitol, near the Caesar" and another "in the Senate in front of the people."[73]

The allusion to Rome was not gratuitous. Like his predecessors at the rostrum, Bulnes centered his argument on the dangerous potential of rhetoric in politics. Prieto was his target because he embodied a style that Bulnes defined by its manipulation of the masses. Bulnes expressed a new, scientific version of rhetorical tradition that was averse to the intervention of popular groups in national politics. Oratory in the early national period had inherited the respectability of religious rhetoric. Early oratory textbooks stressed the formalized interaction between counsel and judge. Violent assemblies and dramatic debates had not been a feature of the independence process in Mexico, as they had been during the French Revolution, and civic discourses, like the one proffered by Prieto from a bench in the zócalo, stressed lofty patriotic teachings and rarely translated into violence. Nevertheless, authorities like Pallares decried the contemporary abuse of eloquence that consisted of addressing the mob rather than judicial officers and subordinating truth to applause.

Public opinion, he claimed, was manipulated by "skillful prestidigitators of common sense."[74] For Bulnes, that kind of populist appeal inside Congress and its link with street violence were dangerous. He described popular assemblies in terms that left no doubt about his views of the lower classes: the common people dominated such meetings "with screams, with obscenities, with spit, with the speeches of a procuress rejected from all brothels, with the impatience of executioners, with the anxiety of petty thieves, with the loud demands of drunkards, with the incoherence of lunatics . . . with everything infectious that can come flying out of dry mud."[75]

These fears evoked classic arguments about the disjunction between means and ends in rhetoric and the role of beauty in politics: since the art's technical aspects were not based on knowledge of the subject matter, persuasion could be based on flattery and other tricks rather than on the intrinsic value of the cause; orators could apply their skills to any purpose, good or bad, as students did in postrevolutionary contests. The critique of romantic eloquence focused on the unholy communion of orator and audience. Pallares explained the power of rhetoric as a function of the speaker's ability to seduce the audience, taking it to the heights of beauty, when in fact it was him who "freely drags and leads" his spectators.[76] The prestige of the orator—his past, his command of language, his physical beauty—could be the decisive factor in determining the success of a speech. Speakers like Ignacio Manuel Altamirano, Guillermo Prieto, and, to a lesser extent in 1884, Díaz Mirón were preceded at the podium by their reputation and popularity. This created a paradox in the positivist critique of romantic eloquence, one in which the puppeteer became the puppet. Bulnes's fellow científico Joaquín D. Casasús, echoing contemporary European ideas, explained famous speakers as a product of their audiences, rather than their intrinsic abilities: "The orator does not exist without the audience that listens to him, without the environment that surrounds him, without the occasion that inspires him."[77] When audience and speaker were one, as in the romantic version, sincerity had higher emotional value, and the speaker was able to steer his discourse according to the reactions of his audience.[78]

The latter observation comes from Gustave Le Bon, a French writer who inaugurated a field of scientific inquiry on the behavior of crowds and who was highly influential among public men of the late Porfirian and early revolutionary periods—to a large extent because of the authoritarian cachet of his theses. Bulnes, Díaz Mirón, and revolutionaries like Salvador Alvarado read him and quoted his works. In his *Psychologie des foules* (The psychology of crowds), Le Bon described a crowd (whether composed of primitives or modern workers) as an organism with specific psychological traits, such as irritability, and inferior intellectual abilities. Thus crowds were influenced by the form of the ideas conveyed to them rather than by their content, and repetition had a more powerful effect on them than reasoning. Words had magical power over the crowd, even as their meaning could be changed to suit political goals. Le Bon's political sociology was reassuring to public men like Bulnes, who saw an expansion of political participation both as a threat to the influence of educated elites and as a resource that could be tapped through a scientific brand of rhetoric.[79]

The political culture of the Porfiriato, however, did not move in the direction of a greater use of eloquence for political ends. After 1884, the dominant temper among those close to power was one of verbal moderation. Díaz himself was a man of few words, and politicians like Manuel Calero and Díaz Mirón were, by contrast, living proof that excessive reliance on the power to mesmerize assemblies did not lead to personal success; in such a vertical system, it was not wise to talk too much.[80] This evolution paralleled that of judicial culture. Codification of criminal law in the latter part of the century preserved the colonial emphasis on the written compilation of evidence; the goal of lawyers was to argue about the application of the law, and an excessive reliance on eloquence in front of a judge could be counterproductive. Personal connections, in any case, were always more effective in obtaining good results.[81] The new moderation had a point of reference in the speeches of Henri Robert (1863–1936), delivered in French criminal courts: they were brief, aggressive, logical, and disposed of "the death flowers of rhetoric."[82] Speakers like Bulnes and, after the Revolution, Luis Cabrera came to be admired precisely because of the incisive rationalism of their form and content— perceived, however, as a style as much as a philosophical stance.

On 12 November 1884, Bulnes articulated these views in the form of a challenge to the primacy of public opinion postulated by the adversaries of the project. Against Díaz Mirón's defense of sincerity over arithmetic, Bulnes proposed "to define the arguments in a more scientific although less literary form"; this meant putting aside rhetorical devices "to impress the Assembly" and presenting "positive facts."[83] Public opinion was the terrain of uncertain knowledge, and Bulnes proposed to disregard it altogether. The following passage describes in a critical tone the representative public sphere associated with the ongoing challenge to the consolidation of the regime: "We are told that you are the representatives of the people: public opinion rejects this project, and you do not have anything to do but obey it. For public opinion to reject something fairly it needs above all to know the question as it is, and to solve it as it should be. And how are we to know if public opinion has fulfilled these conditions? Who decides? Everyone makes qualifications and the press pretends to illustrate them; but if the '57 Constitution gives the press freedom and guarantees, it does not recognize it as interpreter of public opinion."

The people, continued Bulnes, had the right to direct the actions of its representatives through the vote, "but not as a mass, and without offending public morality"—as crowds in Mexico City were now trying to do. The press was only an informal vehicle for sovereignty, and its representativeness was far from perfect: people lacked scientific authority, and public opinion always made mistakes. He expressed a version of national honor as credit, one that would come to prevail later in the Porfiriato, when national finances came to be identified with científico Minister of Hacienda José Yves Limantour's punctilious concern about paying debts and restricting the deficit, thus explaining the return of foreign lenders and investors. The post-1884 lesson was clear: a national reputation of honradez did not come to fruition as the product of open, heroic debate but through the successful control of public opinion.[84]

Yet Bulnes could not escape the linking of opinion and honor that was the key reasoning of the adversaries of the project. In an intriguing sentence at the end of the passage quoted above, he stated, "If anyone, supported by public opinion, tells me that this is patriotism, I, speaking in the name of public opinion in general, will reply that this is honor." Perhaps interjections like these, rather than his critique of rhetoric, explain the applause that followed his speech.[85]

Honor and the Nation

But, with characteristic irony, Bulnes was trying to disassociate honor and patriotism and undermine the notion that public opinion judged both—his adversaries' premises. His attempt was to no avail. The press had already established the basic equation of national and personal virtues: "Nations, just like individuals," wrote *La Patria*'s "Guanche," "obey laws that try to be inspired by the healthy principles of morality."[86] During his speech, Díaz Mirón read from newspapers to convey journalists' apprehension that the national honor was at stake. He defined the state's obligations with morally charged images: the government should not pay the debt now when "the widows and the pensioners are dying of misery; . . . there are public employees who commit suicide because they do not receive their salaries and lack the courage to see the horrible spectacle of their children's hunger." In terms of foreign relations, the preference given to British bonds was insulting because it neglected Spain, "whose generous blood runs and boils in our veins, always ready to be spilled in the name of everything that is noble and great." He concluded his speech with a plea that would reappear in the days after: "Reject the project under discussion and you will save our patria from the abyss and from dishonor."[87] On the opposite side of the discussion, Sierra could only agree: "The patria is lost when honor is lost."[88]

By the late nineteenth century, personalizing the nation had become a central trope of political discourse. Criminologists and public health officials described their program in terms of the preservation of the country's health; historians saw the recent past in terms of integrity and chastity; Sierra depicted Santa Anna as the seducer who left the republic stained.[89] Conversely, statements about personal reputation, such as Santos Degollado's confession and Francisco de P. Vega's pamphlet of 1868, were based on the premise that "individuals, families, cities, and nations sacrifice" for their reputation.[90] Article 658 of the Penal Code of 1871 defined crimes against the nation's honra. Thus, two Roman Catholic journalists were sentenced to eight months in prison in 1888 for criticizing the liberal government's expropriation of church properties. Their attorney argued that accusing them of an offense against the nation rather than against specific public officials was "antilegal and antiscientific," as it did not amount to *ultraje* (insults) against public officers. Yet prosecutors voiced an allegorical understanding of the nation as having personal characteristics such as morality and reputation—traits further demonstrated in conflicts with other nations.[91]

The debates of November 1884 assumed that national honor could not be distinguished from the personal honor of public men. Honor in this context was often called honradez, a person's rectitude, or pundonor, the "honra o crédito" of an individual. On both sides of the debate the word "credit" referred to personal *and* financial reputation. Díaz Mirón said, "For an honorable man and a dignified people, to owe is to pay."[92] Francisco Cosmes, on the other side, asked Deputy Simón Sarlat if it "behooved his honor" to pay his debts and concluded, "Why does Mr. Sarlat believe that the nation's honor is below his own?"[93] The adversaries of the project, however, were more willing to follow this logic to its personal consequences. Giving away the patria's honra, students claimed in a manifesto, was like giving away the honra of wives and daughters. Díaz Mirón criticized Bulnes's proposal to guarantee payment of the debt with a percentage of customs income because it assumed that Mexican customs officials were corrupt. Thus, he asked how "will we reject the calumnies and insults that newspapers from the other side of the Atlantic continuously send our way?"[94] Rectitude in front of foreigners had been a central theme of Santos Degollado's travails.[95] As noted earlier, Porfirian diplomats like Ignacio Manuel Altamirano felt compelled to "take [foreign journalists] to the field of honor."

The debates about the English debt prompted numerous duels and challenges.[96] In the session of 20 November, Viñas (the deputy who "flew" to the chamber after he read the papers and heard discussions in the streets) was provoked by one of the deputies he had mentioned in a speech—although newspapers did not report the outcome of the conflict.[97] The governor of the Federal District, Carlos Rivas, sent his seconds to Deputy Fernando Duret, who had accused him of using the police to influence deputies. The parties in this instance reached an agreement that displeased Díaz Mirón, who would have preferred a duel. He was a friend of Duret's and, two years later, dedicated a poem, "Voces interiores," to him. The following stanza depicts the moral superiority of opposition deputies during those heady days:

> You, who firm and erect at the rostrum,
> like the rock where the lighthouse shines,
> know how to fulfill your duty as a torch
> over this sea where honor sinks![98]

Díaz Mirón described Duret at the rostrum because his role as a public speaker was, in hindsight, more important than his participation in the rather private business of a duel. The conclusion of the debate about debating at the heart of the deuda inglesa episode seemed inescapable: through eloquence, honor, both national and personal, constituted politics. Readers and spectators saw the rhetorical competence of politicians as the main factor in determining the outcome. Newspapers like *La Patria* focused their reports more on the performance of deputies at the podium than on the substance of their arguments. Sierra "was most unfortunate," according to *La Patria*, "not only because of his poor defense of the business at hand, but also because of his clumsy way of speaking."[99] Reactions in the galleries seemed to be based mostly on elocution, yet determined failure or success: Sierra lost control because of the whistling; Luis Pombo suffered because "the galleries did not stop hooting him down"; Cosmes could not overcome similar noises because his "voice was too weak and his figure very ugly at the rostrum"; and Hilario Gavilondo was treated to "a horrible whistling . . . because of the intonation he gave his speech, like a civic oration."[100] Triumph belonged to Viñas—who "has come to pick up in a single bouquet all the laurels conquered by the gladiators for and against the project"—and to Díaz Mirón—who "made the *inglesistas* tremble with the strength of his voice."[101]

Political success seemed to stem from aesthetic evaluation of personal and artistic attributes and from technical competence in the art of rhetoric. Classic and romantic traditions conspired, for the time being, to defeat a scientific critique of oratory. Behind the spectators' and reporters' evaluation of the performance of orators lay the notion of a public sphere that brought together finance, politics, reputations, and rhetoric. The debates of 12–14 November were pregnant with the hope, or fear, that parliamentary battles would spill out of the Iturbide Theater into the capital's streets. The popular revolt which ensued indeed confirmed the practical potential of romantic oratory.

CHAPTER 4

Breaking Lamps
and Expanding the Public Sphere
Students and *Populacho* against the *Deuda Inglesa*

What were the political consequences of the dangerous ascent of eloquence? In spite of the interventions of Justo Sierra and Francisco Bulnes,
the parliamentary debates over the deuda inglesa exposed weaknesses in
the transition between Porfirio Díaz and Manuel González. Although the
official project was approved in general terms on 15 November, discussions and procedural votes on subsequent days showed that several deputies were changing their mind. In order to prevent a defeat, President
González prompted governors to reign in representatives from their
states and ordered loyal deputies to return from their leaves of absence to
replace substitutes who had sided with the opposition—a maneuver resisted by some of these, like Ireneo Paz and Salvador Díaz Mirón, who
managed to remain in place.[1] Finally, seeking to tip the debates in favor of
the official side by eliminating the opposition's sympathetic audience, the
government ordered policemen and soldiers into the chamber galleries.
The move resulted in violence and disorder that started on the floor and
in the galleries of the Teatro Iturbide and spilled out to the surrounding
city streets. The protests forced the government to withdraw the project
on 21 November, a decision that prompted popular celebrations.

The scene inside the chamber during these days showed the regime's embarrassing and unexpected loss of control. The audience, a socially diverse crowd that behaved more like the patrons of popular theater than like those of high-art functions, booed or applauded speakers, loudly intervening in the debates—the scene resembled a "chicken coop," according to *La Libertad*.[2] Most of this animation emanated from students of institutions of higher education in the capital. Students had been in a fighting mood ever since September, when their celebrations of independence turned into an act of disapproval of President González. Their querulousness had lasted into October as their examinations and classes ended. Now, in November, they had come to the chamber a day before the beginning of the debate ready to act as a *claque*. When Sierra gave his ill-fated defense of the official project, they coughed and hissed every time he referred to his conscience and bothered others speakers by making comments and jokes that produced general hilarity and broke their concentration. On the thirteenth, they led spectators onto the floor of the chamber and occupied seats reserved for stenographers, diplomatic representatives, and deputies, ripping off pieces of the building's molding and throwing them at deputies. Other, less dangerous missiles from the galleries included manifestos and petitions. The environment became so hostile that during the vote on 15 November supporters of the project had to huddle around the chamber president's table to avoid the crowd's rage. Policemen in the galleries failed to contain the audience, as students hid behind respectable members of the audience. Some were detained and taken to the police station, although most were released either before reaching the station or after a few hours of arrest during which they made incendiary speeches to the common prisoners.[3]

Thus stealing the scene from the deputies, students took their rebellion into the streets. They spread accounts of the debates and invited the crowd camped outside the chamber's doors to challenge the forces of order. On the fifteenth, for example, after an initial vote in favor of the government's project, students came out of the Teatro Iturbide and marched to the homes of some politicians, returning later to the area near Plaza Santo Domingo and several of their schools. They were followed by "roaring people" (in the words of a chronicler of the events and a student himself) yet did not incite disorder and were dispersed by the police.[4] The size and defiant attitude of the group increased noticeably two days later, on the seventeenth, when the president of the chamber decided to expel the rowdy audience from inside the teatro, triggering violence in the streets that this time included destruction of windows and lamps and even a few deaths.

Meetings, marches, and street battles illustrate the traditional ability of students and orators to expand political participation beyond class divides and spaces of elite sociability.[5] Fed by political gossip, street oratory, and combat journalism, the riots of November 1884 demonstrate the strong nexus between public men and the city's general population that characterized the public sphere of the República Restaurada and early Porfiriato. I want to examine the specific mechanisms and actors that translated romantic ideas about eloquence and integrity into street action. Students at the preparatory and professional schools played a central role in this story because they occupied a unique place in terms both of social status, coming, as most of them did, from struggling middle-class families, and of their relations with two other groups whose political influence surged during these days: respectable women and the urban plebes. In the first and second sections of this chapter I take a look at the social situation of students, and in the third section I analyze collective actions in the space of the capital. I will suggest, to conclude, that the transgression of class and space boundaries during the deuda inglesa revolt signaled the beginning of the end of the historical role of political elites as vecinos, that is, as educated men who lived in close proximity to the rest of urban society and represented its opinions.

The process was obvious to contemporaries. The difficulty of conceptualizing the relationship between elites and the rest of society is marked by the trouble politicians had in finding the correct words to talk about "the people." On 18 November, soldiers and policemen opened fire on the crowd outside the Teatro Iturbide. As shots rang out outside the chamber, some deputies cried, "They are killing *el pueblo* [the people]! Long live the people!" Díaz Mirón invited his colleagues to come out: "Let's die with the people!" Ever a man of action, he went outside the building accompanied by the president of the chamber, Gumersindo Enríquez, who ordered the public forces to withdraw. Upon his return to the chamber Enríquez committed a revealing gaffe: he informed deputies that the police had fired upon "el populacho." Deputy Cordero corrected him: it "is not the populacho, but the pueblo." The pejorative connotations of *populacho* ("the lowest among the plebs," according to the Real Academia) sparked such indignation among the deputies that the ensuing chaos forced Enríquez to suspend the day's session. The following day, he apologized for referring that way to el pueblo. The distinction was important because actions in the streets were based on students' claim to represent the nation's sovereignty and honor.[6]

Higher Education and the Civilization of Politics

That representation was made possible by the complex mix of cultural capital and sociability that defined students' bohemian life. Spectacle was the first reason for them to join the political fray. The debates in the chamber attracted diverse aficionados of oratory. Many students and journalists had secured seats as early as 11 November because they had heard Díaz Mirón was indignant and was going to give a fiery speech.[7] At the end of each session, spectators at the Teatro Iturbide disseminated the most compelling passages of the discourses among those who could not enter—one or two days before press reports. According to *El Monitor Republicano*, there was a diverse crowd in the galleries, "lo más florido [the best] de la sociedad mexicana" from different classes, including women and students from the Escuela Nacional Preparatoria and the professional schools of Medicine, Mining, and Law, "distinguished and educated people [who] expressed their indignation . . . they are the representatives of all the societies that are going to protest against that abuse."[8] Much like press juries, debates turned passive audiences into active publics that represented society's perceptions in spite of social distance.

The proceedings soon ceased to be pure spectacle. The police arrested twenty-five students on 13 November, but that only added fuel to their will to participate: on the fourteenth, they dropped from the galleries a manifesto, signed "El Pueblo," demanding that deputies vote according to their conscience and in defense of "the honor of the fatherland."[9]

Students had such an authoritative voice because they incarnated youth and bohemian sincerity. For *El Monitor Republicano*'s "Juvenal" (Enrique Chávarri), students promised the future redemption of national politics: "Youth! Youth! you alone are the rainbow that spans the cloudy sky of our unhappy fatherland, . . . you, who bring on your forehead the word of the future."[10] Part of "the world of intelligence," their eloquence was an important political asset: student agitators like Diódoro Batalla emulated opposition deputies outside the Teatro by speaking to crowds and writing manifestos.[11]

In contrast to late twentieth-century student movements, student activism in 1884 did not imply a revolutionary challenge to political institutions and social respectability. On 20 November the students formally presented the chamber with a petition, now signed "The students," in which they defined their role in the political process: "The youth of the schools" protest against the project in its character of "loyal interpreter of public opinion." In a simultaneous manifesto to the nation, they promised to act so that "tomorrow national history will say that the generation that rises today did everything it could to save its country from ruin and dishonor."[12] At the celebration of their victory on November 22, they marched peacefully, carrying banners that read "Long live peace!" and "Long live the Constitution! Long live the rights of the people! Long live the right to assemble!" According to the press, ladies in downtown streets saluted the marchers and covered them with a "rain of flowers, wreaths and verses."[13] The social background of most students was not so distant from that of respectable passersby. Leaders like Carlos Basave did come from well-off families. They received medals presented by a group of "Mexican ladies." And when some of them were expelled from the Escuela Preparatoria and others were arrested, they became "political prisoners" and received the economic and moral support of associations from around the country.[14]

It seems paradoxical that students could hold such a central role in public life in a country in which less than a quarter of the population was able to read and write. Pupils in secondary and professional schools, furthermore, were relatively few in the world of Mexican education—1 and 1.4 percent of primary school enrollment, respectively, in 1900. Of the national population of 9.5 million in 1878, a mere 3,375 were secondary school students. There was a rapid increase in student population during the Porfiriato, particularly at the higher levels, which points to one of the reasons for the students' influence in the episode of 1884. The total number of secondary students doubled by 1900, and those in preparatory schools expanded by 122 percent between 1878 and 1900. But with rising numbers came centralization. By 1900 the number of secondary students reached 7,506 in the country at large and 3,928 in the Federal District, which had only 2.4 percent of the national population; of the latter, 2,789 were men, reflecting a gender imbalance that was even greater at the professional level. The numbers for professional schools were in the same range: in 1878 there were 5,552 students nationally and 3,090 in the Federal District, and by 1907 the numbers had increased by 80 and 66 percent, respectively.[15]

Such growth was the result of increasing investment in education, from 3.1 to 6.74 percent of the federal budget during the same period. From the early 1880s through his appointment as the first head of the Secretaría de Instrucción Pública y Bellas Artes in 1905, Sierra was the main promoter of this expansion within the regime. According to Mary Kay Vaughan, his efforts translated into many more primary schools across the country, largely in the capital and wealthier states.[16] Sierra also presided over the creation of the Universidad Nacional in 1910, the culmination of institutional changes at the higher level that had started in 1867, when the government of Benito Juárez set the legal framework for educational reform.

The capital, with its five professional schools, was the center of the educational system; it also had the most professionals and thus more potential teachers: data are sketchy for the earlier period, but by 1900 there were 826 lawyers and 526 physicians in the Federal District, from a total of 3,652 and 2,626, respectively, in the country.[17] Families from the interior sent their children there to get the best possible education. Although Vaughan doubts that the restrictive and expensive higher education of the Porfiriato had a positive impact on social mobility, the spatial mobility that brought children of poor but *decente* families from the farthest corners of the country to the capital was in itself a big step, as illustrated by José Vasconcelos.[18] The national echoes of the deuda inglesa protest were a product of the social, spatial, and political links established by higher education.

Social capital was a factor in centralization, as people's migration to the capital in search of higher education offered the possibility of access to the smaller circles of political influence. Roderi Ai Camp has shown that higher education was central to the recruitment and renewal of political elites. Coming from the same few schools, Mexican politicians tended to identify themselves as members of distinct generations. Compared to their predecessors, Porfirian officeholders were also increasingly teachers (57 percent of them by 1910). As such, notably at the Jurisprudencia and Preparatoria schools, they incorporated younger cohorts into their political networks and introduced them into the culture and sociability of

ruling groups. Politics, after all, could resemble the classroom in its hierarchies, rituals, and fraternity. Several members of the prominent Unión
Liberal in the 1890s, for example, had been on the examination committees of other members. Recruitment was possible because of the small
scale of higher education: the Escuela de Jurisprudencia, arguably the
most important in terms of its contribution to the political elite, had one
hundred students and fifteen teachers in 1900.[19]

A socially unified elite was one of the goals of supporters of public
education. The Escuela Nacional Preparatoria, which opened its doors to
nine hundred students in 1868, was intended by its founders, Gabino
Barreda and José Díaz Covarrubias, to bridge class divisions and create connections among families and "intimate fraternal ties" among students. Such fraternity, it was hoped, would contribute to the greater
goal of ending the perennial infighting and militarism that characterized
Mexican politics. That year, Sierra expressed that hope in a poem contrasting the death of the soldier, "covering in blood his laurel of glory" and
receiving the "marble and bronze that his fame demands," with that of
the "humble student," who receives only "a handful of dirt" as posthumous reward for his sacrifice for humanity.[20] Jokes about uniformed
Preparatoria students marching at the celebration of the battle of Puebla
on 5 May 1884 pointed to the abyss that separated them from the military: students' caps read "E.N.P.," for Escuela Nacional Preparatoria,
but pranksters intepreted the initials as "Estos No Pelean" (These guys
don't fight).[21]

By laying "a common foundation for all to start . . . so that not a single
important fact is instilled in our spirits without first being subject to a
discussion," the Preparatoria, Barreda thought, would offer a social and
methodological solution to the country's prevailing "ideological and political anarchy."[22] Fellowships were a key element of the success of the
project. Many pupils, above all those from the interior, had a difficult
time paying for room and board and books. The cost for the first out-of-
town students who lived in the Preparatoria's *internado* (dormitories)
was two hundred pesos per trimester. Government aid allowed many to
survive during the five years of the preparatory program and six of law
studies and further cemented the bonds of gratitude that mediated their
eventual entry into the political elite.[23]

Elite recruitment, social mobility, and state expenditure account for
only part of the impact of students on public life—and only in hindsight.

In the eyes of contemporaneous actors the theoretical centrality of education within the liberal project of modernization was even more important. This was not the result of a coherent discourse by Barreda or Sierra so much as the product of heated, yet not always conclusive, debates about the contents of such education. Post-1867 regimes had decided to make education and civilian merit the alternative to the traditional primacy of the military in political careers. While in 1878, 36 percent of the federal budget went to the Secretaría de Guerra (Ministry of War) and only 3 percent to education, by 1910 the numbers had changed to 20 and 7 percent, respectively.[24] This budgetary shift was not the object of much debate, although the content of the education to be supported by the state was more controversial—notably as the influence of the Catholic Church was curtailed by the Constitution of 1857.

The Preparatoria was part of a reorientation of public education in which Barreda installed positivism at the center of the educational project of the República Restaurada. Its five-year curriculum was organized around the sciences, beginning with basic disciplines. The humanities received little attention, ethics became a minor section of the course on logic, and Latin and Greek (taught in the past to all students at the predecessor Colegio de San Ildefonso) gave way to French and English. From the very beginning, critics of positivism defined the project as authoritarian, rigid, and lacking in spiritual values. In 1875 Guillermo Prieto promoted and secured the addition of a course on the history of philosophy in order to expose students to a wider range of influences. Catholic publications like La Voz de México were also critical of positivism, but most early criticisms, including those of Sierra, came from the perspective of romanticism and, later, spiritualism—a flexible combination of faith in science and in spiritual change.[25]

Sierra was close to the project (and in 1884 was briefly the director of the Preparatoria) and a liberal, but he was also ambivalent about the ethical value of positivism. He expressed this sentiment in 1908 in a speech in honor of his dear teacher Barreda. A more frontal critique was launched by the Ateneo de la Juventud generation.[26] Defenders of positivism, in contrast, charged the critics with simply rehashing "a romantic imagination" and imitating the "model of scholastic turbulence" of German students. The school's faculty resisted the demands of students and also those coming from external sources to alter the curriculum and the school's everyday discipline.[27]

The Escuela Preparatoria was highly exposed to the tyranny of public opinion. Faculty appointments, examinations, curricula, and even the selection of textbooks were the subject of debates in the press and in government. The Chamber of Deputies approved the creation of the course on history of philosophy and was part of a heated debate in the late 1870s concerning the selection of a logic textbook. A political subtext of these discussions was the perception that Barreda, the director of the school during its first decade, was a remnant of Juarismo. In the early months of González's presidency, after Barreda's death in 1880, the textbook debate raged on, and the new education minister, Ezequiel Montes, proposed a plan that modified contents and would have eliminated the school altogether. The offensive against positivism was supported by a rare combination of old liberals and Catholics "shrouding themselves in the flag of freedom of conscience," according to the historian Edmundo O'Gorman.[28] Journalists, deputies, and students resisted Montes's plan by defending the budget for public education. Resolution was achieved only after a new minister, Joaquín Baranda, who would remain from 1882 until 1901, negotiated the choice of textbooks and gave teachers greater flexibility in how they used them. The education budget was meaningful because it opposed Barreda and later científicos, who saw the German university as a model of an institution funded by the state yet independent, with critics of positivism, who equated freedom of teaching with the privatization of higher education, as in the United States. The school survived, but student actions in 1884 continued to echo wider political battles over higher education.[29]

The textbook debates were a central moment in the intellectual evolution of the country, evidence of the weakness of positivism or of the dilemmas of Mexican identity. Although useful in general terms, these interpretations tend to subordinate an aspect of these discussions that was at the heart of the liberal concern about education, namely, its moral components and consequences. In Barreda's Comtean view of history, in order to transcend the ethical legacy of the theological and metaphysical eras, education needed "to create habits of behavior among students based on scientific prediction, the inevitable foundation of rational activity."[30] Introspection, a central tenet of the romantic outlook, had no value, in Barreda's view. Beyond vague notions of "moral gymnastics," in fact early positivist educators did not concern themselves with moral education, preferring to leave those issues to the influence of the family.

Thus, for example, Barreda and others were against the internado, the boarding system that had traditionally housed preparatory students at the school. They believed it extended the responsibilities of educators into the kind of everyday realms that characterized the expansive reach of a religious education. From the Catholic perspective, this was dangerous precisely because it abdicated the moral responsibility of educators. For old liberals, the lack of interest in humanistic subjects deprived students of classical moral examples. Sierra oscillated, initially opposing the internado but supporting it in the early 1900s, as part of a more ethically ambitious education, "an education of the feelings and emotion, which is what we call moral culture."[31]

Student Recreation as Mobilization

Heriberto Frías recognized, probably better than anyone because of his academic failures, the strong attraction of student life, on the border between youth and adulthood, high society and the commoners, respectable and decadent customs. What could be more attractive, he asked, than belonging to that world of young men

> seduced by the pride of seeing their names in print, by the pleasure of calling themselves bohemian artists and wearing broad cotton ties, of having cheap lovers and drinking the best tequila and the best pulque during the binges offered by their admirers. . . . They . . . told the true intimate story of that prostituted Mexico of politics and plutocrats . . . they revealed the miseries of the great men, their love affairs with operetta singers . . . the secrets of ministers, generals and deputies and . . . their wives and lovers . . . the story of the last golden adultery . . . everything, in sum, that "cannot be told" in a newspaper, and which was almost always the truth.[32]

Students' success at instigating popular protest in 1884 was the product of their liminal situation in Mexican society—codified by their relations with women, as we will see, but also by their ability to move across class and spatial boundaries.

Indiscipline and student activism were the first demonstrations of the ethical failings of positivism that plagued institutions of higher learning ever since 1867. Students' pranks and gay nightlife were traditional from colonial times.[33] However, since the triumph of liberalism, two aspects of student life, both directly connected to the perceived moral failings of positivism, came to dominate perceptions of their role in public life—both surviving into the second half of the twentieth century. Although the two aspects are intrinsically related, I will treat them separately. The first was the ability of students to mobilize in response to a range of issues, from the internado and the teaching style of faculty to more overtly political issues like the deuda inglesa. The second aspect, and the implicit premise of critiques of positivist morals, concerned the famously loose behavior of students, particularly their relationships with alcohol, the urban poor, and women.

Student mobilization at the Preparatoria began within the school itself. In 1868 students rebelled against the holding of some of their fellow pupils in the school detention cells and against the poor quality of the food. They broke a few chairs, locked members of the staff in the building, and issued a call for the people to take up arms in their support.[34] The connection between internal discipline and political demands was more logical in 1875 during a strike that started at the Escuela de Medicina over the expulsion of three students who were part of a smaller protest against the teaching style of the faculty. The movement expanded beyond Medicina into other schools, including the Preparatoria, which also struck. Representatives formed a *comité central* that collected money for students who depended on fellowships, published a newspaper, and organized classes at the Alameda park taught by students and sympathetic faculty. The movement gained strength when several politicians who were opposed to President Sebastián Lerdo de Tejada and probably sympathetic to Porfirio Díaz joined the students and embraced their demand for *enseñanza libre*—freedom of education, specifically, freedom for teachers to depart from the official programs. The attack took aim both at positivist rule and at Lerdo's political control. Among the supporters of enseñanza libre were the intellectuals General Vicente Riva Palacio and Ignacio Manuel Altamirano; both gave advice to striking students, and Altamirano offered his house to ten of them who lacked the means to support themselves. Several upper-class families also gave material support to the strikers. The movement was discussed in the Chamber of Deputies. After a few weeks the strike was lifted when authorities agreed to reinstate the expelled students, although they were not allowed to reclaim their places in the internado.[35]

The combination of academic, ideological, and political motivations behind the strike reflects students' ability to gain a strong voice in the public sphere by using the capital's spaces, media, and social networks. The origin of the rebellion of 1875 was a perceived offense to students' dignity. In their manifestos, the students emphasized the respectability of their movement and embraced lofty goals like a new program of studies, the end of the internado, enseñanza libre, and the creation of an *universidad libre*, autonomous from the state.[36] "Despotism in the schools" was identified with Lerdo de Tejada's alleged political and ideological tyranny. *El Ahuizote* praised the strikers because their movement "reveals noble feelings of abnegation and fraternity . . . unbreakable will, the dignity and energy that belong to a man who cherishes the recognition of his rights." A source of pride was the fact that members of the comité central "have sworn by their honor and their name to sacrifice their career, their future and their family for the realization of the idea that constitutes the teaching of the revolution."[37] Because of its efficient organization and the elevation of its ideals, the movement became a model for future generations of students, including several future científicos.

The Escuela Nacional Preparatoria became the *Escuela Madre* (Alma mater) where most students first met and created strong bonds across future professional divides. Unity acquired political meaning through students' participation in civic commemorations and artistic events. In the early 1880s, for example, Jurisprudencia and Ingeniería combined their celebrations of independence. Students marched through downtown streets but, to show their disapproval of the current government, bypassed the National Palace. President González forbade students at the Colegio Militar to march with the rest of the schools. In September 1884, students openly expressed their rejection of González; in a function at the Teatro Hidalgo, Diódoro Batalla "threw down the gauntlet to power," and Guadalupe Castañares also spoke eloquently, offering to shed her blood if the government responded with violence to her fellow students' civil courage.[38]

José Guadalupe Posada's print "The Mutiny of the Students" (figure 16) presents the combination of nationalism, oratorical skill, spontaneity, and respectability that defined students' incursions into the public sphere during the first part of the Porfiriato. While a student speaks from atop a carriage, an audience composed of men wearing hats and jackets and elegantly clad women wave flags and share the enthusiasm of the orator. In the background, another student addresses a man wearing a peasant's white shirt and hat.

16. José Guadalupe Posada, "El motín de los estudiantes." 1892.

Students' taste for political action was further legitimated by their explicit invocations of the European, especially the French, revolutionary legacy absorbed by many starting at an early age, often through readings in French. The movements of 1875 and 1884 made frequent reference to "old students, who always started revolutions." Their Parisian counterparts in the "Latin quarter" also fought against the internado and had a heroic role in the movements of 1830, 1848, and the Commune of 1871.[39] German students also inspired rebellious Mexicans, with their "scholastic turbulence" and tendency to walk out, but also with their well-known disposition to drink and duel.[40] The German influence nevertheless pointed to the inevitable connection between student activism and moral dissolution. An image that appeared in *La Patria Ilustrada* illustrates this romantic view (figure 17).

The second aspect of student life that seemed to demonstrate the ethical failings of positivism was the immorality associated with bohemian life. Memoirs and fictionalized accounts of personal experience expounded at length on the dissolution of student life. All these accounts prominently involved drug and alcohol consumption, déclassé sociability, and sex—quite derivative of the account of Bohemia formulated in midcentury Paris. In Juan Antonio Mateos's comedy *¡Los dioses se van!* (The gods are leaving) (1877) a student striker rejects his mother's advice, while an older character, Anselmo, bemoans this "youth that exhibits its virility in the foci of social corruption, and its smallness regarding the

17. "Students." *La Patria Ilustrada*, 29 Sep. 1885.

great virtues."[41] Rubén M. Campos's novel *Claudio Oronoz* (1906) is a gaudy narrative of youth, sensuality, vice, and disease. It is difficult to read these testimonies, even Mateos's comedy, without considering the voyeuristic attraction they might have exercised on Porfirian readers otherwise limited to a rather prurient national literature. Frías's realistic *El amor de las sirenas* (The love of sirens), from 1908, is perhaps the clearest example of this genre. Having fun as a student in late nineteenth-century Mexico City, however risky, was a central component of the sentimental education of the political and cultural elite. Bohemia, in other words, did not undermine respectable identities but worked age and gender to build them through friendship and adventure.[42]

In the company of their peers and neglected by their teachers, students suddenly faced the complexities of life in the capital. "Mexico is full of temptations, and when you least expect it you will feel dragged by un-stoppable currents," a fellow student from Nuevo León told Nemesio García Naranjo in 1903.[43] The dissipation occurring in rented apart-ments and lower-class boardinghouses (*pensiones*) was to a large extent the result of the decadence of the internado. Paradoxically, the move-

ment of 1875 was an immoral institution and a perverse legacy of Jesuiti-
cal control over higher learning. The student leader Salvador Castellot
demanded "the abolition of the immoral internado, sacrilegious substitution of the family by the state."[44] From the evidence given above, however, it seems the demand articulated students' desire to escape the control of school authorities and engage in the same intense social life as
their peers. While the education reforms of 1867 maintained the internado in order to protect the morality of students from the interior, they
were the ones who benefited the most from abandoning the small rooms,
direct supervision, and regulated routine of the school, becoming free to
engage in nighttime revels along with their *paisanos* from the same re-
gion. The greatest fun was for those who received enough money from
their parents to be able to afford their own quarters at a private boarding-
house or rent an apartment along with other students. *Capitalinos*, by
contrast, were more likely to remain under parental vigilance. Parents
from the provinces who did not have the means to put their sons up in
pensiones defended the internado because it was a form of financial
support from the government, although they couched their arguments in
moral terms. Barreda countered that those parents who feared the influences students "acquire in the schools through the diverse relations to
which they are inevitably exposed" were trying to make up for their own
failure in providing a solid moral education within the family.[45]

Much went unsaid in these public exchanges. As in Frías's novel, freedom from the internado meant, first of all, the ability to organize orgies.
In the first scene of *El amor de las sirenas*, a group of friends mockingly
imitate the language of high politics as they allocate their tight budget
and buy drinks and food for an all-night party. While absinthe, wine,
champagne, and other fine liquors were desirable, the need to get the
most bang for the buck often led students to drink pulque, fermented
maguey sap. The resulting *crudas*, or hangovers, were difficult to separate from dandified ennui, as the bohemian cruda alluded to social and
physiological dangers. In Frías's view, pulque signified both the descent
into lower-class mores and the spiral down to alcoholism, a continuing
theme in his semiautobiographical novels. He and other authors described the moral and physical decay of young, beautiful students who
ended up sick, prematurely aged, lonely, and depressed. Drugs, especially
morphine but also, for those who spent time in prison, marijuana, were
only one step in the decline initiated by alcoholism, which was also

associated with suicide. A few well-known cases of suicide, one in 1873 involving Manuel Acuña, a twenty-four-year-old literary talent and medical student, and another in 1877 involving Castellot, were cited to demonstrate the failure of the positivist educational project. But the evidence suggests that amorous disappointments had a larger role than intoxicants in pushing young men to take their lives—although the distinction was meaningless in the eyes of most contemporaries: like drugs and alcohol, sex was prohibited.[46]

Another dangerous practice associated with dissipation was journalism. Frías and others lamented the loss of the best minds of their generation, promising would-be physicians and lawyers, to writing in newspapers, just because they could not keep up with courses. They were lured by the meager but predictable weekly pay and the option to maintain "bohemian life with its terrible charms, with its poisons, its drunkenness, its ephemeral pleasures, its miseries, its sloth, its brazenness and its vices."[47]

Freedom from the internado allowed students to wander through the myriad brothels, cafes, restaurants, cantinas, *pulquerías*, and street stalls the city's nightlife featured. Fighting against the internado and for Bohemia meant expanding young men's access to different areas of urban space. Like Mexican flâneurs, they could explore the city beyond the borders set by class divides. More important, they could move to lower-class *vecindades* (tenement houses), where they found cheap rents, including tasty food prepared on the premises, and greater freedom to throw loud parties or come home late. This crossing of social boundaries was easy given the proximity of lower-class neighborhoods north and east of the zócalo, around Plaza de Santo Domingo, close to the Preparatoria, Medicina, and other schools. Even students who could afford a middle-class, respectable pensión preferred a vecindad and its offering of adventure, the company of the common folk, and the chance to "*flanear* (stroll) with slow indifference."[48] Middle-class students engaged in close, often fraternal relationships with members of the city's working classes, particularly if they were paisanos. A student character in *El amor de las sirenas* spends several months in Belem prison and becomes friends and partner in vice with several petty criminals, or *rateros*.[49] While adults perceived this border crossing as another aspect of the transgressive morality of youth, students saw it as expanding their experience of the city's social life, a tough proposition sometimes. In *Claudio Oronoz* Campos combines the voyeurism of literary descriptions of bohemian debauchery with a critique of the literary mythology that built that life: the narrator, Juan Abreu, soon discovers that tenement apartments in the barrios of Mexico City are not as nice as those in Paris, that the local lower classes are vicious and racially decadent, and that students like him are "exotic" in their midst.[50]

The most visible consequence of students' ability to cross spatial and class boundaries was their relationships with lower-class women—once again living up to the bohemian myth. As Mary Gluck has noted, Bohemia was not only a sentimental stereotype but also a vital dialogue with popular culture, a disposition represented by the elegant street image of the dandy. At the same time, however, bohemians expressed an ambivalent romanticism in which women were celebrated as objects of youthful masculine desire while being construed as an object, "la mujer," both pure and distant.[51] The students in Mateos's play go on strike to the cry of "Let's proclaim love, let youth follow its impetus, let's break the dikes and move forward!"[52] Yet Frías and the novelist Mariano Azuela wrote about students establishing relationships tragically condemned to failure as they contradicted the goals of social climbing that brought them to Mexico City in the first place. Feminine characters like María Luisa in Azuela's eponymous novel are not always mere ornaments but complex characters moved by their feelings and sexual desire. They also serve exemplary purposes, however, and often end in the passive role of sacrificial victims, loyal followers, or idealized objects of love, as in Sierra's and Acuña's texts. María Luisa's love for one of the students housed in her parents' humble pensión cannot prevail over a destiny that separates people from different classes: Pancho abandons her, attracted by a wealthier woman, and resumes his medical studies. He sees but does not recognize María Luisa when she dies in the paupers' ward of the hospital, having succumbed to alcohol and disease. The body of the fallen woman being examined and dissected by her former lover is a recurring image in novels of this period. Besides graphically illustrating the material decay of the once-idealized object of love, these images set romantic love and scientific knowledge in contraposition.[53] Writers solved the uncertain place of women in Porfirian testimonies of student life by means of a morality lesson: male student love and feminine lower-class freedom could only lead to disaster, including, for the woman, pregnancy, abandonment, and disease and, for the man, flunked courses, vice, decadence, and journalism.[54]

Forbidden love was, in these narratives, the consequence of uncontrollable masculinity opposed to romance. Students can be hypersexualized males engaged in the destructive sport of seduction, sometimes even against the honor of their mentors' families. Pedro, the main character in *El amor de las sirenas*, attracts many women because, as his friends told him, he owned "the 'wand of virtue' with which he had been born to set on fire and melt women."[55] The victims of seduction were often poor women like María Luisa. Too much sex was commonly associated in these cases with disease, as demonstrated, through the irrefutable evidence of science, by venereal diseases. Sexual libertinage could lead to the low point of finding refuge and feminine friendship in brothels or living off pornographic drawings, as Pedro does in *El amor de las sirenas*.[56] More disturbing, however, was students' seduction of upper-class married ladies whose respectable homes were thus destroyed. Loveless marriage to wealthy widows or young women was another consequence of the irrepressible masculinity of students.[57]

Not all was misfortune, however, and reality was probably less pathological than literature. Sex and love were also tools to build social capital and preserve a safely homosocial public life. Risky access to lower-class women marked the coming of age of young men, their entrance into an adult world in which social life could be isolated from family and friendship could extend beyond the divides of class and gender—all important operations as students entered elite social networks of knowledge and political power. While most female students seem to have been respected by their male peers, the tightly male homosocial student world and the role of sexual adventures in reinforcing that world effectively excluded them from further advancement. The fiery speech of Castañares in September 1884, mentioned above, suggested that women were becoming visible actors in the landscape of higher education in Mexico City, yet still largely excluded from oratory.[58] For Campos's characters, female speech "says nothing," and trying to instill it with reason is perverse: in pure women, "thought is evil."[59] The strict normative divide between the world of sin and the family offered the illusion of a clear moral order, even in the spaces of dissipation: men were forbidden to mention their wife's name at a brothel.

The participation of women in the protests against the deuda inglesa challenged this divide and distinguished the movement from others that occurred later in the Porfiriato. The presence of *señoras* was noticeable in the galleries of the chamber, in the streets during the protests of 21 November, and on balconies the following day as they threw flowers and waved their handkerchiefs at marching students. Several women raised money to give commemorative medals to protesters. Others wrote petitions in which they defended a greater public role for their sex that nevertheless preserved the distance and propriety reflected by the height of balconies. They declared themselves "foreign to political questions," yet, like other sectors of the population, "we believe the time has come to raise our voice" against the abuses of power.[60] In July 1885, several women requested in the same cautious tone that President Díaz release students and journalists from jail. "We are not going to meddle in political matters or high affairs of state," they declared; "we understand that the mission of woman is peace, and that even though her heart must germinate in the love of the fatherland, the most holy of all virtues, both customs and nature indicate for her a passive role in the events that decide the future of a nation."[61] Students' masculinity partly explains this caution. Respect meant preserving one's distance. During the demonstration on 22 November 1884 in celebration of the victory of the opposition, students carried banners that, without apparent irony, recognized the contribution of, yet reaffirmed a respectful distance from, their female supporters: "Long live the *señoritas*! Long live the fair sex! Long live the Mexican woman!"[62] Greater closeness between male oppositionists and sympathizing women would have threatened "both costums and nature" with the dangerous possibility of seduction. The exclusion of women was a price worth paying for the social and cultural capital bohemian students could earn with their bohemian exploits.

El Populacho and Public Men

The most powerful effect of students' ability to cross the boundaries of class separation in both directions was the widespread support they received from capitalinos during the events that started in and radiated from the Teatro Iturbide during those November days. Contemporary descriptions of the riots of November 1884 reflect the subversive mood of a pueblo that challenged authorities and the hierarchical organization of urban space. On the seventeenth, troops fired on crowds of students and lower-class men who threw stones and threatened to engage in hand-to-hand combat. In the days following, crowds of up to three thousand persons, according to *La Libertad*, pelted the windows of residences, businesses, and tramways. Soldiers and policemen chased them with little effect. As in the chamber debates, there was a sense of spectacle in these actions. In between skirmishes, crowds challenged and mocked the troops with comical imitations of bullfights. These street scenes, according to Juvenal, demonstrated the sense of humor and courage of Mexicans and competed favorably with the entertainment of theater, zarzuela, and horse races.[63]

Street rebellion was more dangerous than theater, of course. As crowd violence became widespread, the police and army became more aggressive. A couple of days into the debates two dozen students were arrested, sent to jail, and threatened with transportation to the forced labor camps of Yucatan. Word got out, and soon committees of relatives and fellow students demanded and obtained their release. Days later, however, the arrests numbered in the hundreds (again, none lasted too long), and the army fired on protesters; a few students responded with their own guns, but there were no deaths on either side. More common were slight wounds caused by soldiers' sabers and police batons. Although casualty counts are uncertain, they indicate that only anonymous members of the populacho died. Testimonies differ on the numbers: several students and children died on the eighteenth, when crowds tried to force their way into the chamber, according to *El Monitor Republicano*; by the twentieth, *La Patria* counted eighteen deaths and thirty wounded, although the police chief denied any "mishaps."[64]

Although public security focused on the protection of key areas, repression had little success in redirecting crowds away from the center of the city. The protesters' choice of location in which to stage their actions demonstrated a deliberate although probably uncoordinated effort to subvert the hierarchical relationship between the center and surrounding lower-class neighborhoods. Collective actions usually started in the afternoon as soon as the debates in the chamber ended, radiating from the doors of the Teatro Iturbide to surrounding streets and then to peripheral barrios, where many protesters seemed to come from. The first areas to be affected were elegant avenues like Plateros and San Francisco, a few blocks from the chamber. Disorder and destruction there forced the closing of hotels, cafes, and bars and prompted hurried responses by policemen and soldiers. As the debates went on, actions expanded beyond the initial blocks. On the fifteenth, a crowd marched east on Plateros toward the zócalo, seat of the National Palace and Cathedral. Other groups marched toward popular neighborhoods southwest of downtown. On the seventeenth, a group led by students headed west to the elegant Alameda, close to Díaz's residence on Humboldt Street. In spite of the army's effort to prevent these movements, crowds destroyed streetlights, tramways, and coaches and threw stones at "peaceful people" who observed from their balconies, before moving from downtown to the barrios of Soledad de Santa Cruz and San Juan. Conversely, the celebration after the government withdrew the project initiated in the barrios and converged downtown: the bells of churches distant from the zócalo rang first, and people eventually congregated at the plaza mayor, although the army did not allow them to toll the bells of the Cathedral.[65]

The riot expressed the pueblo's nationalistic assertion of control over urban space and its consumption demands regarding urban infrastructure. The stones hurled at troops and windows probably came from the cobbled streets downtown, an amenity lacking in lower-class neighborhoods, where the streets were of dirt. Recently installed electric streetlights were the object of special violence. Protesters destroyed light bulbs and bent lampposts, leaving "broken skeleton[s]."[66] Downtown lights were operated by an English company. Its contract with the City Council had been the product of contentious negotiations. The company sought protection from competition by restricting the number of gas lamps installed in peripheral neighborhoods, in spite of increasing demand throughout the city and the limited reach and poor quality of its service.[67] Darkness was common in the barrios, but darkness downtown that resulted from broken lamps forced businesses to close and gave an advantage to groups escaping from police and army patrols. By contrast, the government's decision to withdraw the project unleashed a celebration that lighted up the city. Students distributed fliers inviting neighbors to illuminate their houses, and the night of the twenty-first the city's windows were "completely full of colored lights."[68] Fireworks accompanied "serenades of humble people [who] walked the streets playing their guitars."[69] The destruction of streetlights and the rioters' play with darkness and light expressed both nationalist claims and the rejection of class biases in the allocation of urban infrastructure.

Popular control over urban spaces explains a feature of the deuda inglesa riots: the dramatic, face-to-face interactions between the populacho and the capital's public men. The same crowds that vaguely ascertained their rights as urban consumers by breaking lamps could be very precise in expressing their opinions about specific members of the political class. When a deputy made a successful speech, for example, crowds met outside his residence, as they did after speeches by Prieto, Díaz Mirón, and Juan Pablo de los Ríos; they carried Deputy de los Ríos on their shoulders, placing his portrait on a showcase to "pay homage to the citizens who have defended the interests of the people from the ros-trum."[70] A wounded student asked to be taken to Prieto's house so that he could greet him before he died. Many members of the elite during those days openly conducted their social lives around Plateros and San Fran-cisco avenues. The zócalo was a place where one could meet and start a conversation with anyone, from presidents to soldiers. These places be-came the initial sites of popular demonstrations, prompting the closing of bars and restaurants.[71] Some pelted the offices of Sierra's *La Liber-tad* behind the National Palace, and others threateningly shouted, "Die!" outside the home of Deputy Juan Antonio Mateos.[72] In front of Díaz's home, the student Diódoro Batalla gave a speech and commanded the president-elect to respond to popular claims.[73] Students' specific com-bination of rebelliousness and proximity to the elite was clear in their response to Sierra after his defense of the official project. He was booed and threatened in the chamber. In January of the following year Sierra went to the Preparatoria to begin his history course, but five hundred students tried to prevent him from entering the building. Protected by the police and noticeably saddened by the event, he left the premises. Someone in the crowd threw a zapote fruit at him. Carlos Basave and Luis Guillén were expelled as a consequence. Guillén wrote to Sierra to lament the end of his own literary career, yet he claimed a moral superi-ority over both Díaz and Sierra.[74]

The most sensational example of closeness between the city's pueblo and the political elite was the encounters between crowds and President González. A year later, Díaz Mirón would remember that "the Mexican people even shouted in the streets, 'Death to the one-handed Gonzá-lez.' "[75] Unlike Díaz, who did not bother even to look out the window at the crowd outside his home, González was willing to make an appear-ance. An episode that occurred on 21 November is striking. The night of the celebrations, soldiers shot at a crowd trying to break into the Cathe-dral, killing a young musician. Instead of attacking the soldiers, the group lifted the body on a board and walked quietly, in an impromptu funeral procession, to the home of the governor of the Federal District, Carlos Rivas, in front of the Alameda, about eight blocks from the zócalo. Rivas received a committee of students and promised justice in the death of the musician. As shots rang out, Rivas ordered the troops to stop attacking the pueblo. The body was carried into the governor's living room, as were several people who were wounded in the second shooting, to be treated by the governor's mother. President González arrived moments later, accompanied by his son. He contemplated the body, shook hands with people, and awkwardly pronounced some words to ease tensions. He left in his carriage, and the crowd dispersed in silence. González's next stop was the zócalo, where he mingled with the crowd. According to "Juvenal," González demonstrated courage, listening to speeches by people in the crowd and leaving without succeeding in dispersing the crowd.[76]

Why did González feel compelled to confront a hostile crowd? Why did the crowd, conversely, show such restraint in front of the man whose head some had been demanding earlier? The scene is all the more impressive in that his son, Manuel, was a friend of several students yet had fired on the crowd from his horse on the night of the eighteenth. A wounded veteran of the wars against conservatives and the French, the president was able to claim courage as part of his personal legitimacy as a politician even though it was already sullied by public evidence of his marital infidelities and widespread suspicions about his great wealth (figure 18). His wife, Laura Mantecón, went so far as to set up a store at the zócalo to demonstrate that he was not paying her expenses.[77] In calling him "one-handed" people were referring to his martial past, not just mocking him, as some critics of Díaz Mirón complained a year later when the poet remembered the episode. González's authority, in other words, was based on a historically specific kind of republican representation, one based on a notion of honor that stressed integrity and publicity. That notion of honor forced him to attend, in spite of the risks, to the voice of public opinion, whose incarnation during those days was the pueblo of the capital.

Was this pueblo the same heroic actor that in Europe had emerged from a century of revolutionary journeys? Participants in the events of 1884 certainly interpreted them in terms of a Western political tradition of emancipatory rebellion. A book printed by Ireneo Paz shortly after the events proposed interesting parallels: it included the long poem *La machicuepa de la deuda inglesa y recuerdos de ultra-tumba* (Somersault of the English Debt and Memories from the Great Beyond) by Celestino Hourcade, in which a narrator from heaven blames greedy government officials and speculators for the poverty of writers and workers and praises the courage of "patriotic and civilized deputies and stu-

18. Manuel González. © 17257. CND. SINAFO-Foto-teca Nacional del INAH.

dents" who oppose "tainted debts."[78] The crowds that filled the streets over the deuda inglesa fell short of being revolutionary, but Hourcade praised the patriotism of a multiclass movement:

> There may not be nihilists,
> But we have students,
> Brilliant patriots,
> Joined with artisans,
> Of callused hands
> But lovers of the patria.[79]

The sense of respectability and historical importance found in Hour-cade's poem emerges also in the music, theater, and paintings that cele-brated "El triunfo de los estudiantes" (the title of a polka composed by Juan Hernández) across the country.[80] Participants in the demonstration of 22 November intoned the national anthem several times and raised banners that were far from revolutionary: "Long live the right to assemble! Long live the Constitution of '57, article 9! Long live administrative honesty! Long live the dignified representatives of the people!. . . . Long live the pueblo!"[81]

The celebration, in other words, interpreted the defeat of the government as the product not of the alliance of distinct classes but of the crowd's ability to embrace a sense of collective national and civic honor. As time went by, this unity became harder to digest for educated men. Months later, for example, Díaz Mirón wrote a poem, "Voces interiores" (Interior voices), in which he alluded to the movement as an "invasion of mud," yet a "sacred" one because of its struggle against "the executioners / that oppress and vilify Anahuac."[82] Thus, Díaz Mirón contrasted the higher moral value of the masses against the "executioners" who exposed the nation to dishonorable deals. His allegory nevertheless betrayed uneasy feelings about the crowd. "Mud" alluded to the pueblo of the city by identifying it with the recurrent floods that covered downtown streets—just as Bulnes referred to dirty "dry mud" in his description of plebeian oratory. Many protesters certainly came from eastern neighborhoods, closer to the remains of the Texcoco lake and often flooded by muddy waters.

The episode, in other words, was never construed as an egalitarian challenge to respectable men's representation of national sovereignty. The "invasion of muds" itself flooded the city, creating brief, albeit strong, horizontal links among the inhabitants of Mexico City. The groups roaming the streets of the capital during those days linked parliamentarian debates and newspapers, peripheral neighborhoods and downtown spaces, the masses and the elite. Their actions, however, did not make politicians more plebeian; rather, they made the populacho more honorable. The pueblo's physical immediacy to the political class reinforced prevailing notions of republican honor; it influenced decision making by directly expressing its opinions about the reputation of politicians and about the nation's honor. As a public, this populacho was a product of the romantic rhetoric and behavior of speakers and students, yet took their heroism into dangerous political territory.

Aftermath

La Patria saw the episode of 1884 as the awakening of "public spirit," thanks to "forceful knights who do not wander a single step from the path set forth by the heroes of the Reforma."[83] History, with its clear divide between traitors and heroes, was the judge of politicians' ethics. During the debates, Viñas warned that "the vote, gentlemen, will be short-lived . . . but shame and opprobrium will be eternal."[84] Days after the end of the parliamentary debates, the Club de Bohemios de Yucatán, also known as "El club de pelados," promised there would be long-lasting condemnation of Sierra and other Yucatecan representatives in Congress: "Since in themselves and in the eyes of public opinion they are guilty of high treason, may the stigma of shame and opprobrium which they deserve fall on their heads . . . may the people curse them and subject their miserable descendants to the consequences of popular justice."[85] By contrast, during the nationwide unofficial celebration of the students' triumph praise focused on those who had opposed the government's project. Letters characterized Viñas, Duret, Díaz Mirón, and Batalla as "the only heroes of this glorious journey."[86] When they arrived in the city of Veracruz in late November, Díaz Mirón and Batalla were acclaimed with music, meetings, speeches, and commemorative medals.[87]

This democratic proximity (whether threatening or celebratory) between people and politicians was bound not to be permanent. On 22 June 1885 the Díaz administration recognized by decree Noetzlin's arrangement with English bondholders—thus addressing a deepening financial crisis. In spite of manifestos, press criticisms, and speeches by some of the same protagonists of November 1884, there was no popular mobilization in opposition. Judges interpreted the mere description of the events of November 1884 in the press as instigation of violence and arrested and sentenced several students and journalists. Díaz Mirón gave another moving speech, but there was no parliamentary insurrection, largely because the presidential decree did not require the Chamber of Deputies' approval.[88] Aborted protest and aggressive repression showed that the rules were changing and that the spaces for political mobilization and open discussion were closing up. The trial and appeal that followed the arrests in 1885 advanced the new strategies of the Porfirian government against free speech. The suspects were accused of sedition. They were vainly defended in court and in the press as political prisoners.

Díaz was keeping deputies on a short leash, while the police prevented any disorder in the chamber galleries. Díaz Mirón's ambition to spearhead a new movement collapsed in tandem with his failure to be elected to the next Congress. The regime took a more systematic approach to controlling the press. In the remaining years of his government, Díaz prevented the formation of crowds in the central spaces of the capital. The impact of such disorder on the foreign press concerned Díaz, who had to balance the effects of repression against the opinion of newspapers in the United States that portrayed him as a tyrant.[89]

Díaz also succeeded in avoiding discussion of fiscal matters in Congress and in the newspapers, limiting it to the specialized realm of economists within the government. The critical ideas about public opinion expressed by Bulnes and other defenders of the official project in November 1884 became the official ideology. Finance Minister Limantour, a former Preparatoria student but someone who did not like to describe himself as a politician, would eventually become the key player in Díaz's selection of federal deputies.[90] None of this might have happened, of course, had the monetary and fiscal crises that characterized the last years of González's administration not given way to an era of economic growth.

The episode of the deuda inglesa suggests the need to revise the dichotomy drawn between traditional politics and collective actors, on one side, and modern, individualist, opinionated politicos, on the other. The events examined here were an expression of a moral economy, that of the Mexico City populacho, composed of multiple interests and class positions. As a result of the revolt of 1884, future generations saw that there were other paths—potentially broad ones—city dwellers might take in order to exert influence on the political process. Although urban demonstrations were limited until 1911, the right to petition authorities remained a feature of the interaction between the state and subjects under Díaz, and the postrevolutionary regime made of massive demonstrations, in the same spaces disputed by troops and protesters in 1884, the most eloquent exhibition of its legitimacy. Students played a key role in many of these urban movements because they brought city dwellers and national authorities into closer proximity, both morally and physically. Many students, even some quite radical protesters like Carlos Basave, were recruited by the political class, both before and after the revolution of 1910.

Such closeness between subjects and rulers was possible because honor served as the point of reference for public and private interests, shaping the development of the public sphere. It provided a language that linked national politics and personal reputations and allowed for negotiations to take place between actors with unequal power. Both citizenship and the personal authority of public men were linked to residence in a city in which the dictates of opinion were the real tyrant. As a consequence, everyone had to talk and listen to others, even if they despised individual traitors or disorderly mobs. Rhetoric, particularly its modern, romantic instantiation, was an essential tool in establishing horizontal and vertical political dialogues.

To contain the democratic potential of those dialogues, the dictatorship of a man replaced that of opinion. That substitution could be achieved only by transforming honor.

PART III
Taming Opinion

Porfirio Díaz was able to repress protests against the recognition of the English debt not only because of his personal influence, but also because the recent abolition of press juries allowed him to prosecute journalists through criminal judges and thus limit the development and autonomy of the public sphere. This announced a new era in Mexican public culture, one in which public opinion would be part of the modernization of the country, its economy, and its inhabitants' customs.

In the remainder of the book I address the new conditions for public discourse as the result of parallel changes in the penal law and in everyday disputes about honor. Chapter 5 analyzes the transformation in state protection of honor associated with the rise of positivism. The constitutional reform of 1882 that abolished the jury was an effective tool in transforming the Mexican public sphere because it resonated with other legislative changes concerning crimes against honor. Press and criminal legislation became centered on the crime of defamation. Judges applied the Penal Code's definitions of offenses against honor, particularly those that victimized public officials, with flexibility and zeal. Judges and prosecutors invented the "psychological doctrine" to avert criticism of their decisions regarding the subtle causality and interpretation of issues of honor. Journalists were now prosecuted in a more systematic, if less bloody, way. This was largely possible not because Díaz silenced public opinion but because, where honor was concerned, his contemporaries preferred his tyranny to that of opinion. The transformation of honor into an objective, well-defined juridical good with material value, a process also examined in this chapter, created an enduring set of rules for public discourse and a shrinking of the public sphere.

Chapter 6 shifts the book's focus away from the elites and examines common people's struggles to defend their honor in court. Salient in court records is the diversity of actors who cared dearly about their reputations and who turned legislation and judges intended to protect elites to their purposes. The language used and goods disputed in those cases strongly suggest that the concerns about honor and opinion described throughout this book were shared by all sectors of Mexican society, including poor women. Chapter 7 returns to public men and examines the high point and the decadence of dueling. In the context of new views of honor as a good protected by the state, dueling was finely codified and, in the few cases in which duelists were brought to court, carefully examined by judges, political authorities, and public opinion. Honor might have been more valuable than life for some men, but it was no longer clear it could be placed above the law. It is only apparently paradoxical, as we will see, that those men who remembered the Paz-Sierra duel with apprehension saw in the technology of honor, contained in dueling codes, a path toward the emancipation of their lives from the tyranny of honor.

CHAPTER 5

Honor and the State
Reputation as a Juridical Good

After the decree of 22 June 1885 in which Porfirio Díaz recognized the English debt, a group of students who had participated in the protest of the previous year met in front of the Cathedral and decided to issue a manifesto. They raised money to pay for three hundred copies of it to be pasted on street corners and for three thousand copies in a smaller format to be handed out around the city by workers hired for that purpose. The manifesto, dated 3 July and published two days later, invited the pueblo to rise against the humiliating terms of the agreement. Besides repeating the arguments successfully used in the previous year's protest, the students added an explicit accusation of the president for his "shamelessness" and for the "tyrannical and arbitrary" means he had used to usurp the power of the legislative branch. The signatories included Carlos Basave, Luis Guillén, and "several [other] students." The police quickly seized the copies of the manifesto and arrested suspects at the print shop of Benito Nichols. Those arrested included Enrique Chávarri, "Juvenal," of *El Monitor Republicano*, Adolfo Carrillo of the *Correo del Lunes*, the student leader Diódoro Batalla, plus Basave, three other students, and two "artisans." The artisans were soon released because they declared that a "decent young man" had paid them to post the broadsheets.[1]

This might seem like a minor episode in the inevitable consolidation of the dictator. Yet, I will argue, the devil of political control was in the juridical details. It was not obvious that the suspects had committed the crime of sedition as defined in article 1123 of the Penal Code of 1871, since there had been no meeting of more than ten persons or any invitation to forcibly resist the authorities. In carefully crafted speeches, the defense attorneys, Manuel Prieto, Emilio Velasco, and Eduardo Viñas, argued during the trial that the suspects were merely exercising their right of petition. They framed the case as a defense of freedom of speech: the suspects were criticizing an act of authority for the public good but not committing sedition or libel; there was no defamation but ample public evidence that the executive power had usurped the jurisdiction of the legislative branch. The press began to call the suspects political prisoners, and Velasco assigned the case a large historical and moral meaning, claiming upon the judge's finding of guilt that the decision "started an era of political press trials; that is, began the persecution against public opinion."[2] The strategies followed by the judicial authorities announced new practices that would allow the political persecution of journalists in the name of protecting public men's reputation. Velasco listed the irregularities of the trial that jeopardized the suspects, notably Judge Luis Garfias's shifting of the characterization of the crimes from calumny (*calumnia*) to defamation (*difamación*), then to insults (*injurias*), and finally to attacks against officials (*ultrajes a funcionarios públicos*). Ultrajes, in particular, served prosecutors' political goals because they justified heavier sentences and allowed the court to proceed in the absence of a victim pressing charges. Velasco claimed that ultrajes could not be committed through the press because article 7 of the Constitution protected the right to criticize government officials, while defamation, calumny, and insults did not apply since the public life of officials was subject to criticism in the name of "public interest."[3]

The prosecutors, Luis Labastida and Isidro Montiel y Duarte, and Judge Garfias countered that they did not need such high-sounding language to justify a process similar to that applied in other cases against opposition writers in the past two years. Montiel y Duarte invoked the same scientific knowledge about evolution, culture, and race that criminologists used against lower-class transgressors: inciting the people "with the goal of exploring public opinion," he argued, while feasible among the races of England and the United States, was useless in Mexico because the disposition to form legitimate political associations "is not in the habits and uses of the Latin race," whose "acute imagination and impulsive feelings" make any public discussion dangerous.[4]

The government's attorneys introduced a scientific-sounding argument that would be frequently used against the press in subsequent years: the *doctrina psicológica* (psychological doctrine), which held that the decision to typify and punish an act as a crime happened only in the mind of the judge and was not subject, therefore, to discussion by others.[5] Such psychological discretion was necessary in order to enable judges to make the kind of precise, contextualized interpretation of textual evidence that popular juries had performed according to the Press Law of 1868. Judge Garfias stated in the sentencing phase that, since the reform in 1882 of article 7 of the Constitution abolishing press juries, there were no more "crimes of the press" to speak of. Thus, the July manifesto could be read, in the context of the riots of 1884, as containing common insults, calumny, and sedition. He found the suspects guilty of "inciting rebellion" and insulting authorities and sentenced them to terms of up to seven months in prison.[6]

The reform of article 7 indeed "began the persecution against public opinion," to use Velasco's prophetic words, by giving the regime the legal tools it needed to deal with opposition writers through the penal protection of honor. From the perspective of the journalists who were on the receiving end of Porfirian repression, the reform was part of the consolidation of dictatorship, the key chapter in a process that moved Mexican public life away from the ideals held by liberals like Francisco Zarco and Ignacio Ramírez and left freedom of speech in the hands of judges appointed by the very same political authorities that combat journalists were supposed to challenge. In this view, which would later become the dominating historical perspective on the Porfiriato, the autocratic means of Porfirio Díaz betrayed the legacy of 1857 through the chicanery and formalism enshrined in the abolition of the press jury. Recent studies of the press during the Porfiriato, however, paint a more nuanced picture of both repression and corruption by Díaz. I want to add an element to that picture: the legal protection of honor was not just a subterfuge, but an essential component of the consensus that accompanied Porfirian control of the press starting in the 1880s.[7]

The tone of public debates and the style of public men changed in the last decade of the nineteenth century, and combat journalists all but disappeared. The reform of article 7 was not the only means employed by the regime to achieve political control and curb dissent in the public sphere. The centralization of subsidy in one newspaper, *El Imparcial*, ran independent newspapers out of business and contributed to the emergence of a daily press which profited not from polemic but from reliability and of journalists who were employees rather than public men. According to its director, Rafael Reyes Spíndola, the goal of *El Imparcial* when it was founded in 1896 was "to do everything possible to eliminate other newspapers with fewer resources and poor editing."[8] Veterans like Manuel Gutiérrez Nájera denounced the supplanting of the romantic writers of his era by the uninteresting putative "reporter" who walked around the city collecting gossip instead of socializing with elites.[9] The *Monitor Republicano* and *El Siglo Diez y Nueve*, prestigious, venerable liberal dailies, lost their clout and ceased publishing. As for minor publications, the personal influence of the president was enough to stifle them. He could order the termination of a newspaper, even if it had been loyal to him in the past, or simply, through his secretary Rafael Chousal, "pull the bridle" when loyal journalists were stepping over the line.[10] Harassment by local police and *jefes políticos* (that is, without the intervention of the judiciary), exile, and, in a few cases, assassination were not out of the question—although repression took place sporadically and usually around the time of elections.[11]

Criminal court judges were the most important players in the control of the press during the Porfiriato. Many journalists were intimidated or imprisoned under the psychological doctrine and the newfound ability of judges to convict them of crimes against honor. The exemplary impact of these cases came not so much from the force they deployed but from their practical demonstration of the state's new role in the protection of honor: judges could now punish speech, imposing a discipline that was all the more effective because it was based not on fear—a feeling that few public men would be willing to admit anyway—but on the widespread belief that honor was the citizens' right, regardless of rank.

The reform of 1882 and the prosecution of protesters in 1885 epitomize a late nineteenth-century shift in Mexican conceptions of honor, public speech, and privacy—a process that was not exclusively political but had lasting political consequences. Authorities and jurists put forward the notion that honor was a juridical good protected by the state, and civil society accepted it. This criminalization of free speech was particularly successful because it was based on a new, more convincing map of the separation between the public and the private, a map that even combat journalists now seemed willing to respect. Whereas in the recent past honor had been an expansive value that could justify rebellion and the sacrifice of reputation to an autonomous conscience or a higher mission, such as patriotism (as in the case of Santos Degollado), the new notion identified honor more closely with reputation and posited a stronger separation between domesticity and the public realm.

This separation was politically necessary because, even as the authority of Díaz seemed indisputable, the phantom of Degollado and other liberal men of honor still hovered above Mexican politics. They represented a potentially disruptive example in which integrity was placed above family and interests. For the Porfirian advocates of order and progress, modernization entailed new principles where public men's exposure to public opinion was concerned, nothing less than a new ethical code and new political rules. Although capitalist development was a condition for this transformation, legislation and punishment were the privileged expression of the modern persuasion. The objectivity of judicial procedure vis-à-vis those who disrespected private rights was, in this perspective, the best alternative to the unfocused anxiety of romantic views about honor.

The process of redefining honor followed two tracks: the reinvention of honor as a tangible juridical good guaranteed by the state, and the reform of libel legislation, shifting the protection of the law from journalists to public officials. I start with a look at the late nineteenth-century redefinition of honor. In the second section I return to familiar territory by examining the abolition of the press jury and then describe new juridical practices that protected the good name of public officials.

Honor as a Juridical Good

Porfirian notions of honor were born out of the negotiation between old vocabulary and new legal syntax. The process was not a mere exercise of Díaz's patriarchal authority: it involved the rationality of science and a reinterpretation of legal traditions. More than a spurt of modernization, the transformation of honor was the result of a gradual process that began with status-based colonial conceptions, mutated under Mexican views of romantic individualism, and ended in the penal defense of society—which positivism construed not as an association of free wills but as an organism behaving according to objective rules. Focusing only on legislation to tell this story, however, would imply neat breaks between those phases, when in practice colonial, romantic, and positivist ideas often overlapped. During the first decades of Mexico's independent life, Spanish penal legislation stayed in effect and, even after the passing of the Penal Code of 1871, colonial notions of honor remained implicit in upper-class men's ability to defend their status in the name of ethnic and gender hierarchies. Preservation of social difference continued as the main goal of a judiciary that emphasized the publicizing of correction and the restoration of victims' honra, or credit. Judges continued to cite the Spanish *Partidas* and to use the old language. In a case in Tlaxcala in 1876, for example, the judge Francisco Zempoalteca sentenced the offender "a cantar la palinodia imponiéndole perpetuo silencio" (to issue a retraction and keep perpetual silence) and declared the victim to be still "en buena fama" (in good repute).[12] Another sentence from the same year and state, also citing colonial laws, settled a dispute between the governor and a municipal authority by announcing that, after serving a nine-day prison sentence, the president of the Tepeyanco city council "has in no way damaged his *buena fama* and reputation." This was no Tlaxcaltecan eccentricity: a higher court confirmed the sentence, although it struck down the reference to "buena fama."[13] The correction was meaningful. As noted by Ann Twinam, the "hierarchical ethos at the core of colonial society" was predominantly concerned with the public domain.[14] Buena fama, the good name a person bore, assumed not a fixed divide between public and private but the centrality of one's persona. It corresponded with an idea of representation in which sovereignty was personalized and publicly displayed in the figure of the viceroy and other authorities. The colonial stress on public recognition of hierarchies contrasted with modern honor, which was centered on a private realm of self-esteem and an individual right to reputation.[15]

Such a perspective emerged in Mexico parallel with the late phase of romantic ideas about the individual. Like their European counterparts, Mexican romantics believed that the intimate realm, as opposed to inheritance or ascribed rank, was the original source of virtue and public recognition. Particularly during the second half of the century, individualism in Mexico was the product of romantic constructions of the self in constant struggle against the world of conventions and interests. Bohemia was an example of this individualism (see chapter 4), yet one that was contained by the transitional nature of youth. This agonic individualism did not fit the more stable liberal mold because it was not the child of the bourgeois nuclear family and its private realm of feelings, as, theoretically, it was in Europe, but the expression of a heightened sense of the self. For some educated men and women, it meant freedom from social conventions rather than middle-class respectability. In Vicente Riva Palacio's view, "the precious theory of individualism" inspired students to challenge patriarchy and be exceptional—at least during the bohemian phase of their lives.[16] In the European, liberal model, individualism meant the embrace of markers of individuality (such as first names or portraits), introspection (often recorded in diaries), and intimate (domestic) spaces. In Mexico young writers adopted the romantic individualist ethos as a lonely struggle against the misunderstanding of public opinion, which as often turned them toward lyricism and solitude as it pushed them into public battles over reputation. Federico Gamboa preferred, instead of a career in Congress ("a tomb for individual independence"), the relative solitude of diplomatic service, far from the crudity of Mexican social and literary circles.[17] Santiago Sierra's decision to face Ireneo Paz in a duel in spite of his wife's pleas and Justo Sierra's despondent response afterward (see chapter 2) are vivid examples of the dilemma between withdrawal and public confrontation faced by Mexican men of their time. Unlike French romanticism, this late version in Mexico was not defined by the priority of political and social commitment.[18]

Few, however, had the opportunity or the inclination to maintain such proud solitude as Gamboa did—and then only for awhile. Extended family structures and networks of patronage remained dominant in Mexican society, while orality and porous divides between public and domestic life undermined privacy and discouraged the writing of diaries and intimate correspondences.[19] As Justo Sierra realized after his brother died, not everyone could, like Gamboa, Puga y Acal, and Díaz Mirón, brush aside conventions and hold that "the style is the man" because doing so meant permanent conflict and came at a high social cost. As a consequence, individualism in late nineteenth-century Mexico mutated from romantic isolation into a postromantic notion of personal honor as a fundamental right.[20] However rebellious or misunderstood, victims of libel or defamation recognized that preserving individuality was not just a subjective adventure: it meant the defense of a place in society that was always exposed to the judgment of public opinion. The legal definition of honor as a state-protected right in Porfirian Mexico was, therefore, a continuation rather than a rupture with romanticism, and not one associated with more robust liberal freedoms.

Individualism was no longer just a literary construction but a legal one as well, a central component of citizenship insofar as it was also a point of reference for state intervention. The protection of reputation in the first postindependence codes was already centered on individuals rather than on corporations or families. Early legislation against slander referred both to private behavior and reputation as targets of offensive talk, and press legislation punished injurias and other crimes against honor without allowing suspects to prove their claims. In doing so, legislators posited that honor was an immanent, irreducibly private good against which slanderers had nothing to say. Evidence about the alleged charges was not admissible as a defense for suspects because the victim's internal sense of self-worth, rather than any external sign, was the measure of damage. Unlike other juridical traditions, in that of Mexico all victims were presumed to have honor. The colonial notion of honra as an external value associated with social hierarchies and thus contingent gave way in the national era to a definition of honor as an individual, stable value protected by natural law.[21]

The new emphasis on individuals with immanent rights changed the relations between victims and offenders, and between them and the state. Subjective aspects of crimes and victimization became central to the protection of reputations, turning sentiments into legally relevant evidence: just as victims' self-esteem was the ultimate object of damage, suspects' intention to harm was now a constitutive aspect of the crime, and there could be no determination of guilt without proof, however indirect, of that intention. Conversely, suspects whose demonstrable intention was to protect the public good were exempted from responsibility. Knowing the true goals of an offensive statement was almost impossible, however, since intentions, like conscience, belonged in the individual realm. The only rule that seems to have characterized exceptions for the public good was that, for a statement to be civic-minded, humor had to be excluded: satirical and other humorous writings were not protected by the exception of the public good, and political caricature understandably lost some of its edge by the end of the century.[22]

Ironically, the need to probe sentiments and intentions kept the protection of modern honor right in the middle of the public sphere. During the national era, publicity continued to be, as in colonial times, the privileged scene for the negotiation of reputation and self-esteem. Chapter 2 exemplified these negotiations through conflicts among journalists, and the next chapter will show the same thing happening among others. This combination of old and new rules characterizes the specific relationship between the public and the subjective in Mexican public life. The process is not unlike that described by historians of the public sphere in Europe, where the domestic privacy underlying bourgeois identities was itself a product of the public exposure of the household under capitalism, and even the intimacy of the self was created for the benefit of an audience. The very notion of public opinion stemmed largely from the discussion of reputations in the public realm and, according to Rousseau, in turn "engraved [itself in] the hearts of citizens."[23] In Mexico, an intimate realm of sentiment was necessary if an individual was to participate in politics; as in Latin America, in Mexico independence meant the explosion of a politicized public sphere that engaged all aspects of life, including domesticity, reputation, and gender roles.[24] Private and public realms built on each other historically.

As a consequence of this combination of colonial and bourgeois beliefs, of openness and individualism, penal legislation became central in the protection of honor. Any expression voiced about someone, whether public or not, true or false, fell within the purview of the Penal Code. Insults, defamation, and slander were punished in colonial legislation, but the independent era saw a drive to establish more comprehensive definitions. In his introduction to the first comprehensive penal codification in the country, the Federal District Penal Code of 1871, Antonio Martínez de Castro explained the code's articles about crimes against honor as an attempt to establish clear definitions absent from the Press Law of 1868. He argued for greater penalties, above all against defamation, to fit the seriousness of offenses and to prevent dueling. The code referred to both oral and printed communications, made the publicness of the offense an aggravating circumstance, and punished insults more severely when they reflected "an effrontery in the eyes of public opinion." (The contradiction between a Penal Code that dealt with offenses in all media and mandated stronger penalties and a generally lenient Press Law concerned only with printed matter lasted until the Constitutional reform of 1882 abrogated the Press Law and made the Penal Code of 1871 the principal statute for the regulation for public speech.)[25]

The code defined offenses against honor in quite expansive terms, yet still using the old terms of injuria, difamación, and calumnia. Injuria was, according to the code, "any expression pronounced and any action performed in order to express disdain to another or with the goal of offending him or her." Rather than the content of expressions, what distinguished injurias was that the criminal act did not need to be committed in public: the victim had to be present in front of the suspect but no one else. For difamación, by contrast, publicity was required but not the presence of the victim: it was defined as "to intentionally communicate to one or more persons the imputation made against another . . . that might cause him or her dishonor or discredit [*deshonra o descrédito*] or expose him or her to the scorn of anyone." Again, there was no specification about the content of the offense, as difamación included charges "of a fact, true or false, determined or undetermined," including charges made "in equivocal terms." Calumnia occurred when injuria or difamación included the false imputation of a crime.[26] Calumnia, therefore, was the only crime in which the truthfulness of the offensive charge could be relevant, yet only a preexisting judicial sentence was valid evidence for the defense. Otherwise, the code implied the equality of victims in terms of honor and reduced the fact-finding aspect of trials to establishing that the offensive words had indeed been uttered, printed, or implied in a gesture. There was no specific procedure, other than the judge's decision, to establish intentionality. Penalties ranged from eight days in prison for injuria to two years for difamación.[27]

Given such broad definitions, the offense's public nature and its impact on the victim were essential to identify and measure it. Publicity implied the existence of an audience and was therefore more tangible than intentionality. Libel—difamación or calumnia through the press—was the most serious crime because it reached more people and was more permanent in its effects, yet it was not defined specifically in the code. For an offense to be public it only needed to involve communication between two or more persons, together or separately. Nevertheless, a reform to the code in 1902 established that a sentence for public offenses was to be published in three newspapers at the convict's expense. But publicity was not in itself enough to achieve a sentence: the active participation of the victim was also necessary. Unlike most other crimes, injuria, difamación, and calumnia were prosecuted only when a person pressed charges. Only when the victim was the Mexican nation or a public official could prosecutors initiate penal action; and relatives could press charges when offenses affected the reputation of a deceased person. As in other crimes that required a complainant, the rationale was to give victims the option of avoiding further public exposure of private matters.[28]

Despite Martínez de Castro's hope for a clean break with the past the codification of crimes against honor in the Penal Code of 1871 continued to stress publicity, allowed for the presentation of evidence in some instances, and conditioned prosecution on the initiative of victims—all without establishing, in his view and that of other jurists, strong enough penalties. As noted by Elisa Speckman, crimes against honor represented a "fracture in juridical absolutism" that contradicted the liberal state's goal of a single source of justice and law.[29] This contradictory legacy came under attack as positivism finally made its mark on legislation concerning honor. In the perspective of a new generation of jurists critical of Martínez de Castro's classicism, honor was a quasi-material good that had to be aggressively protected by the state. These jurists cited evolutionary explanations to give stronger punishment and state intervention a scientific rationale. Their coherence of purpose was possible thanks to new political conditions that emerged under Díaz's strong-arm administration.

Paralleling positivism's influence on other aspects of social thought, positivist theorists of honor challenged liberal egalitarianism by proposing class-specific conceptions. The lawyer Carlos Díaz Infante argued in 1896 that honor had been valued since ancient times as the reputation of those with virtue and in that role played a part in the survival of the fittest. Díaz Infante cited Herbert Spencer, "the most illustrious contemporary philosopher."[30] Spencer had a deep influence on Mexican positivists in the heyday of the Porfiriato, particularly among the younger cohort, among whom the Comtian influence brought by Gabino Barreda in the late 1860s was weaker. The English philosopher was cited in legal studies, read in courses at the Escuela Preparatoria, and even quoted in novels and during the debates on the deuda inglesa. Spencer was germane because he proposed an objective notion of honor as an "incorporeal property" derived from "moral conduct" that was useful for business and could therefore be measured according to its monetary value.[31] In the interpretation of Díaz Infante, honor was now more objectively defined than in the past: it was "the reputation resulting from mental actions which have taken the form of . . . rectitude, sincerity, temperance"; "public esteem," he added, "is a good that can be owned just like other goods of a tangible nature" and has "a commercial value" of great importance to economic development. A good reputation, concluded Díaz Infante, was the product of individuals' different natures, a possession which they had every right to employ to their advantage and to defend in court.[32]

The new dispensation could reconcile honor and progress without losing sight of honor's dual dimension, both internal and external. In Spencer's view the "ethical consciousness" generated by public opinion, which he also referred to as reputation, played a central role in the growth of maintenance of wealth and therefore in the advance of capitalism.[33] Progress, of course, did not mean egalitarianism. In a study from 1888 about the ethics of contemporary commerce, Spencer argued that self-consciousness was a trait of superior individuals and of "advanced and highly-organized societies." Among the rich, honesty correlated with the broader desire to serve society; wealth, even if inherited, could be a sign of intelligence and other virtues. Publicity took care of deception: when honor (as honra, that is, external recognition) was granted to the wealthy regardless of their "underlying virtues," Spencer observed that a "purified public opinion" corrected the error.[34]

Spencer's ideas offered a general framework within which to modernize the protection of reputation but said nothing about punishment, Mexican positivists' favorite instrument of social reform. A prescription for that objective was found in the work of the Italian penologist Eugenio Florian, often cited in legal discussions and sentences in Mexico. Florian trumpeted the expansion of "the positivist criminal school" to the realm of crimes against honor. According to the founding father of criminology, Enrico Ferri, who wrote an introduction to Florian's book, the classic school of penology had not been able to deal with the recent increase in cases of defamation and libel because of its emphasis on the material aspects of the criminal act, which could be elusive in these offenses. Instead, the positive school was able to apply scientific advances to probe the psychological dimension of crimes against honor. Florian distinguished the objective and subjective aspects of defamation and tackled the psychology of criminals through the methodical observation of their motivations.[35]

Or so he claimed. Rather than attempting a more nuanced understanding of crimes against honor, Florian took the favorite analytical tack of contemporaneous criminologists: he classified offenders. He found most slanderers to be in the category of occasional criminals. Other types, more troubling because of their greater propensity to recidivism, included children, pathological "mattoids," and women, who were the prototypical liar because of "their multiform condition of inferiority vis-à-vis men." Given the "organic" tendency of women and other groups to lie, any exploring of the actual mechanism of their behavior was irrelevant. Florian's focus on the criminal, therefore, fit well with Ferri's and Mexican penologists' demand for harsher penalties against the perceived increase in crimes against reputation. Even though he agreed with Spencer that public criticism of individuals could be useful for society, Florian insisted that strong sanctions were necessary to prevent slanderers from going beyond the corrective function of public opinion.[36]

In spite of its prestigious advocates, positivism had a weaker impact on the legal protection of honor in Mexico than advertised. Earlier penologists had been concerned about the tension between collective needs and individual interests in the definition of slander. Martínez de Castro justified the Penal Code in general as a tool for realizing a new era of stronger social bonds in a country long weakened by suspicion and isolation. Weary of the potential implications of punishment for free speech and implicitly criticizing Florian's limited psychological insight, Ferri proposed that juries decide crimes against defamation—in Mexico this idea was contained in the Constitution of 1857 regarding the press, but it was no longer feasible after 1882.[37] Positivism, in fact, did not bring about a new empirical approach to the relation between internal and external aspects of honor. Psychology, as we will see, justified judges' application of harsh penalties but failed to bridge the gap between public behavior and conscience over which the late generations of Mexican romantics agonized.

Positivism did contribute to define honor as a good of material value, as proposed by Spencer, and to justify stronger state intervention—just as the regime was becoming more aggressive in its handling of urban thieves and rural bandits. Mexican jurists and politicians in the last decades of the nineteenth century agreed that honor was a private good that had to be protected by the state. This was imperative if the country was to look more like other modern nations that were strengthening the protection of honor. Litigants and judges cited cases and legislation from France and England as if they were directly relevant to Mexican cases.[38] Expanding the state's responsibility toward honor in the name of social evolution resonated with the critique of Jacobin liberalism voiced by newspapers like *La Libertad* and by científico ideologues. Their program of "scientific politics" sought to reconcile the defense of the social organism with the liberal tradition of individual rights through the intervention of a strong state. According to Díaz Infante, honor was a more objective idea than the poorly defined notions of morality and public peace used by the framers of the Constitution of 1857. Honor, he wrote in 1896, had been evolving since classical times and had now acquired a concrete role in economic modernization. Reputation was a possession that, even if not possessed in equal measure by all individuals, required equal protection from the state.[39] As in the case of other so-called social problems, only harsher, better defined penalties could remedy the weaknesses of the Constitution and the Penal Code.

Although easy to translate into legal decisions, the redefining of honor as reputation assumed an evolutionary movement (from the romantic, subjective perception of honor toward the objective, positivist notion of reputation) that in practice had not taken place. Mexican public men could not simply conflate honor and reputation. While honor referred to the consideration granted by others, it was both an objective value and a sentiment, a complex possession linked to publicity but also to self-esteem, something valuable as social capital but also, if one recalls Santos Degollado, as the integrity of one's conscience.[40] In theory, legislators and commentators tried to distinguish between injurias (an offense that required only the presence of the victim, thus referring to honor as a subjective good embodied in the victim's sense of self-worth) and difamación or calumnia (public attacks against reputation in which honor was a socially negotiated good). In practice, however, judges and victims, reflecting broader views of honor as a good involving internal and external aspects, seldom separated injurias from difamación. Practice, in turn, shaped laws as much as theory did. Modern penal codes in Mexico do not reflect a clear evolution toward reputation becoming the only object of protection; in fact, honor was increasingly recognized in the classification of crimes: whereas the relevant chapter in the Penal Code of 1871 was entitled "Delitos [crimes] contra la reputación," the positivist code of 1929 and the more pragmatic code of 1931 (which continues in use today) called it "Delitos contra el honor."[41]

Distinguishing reputation from honor was not made easier by the legacy of the Reforma generation, which had established an expansive definition of public life in order to regenerate national politics. During a discussion about freedom of the press at the Constitutional Congress of 1856, Francisco Zarco warned that the "sanctuary" of private life could not be used by judges to defend dishonest government officers.[42] In 1867, Ignacio Ramírez wrote against invoking private life to protect corrupt officials. The legislator, he believed, had to "establish where private life ends and public life begins, and in which cases writers can seize on the defects, vices, and faults of the citizen as a patrimony of publicity and an object of censure." The examples Ramírez provided left very little that was protected on the private side: all character traits that might affect the interests of third parties were public; moral and corporal traits were legitimate objects of the criticism of journalists and the public— "drunkenness, ignorance, imbecility, and even the lack of an extremity become an important business in which writers must take a more active part."[43] Such comprehensive definition of the object of public opinion had tragic consequences for men like Degollado, who could not shield their intimate sense of dignity from a tarnished reputation.

From the Porfirian perspective (less concerned with critical discourse than with order) Jacobin moralism opened the door for public opinion to invade the private life of respectable men. In a debate in 1890 involving, among other newspapers in Mexico City, *El Foro, Diario del Hogar, El Nacional*, and *El Siglo Diez y Nueve*, a judge's sentence against a journalist afforded the opportunity to propose a clearer line between the public and the private, one more consonant with new notions of reputation. In the middle of the debate, Ignacio L. Vallarta was asked to clarify the thinking of the authors of the Constitution regarding the limits of publicity. Vallarta, who had been involved in the constitutional debate on freedom of the press in 1857 and was now a member of the Supreme Court, contributed only a few generalities about the need to maintain the rights of suspects. He recognized the difficulty of demarcating public and private life.[44]

Vallarta's caution betrayed an underlying division: while some in 1890 still defended Ramírez's view of a comprehensive list of the personal traits that might be considered public and, therefore, legitimate objects of discussion, others sought to establish an absolute separation between public and private. Squarely in the first group, *Diario del Hogar* advocated the duty of a new civilian generation to fight for the preservation of liberties by criticizing the powerful in the name of the public good. In the other band, *El Progreso* argued that the press had never been so pure as painted by the Reforma liberals, and the insulting of public officials was not useful because it went against the dictates of *caballerosidad* (chivalry), which always advised discretion.[45] They cited famous extortions of journalists in France and England in support of a restrictive definition of the public realm—although similar abuses were rather scarce in Mexico.[46] A strong, impermeable notion of reputation, applicable to public officials and disassociated from intimate feelings, seemed the best legal tool to prevent those evils.

The debate in 1890 focused on the already extinct press jury, so the tone was rather academic. The interlocutors did not expect a dramatic reversal in the Porfirian regime's increasing reign over the public sphere.[47] Yet the discussion signaled the historical significance of the interconnection between the abolition of the press jury and the legislation to protect public officials' reputations.

Abolition of the Press Jury and Protection of Public Officials

The reform of article 7 of the Constitution in 1882 was the decisive step toward a new protection of reputation. The reform made possible the indictment of the protesters who fought against the deuda inglesa in 1885 and led to the criminalization of opposition speech. Until the liberal triumphs of the 1860s, as noted in chapter 1, conservative or plainly autocratic regimes had abolished the press jury according to political need and without much soul-searching. It was only after the restoration of the Republic and the enactment of the Press Law of 1868 that serious juridical criticism of this protection of free speech began to gain ground. In 1875 Jacinto Pallares formulated the basic objection: the law of 1868 and the Penal Code of 1871 contradicted each other by giving press crimes against reputation a dual nature. While the law of 1868 created a secure realm for public criticism of private vices, the code saw publication as merely a means of communication that did not necessarily entail concern for the public good. The code, in contrast with the law, finely calibrated behaviors (injuria, difamación, calumnia) according to publicity and intentionality. The Press Law did not establish a precise gradation among different offenses and their corresponding penalties, as the Penal Code did. This meant, in one regulation, impunity and greater

protection of defendants for crimes that, in another, were punished severely with a simple sentence from a judge. *La Libertad* provided a vivid
analogy: if a thief steals our watch, we can arrest him and bring him to a
judge; but if "a writer with his pen rips up a piece of our honor" that is not
possible.[48]

Adversaries of the press jury did not explicitly defend censorship but
framed their claims in terms of equality before the law, rationalization of
legal codes, and federalism—all liberal articles of faith. Writing in 1875,
G. Baturoni called press crimes "mixed crimes" and argued against the
special status that the Press Law of 1868 gave journalists. He called it a
fuero (special jurisdiction) which journalists, like other citizens, should
renounce. The word *fuero* evoked liberal struggles against the special
jurisdiction that the church and the army had maintained after independence; their staunch defense of privileges caused, in the liberal narrative,
long, bloody civil conflicts. Parliamentary fuero, which prevented congressmen from being indicted by judicial authorities, was also thought
to be dishonorable, and punctilious men like Santos Degollado were
prompt to renounce it when accused of a crime. Stressing the liberal
pedigree of his criticism, Baturoni argued that regulating press crimes
through criminal legislation furthered federalism by leaving to local and
state officials the authority to deal with transgressions that had local
implications.[49] Baturoni and Pallares agreed that the Press Law was a
failure in that it punished the improper use of the press rather than
specific injuries to "an individual or the entire social body." Quite the
contrary, accusations discussed before a press jury further damaged the
victim's reputation. Finally, other abolitionists argued that the honor of
the judiciary was at stake: it was an insult to judges to say, as Prieto and
other defenders of the press jury did, that criminal courts could not be
trusted to read the press with a finely tuned sensitivity.[50]

One semantic shift, however, prefigured subsequent authoritarian use
of these ideas: Baturoni and Pallares talked about press offenses as crimes
(*delitos* or *crímenes*) rather than as misdemeanors (*faltas*), as in the law of
1868. Abolishing journalists' fuero, in other words, meant they could
now be treated as criminals—a kind of criminal distinguished by their
weapon: publicity.[51] Displacing of the discussion from the defense of free
speech to the punishment of transgressions against reputation was essential if abolitionists ever hoped to defeat a strong tradition of court
protection of journalists' rights. Yet it was not an easy road. A district

court in Jalisco, for example, decided in 1877 that journalists could not be prosecuted under article 1110 of the Penal Code, which punished the inciting of rebellion through print, unless they had already been sentenced for rebellion.[52] The Supreme Court confirmed in 1881 that calumnia, if committed through a publication, was "the exclusive concern of popular juries."[53] As long as the press jury subsisted, judges could not think of journalists as common criminals.

Criticism of press legislation laid the groundwork for swift congressional approval of the constitutional reform that abolished press juries. The project introduced in the Senate invoked criticisms of press legislation that they defined as a fuero, stressed the weaknesses of the law of 1868, and supported a rationalization of judicial authority. Proponents appealed to the protection of citizens' honra as a moral and political obligation. *La Libertad* portrayed the new attitude in terms that contrast starkly with the ethics of combat journalists: "Society demands an effective remedy against the premeditation of journalists of certain caste for whom the honor of people is an object of profit."[54] By deleting mention of the press jury from the Constitution, the new framework would reinforce judges' jurisdiction over all matters of criminal justice and place all press crimes under the Penal Code. The reform also simplified procedures since enforcement would no longer require a regulatory instrument, thus automatically abrogating the law of 1868. The initiative had the active support of President Manuel González, who sent his minister of justice to argue on its behalf in Congress. In spite of angry responses from newspapers like *Diario del Hogar*, the Senate approved the project and sent it to the Chamber of Deputies, which passed it by a vote of 140 to 8 in December of 1882. González and Díaz pressured state authorities to have local legislatures approve the constitutional amendment, and soon a majority did: the reform was enacted on May 15, 1883. Although debates about the consequences of the reform continued for years, the reform itself was not challenged by the Supreme Court and enjoyed the support of Justice Vallarta, perhaps the most influential jurist of his generation, and a considerable sector of the press.[55]

The legislative changes of 1882 reflected a historic shift in attitudes, even among journalists, about state protection of victims' honor. In the perspective of old-style combat journalists and many public men, honor was above the laws of the state. According to the prosecutor José Olmedo y Lama in 1877, individuals' active defense of their honor was governed

EL PERRO QUE HABLA.

La Oposicion actual pintada por ella misma

19. Jesús T. Alamilla, "Today's opposition painted by itself," in *Mefistófeles*, 10 November 1877. Reproduced in Barajas Durán, *El País del Llorón*, 139. Used by permission of the author.

by "laws sanctioned by men's unanimous although tacit consent and could not be broken without risking civil death."[56] Only five years later, during the debates leading to the reform of article 7, the deputies Enrique María Rubio and Ignacio T. Chavez rebuked the supporters of the press jury because, "worried about protecting the writer's fuero, they forget to respect one of the human rights that any well-organized society must guarantee: the honra of each citizen."[57] The focus of reference now was victims and the state's protection of their interests. Even veteran journalists like Vicente García Torres began to demand such protection, as they could now be attacked by lowly reporters through libelous writings.[58] The irony of García Torres, an inveterate object of libel suits, seeking the protection of the state must not have been lost on contemporaries. A drawing by Jesús T. Alamilla from 1877 portrays the new attitude: a ragged old hag with a lantern (perhaps representing opinion) props a skinny barking dog, representing the opposition magazine *El Quixote*, upon a stool labeled "calumnia" (see figure 19, above).

The reform of 1882 opened the door for the criminalization of that mangy dog, but Porfirian jurists still had to reinforce the penal legislation and coordinate constitutional, press, and penal frameworks. That job was not as easy as arresting a watch-snatching thief. According to a majority of the Supreme Court in June 1885, the Penal Code's chapter on crimes against reputation was still "a hybrid, equivocal group of prescriptions that not only differ from each other but also are mutually exclusive."[59] Justices pointed to the multiple contradictions between the Press Law, the Penal Code, and article 7 of the Constitution that were not solved by the reform. As Pallares and Baturoni had noted, crimes committed by the press had a dual nature, being punished by the press and criminal codes at the same time. The reform of article 7 seemed to solve that contradiction by replacing the Press Law with the Penal Code. Yet lawyers defending journalists argued that the law of 1868 was abrogated only in its prescriptions about the jury, but not in other regards: even if a judge now replaced juries in sentencing press crimes, conciliation had to be attempted, and, more important, judges had to apply the lesser penalties of the Press Law. In 1885 an appellate court in the Federal District expressed a retroactive interpretation that eventually prevailed: the code had already abrogated the press law, since Martínez de Castro claimed in its introduction that harsher penalties were necessary in crimes against honor. Thus, the reform of 1882 only confirmed that the Penal Code superseded the Press Law in its entirety.[60] If the issue was the protection of reputation, in other words, punishment passed leniency on the road to modernization.

Greater rigor, however, did not translate into a seamless body of laws. Regarding evidence, for example, the Penal Code, unlike the Press Law, did not allow for the presentation of evidence in most crimes against reputation and in general established more stringent limits to speech— thus effectively contradicting the Constitution. The Penal Code did not distinguish the means (either oral or written) through which the attack against reputation was committed, but the Constitution did so by specifically protecting speech through the press even after the reform of 1882. The correctional judge José María Gamboa (brother of the novelist Federico) acquitted writers for *La Voz de España* accused of criticizing a brewer because even if the Penal Code punished defamation against a commercial firm or industry, article 7 of the Constitution set as the only limits to freedom of speech the respect to private life, morality, and public peace—none of which were infringed by tasting beer. Adding a new layer to the possible contradictions, the reformed article 7 gave states the ability to regulate press crimes. While the Federal District Penal Code was the national model at the time of the reform in 1882, the federalization of press jurisdiction allowed for the passage of harsher press codes like that passed in Michoacán in 1896.[61]

Porfirian jurists tried to skirt these problems, which often led to appeals, by focusing on the victim rather than on the writer. In practice, the problem was first to measure the status of the person offended and, as a consequence, the seriousness of the injury inflicted by libels. Press jurors, who had personal knowledge of complainants and suspects, had served this purpose before (see chapter 1). In common cases of battery, penalties were established on the basis of physicians' reports on the length of time the victim's bodily wounds would take to heal, but there was no equivalent expert testimony to assess damages to reputation. Criminal judges could determine only whether the suspect's statements might offend a generic victim—an almost impossible task since reputation was a relative value.[62] The problem was solved in part by defining more usable victims.

The figure of the public official (*funcionario público*) became the key reference in prosecutions against journalists during the late Porfiriato. While the Constitution made no distinction regarding victims of press offenses, chapter X of the Penal Code of 1871 was devoted to "Ultrajes y atentados contra los funcionarios públicos," as part of title VIII of book 3, on crimes against public order. While *atentado* referred to a physical offense, *ultraje* became a large receptacle for any verbal or written attack against individual officials or government bodies (Congress, tribunals, juries). Ultraje itself had an imprecise meaning and was not defined in the code.[63] Some Mexican jurists distinguished ultraje by the fact that it was committed in the presence of or in writing addressed to the victim; others simply referred to the victim's status. Díaz Infante gave an expansive interpretation: ultrajes meant "any injuria directed privately or publicly, by word, writing, or in any other way, against public officials in the act of exercising his office or because of that office."[64] Beginning in 1882, ultraje stuck in practice, was further refined in legislation, and became an essential tool in prosecutions against the press; prosecutors and judges turned it into a blanket authorization to punish anyone who offended "the Mexican nation" or its representatives.[65]

The new focus on public officials upended the classical legal reasoning that targeted actions rather than persons. The liberal tradition had seen public officials as potential offenders rather than victims and protected free speech on the premise that the border between public and private actions, although clear, was elastic enough to allow combat journalists almost unfettered freedom. "The acts of public officials are of two kinds, private or public, that is, they are either foreign to their duties or related to their exercise; both fall under the domain of the press," argued Emilio Velasco, the attorney for the political prisoners in 1885.[66] Article 7 of the Constitution, after all, said nothing about the public life of officials as a limit to free speech. Thus, according to some jurists, ultrajes as a crime contradicted the Constitution, and appellate judges struck down sentences. The political implications were obvious. "What happiness would prevail," lamented *El Artesano*, "if public men in our country realized how essential it is to purify their behavior in the eyes of the public."[67] Writers defending this tradition cited debates in the Constitutional Congress in which José María Mata had proposed a restricted definition of privacy that would not have protected dishonest authorities. For them, the law had to distinguish "home from palace," and while individuals had the criminal courts, officials had to face "the tribunal of opinion."[68]

The possibility of facing such a tyrant unnerved Porfirian public men, and they set out to erode that liberal tradition. The last two decades of the century saw an increasing emphasis on the radical separation between public and private realms. Public officials as victims were the living embodiment of the separation of public persona from private subject, to the extent that the same man's honor could be attacked and defended according to two different sets of rules. A paradigmatic example was the affair in 1879 in which Salvador Díaz Mirón assailed the governor of Veracruz, Luis Mier y Terán, for his role in the execution of several rebels and in a newspaper invited him to solve the dispute on the field of honor (see chapter 3). The governor avoided a dangerous encounter with the bellicose poet by deferring the issue to an ad hoc "tribunal of honor." The tribunal decided he had no obligation to duel Díaz Mirón since the insults had been cast against Mier y Terán, the public official, not the private citizen.[69] Most conflicts had a more routine quality. Passages of gacetilla in the República Restaurada dealing with small issues like lost accounting books or the illegal butchering of sheep often prompted accusations in front of the press jury in defense of individuals or, more generally, "the honra and reputation of municipal employees."[70] Esteban

Benítez, a high ranking official at the Ministry of War and Navy recognized in 1872 that, owing to his preoccupations in the ministry, "I seldom read the newspapers." Yet he had to invoke a press jury against José González Gordoa, the author of a diatribe against him in *El Monitor Republicano*, lest his silence earn him the reputation of criminal.[71] However busy a public officer might be, he had to keep his eyes on the newspapers because press laws in the República Restaurada considered such attacks personal offenses against which only the victim could initiate legal action.

The reign of the Penal Code since 1882 made possible both a comfortable indifference of public officials toward the press and the aggressive zeal of prosecutors and judges against journalists. Public men were now less interested in publishing pamphlets to defend their decisions, as Francisco de P. Vega did in 1868, and more likely to seek the protection of the penal system. Presentation of evidence no longer preempted charges. Summary procedures became common against lesser-known suspects, and the standards of evidence were lowered, so judges engaged in what Filomeno Mata called "petty revenges."[72] While the Penal Code required demonstration of intentionality (*dolo*) in order to convict for difamación, in cases of ultrajes the existence of such intent was presumed. Contrary to the practice in most other crimes, judges saw the suspect's education as an aggravating circumstance. Prosecutions for insults against government bodies, which in the past tended to peter out for lack of identifiable victims, were now more likely to succeed. In a well-known case from 1890 a criminal judge found the writers and editors of *El Acusador Político* guilty of injurias "against the majority of the Chamber of Deputies." The abstract victim did not prevent a real penalty: José Avalos Salazar was sentenced to eighteen months in prison, fined a thousand pesos, and ordered to learn the trade of shoemaker—a common occupation among prisoners.[73] Even humor was lost. Jesús M. Rábago was arrested in 1884 for writing the following *calavera* (a popular genre in which the person in the verse was imagined to be dead) about a magistrate, Mauro F. de Córdova: "Small in talent and body / It is a shame he no longer exists, / Because he was, in my story, / Criminal, criminologist."[74]

Although vague accusations and harsh penalties were not new, the replacing of press legislation with the Penal Code marked a historical shift in the rules of the public sphere: "the status of the victim" (his or her social standing) became the center of arguments over political and ideological considerations. If in the past the common good justified a free press, now honor was the supreme value, one that had to be actively protected by the state in both public and private realms. For Díaz Infante, the judiciary enforced "the right of the official . . . to demand that the honor emanating from his public conduct be respected" even though this honor remained a "good of [the official's] property."[75] Judges and prosecutors now called ultrajes what in the past had been prosecuted as insults and defamation, even if the statements were only vaguely linked to the victim's post, and independently of the place or situation of the victim at the moment of the attack. The broad interpretive abilities formerly entrusted to press juries shifted to law enforcement officials and in the process assumed an opposite intent. For the prosecutor Luis Labastida, "a simple offensive expression, a simple word that wounds . . . without referring to an act," was reason enough to prosecute.[76]

The highest expression of this newfound prosecutorial power was the doctrina psicológica. According to the doctrine, cited in multiple cases against the press, judges' decisions about what constituted evidence of libel could not be criticized even by higher courts since, "in the absence of any criterion or intelligence able to describe or positively study the psychological phenomenon that takes place in the brain of the judge," the psychical realm in which the interpretation of evidence took place could not be ruled either by precedent or by old or new legislation.[77] This original formulation of the doctrine, by the prosecutor Isidro Montiel y Duarte, justified courts' refusal to overrule the indictment of journalists and students accused of trying to rekindle public opposition to the deuda inglesa, without actually rebelling, in 1885. Judge Andrés Horcasitas agreed that "the psychological function is so free in its interpretation of the results of the inquest" that the only guarantee against arbitrary decisions is not the procedural law but the judge's intelligence.[78] Defense attorneys then and other critics later argued that there was such a thing as a "legal reason" that could be analyzed and proven erroneous and that the psychological doctrine went against positive science, which offered objective rules for the act of interpreting and applying the law.[79]

No objection could effectively counter the doctrina psicológica, however, because it reconciled order and progress with the logic of honor. According to Montiel y Duarte (echoing Justo Sierra's protestation of journalistic integrity years earlier, cited in chapter 2), it was impossible to demonstrate that a judge was acting against his will, "given that not even the clearest intelligence can penetrate the sanctuary of others' con-science."[80] The doctrine was all the more unyielding in that it was itself a paradoxical legacy of combat journalism and its concern for honor. Even his adversaries acknowledged that Montiel y Duarte was a man of honor who had been a combat journalist and had participated in the constitu-tion of the Junta General de Periodistas—a court of honor formed in 1880 to mediate disputes and prevent dueling while protecting the reputation of the trade. In 1885, however, he argued that the "Latin race" had such "lively imagination and the impulsive force of sentiment" that any debate was potentially dangerous.[81] Against unreliable, Latin masses there was no better remedy that intelligent, honorable judges. The doctrina psico-lógica was so successful that decades later journalists saw in the 1885 case the beginning of an era of press repression, while judges continued to refer to it during the remainder of the Porfiriato.[82]

The doctrina became synonymous with arbitrary incarcerations of journalists: Filomeno Mata, reported *El Hijo del Ahuizote*, suffered "a new blow of *psicología*" when he was sent incommunicado to Belem. He was not responsible for the article denounced, but nothing could be done: "Mysteries of Psicología!"[83] Days later the newspaper defined the "Psicología Judicial" as "that new kind of prior censorship which judges on the basis of hypotheses, not established facts, of mere suspicion rather than consummated acts," resulting in arrests of journalists even if they did not attack the private life of public officials they criticized. An elo-quent allegory of the free press entitled "Peligros de naufragio" (The dangers of shipwreck) accompanied the text (figure 20).[84]

If one examines the impact of these new doctrines during the rest of the period it becomes clear that, while the regime became clearly author-itarian, pure politics was never the only rationale for persecution of the press. Most cases against writers centered on municipal politics and involved actors known to (although not always loved by) each other. The weight of honor was never absent in these disputes, and judges played a role that was distinct from that of political authorities—sometimes pro-tecting journalists but more frequently employing the full arsenal of the penal law against them. Criminal records show complex interactions between journalists who were often well connected locally, political au-thorities (such as *prefectos* or jefes políticos and their police underlings), and judges or prosecutors. Victoriano Rodríguez, for example, wrote from the municipal prison in León, Guanajuato, to the lawyer Toribio

20. "Free Press." *El Hijo del Ahuizote*, 4:298, 11 Oct. 1891, 3.

Esquivel Obregón asking for advice and support in reversing the "arbitrary prison term" he had been sentenced to by the local jefe político for writing an article in *El Obrero* entitled "Las dulzuras del periodismo" (The pleasures of journalism). Esquivel Obregón wrote to the political authorities appealing for Rodríguez's release. Yet relying only on lawyers and patrons was costly and ultimately useless, reflected Rodríguez, since his own reputation as a journalist was also being attacked by the rival paper *El Comercio*.[85]

The anecdote, from 1907, suggests that some journalists continued to see their reputation as a central asset, one they could summon in local disputes according to the same basic patterns observed in chapter 2. Editors continued to refuse to name authors of offensive writings, citing their "word as a gentleman," and proudly faced prison.[86] Conversely, even at the apex of Porfirian political control, judges maintained some autonomy. This was part of a tradition firmly established during the days before the abolition of the press jury, when local and circuit judges could grant *amparos* (protection) against arrests derived from local disputes or mediate press confrontations into a "satisfactory explanation"—even if they now enjoyed enhanced authority thanks to the doctrina psicológica.[87]

While the basic rules regarding the honor of writers and victims survived, Porfirian authoritarianism was now able to persecute political criticism as personal insult. Ultrajes and crimes against reputation became central mechanisms to control the press. The examples are numerous: in Monterrey, a passage in *El Norte* accusing a politician in Tamaulipas of being a "traitor to his friends and supporters" was interpreted as injurias by a local judge and upgraded to difamación by a district court;[88] a caricature in *El Padre Padilla* earned Luis Moncayo an accusation for the same crimes, a sentence of ultrajes, and a penalty of one year and three months in prison plus a fine of three hundred pesos.[89] Judges and prosecutors became ill-advised readers and issued harsh penalties, as did the infamous Judge Horcasitas by sentencing Salazar to learn the trade of shoemaker. In spite of the informal right they had to occupy a section of the prison that was separate from that of the other inmates, journalists loathed time inside in close proximity to common prisoners.[90]

Conclusions

Some nearly forgotten episodes of public life, like the repression of the presos políticos in 1885, synthesize historical change. In that case, evolving judicial rules and practices combined with new, allegedly more objective notions of honor to justify repression. This combination suggests a correction to established historical accounts of the Porfiriato as a well-oiled machine that combined persecution and cooptation. In these accounts, the official subsidization of *El Imparcial*, established in 1896, put combat newspapers *El Monitor Republicano* out of business. Publishing articles with no signatures, *El Imparcial* removed an incentive for journalists to gain celebrity and material advantages through polemics; and judges who were lackeys of power did the rest.[91] The image of Rafael Reyes Spíndola, the director of *El Imparcial*, cozying up to power and money contrasted, in these accounts, with the romantic figure of the independent journalist. Set in such starks terms, historical views of cases against the press during these years tend to embrace a narrow putatively political explanation: prosecutions against journalists were dictated by power even if they were framed as the protection of public officials' reputation; honor as an individual value of journalists gave way to honor as an object to be protected to the full extent of the law.

Yet things were not that black and white: Reyes Spíndola continued to fight duels, while García Torres, owner of *El Monitor Republicano*, sued other journalists for libel.[92] Across supposed political divides, a general consensus about the value of private honor and the state's responsibility to protect it turned free speech into a crime. The taming of public men (or, what amounted to the same thing, the taming of public opinion) was a central step in the consolidation of Porfirian control over the public sphere. It took place after the abolition of the press jury but before the hegemony of *El Imparcial*. The judiciary was the most important instrument in disciplining and criminalizing dissent thanks to a new legal construction of honor that measured and protected it as a material good and individual right. Jurists and legislators summoned foreign theories and local examples to build a scientific conception of reputation as measurable in credit and social capital—thus laying out an objective criterion for punishment. Mexicans citizens became more willing to go to court, and the state more eager to intervene.

Honor as a state-protected good did allow for a distinction between control of the political class, largely exercised by Díaz and the científicos through informal means, and the protection of decorum, through citizens' or public officials' right to uphold their reputation. Many agreed with the defense attorney Luis Gutiérrez Otero, who wrote in 1888 that, "in dealing with truly political crimes and criminals, everything should be moderated because their motives cannot be confused with those of common crime."[93] The distinction was clear in the minds of those who supported the abolition of the press jury: protecting reputations was in itself a valuable goal and did not necessarily have to lead to dictatorship.

In hindsight, the political consequences seem unavoidable: the autocratic regime of Díaz survived for so long because it eliminated dissent through extralegal means; the criminalization of journalists operated a subtle but effective shift, making harassment of the press more acceptable, less overtly political. The prosecution of those who opposed the decree on the deuda inglesa in 1885 prefigured what was to come: instead of open discussion and repression, as in the debates and riots of 1884 examined in chapter 3, a new, "psychological" ability by judges to use penal legislation against speech.

The opposition to Díaz failed to secure a realm of open debate in which political authority could be subject to criticism yet maintain a Juarista majesty, above personal interests and disputes. Two powerful forces conspired against free speech during the early 1880s. One was the personalization of political authority around Porfirio Díaz: offenses against him or his appointees were offenses against the regime; their honor was that of the country. As we saw in chapter 3, this was also the reasoning used during the deuda inglesa debates. Another force, one that distinguished Porfirian authority from old-style caudillismo, was the reform and reinterpretation of the juridical framework to protect that personalized authority. The abolition of the press jury and, above all, the rule of the Penal Code and the doctrina psicológica allowed prosecutors and judges to see polemic criticism as ultrajes against funcionarios públicos and to establish a neat separation, in a public man's life, between the public realm (still theoretically exposed to the tyranny of public opinion) and a protected private realm.[94] The separation was harder to trace in the lives of regular citizens (see chapter 6).

The mutation of republican honor I examine here was the condition for the shrinking of political life. While the expansive politicization of life in the early national period gave way to the neat compartmentalization of public and private during the Porfiriato, the economic value of honor became more explicit, thus allowing the state to protect it as property. The privacy of funcionarios públicos further undermined the tyranny of opinion. Yet this mutation was a long agony: the centrality of honor in the courts and on the field of honor endured, even as the political regime consolidated as a dictatorship.

CHAPTER 6

"A Horrible Web of Insults"
The Everyday Defense of Honor

The protection of honor as a right became a central concern for Mexicans toward the end of the nineteenth century, resulting in practices that
both reinforced and modified the legal framework discussed in the previous chapter. Common citizens sought state protection for their reputation and presented compelling testimonies about the role of honor in
their lives. A broad range of conflicts, from insults to defamation, mobilized complainants, who, regardless of their ostensible status, saw honor
as something intrinsically related to their social capital. Judicial archives
in Mexico City and Morelia, Michoacán, contain the names of people of
all classes, many of them poor and female, who fought for their reputation in court. Class bias, of course, persisted: judges and prosecutors
were forced by the new penal legislation to respond to these complaints,
but they were not willing to exert the same energy prosecuting crimes
against reputation as they did other offenses. As usual, the machinery of
the law, which in these cases could be set in motion only by victims'
complaints, did not work very well unless lubricated by money. The
result was a mix of judicial interventions and extralegal negotiations:
complainants couched their demands in words that would obtain results,
and judges reinterpreted testimonies to fit their own evaluation of what
was at stake.

I begin by reconstructing the careful dance between legal institutions and the demands of civil society. Specifically, I discuss the ambivalent role of judges and citizens, paying particular attention to their language and to their negotiations around the multiple goods and relations associated with honor. As a corrective to the male-centered, elite notion of honor this book has been exploring, I conclude with a look at the role of women as complainants and suspects. The performances of men and women in front of judges and against each other provide a critical perspective on the boundaries and rules of the public sphere. Actors sought the publicity of courts because it provided them with a way to defend the honor they saw as a valuable resource.[1]

When the theoretical and legal debates described in the previous chapter are left behind, the cultural consensus that allowed for the taming of the political elite fades. Criminal courts often heard questions that anchored the limits between the public and the private to specific situations rather than to law or principle. Was it legitimate to publish private letters in the context of a legal dispute? or to criticize someone who had not donated money for national festivities? or to attack the wives of two citizens for promoting a religious festivity?[2] I look at how courts tested the limits of privacy and publicity in cases involving actors who were not necessarily public men. These cases open a window on what changed in everyday life when the penal law came to guarantee honor as a juridical good and a right of all citizens.

Honor in this era is no longer the patrimony of elites, according to recent historiography on Latin America. Even slaves claimed their right to a good reputation and used civil and penal courts to defend it. Most current literature, however, takes as its point of departure the elite model of the defense of honor by examining the ways in which the lower classes appropriated codes of behavior only fully developed among the educated.[3] I draw inspiration here from those studies, but I alter that perspective by suggesting that lower-class conflicts over reputation can help elucidate the attitudes of elites by documenting actions and words that the upper classes safely hid from public scrutiny. Mexican courts did not bother *gente decente* (decent people), and the public confrontations examined so far in this book maintained a decorous silence about the private insults and affronts that might have lurked behind them—although that, I promise, will change (see chapter 7).

Common people, by contrast, could not afford such protection for their troubles. Judicial sources offer evidence about the importance of honor and reputation in daily life. The class background of actors in the following cases varies widely, and the press is not the key medium for offenses and their resolution. Yet newspaper articles could offend victims who were not rich or powerful: Pablo Palomino brought suit against Juan Padilla in Guadalajara in 1884, claiming a small text in *Juan Panadero* "attacks his 'private life' and accuses him of 'notoriously inaccurate acts by stating that Palomino stole a herd of twenty skinny pigs.'"[4] This was no parody of elite anxieties, however. Rather than posit a distinct lower-class honor, I propose that the tyranny of public opinion was not the preserve of educated men.

A careful reading of social history bears out this idea. Recent studies have shown, for example, that women and the lower strata of colonial societies fought for their reputation in court and that ethnic, age, and gender hierarchies were not insuperable obstacles in victims' pursuit of justice.[5] Perhaps a more important colonial legacy was a normative regime characterized by pluralism, one in which the state was not the only, perhaps not even the most important, actor in the protection of honor. This fact could be lost from sight if one looks only at legal history. Just as colonial precedent survived in judges' reasonings, gossip and other verbal exchanges and public performances provided alternative, legitimate ways to deal with transgressions. As noted in chapter 5, the bourgeois divide between public and private that informed liberal views was not a central concern in the colonial period, during which complex networks of deference and loyalty bounded ethnicity, sexual mores, and corporate, familial, and individual reputations. Multiple implications of *honor* and *honra* corresponded to multiple values of customs, the law, and the judicial system for diverse social actors.[6] Independence did not mean an interruption in these conditions. Studies of artisans in the nineteenth century and of the emergence of a working-class consciousness later in that century give ample evidence of a widespread concern about respectability, often explicitly articulated as honor. Although historians have identified this preoccupation in their search for collective identities, administrative archives and the popular press suggest that it also operated at the individual level. Working-class sociabilities and institutions and early ideologies of class, which we now know about thanks to the research of historians like Carlos Illades, constituted many terrains on which to conduct the negotiation of reputations.[7]

Judges and Citizens' Reputation

Judicial records are not transparent: they involve the mediation of judicial authorities through their interpretations of behaviors and the law and the participation of multiple actors. Situations and practices recorded in judicial settings were the first to undermine the certainties of the law, as their outcome often occurred beyond those settings. Many trials for injuria, difamación, and calumnia concluded without a sentence; judges routinely changed accusations to less serious crimes; months elapsed without anything happening, at least in court, until the victims dropped the charges. It is not enough, in other words, to see these disputes only through the eyes of the state. As Tamar Herzog has noted for the colonial period, the legal sphere cannot be properly understood if taken as an autonomous realm, isolated from conflicts and negotiations that ran parallel to trials. Just as she finds "social networks, rumor, and systems of reputation" operating in Quito, the evidence from Porfirian Mexico similarly challenges an exclusively institutional approach and the idea of an all-powerful state. Actors here weighed multiple venues before deciding to "bother the authorities." Manuel Córdova, for example, first tried asking his landlord to get Antonia Moya to stop getting drunk and insulting and defaming him every day. Moya refused to leave the building, so Córdova next tried a police inspector, who admonished Moya, to no effect. Moya then sought a reconciliation before a judge, a hearing Córdova refused to attend, instead bringing charges against her in the same court.[8] Besides landlords and the police, multiple actors could arbitrate disputes over reputation: storekeepers, court employees, employers, parents, and other "diverse authorities."[9]

Information in criminal records from 1897 gives a glimpse of the various outcomes of cases for crimes against reputation. Of 177 persons indicted for injuria, difamación, and calumnia that year in the Federal District, 31 were released "por falta de mérito" (for lack of evidence) or because the evidence against them vanished when witnesses failed to confirm their statements; 53 cases ended because the accuser dropped charges. In the cases that reached a verdict, 3 suspects were acquitted and 90 were found guilty. The number of guilty sentences is remarkably high. In the few years between 1871 and 1911 for which information is available on both indictments and sentences handed out for these crimes, the ratio is 4 to 31 on average—not a bad rate of success in comparison to other crimes.[10] The high rate of guilty verdicts in spite of the diversity of outcomes of most cases (including very few acquittals) suggests that victims in crimes against reputation put pressure on the authorities to take their accusations seriously. Victims' intervention was particularly important since trials could span several months. The main factor in delays and a reason for judges' passivity was, in the words of one of them, "the excess of work in this court."[11] Judges had another excuse to be less aggressive in that only victims could initiate legal action for crimes against reputation: their continuing pressure on judges and witnesses was necessary to take cases to their conclusion.

Seeking the protection of such a reluctant judiciary came with high costs for victims, so those who persevered, like Manuel Córdova, had good reason to do so. In another case, Jesús Venegas de Goya sought the advice and assistance of her employer to write her initial complaint against Soledad Cerón, since the services of lawyers were beyond her means. Failure to affix tax stamps to petitions prompted judges to halt proceedings even if, as established by law, victims claimed they were too poor to afford them.[12] A less tangible but also costly aspect of penal action was the publicity that engulfed both sides. When they involved juries or attracted the interest of the press, trials hurt victims' reputations even if they resulted in guilty verdicts. Since witnesses could not be accused for statements made in the context of judicial proceedings, judicial settings revealed information that both parties preferred to keep private. Rosa Rivero, accused of difamación, did not wait to hear from her attorney and asked the judge to find her guilty as soon as possible, so she could pay the fifteen-peso fine and be done with it. Authorities shared this concern about privacy to a fault. The Third Precinct police inspector destroyed letters used as evidence in a case because, he told the judge, "of their lack of significance and because they were written in incoherent and amorous terms."[13]

Once the machinery of justice was in motion, parties had multiple alternatives to sentencing and punishment. Negotiations between the victim and the suspect were time-consuming, and the passage of time surely affected the feelings that had triggered the accusation; the delays led to dropped cases. Such was the case in the dispute between Filandro San Martín and Francisco Espinosa. The judge sent both to the municipal jail for a day, which made possible "some clarifications" and eventually the dropping of the accusations they had leveled against each other.[14] Judicial authorities were not opposed to these alternative outcomes: the Supremo Tribunal de Justicia of Chihuahua advised judges to stop proceedings once the offended party decided that further legal action was hurting his or her reputation, or, alternatively, when they realized that the case itself was becoming a means of revenge for the alleged victim. Judges did exercise considerable flexibility in allowing negotiated outcomes. Rafaela Trujillo stated during cross-examination of her offender, Soledad Heredia, that "her wish is only that her rival would no longer insist . . . and would promise to no longer bother" her. Trujillo accepted Heredia's husband's word that she was not going to be bothered again, and the judge decided that no crime had been committed.[15] Expecting such flexibility, Jesús Castro, in another case, came back before the judge, after his initial accusation, and stated that the suspect's explanations were enough for him "and that my honra, which I believed stained, is still clean, so I no longer ask for more."[16]

Judicial flexibility allowed authorities to preserve decorum. Gregoria Salmerón, for example, claimed that Petra González had paid a policeman fifty cents to have Salmerón arrested and brought to court on charges of insultos. She and other female suspects could put up forceful resistance, refusing to go to court or the police station or even to recognize the authority of the judge. Judge Vidal Delgado, in Nuevo Laredo, had to tell the court clerk to strike out the "insulting sentences" expressed by a defense lawyer against his impartiality.[17] Allowing such statements to stand on record would have made the reputation of authorities another casualty in the already dangerous terrain of disputes over honor.

A common way to exercise flexibility was for judges to change the type of crime under consideration, in effect relabeling the trial. Thus, many cases in which victims initially complained of difamación became injurias when it came to the sentencing. Victims like Manuela Franco de Grower claimed that statements made by Manuela and Mauricia Lemus amounted to difamación because they called her a "prostitute, in public"; the same thing happened with Francisco Giles in his accusation against Rosa Rivero for statements she made in front of customers at his store. Yet in both cases the judges indicted the suspects for injurias.[18] Complaints of calumnia could in turn be downgraded to difamación or injurias to *golpes* (blows that did not cause injuries), but never the converse. Judges could suspend processes if they decided victims' testimonies did not correspond to the crime to be prosecuted.[19] Calumnia, the false attribution of a crime, gave suspects the right to present evidence in support of their statements.[20] Yet judges viewed difamación and calumnia as mutually incompatible and often chose the former, thus weakening the victims' case. Arguing for the compatibility of the two kinds of charges, Vicente García Torres expressed their relationship metaphorically: "Injuria and difamación, or both, are the soul; calumnia is the body, animated by the soul; the whole action [is] raised to juridical life by the reunion of body and soul: as a consequence one could never properly say that body and soul are incompatible."[21] The "soul" was the intention behind the crime, and the "body" was its incarnation in action: the goal was to defame, and the tool was calumnia. Long a victim of judicial persecution, this time, in 1897, García Torres wanted a higher court to use broad discretion to defend his reputation and revise a sentence that had acquitted José Ferrel, another combat journalist.

The language was odd but it fairly represented the absence of neat definitions in practice, where injurias and difamación were almost synonymous and calumnia usually a supplement to the first two in accusations, although not in sentences. Injurias (which required parties to be in the presence of each other and the victim to be offended but did not entail publicity) became the lowest common denominator of all crimes against honor. For the judge Antonio Arnaiz, every instance of injurias was also difamación.[22] Victims mentioned all these crimes in most complaints in order to avoid dismissal of the charges.

A loose application of injurias is found in a case in 1876 in which a Yucatecan judge sentenced the Catholic priest Ireneo Muñoz for injurias because he whipped the corpse of one Baltazar Madera, whose only fault had been to swear the Constitution of 1857.[23] This bizarre case—perhaps an attempt, by both priest and judge, to demonstrate the unity of body and soul postulated by García Torres—points to the main conceptual problem in the definition and enforcement of crimes against reputation: trials had to establish that there had been effective communication between the victim, the suspect, and third parties. Was Madera offended by the whipping? The Penal Code defined difamación as the act of "willfully communicating" a dishonoring imputation, thus tacitly encompassing letters, press, and other media or actions (such as whipping) and stressing objective interactions rather than an all-encompassing notion of publicity.[24] At the same time, "communicating" involved not just the victim but also those who knew her, regardless of their location. As summed up by a defense lawyer, you can only offend someone you know.[25] The problem was whether knowing someone required physical proximity. Persons moved freely across the world, and offensive statements were equally criminal if read in Paris or proffered in front of the victim in Mexico: Carlos Eisenmann argued that he should not have been tried in Mexico for writing a letter that might have damaged Ricardo Kent's reputation because "what constitutes calumnia is communication"—which did not occur until Kent read the letter Eisenmann had written in Mexico when he was in Paris.[26]

Such an evasive notion of communication went against the territoriality that had characterized enforcement of press legislation before 1882, when, as noted in chapter 1, offenders could be tried only in the city of publication. Four years later, a correctional judge in the Federal District, Salvador Medina y Ormaechea, agreed to try in Mexico City the author of a letter written in Chicontepec, Veracruz. The suspect, Cipriano Castillo, claimed he had to be judged in his hometown, Chicontepec, because he had written the letter there. But the prosecutor Manuel Mateos Alarcón argued that the crime took place in the capital, where the person who stood to lose honor read the letter and thereby became an injuria. Reviewing the case, the Supreme Court agreed with Alarcón, thus defining publicity as communication: the defamatory statement "was not known and had not been communicated until the moment it reached public light and circulated through the press."[27] The centrality of the victim that characterized the new notion of honor discussed in chapter 5 was the premise for this interpretation. Communication occurred the instant an article, letter, or offensive statement was received: it was not an ongoing crime that included the acts of writing, mailing, or printing but was committed when and where a victim or audience read the statement. Publicity was no longer a place or a printed paper: it existed and could be prosecuted when the suspect and the victim communicated.[28]

The sentence against Muñoz, the cadaver-whipping priest of Yucatan, was all the more strange as the relationship between the victim and the suspect was fundamental to establishing intentionality and seriousness in crimes against reputation. The penal protection of honor distinguished injuria, difamación, and calumnia by their seriousness, which depended on the relationship between the actors. The suspect's communication with the victim or a common audience implied a preexisting relationship, which in turn was required to prove *dolo*, the intention to harm. Judges could be lenient when suspects demonstrated that they did not know the victim and therefore could not have had an intention to harm her. When the policeman Simón León suggested that his superior Pedro Santa Cruz stole his gun while he was taking a nap at his post, León not only confessed to dereliction of duty but also, in the opinion of the judge, committed injurias because he knew who Santa Cruz was. As this case and the ones examined below suggest, the perceived or real subordination of one of the actors to the other was a central argument in characterizing criminal conduct. The clearest example was ultrajes against public officials (see chapter 5). The crime could be committed and prosecuted by the Ministerio Público only if offensive statements were made "in the presence of the official or in a text addressed to him." Otherwise, the crime was simply an injuria or difamación, and the case had to be initiated by the victim.[29]

Although intended to secure a more aggressive defense of individual rights, penal legislation opened multiple avenues for negotiations and alternative interpretations, as dolo, communication, and hierarchies could be established only in exchanges that went beyond the court. Obligated to protect citizens' honor yet unable to prosecute without prior complaint, authorities often became onlookers as individuals piled up evidence against each other. Because verdicts had to be supported by evidence of the intimate sense of harm inflicted by statements and by the equally elusive intention to cause that harm, judges and actors could discover such factors only by documenting preexisting, public relationships — a process that was seldom discreet or predictable. The figure of the judge receded, and citizens became more active, as disputes could be solved only in the public sphere.

The risk of exposing private life in court did not paralyze urban dwellers during the República Restaurada and Porfiriato. Regardless of their social background or gender, they actively defended their reputation. The condescending attitude of some judges or the biases in the law did not reflect their views of honor. On the contrary, multiple examples suggest that people thought these were serious transgressions that deserved to be punished regardless of the victim's status. Paradoxically, the punitive codification of honor as a right in the late nineteenth century did not mean a more exclusive system but the opposite. Through small disputes, those occurring among poor people, out of the press's radar, one can see the broad

TABLE 4. Information about Persons Indicted for Crimes against Reputation,
Federal District, 1900

Crime	Total Indicted	Women	Have a Profession	Read and Write	Single	Married	Widow	Drunk
				PERCENTAGES				
Injuria and Difamación	43	30.23	67.44	41.86	62.79	32.56	4.65	48.84
All Crimes	18,068	21.02	80.05	18.52	74.99	22.57	2.44	69.79

Source: Cuadros estadisticos e informe del Procurador de Justicia concernientes a la criminalidad en el Distrito Federal, 1900 (Mexico City: La Europea, 1903).

access to honor as a right. For Francisco Llamas Noriega, counsel to two gentlemen from Zacatecas, popular notions about defamation, expressed in simple but clear language, were as important as national and foreign legislations. After making his legal case he added, "It is beyond doubt, then, that the people, by using a similar language, pay homage to the wisdom of the law and demonstrate the justice of its definitions."[30]

If one assumes such coincidence between legal syntax and social vocabularies, judicial sources document a strong, widespread desire to defend personal honor. Official statistics offer few yet intriguing indications of the diverse social backgrounds of suspects. Data compiled by the attorney general of the Federal District for 1900, synthesized in table 4, suggest that suspects in crimes against reputation were less likely to have a profession or trade than suspects in all crimes. The lower number of suspects with a trade may be explained by the fact that women (who tended to report no trade in their statements) were more likely to be accused for injurias than they were, in general, for all crimes. Information from extant trial records confirms that suspects and victims came from diverse strata and that women played a highly important role in these crimes. Suspects, however, were much more likely to be able to read and write than the average suspect (see table 4). Although this might seem paradoxical given their lack of trade and the proportion of women, it resonates with actors' concern about a public sphere that straddled oral and written media—as the analysis of specific cases in the following section will suggest.

Judicial records show victims ranging from lawyers and engineers to merchants and artisans, carpenters, domestic and construction workers —some unable to write, but all willing to publicly defend their honor. Even prisoners, like Enrique Paniagua, would seek legal remedy. In his case, because a visitor to Belem prison accused him, "publicly, in the galleries," of having committed "acts against nature by playing the role of woman with other inmates."[31] Just like prisoners and neighbors, any audience constituted a public for reputations: customers at a *pulquería*, coworkers, students. Antonio Rodríguez, a primary school teacher, pressed charges against his employer, a municipal official, because he had treated him disrespectfully in front of his students. Victims were also collectivities. Rodríguez argued that by attacking his person his aggressor was attacking the honor of his profession. Physicians, according to Dr. J. Alberto Salinas y Rivera, had to act, in his case by publishing an article in *El Foro* in which he warned that "we physicians are in general tolerant, except in what concerns or might concern our professional honor."[32] Personal self-esteem, however, could not be subordinated to professional affiliation. In several cases accusations of injurias and calumnia were the result of internal disputes among coworkers: municipal employees, railroad workers, and even policemen used penal courts to redress suspicions voiced about their honesty or challenges to their dignity. Thus accusations shifted domestic or work-related disputes to the context of criminal courts.[33]

For all these kinds of victims, the intervention of authorities was necessary to prevent further damage to their standing in the eyes of the multiple audiences populating their everyday lives. They did not limit their demands for protection to judges but also included less formal requests and fora. Filandro San Martin, for example, sent a note to the police station in 1896 asking for a plainclothes policeman to help him deal with Francisco Espinosa, who had insulted him. Others simply went to the Ministerio Público to make authorities aware of the defamatory accusations against them, yet without pressing charges.[34] Nevertheless, many cases reached judicial authorities.

How many? Since complaints did not always lead to indictments, crimes against reputation are probably underestimated in official statistics. Although these crimes did not comprise the largest part of the work at police stations and courts, the available evidence shows a steady, probably increasing number of indictments in the late nineteenth century

TABLE 5. Crimes against Reputation Indictments, Federal District, 1871–1885

Year	Dueling	Injurias	Difamación	Calumnia	Ultrajes contra Funcionarios Públicos	Total Offenses against Reputation	Total All Crimes	% Crimes against Reputation
1871	2	86	6	0	50	144	5,456	2.64
1872	0	93	5	1	177	276	6,152	4.49
1873	0	129	7	0	337	473	7,527	6.28
1874	3	308	9	2	266	588	5,757	10.21
1875	1	343	1	5	93	443	5,285	8.38
1876	0	42	1	2	45	90	4,270	2.11
1877	0	101	1	4	253	359	7,576	4.74
1878	1	107	4	3	207	322	7,262	4.43
1879	2	117	3	8	301	431	8,117	5.31
1880	4	285	8	11	602	910	12,080	7.53
1881	5	93	6	5	226	335	9,722	3.45
1882	4	135	11	10	157	317	8,859	3.58
1883	3	87	8	2	106	206	7,573	2.72
1884	4	223	11	2	72	312	6,799	4.59
1885	3	144	7	9	88	251	7,080	3.55

Source: Dirección General de Estadística, *Estadística del ramo criminal en la República Mexicana que comprende un periodo de quince años, de 1871 a 1885* (Mexico City: Secretaría de Fomento, 1890).

(table 5). Based on the earliest available systematic count of criminal statistics in the capital, the table indicates the relative weight of these crimes within the total and their trends during the fifteen years after the passing of the Penal Code. Injurias and ultrajes a funcionarios públicos make up the largest number of cases. If one considers them, plus dueling (always linked to reputation), calumnia, and difamación, crimes related to honor make up an average of almost 5 percent of all cases—not an insignificant number—with a peak of more than 10 percent in 1874. That year and 1880 mark moments of especially intense activity, with 588 and 910 crimes against reputation, respectively—a meaningful number considering the reluctance of courts to take on more work.

The frequency of these crimes seems to have remained steady or increased slightly in the following decade. Table 6 shows the number of cases recorded in Mexico City police stations, and it does not include cases of ultrajes. Although the numbers on average (42.55) are lower than

TABLE 6. Accused of Injurias, Calumnia and Difamación in Mexico City
Police Stations, 1885–1895

Year	Total	Men	Women	Total All Offenses	As % of All Offenses
1885	52	25	27	32,893	0.16
1886	18	9	9	35,421	0.05
1887	15	7	8	34,972	0.04
1888	27	20	7	39,542	0.07
1889	28	18	10	44,377	0.06
1890	23	17	6	44,074	0.05
1891	33	24	9	47,708	0.07
1892	44	36	8	49,577	0.09
1893	64	42	22	43,684	0.15
1894	71	44	27	37,798	0.19
1895	93	42	51	38,577	0.24

Source: Antonio Peñafiel, *Anuario estadístico de la República Mexicana 1896* (Mexico City: Secretaría de Fomento, 1897).

the average total of injurias, calumnia, and difamación for the previous period (163, from table 5), one must keep in mind that they do not include other populations within the Federal District and do not count cases in which complaints went directly to the Ministerio Público, skirting the police—a path that many victims chose to take. The percentage of crimes against reputation here is much lower than that shown in the previous table because police stations dealt with an enormous number of offenders against urban ordinances, such as vagrants, drunkards, and prostitutes. It indicates, nevertheless, an increase in the last three years of the series.

Data on injurias, the category that was recorded most consistently in published statistics during this period, show an increase in the number of cases until the end of the nineteenth century and a decrease during the last years of the Porfiriato (figure 21). Changes in the criteria used to define the indicted explain the sudden variation after 1900, but the line for people sentenced is more stable, suggesting there was no such radical change in 1900. Qualitative evidence and legislation further imply that there was no sea change in attitudes and practices regarding these crimes, and it would be difficult to establish a steady decrease afterward. Twentieth-century published statistics usually do not record

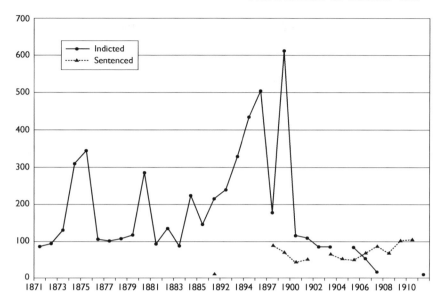

21. Indicted and Sentenced for Injuria, Federal District, 1871–1911.

cases of injurias. In the three years for which numbers are available (1922 to 1924, not included in the figure) injurias constitute a significant 4 percent of all indictments in the Federal District.[35]

In sum: conflicts over honor became the usual fare of police and criminal court work starting with their systematic definition in the Penal Code of 1871. There were peaks of activity in the mid-1870s and early 1880s, and thereafter a steady increase until the turn of the century. Even then, and probably afterward, the frequency of these cases was not negligible, considering that most crimes against reputation resulted from the action of victims rather than the initiative of the state and, as noted, had a high cost in terms of time and money.

Against strong odds, a growing number of people from diverse backgrounds availed themselves of the penal legislation to vindicate their honor. This might come as a surprise if one read elite discourse about honor too literally, but it becomes plausible if one defines more broadly the public sphere in which opinion exercised its tyranny. Courts were but one forum among several in which disagreements and negotiations over individual and collective honor played out. Judicial records are the tip of the iceberg of the contentious everyday life of urban dwellers: conflict was not the exception in everyday interactions but the norm.

The Words and Goods in Dispute

The diversity of actors arguing about reputation echoed the complexity of their vocabulary. Judicial and other everyday life records yield a dizzying variety of signs that could be interpreted as offensive, in an equally diverse number of contexts and media. Rather than being anchored in one definition of honor (which the previous chapter extracted from legal discourse), these records fall inside the porous boundaries of a vague semantic field. Meanings in this field shift according to the audience and to the social capital at stake. Popular practices and words concerning honor offer in this regard an illuminating contrast with the rigid notions embraced by public men. José Arteaga, a scribe by trade, pointed to those vague boundaries when he accused Luisa Contreras not of a specific charge, but of publishing "a horrible web of insults and ultrajes" that impugned him; if anything characterized her words it was their ability to "excite the least susceptible man."[36]

Arteaga knew that the semantic field of honor had a topography of feelings. It was an offensive "web" of accusations and counteraccusations that eventually impelled actors to press charges. In doing so, however, they accepted rules that required them to defend their reputation through rational and nonviolent means, thus making possible the survival of testimonies. It is not surprising, therefore, to hear victims of abuse by authorities demand self-control from those in power. Manuel María Romero denounced the arbitrary acts of authority that landed him in prison, arguing that "the one who acts without the guidance of reason, that is, the one who cannot govern himself, can hardly govern others."[37] Among the powerful, according to the schoolteacher Antonio Rodríguez, emotions lead to abuses, in his case "an outburst of pride . . . and ill-conceived arrogance" by the president of the Tlalpan city council.[38] Yet self-control was not expected only of persons of authority, nor was it a sign of submission among the less powerful. Victims of insultos and difamación underlined their restraint when faced with abuse: despite her limited education and poverty, the market seller María Bonilla "endured with great prudence" the insults from Paula Altamirano.[39] Such control of one's own indignation explains the absence of violence in most of the cases examined here.

The emotional dimension of disputes, however, was inevitable, and actors incorporated feelings into their arguments. For victims, most of whom lacked the education that allowed men like Salvador Díaz Mirón and Justo Sierra to sublimate rage into poetry, the expression of emotional struggle was nevertheless a dramatic argument that alluded to psychology and illness. In earlier chapters we observed how journalists and politicians succumbed to emotions when their self-esteem was attacked by insults or rumors. This was to be expected since honor was as much an external function of publicity as it was an internal product of conscience and sentiment. Explaining their recourse to penal protection, victims referred to a force beyond their control. It was not simply the often-invoked conscience and the tyranny of opinion but, in the words of the imperialist general Manuel Noriega, "another voice, more sacred, that of God himself, that tells me to take care of my good name."[40] The prosecutor José Olmedo y Lama asked for the acquittal of General Alonso Flores in 1878, arguing that "he whose acts are impelled by an irresistible, superior force is not responsible because he did not have the will to choose between action and inaction; he who is first insulted is no longer his own master, his physiological state is altered, blood flows to his brain, his nervous system is overexcited and impels him to execute an action that is truly unconscious."[41] The paradoxical use of the category of "unconscious" here was probably meant to sound scientific, yet Olmedo y Lama's physical description of rage echoed traditional beliefs about the links between moral suffering and illness.[42] While such feelings were nicely articulated by educated men like Olmedo y Lama and Noriega, people from all walks of life shared them: from established merchants and bureaucrats worrying about their credit or authority to working-class women hurt in their *amor propio* (self-esteem) or their *honra*. And worry they did: María Antonia Torres fell ill upon hearing neighbors hurl insults at her daughter, yet managed to get out of bed and press charges against them. She felt "acute pains in her stomach," and the judge who first heard the case was so alarmed that he sent the case to a higher court in Iztacalco, arguing that "because of the sorrow [*muina*] they had given Ms. Doña tonchi [*sic*] she is in the throes of agony, and I therefore send her case to you lest she die."[43] Physical pain was an eloquent way of saying that a person's self-esteem had been wounded.

Outrage might be tangible, but it was not enough to prove a crime had been committed. Amor propio referred to a subjective sensibility that offered no objective means of measuring the wound. José M. Gil y Boizán argued that the accusation of slander against him was too vague since "in the generic scale of the offense there is a long specific gradation . . . whose extension might be greater or smaller according to the susceptibility of the wounded person."[44] Victims found firmer ground for their claims in the web of communications involving real audiences that gave meaning to words and gestures: passersby in the street, students in the classroom, curious readers of the press.[45] Yet communications did not need to be public or verbal to be criminal. A furtive look or a gesture was enough to justify a complaint: "making a violin with the hand" was a common gesture; a stare coming from "an irate visage" could also be interpreted as an insult, the same as sarcastic comments in private letters.[46] Third parties might find subtle signals difficult to perceive, but few doubted that the "fire in a look" could trigger serious disputes.[47]

Words, however, were the most dangerous form of communication. Almost any dialogue, however proper at the outset, contained the possibility of conflict. Using a common expression, witnesses described suspects and victims "quienes se habían hecho de razones" (roughly, "who had availed themselves of arguments"). *Razones* or *cuestiones* degenerated into fighting exchanges, as if words had the will to engage in conflict.[48] The intensity and directness of some verbal attacks left no doubts as to their meaning, as when Rafaela González said about Concepción González, "There goes that cuckolded tortilla maker, daughter of a fucked man, disgraceful whore, vomit-face." The use of the third person sounded ironic but was part of the insult, as it addressed the street audience.[49] Victims' decision to respond was inevitable after such words. If their adversary in Sinaloan politics, the *licenciado* Eustaquio Buelna, "had used less virulent and racy language" against them, Antonio T. Izábal and Francisco F. Izábal would not have responded publicly to his assertions; but now, having been called "ignorant, rude, insolent, disrespectful," they were forced to go on the offensive, even if they could not match "the flowers of his eloquence."[50] Language thus offered an apparently simple way to tell what was offensive. Carlos Díaz Infante proposed that attacks against reputation which did not "use insulting expressions, demeaning terms or invective" be defined as difamación or calumnias, leaving injurias to cover all other utterances.[51] Yet, as noted, victims tended to press charges for difamación, as the borders between accusation and invective, between insult and factual claim, were never clear. Adjectives like "coward" implied a lack of action that was more dishonorable than any action defined as criminal by the law.

The offensive quality of utterances was not always signaled by an excess of language, as in Rafaela González's tirade, but sometimes by its indirect quality. Allusions could be more hurtful than plain insults when their understated tone deferred to a common audience capable of connecting the dots. The more cryptic the statement, in those cases, the greater the knowledge about the victim's ill reputation assumed in the audience. Literary depictions of elites' disputes over honor, however, missed these nuances and stressed the grave consequences of bald words like "treason," "the cruelest insult a man can receive."[52] Good as they were for dramatic effect, such situations ignore the complexity of the semantic field of honor. The romantic novels of Juan Antonio Mateos, the source of the example above, did not capture the equivocal and sometimes furtive gestures exchanged amid theater crowds that, for characters in Emile Zola's *Nana*, subtly communicated opinions about reputations. Although Mexican writers like Mateos, Federico Gamboa, and Heriberto Frías admired Zola, their characters were rarely defined by ambiguity; more often they had either a perfect sense of honor or none at all.[53]

Records of conflicts show that the dangers of irony, by contrast, were present in everyday exchanges. Victims did not have to enjoy wealth or status in order to be sensitive to allusions or to "a smile poisoned by irony."[54] Petra Maldonado de Valdez accused Eleodoro Zuñiga of insultos and difamación as a result of a conflict that began to escalate one day when she asked Zuñiga to return a gun that belonged to her husband; Zuñiga responded that "he had two pistols, so which one did she want."[55] Though framed as a humorous double entendre, the statement forced Maldonado to respond because it implied her availability for extramarital affairs. The problem with irony is that it required an audience in order to be deciphered. For Licenciado Francisco Llamas Noriega, even calling a woman "beata" (sanctimonious) could be offensive since "the circumstance of a word or an act to be insulting depends in large degree on opinion, on customs, on social beliefs. It wounds reputation and *fama* whatever the world . . . understands and decides has [been] wounded . . . according to the contemporary ideas that make for the common doctrine." Noriega interpreted "beata" according to the word's "ironic definition given by the Dictionary of the Spanish Language."[56] His point, ultimately, was that the audience decided what was offensive on the basis of its relationship with the actors. When offenders used irony, victims had to respond all the more rapidly because the disguised insult suggested their inability to see what the rest of the audience could. In case of doubt, it was better to err on the side of interpretive caution: the licenciados Juan B. Alaman and Tomás Noriega demanded the intervention of a judge to require Joaquín Trejo to explain the meaning of sentences he uttered that explicitly reckoned their "honorabilidad" yet could involve "a hidden attack to honra and reputation."[57]

The public venue courts provided a way to uncover the meaning of words. Trials and interrogations, however, made conflicts and accusations more public, turning irony into sarcasm. Actors were aware of this, yet still saw publicity as a way to restore reputation. In some cases, the informal or legal arrangement of the case involved the publication of a satisfactory explanation of the meaning of words; in others, the victim directly addressed the public to put all the facts on the table. Juan Potts published a pamphlet, like many others, "to the public" after Federico Ferrugia Manly's failure to publish the explanation he had promised. The pamphlet transcribed the judicial proceedings in the case, so "society will judge on which side reason lay"—including the accusation that Potts had poisoned his brother for money.[58] I described earlier the importance of publicity to elite men, but evidence from everyday crimes against reputation shows that even women of the lower classes saw in judicial venues an option to direct the interpretations of the public. María Guillen brought charges against Cayetano Tovar because he published a paragraph in the *Monitor del Pueblo* in which he claimed that Guillen was a "heartless mother" who mistreated her children, engaged in scandalous behavior, and constantly threatened neighbors at her tenement. Tovar, who was arrested, declared that he published the paragraph "in agreement with his neighbors" in order to put pressure on the landlord to evict Guillen. She, on the other hand, claimed that the publication had been part of continuing verbal and physical attacks against her. Tovar had told Guillen's son "that she was a clandestine whore [and] that he was going to put her in the newspapers so she would be shamed." She dropped the charges a few days later "since Cayetano Tovar offers her in the presence of judicial authorities the publication of a text in which he will express that nothing he had put in the newspaper was true . . . and will also withdraw the insults he rained upon her," promising also to pay the costs of the case.[59] However embarrassing, debates and explanations in the controlled publicity of judicial courts could dispel the threat of ironic words.

But more than words were at play. Cases of injuria, difamación, and calumnia in criminal courts reveal the great diversity of goods and relations associated with the defense of honor. A look at words only, direct or ironic, would fail to explain why some people went to court to denounce crimes against reputation and others did not. By identifying the material and symbolic goods threatened by the exchanges cited above one can explain why socially diverse actors availed themselves of judicial protection. Social capital is useful here as a broad category that recognizes the links between cultural and material resources in mobilizing support. But what specific historically and locally contingent realities were referred to by insults and defamations?

Fama pública was the personal attribute most commonly mentioned by those involved in these cases because it was the one that could be assessed most objectively by legal authorities. From the schoolteacher attacked in front of his students to the woman accused by her neighbors, fama pública was something that could be destroyed and had to be defended as a personal possession. The category combined the authority of legal codes and precedents with public opinion's power over daily life. Judges cited fama pública as relevant evidence that could reinforce other forms of proof at the time of sentencing.[60] Having the fama pública of a criminal was not in itself a crime, according to the Penal Code, yet police sometimes used emergency legislation issued during the República Restaurada in order to arrest those who had such a reputation. Providing evidence of fama pública, suspects like Antonia Moya gave the judge a letter signed by her neighbors supporting her claim to be "honest, of good behavior, and peaceful," while others simply cited common knowledge about their morality or political leanings.[61] Fama pública was in turn also a product of trials, a good that victims or suspects could recover after a favorable sentence. Cirilo Montes, president of the Tepeyanco City Council was found guilty of disobeying authorities in 1876, but the sentence also stated that he had already served the penalty he deserved while waiting nine days for the ruling, adding that the outcome "has in no way damaged his fama and reputation."[62]

Fama pública forced actors in judicial settings to grapple with the difficult task of establishing objective knowledge about public opinion. There were no strict trial rules in this regard. The public defender Agustín Arroyo de Anda presented clippings from Mexican and French newspapers as proof of Jorge Carmona's fama pública as the perpetrator of the homicide of Manuel Bolado.[63] However defined in juridical discourse, the measure of fama pública's objectivity was the good reputation of its sources. In a press case about anonymous pasquinades in Texcoco, the defense attorney Manuel Jiménez argued that "the vague statements by six witnesses, which have erroneously been passed as fama pública," could not be considered sufficient to indict Cruz Balcázar, who could cite his own "buena fama." Jiménez added that respected authors admitted fama pública in civil cases, but criminal trials had higher standards of evidence. Fama pública, he continued, had to come from "definite persons, serious, honest, trustworthy and disinterested, [and] should not be considered [if it] comes from malevolent, suspicious, and interested persons."[64] Antonio Díaz Soto y Gama, then a law student, recommended a proactive approach: "Go to the testimony of his contemporaries and countrymen."[65] The results were statements about actors' "genius" or "customs"—public opinion's knowledge about their behavior and character.[66] One rule was general: to be objectively assessed, fama pública had to preexist the case and be an intrinsic attribute of actors: "uniform, constant, perpetual and incontrovertible so that a fama cannot be destroyed by another fama."[67]

Beneath judicial fact-finding, however, fama pública was fickle and could be conveyed and changed in subtle ways. Here the evidence is less direct but still suggestive: an article in a newspaper in Orizaba revealing the work of "one so-called" Sesma as brothels inspector; Tomasa Núñez knocking at Luis Esquivel's and Antonio Campos's door and calling them cuckolds; Gregorio Velasco giving "malas ausencias" (literally, "bad absences"; probably "bad-mouthing behind his back") of Claudio Miranda by declaring in a store that he suspected him of being a thief.[68] Fama pública could deteriorate rapidly if not actively protected, with serious impact on social standing and leaving no option but to respond. Antonio Quirós told Rafael Chousal, Porfirio Díaz's secretary, that "I think everything is lost for me" if gossip caused Chousal to "abandon or forsake me."[69] While the exchange between Quirós and Chousal was part of the networks of patronage that defined Porfirian rule, fama pública could also hurt professional reputations and expose individuals to legal attacks.[70]

The notion of credit, closely related to that of fama pública, was a more tangible expression of the material importance of honor. The connection between foreign credit and national honor was the central point of contention in the debates about the deuda inglesa (see chapter 3). Credit was the key to Spencer's theories about reputation and capitalist progress (see chapter 5). According to the Italian jurist Francesco Carrara, often cited by Mexican lawyers, there were three components of honor: the feeling of one own's dignity, the good opinion among others about one, and "the inherent power of a good reputation to provide certain *material advantages*." Crimes against honor undermined this "power" when they resulted in a loss of credit.[71] From merchants and professionals to bakers and pulque sellers, a stained reputation had a price, even if difficult to quantify; a bankrupt French citizen claimed that "my honra and reputation . . . are the only invaluable goods I possess."[72]

Commercial reputations were disputed in a broad diversity of media, from newspapers and trials to letters and hearsay. Francisco García, the owner of a bakery, brought a complaint against an article in *El Monitor Republicano* concerning his tax payments. Two *pulquería* owners squabbled about reputations and their impact on their business. José Juárez, accused of forging a note, interpreted an accusation in front of civil courts as a criminal attempt to hurt his reputation, causing him "damages of great cost" vis-à-vis other lenders.[73] Information easily crossed from the written to the oral realm. Manuel Posada accused Andrés Gómez of difamación because of a letter that indirectly referred to the rent owed for some lands, prompting a third party to invite Posada to "clarify this business so your reputation will not suffer."[74] Letters inspiring rumors could come from as far away as Paris or Ciudad del Carmen, Campeche. The most urgent response was required when patrons were the audience. Francisco Giles accused Rosa Rivera of defamation and obtained a retraction of her statement, made in front of his wine store customers, that "[Giles's] house was a thieves' den . . . and that she would say so loudly and quietly so whoever did not know it would be informed about it." Giles claimed that Rivera, "besides exposing me to public discredit and hurting me commercially, unjustly attacks my well-established reputation, and that of my family and dependents."[75] But discredit also could come from "deplorable family dissent."[76]

The spread of personal information was justified as the public's need of to know the financial status of debtors, "so that nobody claims ignorance."[77] Some victims could be so sensitive as to sue for difamación because of publication of the fact that they had borrowed money. Eugenio de Saint Laurent brought such a suit, but the judge ruled there was no crime since the information published by *Le Petit Galoir* included the fact that he had paid off his debt. Recognizing the complainant's legitimate concern, however, the judge added, "It can never be said that someone is dishonored or discredited, or is exposed to disdain when, pressed by some emergency, he requests from some of his friends a loan, that he then pays religiously."[78]

As Porfirian stability encouraged investment and business involving Mexicans and foreigners, the association between honor and credit became more complex and strong, not a simple nationalist claim or a purely personal attribute. The association was already present in a decision made by a press jury in 1879 against a French company that sued *Le Trait d'Union*, published in Mexico, for an article that "attacks the commercial reputation of our firm" and its honra, causing discredit. The jury dismissed the charges, opining that the publication "contains no attack against private life, morality or public order."[79] Economic development, for positivist thinkers, meant a new emphasis on the economic rationality of actors, opposed in Mexico to the feudal mentality of *hacendados* and the laziness of Indians. This translated into an effort to separate credit from honor. In 1895, Emilio Rabasa wrote that moral persons (such as companies) did not have reputations and therefore could not sue for defamation, as an individual merchant could. "Honra and credit," stated Rabasa, "are entirely independent; social contempt is declared against one who does not have honra, but not against the one who lacks commercial credit." The hypothetical example he offered deliberately contrasted with the romantic notions of integrity held by journalists and employees (see chapter 2) and criticized by Rabasa the novelist: "An honest man, very honorable, very wealthy in personal gifts (reputation), if he does not have properties and lives off the little income from his personal work, will not have credit in the banks or commerce. By contrast, a man despised by everyone; a complacent husband, without any honra, if he has strong capital and has always fulfilled his financial commitments, will have great commercial credit."[80] Although correct from the commercial point of view, Rabasa's reasoning could not have satisfied the victims who continued to present complaints against slanderers on the assumption that their personal reputation had a direct bearing on their success in business, and vice versa.

Everyday Relations and the Centrality of Women

Credit and fama pública were practical expressions of modern ideas about honor as a juridical good (see chapter 5). An objective definition of honor was useful as Porfirian rule established discipline over the political class and guaranteed its commitment to capitalist development. Neither credit nor *fama pública*, however, set the limits of the semantic field of honor as it emerged from everyday conflicts, where the reach and power of public opinion shifted according to the context and "the contemporary ideas that make for the common doctrine." In other words, the social capital that actors protected was not a stable identity or a measurable quantity, as judicial authorities hoped it would be, but consisted of social relations and individual agency. Families held it as much as individuals and firms. Thus it was constantly and publicly evaluated, challenged, and defended in the form of relationships.[81]

Victims could be suspects' neighbors, relatives, or spouses, and offensive statements could refer to members of the family or to friends or customers as much as to victims' own behavior. Thus, Rosa Rivero calling Francisco Giles's store "a thieves' den" was implicitly an accusation against his patrons, "some peons who were there."[82] If in these cases reputation and business seemed obviously linked, in others the actors are related by family ties. Conflict in these cases involved a challenge to the hierarchies or intrinsic harmony of those ties. Francisco Repetto told his sister-in-law Ana E. Nieves de Repetto his formal accusation was necessary so "you listen to me not as a relative but with the necessary equity."[83]

Relations were also built on spatial proximity, either in residences or in other spaces of everyday life. When neighbors were involved the shared use of space itself was often the point of contention. Antonia Moya verbally abused Manuel Córdova because he cut the clothesline where she hung her laundry; he said it prevented him and other neighbors from using the building's stairs. Prison was another space in which the combination of residence, work, and sociability caused tensions articulated in terms of the defense of honor.[84] Tenement buildings, called *vecindades* in Mexico City, created the conditions for disputes because their layout was the haphazard product of the partition of old buildings and because their absentee landlords were reluctant to get involved in tenants' disputes. Coexistence generated small conflicts that escalated over time and involved multiple relationships. Rafaela Trujillo and Soledad Heredia exchanged insults and blows after they punished each other's dogs. Class difference was an underlying factor in this case: Trujillo had decided, before the dog incident, "not to be her [Heredia's] friend because it was not convenient for her education and for her daughters."[85] Yet they had to live together, generating the long-standing tensions that culminated in criminal accusations. Tensions between status and intimacy were highly discernible in disputes involving employers and their domestic workers. In their family, work, and residency, domestic workers could be challenged but also protected by their employers. Just like dogs, children, customers, and construction workers, domestic employees were subject to others' control over their private spaces and therefore over their status.[86] Ricardo Domínguez fired M. Refugio Rodríguez because she got drunk in public, to which she countered, in court, that she had not received her full pay and that Domínguez and her sister slept together "as if they were husband and wife" and made suspicious noises at night.[87] Regardless of the truth of her claims, Domínguez's accusation of defamation against Rodríguez demonstrated his precarious control over intimacy.

Domestic and common spaces, which actors construed, respectively, as private and public realms, were thinly separated, and several disputes about injurias were but negotiations over that largely symbolic separation. Loreto Jiménez was at home with her son Jacinto Rocha when her "neighbor and sister-in-law," Macedonia Suárez, "while passing in front of [her] door, said here they are these sons of a bitch cuckolds, damned be the soul that delivered them." Rocha came out of the house and demanded that Hermenegildo Suárez control her sister. Hermenegildo, in turn, tried to pick a fight with Rocha, but he went back inside his home and was not allowed to leave by his mother. Women's refusal to engage in violence (and men's sequestering themselves behind doors shut by women) caused these cases to turn up among those for crimes against reputation rather than amid battery cases in which the use of violence became the object of judicial inquiry.[88] Accusations in crimes against reputation represented efforts to restore (or create) a separation between intimacy and public utterances about reputation. For most inhabitants of Mexico City and other growing cities at the end of the nineteenth century, that separation was a luxury they could defend only in the theoretical neutrality of courts. The separation was particularly difficult for Jiménez, Rocha, and the brothers Suárez because they were united by kinship but estranged by proximity.

Reputation was also negotiated in public spaces in which encounters seemed a product of chance. As on stairs and patios, in streets and cafes actors were acutely conscious of the audiences that might hear negative statements. However fleeting and formed around seemingly random exchanges, these audiences were able to broadcast opinion. José Rodríguez

Sámano, for example, went to great lengths to find out who initiated a rumor about his failure to pay a group of musicians. Witnesses declared they heard the complaints at the corner of the Teatro Ocampo, in downtown Morelia, as they were leaving Mass. Other cases started with brief meetings at a corner of the town's plaza or at the market while buying *romeritos* (suadeda torreyana) on Holy Friday. These situations triggered gossip or verbal battles not so much because they embodied longstanding relations but because those places were consequential in the definition of personal reputations. Criminal charges expressed actors' competence to read the diverse signs that influenced public opinion and their ability to respond quickly to those signs. A paragraph in a French newspaper was of no concern to most of its readers but became a headache for Ignacio Manuel Altamirano when Gustavo Baz read it aloud at the Cafe Tortoni in Paris in front of Baron Gustave Gostkowsky of Mexico and some French journalists and friends. Baz explained that the conversation had been in Spanish so no one else could understand it, but Altamirano and his friends were so incensed that one of them came close to beating Baz later at another bar. Even chance encounters between passing strangers were of consequence.[89] However fleeting and anonymous the situation, high or low the actors, these moments in public spaces were laden with significance. A swift response to defamation or insults was recognition that there were no chance encounters really and that opinion exercised its tyranny anywhere audiences gathered.

The diversity of relationships and spaces at play in these conflicts nevertheless reveals unexpected gender and class regularities. The evidence from everyday conflicts over honor would not truly balance the elite-centered analysis of earlier chapters if one did not look closely at the central role of women in disputes regarding reputation in court, where they appear often as victims or suspects. They represent 39.32 percent of those arrested for injurias, difamación, and calumnias in 1885–95 (see table 6), 43.50 percent of those indicted in 1898, and 30.23 percent in 1900 (see table 4). These percentages depart from those of all other offenses, in which women usually constituted about a fifth of the accused. Explaining the greater frequency of female participation sheds light on the uses of reputation across class divides.

The behavior of men and women in theses cases was surprisingly similar. Women actively engaged in public disputes over their own honor and that of their families without the need of men's intervention, and in some cases challenging it. In doing so, they struggled to achieve greater visibility in court and in other zones of the public sphere. Wives could speak in court in the name of their husbands too: the wife of the exiled imperialist minister Manuel Siliceo came forward to defend him in court in a case in 1868, introducing herself to the judge as "I, his unhappy wife, by nature and law the defender of his honra."[90] Ana Lidia García Peña found that nineteenth-century court disputes among spouses in Mexico City provided the opportunity for women to resist male domination under the guise of individualism. That outspoken role was acknowledged by judges, who gave women severe sentences, as many complainants saw the punishment of female offenders as the restoration of their reputation: after her sister-in-law María Antonia Viveros was sentenced to six months in prison, María Socorro Zavala claimed to have "obtained vindication before society and my husband for the serious ultraje that Viberos inflicted on her."[91]

Like men, women accused of crimes against reputation came from diverse social backgrounds, including the lowest strata of Porfirian hierarchy. Market sellers could accuse each other of injurias after exchanges like the one between Paula Altamirano and María Bonilla—in which Altamirano said, "Here comes the *soldadera* [soldier's companion], cuckolded whore who is entangled with her compadre."[92] Like those of men, the voices of women carried weight in public opinion: the comments Rosa Rivera made in Francisco Giles's wine store could hurt his business. And as much as men, women could resist the intervention of authorities: while a policeman was able to take Rivera to the police station, other female suspects flatly refused to appear in front of judicial authorities. Laura Altamirano simply walked out of court, to the judge's astonishment.[93]

Received interpretive models still define honor, above all, by men's control over their spouses. Paradoxically, these theses go together with the notion that there were different conceptions of honor for men and women: male honor equals control over women and publicity, and female honor is domestic silence and chastity. As noted in the introduction, these explanations derive from the classic Mediterranean notion of honor formulated by anthropologists like Julian Pitt-Rivers and adopted by many historians in Latin America. The model's essential variable is power, positing a stark sexual distinction in terms of the ability to control the rules of the game. The problem is that such structural inequality of power makes it difficult to understand the historicity of both resistance and domination. Anthropologists are increasingly critical of such fixed dichotomies, and recent ethnographic work has complicated the equation, making gender difference less determining and actors' use of normative models more flexible.[94] The idea of a woman's honestidad had clearer gender implications than honor or honra. While men were *honestos* in regard to their trade or business, *mujeres honestas* had in *putas* (whores) an all-encompassing opposite. But language can create a deceiving sense of order. If one looks at the actual circumstances under which male and female actors went to court for crimes against their reputation, a strictly gendered view of honor (male integrity versus female chastity) is not enough to explain the willingness of poor women to seek legal remedy. Fidelity was indeed a frequent theme in disputes involving women, but not one that left women speechless and passive.

The evidence from Porfirian Mexico is best understood, and the Mediterranean model best corrected, if one keeps in mind the interconnections between class and gender difference. Judicial sources show that women, in their disputes, were more likely than men to bring class difference into sharper focus by exhibiting the precarious boundaries of the private in everyday life. The strong presence of women in disputes was unmistakable in the domestic space of home or tenement, where men played a subordinate role or were absent altogether. Even in cases in which men were involved, women spoke their minds and did not refrain from uttering offensive remarks or complaints against men, as in the case of the neighbors and sisters-in-law Loreto Jiménez and Macedonia Suárez. Men could acquire a more visible role as conflicts moved from domestic spaces into court: in one case the husband of the victim pressed charges, even though he had not been an actor in the dispute. This might have been a strategy to counteract the limits traditionally imposed on women's autonomy in the judicial realm. Bringing charges against another woman who had insulted her, Jesús Venegas de Goya showed the judge the following note signed by her husband: "I authorize you to seek vindication in criminal court . . . so your honor remains in good standing."[95] Men's belated arrival at trials in which women were the main actors was also a way for men to make clear that fights among or with women were not subordinate or parallel to male disputes. This was obvious in cases resolved after the male suspect offered explanations directly to the victim's husband.[96] In the eyes of the public, autonomous, quarrelsome women were an indication of an absence of masculine control over the household—regardless of the precarious divide between public and private dictated by material conditions in lower-class residential areas.

Exhibiting intimacy in court characterized lower-class women's uses of honor. They worried men because their visibility in criminal cases about reputation contrasted with the discretion expected from upper-class women. The female struggle to have a public voice in the negotiations of reputation is difficult to find in press accounts, parliamentary debates, and other male-dominated records. Condescending caballerosidad and the rituals of dueling further hindered women's intervention in elite conflicts. Literary sources echo these biases: they tend to erase women as autonomous actors from scenes of sociability by depicting them, instead, as passive objects of reference for male disputes. In Juan Antonio Mateos's play about rebellious students, one character defines his daughter's pregnancy as a threat to his honor. Yet he vows revenge against the seducer in such a way that no one would know her role: "I will make up something to cleanse my offense without your name appearing or getting involved," he tells her.[97] A similar reluctance to name a woman appeared in elite men's testimonies about duels (see chapter 7). Some judicial evidence suggests, however, that elite women could bring private disputes to court and invite publicity and that, like elite men, they could respond to assertions made in the press and at the theater.[98] In general terms, however, the available judicial record concerning women's reputation inverts that of men: we know more about female working-class actors than about their elite counterparts.

The subtle differences between men and women regarding honor begin to be discernible. One difference that emerges markedly from the evidence is that the language of disputes tended to refer, in the cases involving women, to sexual propriety. Most accusations exchanged between women alluded to sexual morality—"syphilitic whore, daughter of a bitch," Macedonia Suárez called Loreto Jiménez. Yet such gendered language often appeared in disputes that had nothing to do with sex, even as they may have involved relations with men. The neighbors of María Guillen called her a "clandestine whore" when fights took place in the vecindad, but in the newspaper they accused her of beating her son.[99] Puta was the most common word, yet the actual practice of prostitution was never conclusively demonstrated. It seems more useful to understand puta (and cognates like *chingada*, *cuzca*, *fruta*) in a broader sense, as statements about a woman's duplicitous relationship with neighbors, family, and men. "Syphilitic whore" was doubly clear in this regard because it referred to the venereal diseases that made prostitutes a perceived threat to men. Criminal complaints seemed less interested about the factual truth behind such words than about their potential effect in public: María García "feels gravely offended in her reputation" because Ricardo Ruiz Esparza called her puta in front of her husband.[100]

Even though women's reputation was not based solely on sexual behavior, they had to tread carefully across a semantic field of honor charged with sex. M. Concepción Silva was a puta, claimed a neighbor, because she was carrying the baby of a man who was not her husband. Silva countered that her marriage was legal, acknowledging that the status of her marital life, rather than the pregnancy, was really the issue. She had to be explicit because such defamations could undermine the legitimacy of lower-class partnerships, whose legal status was suspect anyway. María Vazquez lamented that similar accusations had "produced in the heart of my husband the poisonous reptile of jealousy," and he "has felt the impulse to punish me with rigor."[101] Men's infidelity was one form of punishment—even though adultery was rarely the content of calumnia against them. The female adjective cabrona, which I have translated as cuckold, by contrast, was a very frequent addition to offensive tirades against women. The cost of a damaged reputation could be a deteriorated relationship with a spouse, as María Vázquez feared, but also the loss of control over the domestic realm. Soledad Heredia called Rafaela Trujillo an "old alcahueta [procurer] who offers her daughters to married men, panther of San Cosme."[102] Accusing a woman of being an alcahueta framed her relation with her children in terms of prostitution and suggested her failure as a mother.

This was serious defamation, and, like men, women could respond violently. Heredia's harangue ended in a fight in front of several neighbors, who eventually had to summon a policeman. Judicial records of battery show that women were not above pummeling their antagonist with their hands. Rather than in mortal violence or knife wounds, however, their fights usually ended in one or both parties being "beaten and disheveled" but not seriously hurt.[103] It would be a mistake, however, to construe this relatively harmless violence as just a way of preventing "real" masculine violence. Men, after all, engaged on their own in the most elaborate dance of all to avoid violence: the duel and its informal equivalents. It may be, however, that women were as likely as men to seek vindication of their reputation through penal courts because they did not see violence as a useful alternative. Data from other contexts do suggest that violence was mostly a resource of men, one they often used against women.[104] If this is the case, lower-class women had a meaningful point in common with elite men: they used legitimate nonviolent methods to deal with conflict, even as they were highly concerned about public opinion. As in the case of elite men, a negative correlation between women's participation as suspects in cases of homicide and battery, on the one hand, and their involvement in crimes against reputation, on the other, explains their presence in the cases examined here. Class in combination with gender, in sum, might account more strongly than biological difference for the use of violence.

Conclusions

The disputes examined here present several stark diversities: of actors and their backgrounds, of situations in which conflicts emerged, of languages used to offend others, of goods at stake. This apparent dissonance contains several useful lessons for understanding elite disputes. One lesson concerns women's role. The cases examined show that women were active in criminal courts and that they used the discourse of honor to defend their autonomy both in the domestic and public realms. When women were offended by language that referred to sexual practices, they defended a social capital that was not based on those practices but on their relations with relatives and neighbors. Sex and, consequently, honestidad provided a language for talking about individuals' value as measured by their communities and for diminishing or defending that capital.

Another lesson concerns the porous borders of the semantic field of honor. Fama pública and credit were tangible expressions of social capital, but there were also less concrete relationships and spaces that had to be defended as part of a person's or a family's reputation—even if the word *honor* did not appear in all judicial records.

Finally, there is an important lesson about class and honor. The following pages suggest that, rather than moving down from elite attitudes to popular customs, a social analysis of honor in everyday life can productively focus on goods and languages found across social divides. Publicity was not just an instrument of journalists to amass social capital: it provided other, less famous actors with an avenue for vindication. In spite of judges' class bias, people of all backgronds were willing to undergo the expense and potential humiliation of going to court in order to defend their reputation. Even if not quite democratic, the court system was a legitimate enough venue for the resolution of disputes—and it affords a documentary glimpse of everyday life and of the workings of the public sphere in spaces often neglected by historians.

On the surface, class difference could be expressed as the distinction between public men, who were interested in politics and using the press, and the rest of the people, who were concerned about petty gossip and referred to penal authorities. If one digs deeper, however, one sees all actors balancing their self-esteem and reputation in the public sphere. Only the degree of completeness of the records distinguishes them, and even then working-class women seem to be better documented than well-to-do women. The evidence as a whole, however, proves the centrality of honor (as legal right, as perception of the self, as reputation) in the relationship between civil society and the state and in the construction of social capital in the public sphere. Such centrality could not have occurred if only the educated had valued honor. Therefore, one cannot understand people's appeal to the state for protection of their honor as an act of pure resistance: in embracing the rules of the discourse of honor, all had to assume their consequences too. The tyranny of opinion worried everyone.

CHAPTER 7

"One Does Not Talk to the Dead"

The Romero-Verástegui Affair and the Apogee
of Dueling in Mexico

On the afternoon of August 9, 1894, José Verástegui died on a field in the outskirts of Mexico City. Colonel Francisco Romero, who had shot the bullet that pierced Verástegui's broad chest, ran toward him and tried to say something. General Sóstenes Rocha, the field judge in the duel, told Romero that Verástegui was dead and "one does not talk to the dead." The phrase was a fitting corollary to the conflict: a duel was a matter of life and death, and a belated word of friendship meant nothing when honor had proven more important than life. The Verástegui–Romero encounter became the most famous duel in Mexico. It involved two public men close to the government and the wife of a third; it was openly discussed in the press, in the Chamber of Deputies, and in sensational jury audiences that lasted several days and resulted in Romero being sentenced to three years in prison.[1]

The case signaled the moment of dueling's greatest prestige but also the beginning of the end of that practice as a legitimate way of solving disputes among public men. The contrast with the duel between Santiago Sierra and Ireneo Paz (see chapter 2) was clear to contemporaries: whereas the encounter in 1880 had been the result of a press polemic, this one was triggered by a chance encounter at a soirée in a beautiful lady's home; privacy had not been a factor in the first but was embarrassingly exposed in the second; while the first had taken place in the years when Porfirio Díaz was beginning to cement his authority as president, the second ran counter to the discipline the caudillo imposed on the political elite; nobody had been punished in the first, but parliamentary and judicial debates swirling around the second and the sentence given Romero expressed broad rejection of a practice that undermined the decorum of decent society and denied the state's new responsibility to protect honor as a juridical good.

This was the anticlimactic end of an era. In the last decades of the nineteenth century, dueling had acquired new meanings for Mexican elites. Military men, politicians, and journalists fought duels, and codes of honor became guides for the behavior and speech of public men. Dueling demonstrated the Mexican upper classes' embrace of European progress: as in the United States, France, and Germany, in Mexico dueling coincided with greater concern about personal reputation in public settings.[2] At the same time, dueling revealed, perhaps better than any other cultural product, the contradictions of Mexican ruling elites' embrace of modern politics. They construed the duel as a prestigious gesture of modernization, yet they also used it to preserve hierarchies, as it expressed their privileged claims to respectability in a context in which honor was coming to be recognized as a right of all citizens.

Dueling was useful in the process of defining and consolidating a unified political elite since it gave evidence of the courage of men who had not taken part in any of the wars that covered men like Díaz and Rocha with laurels and demonstrated equality among public men. By establishing the honor of congressmen, public officials, military men, and journalists, dueling played a central role in setting up rules that excluded most people from public life. Despite the provisions of the Penal Code, duelists were seldom punished.

But things changed that afternoon in 1894. As legal practices and attitudes about reputation evolved and public life became more sedate, the propensity for violence of some well-known Porfirians, like Romero, came to be seen as an undesirable alternative to the legal protection of honor. Opting for a duel implied that honor was above the written law and, in some cases, above life itself—disturbing evidence of the tyranny of opinion.

Dueling and Modernity

For its apologists, dueling was inevitable because it was both a custom with deep historical roots and a modern solution that showed the affinities between Mexico and the most advanced countries in the world. Duels had been rare in Mexico before the República Restaurada, even though personal conflicts were not strange to public life. Situations that later in the century would have resulted in a challenge used to be solved behind closed doors. As late as the 1850s, even as dueling was already common in Europe, it was frowned upon by "opinion and customs" in Mexico.[3] But the triumph of liberalism brought new attitudes. By the early 1870s, Antonio Martínez de Castro stated that duels in the country were frequent. He believed punishment could prevent dueling and devoted a chapter of the Penal Code to it.[4] Diverse evidence, however, shows an increasing resort to dueling in the last decades of the century. Official statistics of criminality count thirty-two convictions for dueling between 1871 and 1885 in the Federal District—nineteen of them between 1880 and 1885.[5] After 1885, published statistics fail to list a single case, probably owing to prosecutors' reluctance to intervene. Other attempts to count duels, however, support the impression of increasing frequency in the last decades of the nineteenth century. In 1894, for example, the lawyer Manuel Lombardo cited newspaper reports of forty-three duels resulting in wounds or deaths since 1871.[6] Given the secretive nature of dueling and the benign neglect of authorities, it is not possible to establish how many cases are left out of these counts. Many were not reported in the press because, according to La Libertad in 1884, "Nowadays we journalists are used to the system of small duels in which no blood is shed."[7] Duels were "held repeatedly," in Rocha's view, and in 1894 he admitted to having participated as padrino (second, literally godfather) or juez de campo (field judge) in more than a hundred.[8] Angel Escudero's authoritative but hardly systematic El duelo en México, published in 1936, reviewed seventy-eight cases (table 7). In Escudero's account the years in which the most duels took place were 1892 (eight cases) and 1893 (seven)—although he might have been biased in favor of more recent cases in the capital. Duels were certainly few in comparison with other violent crimes, and duels in Mexico probably occurred less frequently, at least in absolute terms, than in France, Germany, and Italy.[9]

TABLE 7. Mexican duels according to Escudero

Date	Duels[a]
1850–1859	1
1860–1869	8
1870–1879	2
1880–1889	10
1890–1899	24
1900–1909	0
1910–1919	1
1920–1929	3
No date	29
Total	*78*

Source: Angel Escudero, *El duelo en México: Recopilación de los desafíos habidos en nuestra República, precedidos de la historia de la esgrima en México y de los duelos mas famosos verificados en el mundo desde los juicios de Dios hasta nuestros días, por el maestro de armas* (Mexico City: Mundial, 1936).

[a]Escudero listed duels celebrated in Mexico City (N = 69), in other Mexican cities (6), and in France (3)—the last being duels in which one Mexican had been involved.

Dueling in Mexico had historical resonance because it linked men like Romero and Verástegui to ancient traditions of the Nordic races of ancient Europe and, at the same time, demonstrated that the changes taking place in Mexican society were unmistakably modern. Rocha, for example, admitted that dueling was a "social disease" but nevertheless useful to honorable men in creating new friendships.[10] The practice of dueling in France could be interpreted, from Mexico, as evidence of the advance of "new freedoms" that inevitably generated disagreements and as an expression of a modern nation's obligation to continue breeding a "spirit of dignity" among its men.[11] Any attempt to eradicate dueling was therefore bound to fail, just as in other "civilized countries, because it opposed progress."[12]

Dueling was a novelty that claimed deep roots. "Few customs like these," argued a Spanish writer "can offer a nobler origin or a cleaner ancestry," as it came from the north with the Germanic invasions of the Roman empire.[13] It eventually lost the juridical value it enjoyed as an ordeal, and while Spanish laws banned it "opinion" kept it alive in Mexico and other Latin American countries.[14] For the few who opposed the practice that same long history could be told as one of repeated state prohibitions and punishment. Catholic authors condemned dueling as an aristocratic legacy that, in addition to being sinful, undermined authentic democracy. In 1869, José María Rodríguez, a physician and member of the Sociedad Católica, published a pamphlet against dueling. He defined it as one of "the perverted customs that human depravity has inherited from ancient times."[15]

Ancient origins were less relevant, both for critics and apologists, than the moment that defined dueling as a modern practice: the French Revolution, when dueling ceased to be the exclusive territory of the aristocracy. Part of the same liberal narrative that included freedom of the press, dueling was also a sign of progress akin to modern science. According to Romero, the practice no longer had a religious meaning: "Our century is more positivist than the Middle Ages. . . . We rather trust the sword."[16] In this liberal perspective, which seemed to imply a critique of romantic historicism, the Catholic Church's condemnation could only be construed as further proof of the progressive meaning of dueling.

Dueling cemented the historical and racial leadership of Mexican men of honor by confirming their fraternal links with rivals from other civilized countries. Duels between Mexicans and foreigners had a special interest during this period when the country was eager to attract culture, capital, and technology from abroad. Patriotism was the cause in some cases: a Mexican dueled a Spaniard who had failed to stand up during a performance of the Mexican national anthem; a similar reason prompted a duel in Paris involving a Mexican citizen. Ignacio Manuel Altamirano contemplated issuing a challenge as a way of dealing with *chantage* experts who tried to stain the honor of Mexico and its representatives in the French press. Most of the duels between Mexicans and foreigners, however, referred to points of personal honor, thus demonstrating that Mexicans could be international men of honor who shared a precise knowledge of the rules of dueling with their counterparts. Such conflicts were not xenophobic reactions but expressed Mexicans' cosmopolitanism.[17] Educated men in Mexico read about famous duels in newspapers, hired foreign fencing instructors, and held codes and famous cases from abroad to have the same relevance as their national counterparts. France had a considerable cultural influence, but merchants, bankers, and industrialists from Germany were also visible participants in the world of

Porfirian elites. Few among them could fail to notice a German student who "had returned from Heidelberg with two purple . . . knife wounds in his rosy face."[18]

The absence of dueling in England, the other modern nation par excellence, posed a problem for this genealogy. As usual, racial theories came to the rescue of inconsistent ideologies: Alfonso Láncaster Jones, defender of Rocha in the trial in 1895, argued that Mexican customs come from the "arrogant Spanish nobility [*hidalguía*] and the rough Aztec courage"; thus boys are trained from early on to fight and "stand up." "The Latin race," he added, was different from the English, "because of its temper, its susceptibility, its education, its atavisms, its customs, its ideals, and even its defects." Such disposition tied the Mexican nation to the honor of its leading men since "the legacy of the national character comes from the warriors and from Medieval knights; [and] the primitive spirit of the more cultivated and high classes was tempered, like the steel for combat, in jousts, tournaments, and *palenques*."[19]

Class, as usual, was more important than race. Although a few aristocrats appear in anecdotal evidence about Mexican duels, dueling was mainly part of a bourgeois claim to social respectability, a claim that was especially relevant in a fast-changing urban society such as that of Mexico City, where social hierarchies were no longer obviously expressed by ethnicity, demeanor, or titles of nobility. Arguing for the usefulness of dueling, Colonel Antonio Tovar gave an example of the situations and fears associated with the defense of dignity in the capital. "A gentleman," wrote Tovar, "goes to the theater in the pleasant company of his young, beautiful wife, whom he loves." As they are leaving, someone says, "*¡Me gusta!*" (meaning ambiguously both "I like her" and "I like it"). The gentleman has three options. He could engage in a fight on the spot, which would lead to a judicial process, a "social scandal, and the corresponding open-air comments." This option would expose the lady to the obligation of testifying in front of a judge and a court audience. "Is this morality?" asks Tovar. Alternatively, the gentleman could file a civil suit, but this would result only in a fine, and, continues Tovar, "Is this reparation?" Or he could challenge the scoundrel to a duel, which would be more discreet but legitimate enough to allow the gentleman to continue patronizing the theater and would make his wife "proud to have as a husband a man who possesses the necessary dignity and courage to make her respectable and respected." The answer, for Tovar, was obvious: the third choice was the dignified response to vulgarity.[20] Most challenges recorded in the sources were indeed prompted by an offense at a public function, such as the theater or a ball, places where the presence of women was important, even if they did not include people from diverse social classes. The pattern suggests the role of dueling in establishing a progressive respectability for the claims of patriarchal rights.[21]

A close look at the Romero-Verástegui case of 1894 shows that theory and history were not always sufficient to afford respectability and that dueling no longer guaranteed discretion. The duel was a transparent example of a public conflict caused by private relations between two men and a woman—too transparent, perhaps, for a society that valued decorum. That much can be gleaned from newspapers like the *Los Angeles Times*, which did not have to be so discreet as its counterparts in Mexico City, and by word-of-mouth accounts divulged in court statements. The conflict began in the house of Natalia Gutiérrez Zamora de Barajas, the beautiful wife of Juan Barajas. As he did every night, Francisco Romero approached the house to have dinner with the family, which had a quite intense social life. From the sidewalk, through a window, he overheard a conversation between Natalia Barajas and Licenciado José Verástegui; Verástegui was criticizing Romero. Romero entered the house and subtly signaled to both interlocutors that he was angry. The following day he sent a letter to Verástegui demanding that he explain his words. Verástegui destroyed the letter immediately after reading it, for fear it would be seen by his family, but pieces of a draft written by Romero were presented at trial. In the letter, Romero accused Verástegui of using his public office, as inspector del timbre (postmaster general), for "the triumph you have achieved in the erotic tournament"—implying that he had been able to gain Ms. Baraja's favor by offering her husband a job in the federal government.[22]

Romero denied that Barajas was the cause of the quarrel, but public opinion saw the opposite as the obvious state of affairs. Testimonies, including those of the Barajases, confirmed that they routinely welcomed male and female visitors into the relaxed environment of their home, and that Barajas was so beautiful that it was logical she would arouse "mad passions." Juan Barajas admitted that his wife and Romero had had "relations of intimacy" for two months and that she had a "boyish" but not a dishonorable character. Although the term "intimidad," meaning close friendship, had no sexual implications, the jury audience expressed sur-

22. The Barajases.
El Hijo del Ahuizote,
14 Oct. 1894, 1.

prise at the revelation, prompting Barajas to clarify that he was always present when Romero visited his wife. In her written statement, Natalia Barajas acknowledged that she liked to joke with Romero, sometimes incurring the disapproval of her husband, but stressed that "those relations never passed the limits of friendship." The prosecutor, however, advanced the thesis that she had caused the duel and described her character as being "not discreet or prudent at all," stressing that her house was always open for anyone to come in.[23] The statements the Barajases made during the process caused them to be sued for defamation, adding to their ridicule, as expressed in a published caricature titled "Marriage in Flight" (figure 22). Natalia Barajas's beauty and irresponsibility, Juan Barajas's lack of control over his household and his wife, Romero's jealousy, and Verástegui's shame before his family made it quite easy to explain the duel, in spite of everyone's reluctance to go on record about its cause.

The affair exhibited the blurred limits of what could be said in public. When the seconds for both duelists arranged the duel they agreed to keep its causes secret. This allowed the prosecutor to accuse Romero and the seconds of participating in a duel for dishonorable reasons, since only a challenge to defend the honor of a wife or a daughter was morally, if not legally, acceptable. The same argument was presented by Genaro García, the attorney for Verástegui's wife, who successfully sued Romero in order to obtain monetary restitution and to "defend the memory of her unfortunate husband shamefully disgraced by the same individual who took his life."[24] Gentlemen, however, were not expected to offer explanations. In the words of the Spanish author Enrique de Sierra Velenzuela, "Society not only sanctions the duel but demands it" when the conflict "stems from very grave offenses against honor which laws cannot repair, and which publicity would only turn into a new martyrdom for the offended; when the audacity of a seducer stains the name of an honest family; when the marital bed is trampled and vilified, or when the veil of a false friendship covers a vile adultery."[25]

Things were not so stark as Velenzuela's nightmarish description might suggest. Taking the actors in the Romero-Verástegui story at their word and looking at other cases, one might conclude that the common origin of disputes ending in duels was not adultery so much as duelists' concerns about their performance in heterosocial settings. It was not Juan Barajas who issued or accepted a challenge, after all, though he did acquire a reputation as a *cornudo* (cuckold) after the scandal, but two men who seemed to have less to lose. Their problem was not the woman herself but their control over public perceptions of their relationship with a woman.[26] In any case, caballerosidad (in this context, gentlemen's obligation not to acknowledge the involvement of a lady) sets an insurmountable limit to the historian's ability to confirm this hypothesis: silence condemned Natalia Barajas as much as it protected her matrimony.

Dueling Above the Law

A noble burden for men, dueling was the most vivid sign of opinion's tyranny. Even as honor was now construed as a legal right, its protection still could not be completely guaranteed by the state. Alfonso Láncaster Jones described the dilemma faced by men of honor who also thought of themselves as law-abiding citizens: "The written law tells us: if you fight a duel, even with all the solemnities and requirements that normalize the most loyal and chivalrous encounters, I will take away your liberty. Society tells us: if you do not fight a duel when in my concept you should do it, I will take away your honra, I will throw you out of my midst . . . with the lash of my ignominious disapproval."[27] The Verástegui-Romero trial was an example of this tension between law and mores. Duels had been illegal since 1871 because, as Antonio Martínez de Castro explained in a true republican vein, duelists did not have the right to "avenge their injuries through the usurpation of public power."[28] At the same time, defense attorneys successfully argued that dueling was sanctioned by public opinion. Láncaster Jones openly asked jurors not to follow the letter of the Penal Code and reminded them, inaccurately, that "since our current trial system was established, there has not been a single verdict against the few duelists brought to trial."[29] Sure enough, even though many people had heard about the duel and the press published the details of Verástegui's death, including a print by José Guadalupe Posada (figure 23), everyone indicted in the case, except Romero, was acquitted.[30]

Láncaster Jones's reasoning laid out the axiological premise of all arguments and practices concerning dueling, that is, that honor was above the law. In Velenzuela's words, the duel survived prohibitions because "It rested on honor, that elevated feeling of man's dignity, against which laws have always fought in vain."[31] Enrique Pérez Rubio, the attorney for the physician present at the Romero-Verástegui duel, argued before the jurors in terms familiar to press juries before 1882: "You do not represent legal justice, but social justice, you should forget legal prescriptions and declare that Dr. Casimiro Preciado only fulfilled his duty"—which they did.[32] Influential men represented public opinion in their approval of dueling. "Many very high public officials," army officers, "a large number of jurists, journalists," and "other honorable individuals incapable of advising or committing a common crime," claimed Láncaster Jones, supported Tovar's Mexican code of honor, a code that informally regulated an illegal practice.[33] Duels, others argued, were based on a contract that had been signed or verbally accepted by the two parties and their seconds, making it as serious an obligation as any imposed by law. Finally, the code of honor could not help but ignore the Penal Code because dueling obviously contradicted the liberal belief in the universality of the law. Only honorable men could duel. Tovar's code banned from the field

23, 1 and 2. The Verástegui-Romero duel by José Guadalupe Posada.

of honor anyone who had suffered "the smirch of a judicial sentence" or had been declared a "professional gambler."[34]

Mexican duelists and their accomplices had no qualms about breaking the law, not only by participating in duels but also by uttering the most improbable lies afterward. Those involved in Verástegui's death invented diverse stories for the police and the newspapers: that the victim's gun went off as he was cleaning it (the bullet entering under his right armpit and lodging in a lung), or that he had fallen down the stairs, triggering the gun (now in his pocket). The law and the truth were to be avoided because they produced unwanted publicity. Tovar's description of the options facing the gentleman whose wife has been offended in the theater amounted to a license to lie. Other authors and many upper-class Mexicans agreed that the judiciary in Mexico could be swayed by wealth—which, as they all knew very well, was not the same as honor. Regular people, as we have seen, did use the courts to solve matters of honor. For some upper-class men, however, this was not enough: existing legislation was "meager and powerless" to punish offenses against honor and therefore deserved no respect.[35] Courts of honor, which in other countries provided a semilegal judicial setting in which to decide offenses, were not so authoritative in Mexico. Men of honor found it more rational to aggressively break the law, turning the duel itself into a punitive method by which duelists could prevent offenses, and then to lie through their teeth.[36]

Not that these men really had anything to fear from the law. According to General Rocha, the Mexican government and governments of other "enlightened peoples . . . tolerate" duels, although they make sure they take place "under the best circumstances of equality . . . and in consonance with the prescriptions of the codes."[37] The Penal Code of 1871 had an entire chapter on dueling, going into considerable detail to describe punishable behaviors. Rather than simply banning those behaviors, the code acted as a commentary on nonlegal dueling codes, assuming that suspects knew them and, in general, allowing considerable leeway for the defense of upper-class honor. The code, for example, mandated judicial authorities to prevent combats by mediating between the parties and formalizing negotiations in notarized acts—thus recognizing the seriousness of duelists' motives. The penalties for wounding or killing were reduced if, as prescribed in dueling codes, witnesses had been present and the weapons had been properly chosen. The maximum punishment for a duelist who killed his rival was six years in prison and a three-thousand-peso fine; they paled in comparison with the penalties, including death, meted out in common homicides. Evoking customary rules, the code distinguished between the duelist who had provoked the confrontation and the one who had been provoked and included penalties for witnesses and physicians, well-established roles in the codes.[38]

These provisions ran counter to the general increase in the severity of penalties and in state intervention that characterized nineteenth-century codification. The Penal Code of 1868 of the State of Veracruz, for example, had established a broader definition of dueling, without references to so-called proper procedures or to suspects' roles, and set stricter penalties. By contrast, Martínez de Castro noted that dueling was "a social need" that the law could not penalize in the same way it punished a fight, in which contenders are "drawn by the irresistible force of vulgar preoccupations." Thus punishing the duel too harshly "would collide with public opinion" and would deprive the nation of "very respectable men."[39] The goal of the Penal Code, in sum, was to regulate a socially accepted, albeit illegal right.

Class bias in the enforcement of the code enabled the lying and cheating of upper-class suspects. Francisco Bulnes, no stranger to duels, criticized Mexico's distorted justice. "After his homicide," explained Bulnes, "the duelist is usually acquitted . . . and he is considered more honorable than ever; while the humble man who commits the same crime in a fight, without advantage, is sentenced to twelve years in prison for homicide . . . and loses his reputation for the rest of his life."[40] The Code of 1871 alluded to suspects' status, but Bulnes's criticism, as usual, touched on a deeper truth. According to a tacit and unquestionable rule, people who possessed wealth or political clout had to be spared the embarrassment of being arrested. In 1894, the respected jurist Jacinto Pallares confessed before the Federal Congress that "personal considerations" had once spared him prison and "the shame of being registered in prison records."[41] It was obvious, by contrast, that no lower-class suspect would expect such "personal considerations," much less seek leniency by claiming that he or she had engaged in a duel. Even though many street fights emulated the basic rules of the duel by involving witnesses and equal weapons and avoiding the intervention of the police, the authorities never referred to them as duels and saw their relative simplicity as evidence of spontaneity. According to Tovar's *Código nacional*, educated men solved their quarrels by dueling, while "men of the lower strata . . . solve theirs with a knife or with their teeth in the middle of the square."[42]

Elite affairs of honor were widely commented upon and discreetly applauded. In 1896, one of the first motion pictures ever made in Mexico, "Un duelo a pistola en el bosque de Chapultepec" by the Lumiére brothers, involved a reenactment of the "Romero-Veraza" [sic] duel. A review of the film prompted Colonel Romero to sue the newspaper El Globo, disingenuously arguing that he was not the Francisco Romero portrayed in the movie.[43] But the movie itself was not attacked, and for added realism actual policemen participated as extras. The authorities also protected real duels. In a case from 1884, the nephew of the governor of the Federal District obtained the help of rural guards to prevent any external intervention in the combat he was about to engage in. Presidents González and Díaz authorized the celebration of at least two duels. Díaz had initially ordered the director of the Colegio Militar in Mexico City to prevent a student from participating in a duel, but a fellow veteran of Díaz's from the French intervention war, General Carlos Pacheco, convinced the president to allow the affair to proceed so that Pacheco's protégé, one of the duelists, might defend his reputation; Pacheco argued that if Díaz's own son was in that situation he would do likewise.[44]

Willing to accept such reasoning, protectors of order turned a blind eye to well-known cases. Few duels were prosecuted, and those that were showed a great deal of respect toward the suspects. Juries, composed of well-off men who did not want to miss the drama, tended to be sympathetic toward suspects, since usually there was no victim for the crime. In 1874, for example, Eduardo Molina, Luis Amato, and the witnesses in their duel were brought to trial. The suspects were the only ones to testify. All of them declared that nothing had happened and that the wounds suffered by Molina and Amato had been caused in an accident. The jury took fifteen minutes to acquit everyone.[45] Defending Romero's parliamentary immunity in the Chamber of Deputies, Manuel Lombardo reasoned that since the Penal Code's regulations on dueling had not been employed and article 183 of the Constitution abrogated any penal law that had not been applied in the past ten years, it followed that dueling was no longer sanctioned by the law—although Bulnes countered that even if article 183 abrogated the code's articles concerning the duel it did not do the same for battery and homicide. Even when they failed to follow the ceremony of dueling, courts still protected elite men who used violence in public. With a single bullet to the forehead, General Alonso Flores killed Refugio Guerrero on a main street of the capital during a dispute that had originated in Tampico. In well-attended jury audiences Guillermo Prieto and others speakers celebrated Flores's character, and even the prosecutor asked for his acquittal, claiming that Flores had been "driven by a feeling that, even if disapproved of in the moral realm, is accepted in the social realm."[46]

Neither law nor authority mattered when it came to issuing or accepting a challenge. Public men's choice in that regard, or, more precisely, their lack of choice, could only be understood as the inexorable confluence of social obligations and internal motivations: both conscience, as in Verástegui's case, and passion, as in Romero's. A character in a novel by Juan A. Mateos put it in melodramatic terms when challenging a friend: "[I feel] crazy for my name, crazy for my honor!"[47] There was a subtle economy to that loss of control, however. Blinding rage excused Flores when he killed Guerrero on the street, and it justified challenges, but it did not apply to the performance of the duel itself. As a consequence, the self-defense argument tried by Romero's attorneys in 1894 did not work: seasoned public men like him were expected to keep a clear head even in moments of the greatest danger and follow the dictates of dueling codes. Rather than a bullet, they were supposed to fear "opinion, that invisible executor of the cruel sentences of society."[48] Romero, explained Heriberto Barrón, was in fact afraid of "receiving the shameful stigma of coward from society."[49] Perhaps he was remembering a tragic example of such fear: Colonel Juan Espinoza y Gorostiza had been accused of cowardice for retreating during a battle against the French; he remained "overexcited" afterward and killed a subordinate who questioned him in another action. Espinoza y Gorostiza died in 1868 in a duel with a one-time friend, and his epitaph was witness to his sad success in avoiding the stigma of cowardice: "Glory keeps his name amid laurels / and Friendship, amid tears, his story."[50]

Dueling was inevitable because honor was more important than life. Even the death penalty would not deter dueling; as Juan N. Mirafuentes wrote, "What influence can it [the death penalty] have over someone who feels compelled to fight for a cause that makes him despise existence?" Some offenses, he added, "inflict a pain greater than death."[51] Men's willingness to sacrifice their life to an evasive good bespoke an idealism that transcended individual existence and contradicted "our own strong preservation instinct."[52] Verástegui and Santiago Sierra surrendered the welfare of their families, and others, like Espinoza y Gorostiza, sacrificed friendship—the strongest link of affection between two men, that supreme treasure in Porfirian sociability. The deaths themselves were beyond words of affection (as Rocha reminded Romero as he was trying to speak to a dying Verástegui), but not beyond dishonor (as Verástegui's widow demonstrated by suing Romero in defense of her husband's reputation). Honor, in the apt words of Sierra Velenzuela, was one of the "many tyrannies that public opinion exercises over the character of societies."[53]

The Technology of Honor

Even if they could be triggered by passion and lead to tragedy, duels were not only a path to sacrifice but also a method to impose reason and discipline. Bulnes embodied the apparent contradiction: in an undated note found in his archive, he recognized that "I cannot be a martyr precisely because I strive to be rational" and that he was not predisposed "to prove with sacrifice the sanctity of my convictions."[54] Yet he was a duelist, too, because there was a strong rational component to the practice. The most enduring cultural legacy of the duel among Mexican elites was its codification of individual behavior and public disputes through a technology that shaped bodies and minds. The men who abided by the complex rules of codes of honor deserved as much respect for their knowledge and self-control as they did for their courage. Learning those rules required study, examples, and friends.

There was plenty to study. During the last decades of the nineteenth century, several texts concerning the duel appeared in Mexico, notably Colonel Antonio Tovar's *Código nacional mexicano del duelo* (1891), in addition to translations of European codes and fencing manuals.[55] All of these codes were easily available; educated men who claimed not to know them, as Juan Barajas did in his testimony in 1895, were reminded, in his case by Bulnes himself, that they were so readily available "you can smell the laws of the duel."[56] These were laws indeed, and as such they offered criteria by which to judge duelists and their partners. During the trial against Romero, the accusation constantly cited Tovar's *Código nacional*, often to demonstrate that suspects had not properly followed its dictates. Tovar himself attended the audiences. Suspects and defense attorneys referred to the authoritativeness of his code in order to explain that the duel had been fought honorably. But questions asked by the prosecutor and the judge exposed their incompetence in following common standards: from the dishonorable behavior of a vengeful trouble-maker, Romero, to the passivity of a cornudo, Barajas, to the ignorance of several padrinos. Specifically they failed to use the code of honor to prevent violence by attempting a negotiation and even admitted to arranging a combat whose cause was secret—something frowned upon by many codes. Rocha was less exposed to these criticisms, as he was one of the most experienced men in the practices and codifications of honor in the country; yet he too faced tough questions concerning the harsh rules of the encounter, the weapons used, and his dinner with Romero the day before the duel.[57]

Rocha's wisdom was central to the trial because, even if you could "smell the laws of the duel," the multiplicity of overlapping codes required considerable knowledge to put them into practice. The letter of the codes remained somewhat arcane for most people. More than through written regulations, rules were conveyed through fencing classes, shooting-range practice, and the participation of seconds. Experienced duelists such as Rocha and Romero transmitted knowledge by example to those who shared their social life. Paradoxically, public men embraced the technology of honor with the same progressive faith with which they applied science to politics and social reform. The positive belief in the sword, to use Romero's phrase, could replace the metaphysical dictates of the civil and criminal law without actors falling prey to passion or spontaneity.[58] The technology of honor was a modern disposition learned not in books but in life, by observing how knowledgeable men conducted themselves in dangerous situations.

Through smell, text, or tradition, the greatest concern of Mexican interpreters and observers of honor codes was the instruments and performance required to guarantee a level playing field. Thus, for example, they went into considerable detail on the specifications of the weapons to be used, particularly guns. Forty-two of the seventy-eight duels examined by Escudero involved pistols. Preparing, loading, and selecting pistols was an intricate process, one that emphasized the participation of padrinos and a juez de campo knowledgeable in the multiple tools that accompanied dueling pistols in their elegant cases. The operation was laborious, conveniently leaving some time for a reconciliation. Though easier to wield than swords, dueling pistols in effect excluded common people from engaging in duels. Deliberately useless for other purposes, a good set of dueling pistols could cost from four or five hundred pesos.[59]

Dueling pistols were not as effective as other firearms because their barrels were smooth inside: the bullets therefore did not spin and thus were less accurate and less penetrating. Unlike swords, the pistols could be used without much previous training and regardless of the contenders' physical aptitudes. Dueling pistols, in sum, were thought to offer a less predictable outcome while still testifying to the courage of the combatants. Romero's defenders went so far as to argue that dueling pistols were safer than other weapons and should be considered as instruments not of a voluntary crime, but of accidents. Even when pistols were used, however, any departure from the norm that would give one of the duelists an advantage was shunned. A duel was aborted in 1906, for example, when the seconds of the challenged party found out that his opponent, a Cuban diplomat, was extremely skillful with a revolver.[60]

Men of honor did not dismiss training, yet they carefully avoided investing too much effort in the conditioning of their bodies. Romero declared at his trial that "the handling of weapons is useful to resist force, to repeal insults and to maintain dignity and honor." Fencing instructions were widely available, but there were only two firing ranges in the capital, both of which were popular places, functioning as meeting places where friends gathered.[61] In fact, Romero and Verástegui ran into each other hours before their fateful duel at Francisco Macedo's shooting range. Although Romero was a regular there, witnesses declared that Verástegui also proved to be a good shooter during that final practice; he had some experience with firearms in his previous position as a customs officer in the north of Mexico. These statements were probably intended to counter the prosecutor's suggestion that the two men's training had made a difference, since Verástegui had not used a gun in years, did not frequent the shooting range, and had no choice but to use pistols since his administrative job had made him *poltrón* (flabby)—a euphemistic way of saying he was too weak and overweight to use a sword.[62]

If proper procedures were followed, it was easier for seconds to preserve the equality of a pistol combat than of two fencing rivals. The distance between the duelists and the timing and order of shots were codified, thus providing clear criteria by which to judge an honorable performance. Among the multiple alternative ways of organizing a pistol combat, duelists in Mexico preferred the variant in which the adversaries fired on the cue of a hand clap, with a limited number of repetitions if the bullets missed their target. This method was also used by Frenchmen, whereas Germans stressed shorter distances and prided themselves on the higher mortality rate of their duels, opposing that against French feebleness. In Mexico, the use of the most extreme variation—reducing the distance after each shot and continuing until "obtaining results"—was deemed recklessly dangerous. In the Romero-Verástegui duel, Rocha and the seconds had decided to stop the combat after one round of shots, in contravention of the rules initially set during the negotiations; yet they failed to inform the duelists before the first round, and after that it was too late—although their statements in this regard may have been an attempt to avoid penal responsibility.

Details were important. During the trial, the simultaneity of the shots exchanged between Romero and Verástegui came under discussion. Some witnesses declared they had heard two separate shots, suggesting that Romero had fired first. Rocha and the other suspects insisted the behavior of both duelists was honorable and explained the separate sounds as an acoustic phenomenon. But they stood on shaky ground. The prosecutor further insisted on the inability of the participants to keep an even field by noting that, against the norms, the barrels of the pistols used in the duel, which belonged to Rocha, had rifling, thus giving an advantage to the best shooter.[63]

Padrinos were always in a bind because they had to make sure that a duel was truly dangerous even while preserving its method and fairness. If they represented parties in an affair, they also represented public opinion on the field of honor and were themselves the object of opinion's judgment. Senator Apolinar Castillo, for example, made it clear to everyone who asked that he would have not represented anyone other than Verástegui because "at his age and social position he did not like to intervene in duels of little import."[64] As a general rule, it was not proper to accept an appointment before having sought explanations from the adversary or indications, through "trusted friends," that the causes of the duel were serious and did not involve posturing. Romero and Verástegui had to ask several friends before finding their padrinos, treading carefully through the intricate networks of loyalty that constituted the Porfirian elite. Romero, for example, first asked Senator Antonio Arguinzóniz about his relation to Verástegui. "I love him as a brother," responded Arguinzóniz; Romero did not explain to him what kind of business he needed to arrange and moved on. Romero then thought about General Márquez but chose not to ask him "because I had earlier provided him with a service of this kind and I feared he would say that I was charging him for the favor."[65] He finally received help from Senator Lauro Carrillo and Manuel Barreto, although he had to give written instructions to Barreto because of his ignorance about dueling. The decision to seek and provide help was not just a function of specialized knowledge, but also a result of the trust between duelist and padrino, a tie that could, if necessary, be revealed to the public. Romero later wrote a letter to Carrillo and Barreto, published in the newspapers, in which he thanked them for "the great honra you give me by coming out as guarantors of the truth of my words."[66]

It was a favor indeed: the second, although rarely prosecuted, had to invest his own reputation in setting up and obtaining an honorable outcome, through either reconciliation or combat. Otherwise, he risked incurring the ire, and even a challenge, from his *ahijados* (literally, godsons), who could accuse him of selling their honor cheaply. Padrinos could also be dragged into a new dispute against the opposing seconds and were sure to spend days in negotiations, which could not be postponed if unwanted publicity was to be avoided. More important, perhaps, was the personal investment of the padrino in his ahijado. This made the padrino's position more delicate because he could not have strong feelings toward the adversary nor be unduly loyal or indebted to his ahijado, lest he be a poor guarantor of his honor. In the codes of the marquis of Cabriñana and the count of Chatauvillard, the second had to be able to "keep the utmost secret about their conversation [with the duelist] and to obtain the most intimate confession of his thoughts."[67]

Knowing too much about the causes of the duel, however, could undermine the padrino's ability to negotiate with the other party. This became apparent in the Romero-Verástegui case since both men refused to divulge the origin of their dispute. Engaging in a dispute with dishonorable causes could damage the seconds' reputation. Romero hinted this could be the reason for his refusal to reveal the contents of the letter he sent to Verástegui, which Verástegui destroyed but referred to when he challenged Romero. During interrogation, Romero tried to finesse the problem by saying that what he heard outside the window at the Barajases' home "contained very serious offenses against him and other persons whose names he does not want to uncover."[68] Verástegui's seconds did not like negotiating a duel being contemplated for "secret causes" but accepted Romero's argument as a way of avoiding further involvement in an issue of more serious implications than the love of Natalia Barajas, such as a political dispute. Discretion, after all, could always be justified in court on moral grounds. In Mateos's words, some causes could not be mentioned at trial because it was not right to "extract a secret from the dead."[69]

The problem with secrecy was that seconds needed to know the causes of an affair in order to perform one of their most important duties, classifying offenses. This was necessary to establish whether a reconciliation was at all possible and, if not, what kind of duel was to be fought. The assembly of seconds, usually two per party, was in itself a "tribunal of honor" that determined the causes and implications of an affair.[70] The two adversaries had to give ample power to their seconds in this regard, signing *cartas poder* (proxy) that put their fate in their hands. Codes recognized the difficulty of establishing the seriousness of offenses, as the issue ultimately depended on the parties' circumstances and self-esteem. They nevertheless provided a rough classification, one in which physical contact was the most serious offense, followed by public attacks (that is, witnessed by more than three persons), and finally those that were private and only affected self-esteem or susceptibility.[71] A slap to the face, even if only attempted, was so serious that it prevented journalists from shifting responsibility for an offensive text onto another colleague—otherwise a common practice to avoid prosecution. Conversely, a man who failed to respond to another who *abofeteó* him (slapped, although the term euphemistically included stronger blows) lacked honor. José Ferrel reminded Vicente García Torres of this in a provocative piece in which he claimed that a longshoreman had hit García Torres and that he had failed to respond.[72]

Seconds had to establish who the offended party was—not a simple question, since even hand gestures, drawings, letters, or nasty glances could be considered offensive; in the words of Juan N. Mirafuentes, "There are many insults almost imperceptible in the eyes of a third party, but that can deeply hurt the offended person's heart." The initial aggression was the most important one, and all those that followed it, however serious, were its consequence—except when an insult was followed by a blow.[73] Establishing causality was crucial because the offended party had the right to choose the weapons and terms of the duel.

In the case of the Romero-Verástegui duel, as in many others in all likelihood, causality was not obvious: Romero was offended by Verástegui's words and wrote and threatened to publish a sarcastic letter which, even if failing to elicit a satisfactory explanation, forced a challenge. Negotiations among seconds could become debates about actions and responses among the parties. There was nothing to negotiate, other than the time and place of the duel, if the offense had been physical, but in most other cases finding the ultimate cause of an affair entailed complex disputes that were not always satisfactorily resolved. The recorded minutes of one such negotiation, found among Bulnes's papers, are revealing: marked by multiple corrections, erasures, and stricken names, the document established that

> 1st. Consulted, the undersign state that Mr. Gutiérrez Nájera should not duel because of having made a historical observation regarding the diseased general Garibaldi.
>
> 2nd. The idea of "severely punishing" refers to Mr. Nágera, not to us, who have not offended or been offended. . . .
>
> [deleted: 3rd.] Mrs. de Cavero, D'Agustini [deleted: and Signorelli] state that they did not mean to offend Mrs. Lizardi, Kammeken, Bulnes, Castellanos y Garcia when they said that the challenge would be solved on the border because of the police, since they are sure that they are true gentlemen and that they would never appeal to authority to prevent a combat of honor.[74]

The document lacks contextual information and is cryptic, but it sums up the complex duties of duelists and their seconds: to explore the origins of a dispute, to settle on the true meaning of a few words, and to clarify the intention of those involved in the negotiation, stressing that they never doubted each others' willingness to arrange a proper duel and to avoid, at all costs, the intervention of the state.

Dueling and Politics

In spite of evidence of Porfirian authorities' sympathy toward duelists, it was essential for them to maintain some separation from the state, if not from politics. The paradox in Mexico was that the historical apogee of the practice of dueling was reached at a time when the national state was consolidating its power and beginning to codify many aspects of life. Men of honor dreamed of having an autonomous and egalitarian field on which to solve their disputes with courage and rationality—two values that were not always compatible yet still reigned over political life. But Porfirian public culture was rapidly changing, and one can see the infamous Romero-Verástegui duel of 1894 as evidence that now, to use Hobbes's words, "Honour consisteth onely in the opinion of Power." Dueling, as men of honor found out, could not survive the ban of a strong state and the disapproval of society.[75]

The codification of Mexican dueling, signaled by the publication of Tovar's book in 1890, was in fact the beginning of a process of erosion of the legitimacy of the duel. Politics had made its heyday possible. Dueling served as a tool to unify the political class under Díaz but became a liability when it threatened to publicize political disputes inside that elite. The 1890s saw the consolidation of the científico group around Díaz. If one reads the Verástegui-Romero duel with an eye to its political context one can see that the 1894 trial served as a clear warning that pride and autonomy had their limits, even if reputation continued to play a central part in the career of public men. Loyalty and circumspection (the científicos' style, but one not to the romantic's taste) were now at a premium.[76]

Dueling expressed equality, openness, and cohesion among the Mexican political elite. For Escudero, fencing and pistol training "diluted social and age differences . . . into open camaraderie."[77] A challenge accepted implied that the two rivals were of the same status and knew the modern codes of dueling well. As stated in the document signed by Bulnes and others, negotiations preceding the duel and the ritual of combat itself were based on the premise that honor presided over the behavior of all contenders. An honorable fight, regardless of the outcome, would result in the restoration of both men's reputation and often their reconciliation, if not a new friendship. Since many encounters in Mexico resulted in minor injuries or none at all it was common to see Mexican rivals walk off the field as "excellent friends."[78] Dueling brought together groups and individuals who had been bitterly divided by war and ideology. It also established ties between civilian and military men, thus bridging another important internal divide between young cohorts and veterans of the Reforma and French intervention wars like General

Rocha. By playing according to his rules, others could assert their own claim to the values of courage and honor associated with his prestigious past—which may explain the large number of duels in which Rocha was involved. It is telling that the highest frequency of duels recorded by Escudero and published statistics coincides with the era of supposed reconciliation with conservatives and with the ascendancy of the cien-tíficos in the early 1890s.[79]

Professionalization of the military was part of this political process. Porfirian reformers sought to impose values of discipline and scientific knowledge on armed forces characterized by scarce cohesion. Civil wars and foreign intervention at midcentury, according to Justo Sierra, had created an army of "courageous officers, fanatics, terrible men of war in the full extension of the term" who were usually disdainful of civil govern-ments.[80] After the defeat of the French, the ambitions of the veterans had to be tamed through careful administration by Díaz himself, but also through the introduction of European military technologies and organi-zational techniques, Germany in particular. Dueling became part of the ethics of Mexican officers, as witnessed by the story of Espinoza y Goro-stiza, noted above. Commanders protected and encouraged duelists in uniform, duels escaped the scrutiny of the law, and officers were dis-missed for refusing to fight. The military code of justice included articles on dueling, and Rocha's manual for Mexican soldiers, *Enquiridión*, de-scribed the rules of dueling that every officer should know. Both Ve-rástegui and Romero had military commissions, even if they held civilian posts at the time of their encounter: Verástegui had fought for Juárez and had been a member of the court martial that sentenced Maximilian to death, and Romero, who was several years younger, had been educated as an engineer at the Colegio Militar. One of the statements that triggered Romero's indignation at the Barajases' home was Verástegui's claim that a potential promotion of Romero to the rank of general (earned by support-ing the candidacy of General Martín González to the governorship of Oaxaca) was going to diminish the prestige of the army. Romero argued in his letter that by offending the Mexican army Verástegui was being disloyal to an institution of which he was a member.[81]

Rather than military discipline, however, public exposure of political motivations was the key element in the context of this and many other conflicts. Verástegui said that Romero was a *periodiquero* (cheap jour-nalist, newsboy) who slavishly flattered González in the press in an attempt to gain advancement. Echoes of combat journalism could be heard throughout the affair. Romero wrote the letter to Verástegui from the offices of *El Relámpago*, which he had owned until recently. The meetings between the seconds of the two parties took place in the offices of two other well-known newspapers, *El Partido Liberal* and Rafael Reyes Spíndola's *El Universal*.[82] As we saw earlier, dueling was an ever-present possibility for journalists, whose honor and influence it acknowledged by placing them on the same field with other public men (see chapter 2). Tovar's *Código nacional* listed the press offenses (including caricatures) that could justify combat. The implicit responsibilities of newspaper editors involved responding to challenges from those offended by unsigned articles. These rules did not disappear with the disciplining of combat journalism and the consolidation of the regime's control of the press after the elimination of the press jury in 1882. In 1897, for example, Francisco Montes de Oca, the director of the liberal penny papers *Gil Blas* and *El Popular*, accused *El Imparcial* of receiving subsidies from the government—a fact amply documented later on. Montes de Oca faced *El Imparcial*'s director, Reyes Spíndola, on the field of honor; Rocha was one of the witnesses, and no one died. Such affairs were not merely a vehicle for censorship: as noted in previous chapters, the regime had more direct and efficient ways to silence independent journalists. Neither was dueling a way to recover freedom of speech: it simply gave journalists such as Montes de Oca greater prominence, by introducing them into the group of public men concerned about honor.[83]

Dueling similarly enhanced the role of members of Congress in public life. In the 1894 case, Romero was a deputy, as was Ramón Prida, second of Verástequi, while Castillo, as noted, was a senator. According to the historian François-Xavier Guerra, the Federal Congress during the Porfiriato was an honorific showcase for the political elite but hardly a true political venue or a representation of the people.[84] The honorific function was more important than Guerra believed, however. A parliamentary seat, ultimately granted by Díaz, rewarded and incorporated military commanders into the political elite and elevated civilians. Parliamentary discussions could be quite stormy and personal, as in the deuda inglesa debates of 1884, and constituted a highly visible forum for the discussion of honor and the accumulation of further prestige. Congressmen were often involved in duels, and the threat was present in several debates throughout the Porfiriato and after the Revolution.[85]

It is not surprising, then, to see in the Romero-Verástegui affair signs of political tensions. Hinting at the political importance of the case, Senator Castillo declared to great applause on the floor of Congress that he relinquished his congressional immunity so that "the Administration could rescue its sense of decorum."[86] Manuel Flores elaborated on this interpretation during the debate preceding the almost unanimous vote that stripped the suspects of their parliamentary immunity so they could be tried: in the name of "the new political generation" he argued that this was not a traditional fight between clericalism and liberalism, but a struggle between virtue and vice. Thus, Congress's decision had to be reasoned and avoid "the revival of the tumultuous methods of combat politics."[87]

Romero and the other suspects suggested that the reason for the duel was "una cuestión de faldas" (a matter of skirts, by which they did not mean their own, of course). Verástegui seemed to confirm this when he explained to his seconds why he had destroyed the letter. The prosecutor accepted the explanation because he wanted to prove that the duel was prompted by dishonorable causes. Under questioning, however, witnesses and the indicted admitted that there was more to the conflict than the affection of Natalia Barajas—or that her affection meant more than the "erotic tournament" mentioned in Romero's letter. After all, Juan Barajas had ongoing business with both duelists involving their privileged access to federal authorities, particularly the Ministry of Finance. The two explanations (*faldas* and politics) were, in other words, entirely compatible.[88] The insulting words overheard by Romero included mention of the governor-elect of Oaxaca, General González, who had defeated Rosendo Pineda, a member of the científico group, in the election. Verástegui, who was close to this group, called González an "indio tonto" (silly Indian) who had been elected in Oaxaca because of Díaz's influence, and he went on to complain about corrupt members of the current administration.[89]

Beyond González, however, it seemed Verástegui had mentioned names that could not be named during the trial. In his final speech to the jury, Prida's defender, Manuel Flores, promised to dismiss the idea, circulating among public opinion, "that this is a political affair, that you are to decide on a dispute between a group (which they call científico) and some personalities opposed to them." Yet his speech seems to have been cut short, and he did not offer any evidence to support this claim—as if merely recognizing a political interpretation as possible was in itself dangerous.[90]

Romero and Barajas declared that other names cropped up in Verástegui's offensive comments that night, but they refused to be more specific. Romero said there was a mention of "names which I have been keeping secret from the beginning. . . . because it is not a secret that belongs to me, it is a secret that belongs to the deceased, and since he did not reveal it, it is not proper for me to do so."[91] It was indeed a problem for Verástegui. Castillo attempted to defend his late friend's loyalty to the government against "rumors that stain Mr. Verástegui's memory, depicting him as ungrateful to his superiors, as a slovenly and disloyal employee for an administration which he served during many years and from which he received clear benefits."[92] Even Heriberto Frías's novel *El último duelo* (The last duel), based on this episode, was indirect about its political causes: the book placed the story in the administration of Manuel González, probably to defuse the implications of government corruption, yet combined a romantic plot with references to "political things."[93] Along with the racist comment about Martín González and the criticism of Romero's promotion, these clues suggest that Díaz himself had been mentioned—although we will never know for sure.

It was obvious to all, even if never spelled out, that the affair betrayed tensions within the government between ascending científicos, most notably José Y. Limantour, minister of Hacienda, and groups closer to the military. Barajas's business schemes fell within Hacienda's purview, and Verástegui's job as inspector del timbre place him close to Limantour's efforts to modernize tax collection in the country. Romero, in turn, was affiliated with other sectors of the government, although he was also a steadfast Porfirista. Sóstenes Rocha was a maverick, always engaging in duels and journalistic polemics and at times close to and at times an adversary of the científicos. The decision to punish Romero but not the others could be interpreted as a product of Limantour's growing influence in Díaz's inner circle. The jury found the suspect guilty of murder in a duel in which he had been the challenger, and the judge sentenced him to four years and three months of detention in Belem prison, an eighteen-hundred-peso fine, and annual payments of forty-five hundred pesos to Verástegui's widow, in addition to covering the expenses of the funeral and the civil suit. The verdict was hailed, even in American newspapers, as a decision that would change the rules of future prosecutions of duelists.[94] At the very least, it signaled to all political groups the need to maintain internal struggles outside of the public eye.

Reflecting on the episode decades later, Bulnes was not so sure modernity had prevailed. A few months after the verdict, President Díaz decreed an amnesty for all prisoners guilty of dueling—that is, Romero, who was released. Bulnes, a científico, saw the amnesty as a way for Díaz to save face while confirming his disposition to engage in "political thuggery," thinly disguised as matters of honor, to control political dissent.[95] Romero certainly fit the description of a thug: Genaro García characterized him as a "professional duelist, who spends long hours at the shooting range and fencing schools, who has been a second of more than a hundred duelists, who insults publicly."[96] The minister of Justicia e Instrucción Pública Joaquín Baranda, claimed Bulnes, was behind an inside plot against the científicos. Since the científicos had not yet established control over the press with *El Imparcial* and were "serious persons who avoided fights and disapproved of duels outside the laws of honor," Baranda employed a group of combat journalists to provoke polemics and challenges against them, resulting in at least three duels involving científico writers.[97] Baranda fell from grace later, but, as the subsequent political history of the regime would demonstrate, Díaz never allowed the científicos to gain complete control over the system; he constantly encouraged men of honor who had a military background, like General Bernardo Reyes, to nurture political aspirations against them. Romero's amnesty was part of this game.

A narrow political interpretation, however, fails to yield the full historical value of the Verástegui-Romero affair. Dueling became less frequent after 1895 because the verdict, even if undermined by Díaz's amnesty, signaled the strength of attitudes critical to the preeminence of honor in public life. Attorneys on both sides at the trial had predicted that a guilty verdict would usher in momentous transformations regarding dueling.[98] And even those critical of the regime, like Miguel Cabrera's *El Hijo del Ahuizote*, mercilessly mocked duelists. A poem entitled "Epidemia de duelos" condensed the ridicule of recent events and the contradictions of "this century, of lights":

The hard-working man who does not want to go
To the field where he has been challenged
To endure whatever comes about,

Is criticized by black and white alike,

As if he had committed a crime,

Even though he is in fact peaceful and honest.

And those who did respond to challenges, if they were unskilled with weapons, turned "the field of honor into a graveyard."[99] The cover of an earlier issue of the paper (figure 24) pictured contemporary dueling as a rather pathetic mix of masks representing comedy, parody, and tragedy.

The notion of honor as a supreme value that was worth the highest sacrifice began to be replaced by one that stressed the right to protection of reputation and domestic peace. Under a regime that was itself more interested in discipline than heroism among the political class, honor seemed now to be reduced to "the opinion of Power."

Thus, a better explanation of the demise of dueling should examine the intersections of political and cultural factors expressed by *El Hijo del Ahuizote*'s arguments. The first one pertained to political customs. As in other societies, such as Germany and Italy, the decadence of dueling seemed linked to changes in political culture that, in turn, influenced governments' willingness to protect duelists. It is ironic to hear Bulnes, a científico who did not think much of the Mexican masses, criticize the duel as an antidemocratic institution, as he did during the trial. Yet his argument echoed those put forward against the press jury: the practice created a caste of men above republican equality, prone to violence, and averse to the rule of law. The best antidote, following the example of England, was effective legal protection of reputations, particularly if focused on public officials and relying on criminal courts. There was, however, a dangerously democratic aspect to dueling: If the strong-hand rule of Porfirio Díaz was the opposite of the anarchy of multiple strong caudillos during the early independent period, dueling countered progress by spreading the legitimate use of force.[100]

There was a second, moral argument underlying that of political modernization. Ever since the early growth of dueling, critics had denounced the "scarecrow of honor" as the opposite of Christian values and moderation.[101] The duel was unnecessary, in their view, if everyone agreed that "honor based on virtue is also invulnerable."[102] Good men could maintain virtue, an internal and spiritual good, without the use of violence. In the language of Justo Sierra, Jacinto Pallares, and other secular ideologues of the *pax Porfiriana*, this sentiment was expressed as the sovereignty of "our intimate being," that true self that despised "this pharisaic organiza-

24. "Social Masks." El Hijo del Ahuizote, 19 Aug. 1894, p. 1.

tion of moral murder."[103] This anxiety about the tyranny of opinion resonated with new concerns about the optimal moral conditions for capitalism (see chapter 4). These views denounced the irrationality of a system that sought to settle debts through the meaningless victory found in death: What good was satisfaction for a family without a father? Honor rationalized as moral capital (as proposed by Herbert Spencer) made more sense than the ethereal and ultimately tragic calculations of men like Santos Degollado. The result was a tempered, less romantic articulation of conscience. The prosecutor in the Verástegui-Romero case, Federico Peraza Rosado, distinguished between an "hombre honrado" and an "hombre honorable." The hombre honrado is "that person who fulfills the duties imposed by society, be it by religiously paying the rent, be it by attending to the subsistence of his family." By contrast, the hombre honorable is "that person with a more or less developed susceptibility" who would, for example, challenge a stranger who accidentally steps on his shoes in the street.[104]

The view that dueling had moral legitimacy was no longer unanimous, it seemed, but contingent on the attitudes of diverse publics. Prida recognized, during the trial, that if the duel between Verástegui and Romero had not been arranged, "supporters of dueling" might have seen the affair as shameful, but those who were now suspects "would have been praised by those who do not support dueling."[105] Peraza Rosado argued that there were three societies in this regard: the small group of duelists, true apologists of crime, whom he compared to prostitutes and gamblers in their calculating cynicism; those brutes who respond to offenses without thinking and use violence without the formalities of duel; and a majority of "sensible people" who disapprove of dueling as an uncivilized custom.[106] If one looks outside the texts produced by those in the first group (who have received the most attention in this chapter), one can catch glimpses of men who simply ignored the codes and refused to fight, without any loss of self-esteem and, in some cases, even good-humored celebration afterward.[107] This argument, seldom explicit, pitched the spirit of aggressive, troublemaking thugs like Romero against the pleasantry of social life in, for example, the soirées at the Barajases' home. Such civility was more representative of the ways in which the Porfirian elite wanted to see itself: amid elegant humor, good food, and music, smart, well-off men, and beautiful, smiling women.

There was, finally, a third argument against dueling that was less explicit than the moral and political ones: the ambivalence among Porfirian public men over the physical aspects of the practice. From the beginning, dueling and training in the use of weapons had been praised as habits that buttressed masculinity. The fights of children would inevitably grow to become adults' disputes about "the female" in which, according to Láncaster Jones, men learn to see "in physical struggle a duty of virility."[108] Yet there were some inconvenient aspects of this physical logic that undermined equality. Tall men, for example, could withstand attacks in a sword duel by simply keeping their arm straight; and "a Herculean man" could wipe out a small one in hand-to-hand fighting but would tire faster in fencing encounters—as Verástegui admitted when instructing his seconds about the choice of weapons.[109] Although pistols provided a degree of equality, they required dexterity and, ideally, a lean profile to offer a smaller target. Verástegui paid dearly for his robust figure.

Fistfights were a constant if generally despised possibility. The novelist José López Portillo y Rojas explored bodily differences and the instability of honor in his 1919 *Fuertes y débiles* (The Strong and the Weak). Two characters, one of them a big, strong hacendado and the other a lean, cosmopolitan *catrín* (dandy), get into a bloody fistfight that, predictably, is won by the hacendado. A challenge ensues, but the hacendado refuses it, arguing that the brutality of all fights is the same, whether in the form of boxing (whose rules the two men knew but ignored during the fight) or through a more stylized exchange on the field of honor. A duel, he claimed, was a farce, or at best no better than any other form of fighting: "A fight is a brutal thing, and men, when we fight, are nothing more than beasts."[110]

Class distinction was an implicit factor in criticisms of the centrality of the body in dueling. The duel had an unfortunate similitude to the practices of lower-class men, the same men whom positivism identified with brute force and other animal attributes that made certain races, like the Mexican Indian, well suited for hard manual labor. In the biological notions espoused by positivists, the physicality of dueling, even if beneficial in terms of national masculinity, undermined the social classifications that propped up their assumption of their superiority. And gender distinction was also a cause of concern. Multiple references to fights among women as distorted mirrors of men's combats expressed a similar anxiety: anyone, even women and poor men, could fight and potentially claim the mantle of honor, as they already did in court.[111]

In historical terms, finally, dueling was a futile exercise. Too great an emphasis on fit bodies and the generous shedding of blood inevitably revealed that Porfirian men of honor could never really emulate the heroic legacy of the Reforma generation: nobody could match Manuel González's or Carlos Pacheco's selfless sacrifice of limbs in the defense of the patria.[112] Previous chapters offered partial views of the construction of a modern masculinity among Porfirian public men: the bohemian freedom and sexual escapades of journalists and students, the beautiful persona of orators, the proud rights of defamation victims. Strong bodies were only a minor aspect of that construction. Thus, the technology centered on the duel sought to avoid athleticism rather than making it a requirement for public men. The robust bodies of Verástegui and many of his contemporaries bespoke a more organized, stable sense of their place in public life.

Epilogue

The Romero-Verástegui case marked the beginning of the end of dueling in Mexico, and with it that of the entire complex of attitudes that tied honor to the development of the public sphere. Yet it would be wrong to assume an overnight change in the dispositions of public men. There were duels and challenges after 1895. The battle between científicos and Reyistas in the late years of the regime, for example, was articulated in terms of honor and came close to provoking a challenge at the highest levels of government. The aging dictator and the peaceful Limantour weathered that storm, but they could not survive a revolution. After civil war started, in 1910, the duel definitively lost its ability to regulate the use of violence by the political elite—the impact was comparable to that of the massive violence of World War I on European societies. Since the honorable use of violence was now broadly distributed, the duel's ability to signify social status was lost. The restrictive and symbolic function of dueling pistols in Mexico eroded after the "bullets' party" in battlefields and urban centers. Guns became increasingly common in fights that had formerly been resolved with knives, and soldiers of humble origins, such as Pancho Villa and Rodolfo Fierro, mastered their use.[113] The culture of the political elite also changed. In the view of the American historian of revolutionary Mexico Frank Tannenbaum, "The political philosophy of Mexico is saturated with the belief in violence, both for electoral purposes and to effect social change."[114]

A limited role for dueling in public life nevertheless remained after the revolution. The language of denouncing, challenging, and even fighting adversaries was common during the 1920s, when Congress and political parties had a central role in the construction of postrevolutionary legitimacy. Congressmen carried guns and, when discussions became too intense, had to take their quarrels onto "the field of honor."[115] Some postrevolutionary political legislators sought to preserve the preferential treatment of duelists inherited from the Porfiriato. The Penal Code of 1929 maintained the 1871 code's articles about dueling and added the establishment of a Court of Honor entrusted to mediate disputes between potential duelists. The Penal Code of 1931, passed as a more pragmatic alternative to the positivism of its predecessor, eliminated the specific regulation of dueling but maintained it as an attenuating circumstance in cases of battery and homicide.[116] Official protection for Mexican duelists, however, was gone by the 1920s. The few late cases of dueling after the revolution show fear of the police among those involved. In 1925, according to Escudero, a group of respectable and influential gentlemen had to find refuge in the backyard of a deserted summer house in San Angel Inn in order to celebrate the last duel in his account. The report by *Excélsior* read like an epitaph: "This duel caused a deep sensation in our social circles, not only because of the situation of the contenders, but also because these are events that had been eradicated from our customs many years ago, and we can see that half a century has passed since the last and famous duel between Mr. Verástegui and Romero."[117] Nobody was prosecuted and nobody died this time because honor no longer merited either the benign neglect of the state or the ultimate sacrifice of life.

Conclusions

When Santos Degollado chose to sacrifice his life in order to restore his good name, he faced an obligation which Mexican public men in the following decades hoped never to face again. Honor, however, remained the cardinal value for them during the República Restaurada and early Porfiriato, both in politics and, one imagines, in personal life. They wrote and spoke about it and sued, fought, and even took the streets to defend it. This book has followed those men's (and many women's) continuing struggle to grapple with the tyranny of opinion. Although most claimed to obey that strict ruler, they also dreaded its intransigent judgment over their public and private lives. But they could not do otherwise because they also hoped to build a political order in which the ability to speak for society was regulated and earned according to the laws of honor. These laws concerned journalism, parliamentary work, students' exuberance, the penal protection of reputation, and dueling. Yet norms were only the first level of political life: values, attitudes, and practical dispositions reflected the embrace, or rejection, of the tyranny of opinion among men and women. This book approaches the individual level of that dictatorship mostly through testimonies of conflict and negotiation. Public exchanges (in the press, in Congress, in the courts, and on street corners) illustrate the dialogical character of Mexican politics, even after the consolidation of Porfirio Díaz as ultimate arbiter of all disagreements. Codes and practices of honor, in other words, can be fully apprehended historically only if situated in a political system in which conflict was the norm.

This book is an effort to understand Mexican politics from a legal, social, and cultural perspective. Given the extensive reach of politics during the nineteenth century, such an effort could be conceived only on the basis of a selective use of the vast corpus of judicial, press, and literary sources. One hopes other scholars will uncover the weaknesses of the research behind this attempt and propose other ways to assemble the pieces—the most benevolent kind of criticism. There is much work to be done, for example, on the ways in which women used modern notions of honor to seek greater access to political and social agency. An entire dimension of life, domesticity, was a terrain for the negotiation of honor between actors, one that from the outside might be seen as inexorably unequal because of gender, age, and class difference. Those negotiations, I propose, happened at the outer margins of the public sphere, where intimacy revealed itself not as an inherent attribute of family life but as the product of public opinion's judgment. This book only touches on that realm, trying to reproduce and engage the language of its sources rather than analytically reduce it to an oversimplification.

Political history, including not only institutional analysis but also good old narrative, is fertile terrain. The work of Daniel Cosío Villegas informs the chapters above, which propose a critical take on his reading of the press and on his isolation of politics from the rest of social life. Such a perspective might have been healthy at the time he wrote, halfway through the twentieth century, but it seems now a dream of the past. Rather than his faith in the inevitability of democracy, this book borrows Cosío Villegas's sharp gaze to reveal Mexican elites' duplicity between liberal credo and authoritarian customs.

An economic subtext in my chapters builds that critique of political history. Rather than to a unifying thesis, I refer to a loosely connected string of ideas that hopes to justify further research and dialogue. The evidence examined in this book suggests the historical and cultural specificity of the articulation of economic interests. Chapter 1, for example, showed how public men hoped to counter institutional instability with firm rules for public opinion. If inherited status no longer accounted for honor (or not fully, at least), publicity was the inevitable mechanism through which to judge individual honors and establish trust. However profuse the regulations and deep the local roots of the press jury, the court of public opinion was not an even playing field. Journalists, examined in chapter 2, had a double relationship with public opinion. They shaped it with their writings but were also subject to its decisions regarding their own personal worth. Embracing this ambiguity, combat journalists saw the public sphere as a realm for the negotiation of their reputation. Specifically, they saw conflict in the press as a way of accumulating social and cultural capital that would translate into personal advancement—or into marginalization. The public sphere as a market of reputations was also in the minds of the orators examined in chapter 3. They were even more deliberate than journalists in translating social and cultural capital into political capital. Rhetoric was, for them, an instrument with which to construct their persona, but also a powerful weapon in the political battles that preceded, and failed to stop, the consolidation of that master of silence, Porfirio Díaz.

The episode of the deuda inglesa, examined in chapter 4, showed that there was no discontinuity between the honor of public men and that of the country. Thus, the language of honor was not metaphorical in discussions of the nation's credit, and it could lead from press and parliamentary debates to street riots and to tense encounters between politicians and the crowd. Within the political elite a consensus about the identity of national honor with the dutiful payment of the debt began to prevail— even if that seemed to contradict the patriotism that had recently made possible the defeat of foreign invaders. The episode revealed the limits of the romantic model in regard to the reign of public opinion as judge of personal and collective credit. That chapter also examined a specific articulation of economic interests encompassed in the notion of Bohemia. The pursuit of social capital by journalists and students, who were always at the margins of poverty and ambition, was rational: they could become members of the political and cultural elites thanks to the connections and prestige they built during youth, that period when economic disinterest coincided with urban sexual explorations and homosocial fraternity.

As the country embarked on a stable and systematic experiment of capitalist growth, the reforming of the rules for the negotiation of personal honor was the necessary counterpoint to the reform of institutions and policies that would lead to the restoration of the national credit. The transformation of honor into an objective good took place at the collective and individual level during the 1880s. Chapter 5 described how the penal protection of reputations, which replaced press juries and undermined the court of public opinion, constructed a more objective notion of honor. In the internal realm of individual citizens, men and women, rich and poor, honor began to be defined and defended more explicitly as a reputation that guaranteed credit. A good reputation was necessary if citizens were to thrive in an economy increasingly characterized by anonymous monetary exchanges in the open realms of city streets and international markets. From social capital, honor came thus to mean just capital. Chapter 6 looked at how people used courts to defend that asset. During the last two decades of the nineteenth century there emerged a specific configuration of the links between the public and the private, personal and collective interests, individuals and the state. The new system had political, cultural, and social dimensions that this book opens for examination. The tyranny of opinion was the most visible regulatory mechanism of a moral economy that in part survives even today.

Chapter 7, however, showed that it was impossible to calculate precisely the cost of honor because, however objectively defined, it could still come at the expense of life. The decadence of the duel was a sign of a deeper change in public culture and notions of the self in Mexico: some things could not be judged publicly, and the restoration of privacy and a protected sense of self-worth were, if boring, ultimately beneficial for all. The moral economy of public and personal life that drove Santos Degollado to his demise was now less tyrannical as violence came to be associated with the thuggery of a few men. To have a name and to keep one's word, and to trade these publicly, were no longer central aspects of political life. The potential contribution of these insights to other studies of economic behavior might justify the endeavor. Examining the texture of personal interactions will be useful in a critical examination of the cultural construction of interest and trust and of institutions' role therein.

Women, domesticity, political narratives, moral economy: I have tried to say something useful in these three realms, but my efforts will be successful only if they become part of a broader conversation. The conversation begins, of course, with the evidence. The basic thesis of this book— that honor occupied a central place in the system of values that structured public life during the República Restaurada and early Porfiriato—can be challenged and contradicted using the same kind of sources I have summoned. A very synthetic list of my findings suggests one way to fit the many pieces of the puzzle: as soon as Mexico broke its ties with Spain and during the ensuing decades of struggle to preserve independence and integrity as a nation, its political elites tried to find a way to reconcile free speech with respect of personal reputations—since political parties and Masonic lodges did not have all that much reputation to lose. The undertaking involved a systematic codification of two equally important rights: free speech and honor. Such a project implied—and this was probably its most traumatic aspect for Mexican elite men—embracing a modern notion of honor in which inherited status was of relatively small importance in the inexorable eye of public opinion. The concept of public opinion emerges from this narrative not merely as the expression of popular sovereignty on issues of common interest—as in the usual definition of the term in political history—but also judgment on individuals by the community.

Modern honor (egalitarian, publicly negotiated, more democratic and flexible than in the colonial past) and public opinion (of multiple voices and themes) were not easy to manage. They combined in explosive ways when Congress debated the deuda inglesa or when, on a smaller scale, people of all social backgrounds argued over their reputations. The era studied in this book involves the high point of that combination, after the triumph of liberalism made it possible to start building a public sphere in which violence would not be the ultimate solution for dissent. Simultaneously, however, a growing sector of politicians, lawyers, and letrados began to voice concern about the subversive effects of the tyranny of opinion. The abolition of the press juries in 1882 was the most meaningful moment in the process of taming honor and public opinion. The systematic enforcement of the penal protection of honor defined as a juridical good was a coeval transformation. Together with the consolidation of a political regime that administered the press and judges and arbitrated disputes, these changes were the final stage in the building of a more disciplined yet no less honorable public life that endured until the revolution—one in which the intersection of honor and public opinion would be more manageable than in the recent past.

The story does not have a precise beginning or end. Honor continued to be central, particularly for Mexican elites but also for working-class men, for many years afterward. Masculinity and honor remained "naturally" associated. Not too long ago, the eminent historian Edmundo O'Gorman tried to define the Mexican being as "the beauty and abnegation of the woman; the extraordinary sexual potency of the man, his daring courage in the face of danger and his punctilious dignity when faced with insult. And, at another level, the proliferation of very pure heroes, lay saints who leave, for the guidance and consolation of future generations, a legacy of example and sacrifice, of statements of edifying patriotism."[1] My thesis is that O'Gorman's gendered language of honor has deep ideological roots and long-lasting political consequences. As I began to write these conclusions a journalist named Lydia Cacho faced judicial threats and harassment justified by libel laws that had not changed much since the nineteenth century. With the support of the governor of the State of Puebla, Mario Marín, the businessman Kamel Nacif planned to use the indictment and arrest of Cacho as a setup for attacks against her in prison. The plan failed thanks to the intervention of female prison guards and to the reaction of a public that would no longer bear such abuses. The crimes of difamación and calumnias were finally abrogated in the Federal Penal Code in 2007, and Cacho was able to vindicate herself when the real reason for the judicial harassment carried out against her was identified—her courageous charges of pederasty against several powerful men. A man's reputation no longer justified the silencing of a serious journalist.

The story of Lydia Cacho and those of other journalists recently accused of libel by public figures show that honor still plays a role, although much diminished, in the process of building a strong public sphere. This book's thesis that honor is the keystone in the construction of the Mexican public sphere still has considerable relevance today. On July 16, 2006, probably more than a million people in the streets of Mexico City demanded that their votes be recounted, potentially turning a disputed presidential election in favor of the candidate of the left, Andrés Manuel López Obrador. Walking among them on Reforma Avenue, one could not but think that the fight was less about the decision of the electoral court that would adjudicate the complaints of the opposition (against them, as it turned out) than about the media's coverage of campaigns, candidates, and the preliminary outcome of the ballot. The crowds cheered in front of large video screens, chanted in protest of the television duopoly, and applauded the names of journalists like Carlos Monsiváis (who spoke to the crowd) and Rafael Barajas, "El Fisgón"—both of whom are also historians of liberalism in the era of Juárez and Díaz.

In other words, the struggle for democracy has become, again, a struggle for access to the public sphere. The demonstrators seemed to know that there cannot be a legitimate electoral outcome if the possibility of an egalitarian and rational dialogue is canceled beforehand. The old liberal struggle between reputation and free speech is still there, however. In view of the negative campaigning against López Obrador in previous months and also of the accusations against Lydia Cacho, there cannot be a strong public sphere if there is not in addition a reconsideration of the rules that limit opinion's power over citizens' reputations. Punishment is no longer the best means of solving the problem, but it is too early to tell how the public sphere can regulate itself when state, parties, and large corporations have such control over the media. The liberal dilemma cannot be solved, this much we know, if we do not examine the historical contingency of honor and the public sphere.

This book is about the historicity of reason in the Mexican context. From the methodological point of view it proposes a study of politics that crosses traditional disciplinary boundaries and examines the ethics of communication between multiple, unevenly empowered actors. The intentions behind politicians' decisions are, from this point of view, less relevant than the disputes on the public record over the consolidation of a democratic or authoritarian regime. In the late nineteenth century, those disputes focused on honor as the key to represent public opinion, to enjoy personal and ideological authority, and even to define reason. That was how the Díaz regime truncated the democratic expansion of the public sphere: appropriating honor to silence dissent and to solidify class and gender hierarchies in the name of science. When the revolution brought him down, the Mexican public sphere was too narrow to effectively channel popular mobilization. The civil war made possible a new political order that was more integrative, able to spread a political language that gave voice to groups formerly silenced by power. Yet the postrevolutionary regime was also characterized by an effective control of the press through cooptation, some repression, and a Press Law passed in 1917 that was particularly severe in its protection of reputation. Although the law was not aggressively enforced, it was clear to journalists and readers in the twentieth century that the private lives (and interests) of politicians were off limits to the examination of public opinion.

Only in the latter years of the twentieth century and the beginning of the twenty-first do we see, in cases like Cacho's, a strong challenge to that tacit limit to public debate. The result, not surprisingly, has been a revival of honor as a juridical good. If we try to put the Mexican present in historical perspective, it seems more important than ever to test the public sphere as an analytical category. Doing so allows for a more comprehensive examination of politics, one that involves the study of culture and gender in addition to the social factors commonly cited to explain hegemony and resistance. Asking questions about communication is not simply a way of dissolving the boundaries of political analysis. It can be a positive contribution in the effort, for example, to build a more systematic bridge across the big historical break of 1910.

The dispute over the rules and the membership of the public sphere is a thread that runs through Mexican history ever since independence, if not before. It is not the only dispute of national dimensions, of course, and it is probably not the one that will revitalize a teleological narrative from an autocratic to an open system—that, at least, has not been my intention. But, as I have stressed throughout this book, neither was power ever able to completely transform public opinion into an instrument of domination and conformism. The explanation I offer is that public men never quite agreed to emancipate themselves from the tyranny of opinion. As a result, the political history of the country cannot be told simply as a history of power (or, the same thing, one of power and resistance) because power as an analytical category cannot account for the tensions between the external perceptions of an individual and the intimate realm of *conciencia*—that voice telling Santos Degollado that there was no escape. This book attempts to bring those two realms together in a historically meaningful way.

Whereas my goal has been to make our historical understanding of politics more comprehensive, and probably also more complicated, the political desire behind this book is simpler to define. It consists in following the guide of Jürgen Habermas and others toward a recovery of reason as the most important value for dialogue in the public sphere. Reason might sound like a sorry anachronism from those who, rightly so, see exclusion as the central problem of the contemporary cultural, economic, and political order. Reason has been invoked too often as the justification of market-driven policies that have the net effect of increasing inequality while preserving the silence imposed on certain groups on account of their alleged or implicit intellectual inferiority. But I would like to conclude by invoking a notion of reason more akin to that held by some Mexican liberals of the nineteenth century: a common language that would exclude violence while creating a universal public able to participate on a level field of discussion. Reason, in other words, not as an attribute of identity but as a tool of communication and recognition. As Monsiváis said to the crowd in July 2006, "In politics, the opposite of hatred is not love. . . . The opposite of hatred is the systematic exercise of reason."[2] Understanding the history of reason can be useful in choosing between the bifurcating paths open to Mexican democracy today: that of exclusion and that of effective dialogue.

NOTES

Abbreviations

ADSG   Archivo General de la Nación, Fondo Antonio Díaz Soto y Gama

AGN   Archivo General de la Nación

AHDFJ   Archivo Histórico del Distrito Federal, Justicia Jurados de Imprenta. Cited as AHDFJ, (volume or box), (folder or legajo), (document, when specified).

AHSTJM   Archivo Histórico del Tribunal Superior de Justicia de Michoacán, Primera Instancia Penal, Morelia, Morelia. Cited as AHSTJM, (legajo), (document).

AL   Archivo J. I. Limantour, Condumex. Cited as AL, (series), (roll).

ASCJN   Archivo de la Suprema Corte de Justicia de la Nación. Cited as ASCJN, (box), (legajo), (folder), (year).

BCN   Fondo Basave del Castillo Negrete – Centro de Estudios sobre la Universidad, Universidad Nacional Autónoma de México. Cited as BCN, (box or legajo), (folder or document), (page).

CP 1871   Código penal para el Distrito Federal y Territorio de la Baja-California sobre delitos del fuero común y para toda la República Mexicana sobre delitos contra la Federación.

CPD   Colección Porfirio Díaz, UIA. Cited as CPD, (legajo), (document).

DDCD   Diario de los Debates de la Cámara de Diputados. Cited as DDCD, (legislature), (pages).

DH   *Diario del Hogar*

EA   *El Ahuizote, parte política*

EF   *El Foro*

EHA   *El Hijo del Ahuizote*

EN   *El Nacional*

FB   Archivo General de la Nación, Fondo Francisco Bulnes. Cited as FB, (box or volume), (folder).

JSM   Colección Justo Sierra Méndez—Centro de Estudios sobre la Universidad, Universidad Nacional Autónoma de México. Cited as JSM, (box), (folder), (page).

LL   *La Libertad*

LP   *La Patria*

LVM   *La Voz de México*

MR   *El Monitor Republicano*

RCH   Fondo Rafael Chousal—Centro de Estudios sobre la Universidad, Universidad Nacional Autónoma de México. Cited as RCH, (box), (file), (page).

RLJ   *Revista de Legislación y Jurisprudencia*

SDC   Santos Degollado Correspondence, Benson Latin American Collection, Austin. Cited as SDC, (folder), (years).

TSJDF   Tribunal Superior de Justicia del Distrito Federal. Cited as TSJDF, (box), (year), (folder), (type of crime).

Introduction

1. Degollado to Gen. Jesus Ortega, Lagos, 2 October 1860, SDC, 1, 1856–76; Sierra, *Juárez*, 225–32, 141, 136–37. Sierra mistakenly has the funds going to Manzanillo. See British, French, and Spanish Consuls to Miguel Azúa, Gov. of Zacatecas, 15 September 1860, SDC, 1, 1856–76.

2. Sierra, *Juárez*, 225–32, 141, 136–37.

3. Gilberto Moreno, "El Sr. General Don Santos Degollado," undated transcription of an article, in SDC, 2, 1861–1907. The first bullet to hit Degollado, a report noted, may have come from his own troops. Francisco Zarco, "La muerte del Sr. Degollado," transcription of article published in *El Siglo Diez y Nueve*, 18 June 1861, in SDC, 2, 1861–1907.

4. Sierra, *Juárez*, 225–32, 141, 136–37. From Degollado's words and throughout this book, I translate *honra* as "honor." *Honra* is defined according to external perceptions as "la buena opinión que se tiene de una persona, esa opinión no se destruye sino afirmando de esa propia persona algo que contrarie ese buen concepto de que goza." *Informes producidos*, 10. It does not have an English equivalent that would suggest this emphasis on reputation. On Justo Sierra (1848–1913) see chapters 2 and 3. Degollado was born in 1811 and died in 1861. A testimony of his willingness to clear his name, with the help of one of his sons, in Degollado, *Defensa ante el público*. An interesting biographical account in "Apuntes relativos a Don Santos Degollado, escritos al parecer por D. José Ma. Marroquin," SDC, 2, 1861–1907.

5. RLJ (January–February 1894), 101. Jacinto Pallares (1843–1904) was also a lawyer, as was Vallarta (1830–93). Generational classifications are approximate. Justo Sierra, argued Puga y Acal, fell in between those two generations. "Prólogo a Lirismos de Antaño" [1923], in Puga y Acal, *Los poetas mexicanos*, 152–53.

6. Sierra, *Evolución política*, 295; Francisco W. González, "Boletín," MR, 24 February 1886, 1. For an image of a journalist and heroic guerrilla fighter, Frías, *¿Águila o sol?*, 18. In the following pages "public men" refers to those who addressed the public in different capacities, including journalists, congressmen, and other elected officials; "political elite" refers to those with the ability to influence political decisions. The first was more commonly used by the subjects of this book. See, e.g., "Cartas de Junius. A un aspirante a gobernante. Diccionario político, literario y mundano para uso de los tontos o sean los aspirantes a hombres públicos," LL, 4 January 1884, 1.

7. The identity afforded by age was never questioned. Sierra defined his cohort as "Somos los que rodeamos a aquellos que han quedado de la inmortal Reforma santa generación." "Improvisación" [1876], in Sierra, *Obras completas*, 1:377.

8. See, e.g., Cosío Villegas, *La República Restaurada*; Cosío Villegas, *El porfiriato*; Carmagnani and Hernández Chávez, "La ciudadanía orgánica"; Roeder, *Juárez*; Guerra, *México*; but see Mallon, *Peasant and Nation*; Knight, "Weapons and Arches." Mexican political history as the careers and characters of a few central men, easily boiled down to a self-contained game of names and power, in, e.g., Krauze, *Porfirio Díaz*; González y González, *La ronda de las generaciones*; Prida, *De la dictadura*. See also Cosío Villegas, "Octava llamada particular," in Cosío Villegas, *El porfiriato*, xv.: "de las guerras de Reforma e Intervención sale una pléyade de gobernantes que si bien podían diferir, y difirieron, en su trasfondo personal y aun sensiblemente en edad, habían vivido durante una época histórica que les deja una marca común tanto más perdurable cuanto que todos ellos, a su vez, ayudan a forjarla."

9. Yáñez, "Don Justo Sierra," 50.

10. Frías, *Episodios militares*, 184; Sierra, *Juárez*, 69. See also Vázquez Mantecón, *Santa Anna*.

11. Sierra, *Juárez*, 64, 68, 556.

12. Sierra, *Juárez*, 64. For the concern about honor among other members of the political elite during this period, see Vázquez Mantecón, "El honor y la virtud," 22–24. On the moral meaning of Balinese cockfight, see Geertz, *The Interpretation of Cultures*.

13. See Frías, *Episodios militares*, 184, 201. See also Sierra's last chapter of his work on Juárez, "Los tres grandes hombres de México," Sierra, *Juárez*, 553–65. On monarchism, which historians are increasingly reluctant to dismiss as anomalous, see Pani, *Para mexicanizar*; Soto Estrada, *La conspiración monárquica*; O'Gorman, *México: El trauma de su historia*; Rojas, *La escritura*; Palti, "Introducción."

14. Sierra, *Juárez*, 128. See also Garner, *Porfirio Díaz*; Bazant, *Alienation*.

15. Prida, *De la dictadura*, 31.

16. French revolutionary politicization meant the expansion of the public realm, the expectation of an internal change among citizens ("replacing honor with virtue," according to Robespierre), and the increasing seclusion of women in the domestic sphere, resulting in "the development of a more sharply differenti-

ated private space in the early nineteenth century [and] an impetus for the romantic withdrawal into the self." Perrot, *Private Life IV*, 13, 14, 22. The "país político" was contrasted to "el pueblo, socialmente considerado" in Sierra, *Evolución política*, 373.

17. *El libro secreto*; Hermann, *Con Maximiliano*. See also Macías González, "Mexican Aristocracy."

18. Quoted in Prida, *De la dictadura*, 26–27, 29, 38. For Díaz's resentment of Juárez and ambivalence between private and public life in 1867, see Cosío Villegas, *La República Restaurada*, 202–03, 207–08, 216; Garner, *Porfirio Díaz*.

19. Buve and Falcón, *Don Porfirio presidente*; Coatsworth, *Los orígenes*.

20. The political significance of Mexican romanticism has been largely neglected by the historical literature. For an exception, see current work by Carlos Illades in *Nación, sociedad*. But see Berlin, *Las raíces*. Latin American romanticism characterized by its political focus in Carilla, *El romanticismo*, 1:23. For an early effort to define Latin American romanticism, stressing "los sentimientos de amor, honor, patriotismo y religión," and its liberal inspiration, see Vallejo, *El romanticismo*, 17, 23. See also Puga y Acal, *Los poetas mexicanos*, 32; McGann, *The Romantic Ideology*, 107; Sommer, *Foundational Fictions*, 102; Parker and Peers, "The Vogue of Victor Hugo in Spain," 36, 37, 40.

21. Pizarro Suárez, *Obras*, 1:288.

22. Chandler, *England in 1819*, 175, 194; Porter and Teich, *Romanticism*, 1–6, 37; Picard, *Le romantisme social*, 53; Sommer, *Foundational Fictions*.

23. Porter and Teich, *Romanticism*, 260–66, 278; McGann, *The Romantic Ideology*, 134–36, 114, 39; Shelley, *A Defence of Poetry*, 90; Picard, *Le romantisme social*, 50, 65, 77; Kaiser, *Romanticism, Aesthetics, and Nationalism*, 5, 9.

24. Zarco, *Escritos literarios*, 231; "¡Oh patria idolatrada, yo en tus quebrantos, / ensalcé con ternura tus fueros santos, / sin arredrarme; / tu tierra era mi carne, tu amor mi vida, / hiel acerba en tus duelos fue mi bebida / para embriagarme!" Guillermo Prieto, "Cantares" [1889], in *Los Poetas*, Nuri de la Cabada and Luis de la Cabada, webmasters, accessed 22 January 2008, http://www.lospoetas.com/prieto/prieto1.htm.

25. The paradigm was formulated, from the perspective of poetry, by Octavio Paz in *Generaciones y semblanzas*, 41–42.

26. Abrams, *The Mirror and the Lamp*, 22.

27. For a useful warning against confusing "honour in its substantive and its analytical senses," see Wikan, "Shame and Honour," 645. I use "theory" following the suggestion of Michael Herzfeld and Michael Taussig to place subject's knowledges on the same theoretical plane as scholarly models. Rather than theory, they refer to the theoretical value of the subjects' own categorization of their reality. Herzfeld, *The Poetics of Manhood*, xiii; Taussig, *Shamanism*. "It is rather in ethnographic particularism that we should seek, without any sense of paradox, those theoretical insights which the reductionist generalisation of glossing can never yield." Herzfeld, "Honour and Shame," 349.

28. Gutiérrez, *When Jesus Came*, 178, 194, 206. Honor as being "at the apex of

the pyramid of temporal social values and it conditions their hierarchical order," Peristiany, "Introduction," 10. For honor as exclusive upper-class concern, Socolow, *The Women*, 8–9, 78–79; Uribe Uran, *Honorable Lives*. But see Stern, *The Secret History*; Johnson and Lipsett-Rivera, *Faces of Honor*.

29. On the increasing concern about honor among the political elite in Spain in the seventeenth century, Maravall, *Poder, honor y élites*. See also Stern, *The Secret History*, 9, 15; Seed, *To Love, Honor*; Castelán Rueda, *La fuerza*, 39. According to the *Diccionario de autoridades* (1734), "honor" is defined as "honra con esplendor y publicidad" and also "reputación y lustre de alguna familia, acción u otra cosa" and "obsequio, aplauso o celebridad de alguna cosa"; "honra" means "reverencia, acatamiento y veneración que se hace a la virtud, autoridad o mayoría de una persona," although it also included masculine "pundonor" and feminine "integridad virginal." "Honestidad" is defined in terms of behavior as "la compostura, modestia y moderación en la persona, en las acciones y las palabras" but also "moderación y pureza contraria al vicio de la luxuria." "Honradez" emphasizes male virtues: "Aquel genero de pundonor que obliga al hombre de bien a obrar siempre conforme a sus obligaciones, y cumplir su palabra en todo." Real Academia, *Diccionario 1734*. "Pundonor" is "Aquel estado en que, segun las varias opiniones de los hombres, consiste la honra o crédito de alguno." Real Academia, *Diccionario 1737*. For a discussion of honra and honor, see Johnson and Lipsett-Rivera, "Introduction," 3–4.

30. Twinam, *Public Lives*. Víctor Uribe applies a Weberian version of honor as status to examine the rewards of bureaucracy and the adjudicating role of the state: the greater the proximity to the upper levels of the colonial regime, in his view, the greater the personal and familial honor. Uribe Uran, *Honorable Lives*. See also Burkholder, "Honor and Honors." For honor and the rules of court society, Elias, *La sociedad cortesana*.

31. The Porfirian Federico Gamboa wished his son to become an "honorable y honrado" man, a "caballero a la antigua . . . de los que ya nada más van quedando borrosos y vagos en el recuerdo de los descendientes de las familias linajudas, y en los cuadros vetustos de los museos y catedrales." Gamboa, *Mi diario III*, 11. Gamboa later depicted his poverty as a sign of his *honradez*. Gamboa, *Mi diario VI*, 188. For the cultural and political influence of the Mexican aristocracy, see Macías González, "Mexican Aristocracy." Eighteenth-century *cuadros de casta* were imaginary depictions, mostly for foreign consumption, of a society in which interethnic marrying was diluting neat racial categories, wealth did buy honor, even whiteness, and European parvenus rapidly climbed the social ladder. See Twinam, *Public Lives*, 33; Twinam, "The Negotiation of Honor," 77–78; Gutiérrez, *When Jesus Came*, 176–77.

32. Pitt-Rivers, "Honour," 21.

33. Ibid., 27; Stewart, *Honor*, 16. Stewart distinguishes "subjective honor" from "objectified honor," named "honra" in Spanish. Ibid., 15. "Honour, however, is only irrevocably committed by attitudes expressed in the presence of witnesses, the representatives of public opinion. . . . Public opinion forms therefore a tri-

bunal before which the claims to honour are brought, 'the court of reputation' as it has been called, and against its judgments there is no redress." Pitt-Rivers, "Honour," 27. The *Diccionario de la real academia* (1869) places publicity and opinion as the key to its definition of "honor": "Carácter moral, que resulta del religioso cumplimiento de los deberes impuestos por la sociedad o la opinión. Gloria o buena reputación que sigue a la virtud, al mérito o a las acciones heroicas, la cual trasciende a las familias, personas y acciones mismas del que se la granjea." Real Academia, *Diccionario 1869*.

34. Gilmore, *Manhood in the Making*, 27; Wikan, "Shame and Honour," 642. A clear statement in Bourdieu, "The Sentiment of Honour," 219, 223. Wikan sees that as a bias in Mediterranean anthropology. "'Honour' is bound up with male ideology," Wikan, "Shame and Honour," 638. For an example of the symmetry between male/female and honor/shame, see Gutiérrez, *When Jesus Came*, 209.

35. Although he avoided honor as a reference for analysis in *Poetics of Manhood*, his book offers a useful model for understanding the local construction of subjectivities and ethical codes—which in late nineteenth-century Mexico explicitly centered on the notion of honor. Herzfeld, "Honour and Shame," 349. See also Gilmore, *Manhood in the Making*; Gilmore, "Introduction."

36. For a critique of the "Mediterranean society" model, see Fiume, *Onore e storia*; Davidson, "Dover, Foucalt," 29; Gilmore, "Introduction"; Herzfeld, "Honour and Shame."

37. Taylor, *Magistrates*, 645n101. For John Peristiany, for example, "Honour and shame are the constant preoccupation of individuals in small scale, exclusive societies where face to face personal, as opposed to anonymous, relations are of paramount importance and where the social personality of the actor is as significant as his office." Peristiany, "Introduction," 10. For another attempt to apply the model, see Wyatt-Brown, *Southern Honor*. On modern honor, see Nye, *Masculinity and Male Codes*; Reddy, *The Invisible Code*; Spierenburg, *Men and Violence*.

38. Fonseca, "Philanderers, Cuckolds"; Prieur, "Domination and Desire"; Stern, *The Secret History*.

39. Johnson and Lipsett-Rivera, "Introduction," 2, 5, 6, 7, 12; Burkholder, "Honor and Honors," 34; Twinam, "The Negotiation of Honor," 72–73; Stern, *The Secret History*. Honor is a "complex of values and behaviors" not transferred without changes, "seldom absolute, but rather subject to negotiation"—quoting Elizabeth S. Cohen. Twinam, "The Negotiation of Honor," 72. These authors criticize Patricia Seed's use of drama to reconstruct a picture of honor that is too normative. Yet her study of conflicts over marriage points to important changes in the meanings of honor and the role of the state in enforcing morality and patriarchy through the colonial period; Cook and Cook, *Good Faith and Truthful Ignorance*; Seed, *To Love, Honor*.

40. See Bourdieu, *Meditaciones* 220; Bourdieu, *Outline*, 178, 181. A useful review in Portes, "Social Capital."

41. Verdo, "El escándalo de la risa"; Chambers, *From Subjects to Citizens*. For

the survival of honor and its expansion to lower strata, Johnson and Lipsett-Rivera, "Introduction," 14; Peter Guardino, "'We should not be made unequal': Afro-Mexicans and National Identity in 19th-century Mexico," presented at the symposium "Common Vocabularies, Different Perspectives: New Political History on Nineteenth-Century Latin America," New York City, May 2007. For honor as a motivation for lower-class violence after the triumph of liberalism, Piccato, *City of Suspects*, 80–81. For a pathbreaking study linking public opinion and honor in a Mexican society, see Greenberg, *Blood Ties*, 5–6, 225.

42. Chambers, *From Subjects to Citizens*; Annino, "Cádiz y la revolución territorial"; Lempérière, "Reflexiones"; Guerra and Lempérière, "Introducción"; Carmagnani and Hernández Chávez, "La ciudadanía orgánica"; Granados, "Calpultin decimonónicos"; Lira, *Comunidades indígenas*; Guardino, "Barbarism or Republican Law?"; Forment, *Democracy in Latin America*.

43. Wikan, "Shame and Honour," 645; Sedgwick, *Between Men*. Examples of the literature on machos, working women, and lower-class culture include Lomnitz, *Networks and Marginality*; González de la Rocha, *The Resources of Poverty*; Gutmann, *The Meaning of Macho*; Gutmann, "Los hijos de Lewis"; Gutmann, ed., *Changing Men*; Lewis, *The Children of Sánchez*. On homosociality and homosexuality, Irwin, *Mexican Masculinities*; Irwin, McCaughan, and Nasser, *The Famous 41*; Prieur, *Mema's House*; Prieur, "Domination and Desire." For an excellent description of night life and masculine sociability, González Rodríguez, *Bajos Fondos*. Among the best studies of women in Mexico during this period, see Ramos et al., *Presencia y transparencia*; Arrom, *Women*; Vaughan, "Modernizing Patriarchy."

44. Castelán Rueda, *La fuerza*, 71, 85. On the changing meaning of "the public," see Lempérière, "Reflexiones." "In this milieu, the idea of public opinion would refer to the 'reputation' that a given leader enjoyed, the prestige that allowed the individual to 'represent' the community and serve as the nexus with the other bodies that together formed the nation." Palti, "Recent studies," 258. See a suggestive approach in Verdo, "El escándalo de la risa."

45. Connell, *Masculinities*, 99; Stewart, *Honor*, 140. For the "bodily rhetoric of honour," see Foucault, *Discipline and Punish*, 135. On the uncertainty inherent in manhood, see Gilmore, *Manhood in the Making*, 27; Wikan, "Shame and Honour," 642; Fiume, "Onore e storia," 9. But see Bourdieu, "The Sentiment of Honour," 219, 223; Zedner, *Women, Crime*, 12.

46. An example in Sierra, *Obras completas*, 2:147; Sedgwick, *Between Men*. See also Wikan, "Shame and Honour," 638; Herzfeld, *The Poetics of Manhood*; Butler, *Bodies that Matter*.

47. Degollado to Gral. Francisco Casanova, San Pedro, 3 June 1858, and Degollado to Ignacio M. Guerra, Guadalajara, 9 November 1858, both in SDC, 1, 1856–76. Yet he also criticized those who, amid political debates, neglected "la ley fundamental que veda imprimir escritos contra la vida privada." Degollado to Minister of Guerra y Marina, Gral. José Gil Parte Arroyo, 10 April 1860, in SDC, 1, 1856–76.

48. Chartier, "Opinion Publique et Propagande"; Ozouf, "Le concept d'opinion publique"; Rojas, *La escritura*; Guerra, "De la política antigua"; Baker, *Inventing the French Revolution*, chap. 8; Habermas, *Structural Transformation*, chap. 4; Chartier, *Cultural Origins*, chap. 2; Chartier, *Espacio público*; Furet, *Penser*. For the origins of public opinion in trials against Jansenist priests, Maza, *Private Lives*, 37. But see also Kershaw, *Popular Opinion*. For the transformation of public opinion from a tribunal of reason to representation of the "public spirit"— unanimous, coeval to national sovereignty, expressed not so much as a debate but as the intuition of political leaders, guided by a strong state, and eventually replaced by "public order"—see Ozouf, "Espíritu público." As part of urban politics, "opinions" were all plausible, arguable, and investigated by the political police. Farge, *Subversive Words*.

49. Studies of Latin America before the era of mass media interpret the contradictions between the public spirit and diverse opinions as a manifestation of the dominating tension between the ancien régime's collective sociabilities and the individualism of the modern era. At the same time, these studies see the building of public opinion in Latin American countries as a progressive expansion of the restrictive public space (not necessarily the public sphere) of the upper classes. For recent discussions, see Guerra and Lempérière, *Los espacios públicos*; Annino, "Ciudadanía versus gobernabilidad"; Sábato, *The Many and the Few*. See also Palti, "La transformación del liberalismo"; Mallon, *Peasant and Nation*.

50. Chambers, *From Subjects to Citizens*; Lomnitz, *Deep Mexico*.

51. Palti, *La invención de una legitimidad*, 52–53; Palti, "Las polémicas." I have a fundamental debt to Palti's insights. See also Fernando Escalante's discussion of public opinion as part of the Mexican political elite's "imagining" of citizenship: unanimous, reasonable, limited to a narrow, self-referential group of men. Yet, as Escalante shows, writers saw public opinion as both the support of republicanism and an obstacle to despotism, thus the continuing subsidy of newspapers. Escalante, *Ciudadanos imaginarios*, 259–78. A critique in Palti, "Recent Studies." See José María Luis Mora's ideas in this regard in chapter 1.

52. See, for example, Illades, *Hacia la república*, 73; Anderson, *Outcasts*.

53. Rousseau, *Lettre à d'Alembert*. See also his preamble to *Discourse on the Origin and Foundations of Inequality among Men* (1755) in Rousseau, *Basic Political Writings*, 28. Thus, even though Rousseau criticizes the "extravagant" logic of dueling, he notes that "the law cannot force a person to dishonor himself." Rousseau, *Lettre à d'Alembert*, 144–46. See also Farge, *Subversive Words*, 61. On theater, Sennett, *The Fall of Public Man*.

54. Rousseau, *Basic Political Writings*.

55. Habermas, *Structural Transformation*, 27. First German edition published in 1962.

56. See Habermas, *Theory of Communicative Action*.

57. Habermas, *Structural Transformation*; Chartier, *Cultural Origins*; Melton, *The Rise*; Hurd, *Public Spheres*; Nathans, "The French Revolution in Review." For Latin America, Chambers, *From Subjects to Citizens*; Palti, "Introducción";

Guerra and Lempérière, *Los espacios públicos*; Lomnitz, "Ritual, Rumor." I discuss that literature and the model itself in Piccato, "Public Sphere."

58. For further discussion of the usefulness of the model in the Mexican case, see Piccato, "El parlamentarismo." On the exclusions from the public sphere, see Eley, "Nations, Publics"; Hurd, *Public Spheres*; Chartier, *Cultural Origins*, 22; Calhoun, "Introduction," 3. Particularly useful is Habermas, "Prefacio." On republican honor, Nye, *Masculinity and Male Codes*. For the idea of a "democratized honor," see Reddy, *The Invisible Code*. A necessary reference is Johnson and Lipsett-Rivera, *Faces of Honor*. For the need to transcend the "false opposition between public and private spheres," see Goodman, "Public Sphere," 1, 12.

59. J. H. González and Alfredo Chavero to Benito Juárez, Mexico City, 18 September 1876, SDC, f 1, 1856–76.

PART I. *Travails of Opinion*

1. *La Linterna*, 2 April 1877, reproduced in Barajas Durán, *El país de "el llorón,"* 112.

2. Rabasa, "Moneda falsa," 333–34.

3. On the relationship between journalists and politicians, see Cosío Villegas, *El porfiriato*; Escalante, *Ciudadanos imaginarios*, 271–77.

4. Cosío Villegas, *La república restaurada*, 53. Similar readings in Barajas Durán, *El país de "el llorón"*; Monsiváis, *Las herencias ocultas*.

5. Cosío Villegas, *La república restaurada*, 69–70, 351; Cosío Villegas, *El porfiriato*, 1:419. The thesis resonated with Cosío Villegas's attitudes on the "abuses" of freedom: Marxists were excluded from the seminar that produced the *Historia moderna*. Cosío Villegas, *La república restaurada*, 28; Cosío Villegas, "Primera llamada," in Cosío Villegas, *La república restaurada*; Roeder, *Hacia el México moderno*. On Cosío Villegas's "undue reliance on newspapers" in the *Historia moderna*, see Hale, "The Liberal Impulse," 487–89. For recent studies that return to a close, albeit more sophisticated use of the Iberoamerican press, see Alonso, *Construcciones impresas*.

6. See Guerra, *México*; Toussaint Alcaraz, *Escenario de la prensa*. An important antecedent in Valadés, *El porfirismo*. For the symptomatic absence of journalists, see Romana Falcón, ed., *Actores políticos*; Roderi A. Camp, ed., *Los intelectuales*. On the separation of political explanations in the *Historia moderna*, see Hale, "The Liberal Impulse," 493. For a useful discussion of *pensadores* and historically defined intellectuals, see Miller, *In the Shadow of the State*, 4–5.

7. The impact of Francois-Xavier Guerra's latter works is decisive here and, through them, the approaches of Francois Furet and Jürgen Habermas. Guerra and Lempérière, *Los espacios públicos*; Guerra, *Modernidad e independencias*. A good example in Delgado Carranco, *Libertad de imprenta*. See also Pani and Castro de Salmerón, *Conceptualizar*; Castro, *Tipos y caracteres*; Rojas, *La escritura*; Castelán Rueda, *La fuerza*. Critical takes in Palti, "Los diarios y el sis-

tema político"; Piccato, "Public Sphere." As the evidence below suggests, however, Mexican newspapers should not be seen, at least not predominantly, as a Tocquevillian measure of associationism. Drescher, "Tocqueville's"; Forment, *Democracy in Latin America*.

8. This means mainly writers and publishers. On other workers related to the industry, such as typists, see Illades, *Hacia la república*, 109, 167–72. See Bravo Ugarte, *Periodistas y Periódicos*; Ochoa Campos, *Reseña histórica*; Ruiz Castañeda et al., *El periodismo en México*, 217–19; Barajas Durán, *El país de "el llorón."* A good analysis of the trade of writers in Ortiz Monasterio, "La literatura como profesión." See also Camarillo Carbajal, *El sindicato de periodistas*.

1. Setting the Rules of Freedom

1. Fontana, *Benjamin Constant*, 81; *Principes de politique* [1815] in Constant, *Œuvres*, 1077–78.

2. José María Luis Mora, "Discurso sobre los medios de que se vale la ambición para descubrir la libertad," first published in *El Observador*, 20 June 1827, in Mora, *Mora legislador*, 92–93.

3. On the second group, see as examples the works of Peter Guardino and Karen Caplan. On the first, also as examples, see Antonio Annino, François-Xavier Guerra, Annick Lémpèriere, Rafael Rojas. On Constant's influence on Mora, see Hale, *Mexican Liberalism*.

4. Thus the focus on governance does not imply a neat division between sovereignty and the purely instrumental "art of government." Foucault, "Governmentality."

5. Constant, *Oeuvres*, 1180, 1219. On freedom as the boundary between public and private spheres, Todorov, *Benjamin Constant*, 37.

6. Mora, "Discurso sobre los medios," in Mora, *José María Luis Mora*, 92–93. For opinion expanding beyond elites in early national times, Guerra, *Modernidad e independencias*, 288; Rojas, *La escritura*, 45, 88.

7. Reyes Heroles, *El liberalismo*, 1:330. An essential reference in the subsequent discussion of public opinion, including a discussion of the inherent contradictions of liberal public opinion, is Palti, "La transformación del liberalismo." For the "diversas facultades físicas y morales con que la naturaleza ha dotado a cada uno de los hombres" and the "igualdad quimérica" proposed by Robespierre and Marat, see Mora, "Discurso sobre los medios," in Mora, *José María Luis Mora*, 93.

8. Mora, "Discurso sobre la libertad de pensar, hablar y escribir" [1827], in Mora, *José María Luis Mora*, 86. Human understanding could be obscured by interests and passion and it could change with age, but, stated Mora, it was also "noble en sí mismo." Ibid., 87.

9. José María Luis Mora, "Que las autoridades eclesiásticas respeten las leyes sobre libros prohibidos," first published in *El Sol*, 30 September 1824, in Mora,

José María Luis Mora, 31. Mora saw open discussion in the press as an effective balance to the secretive and divisive modes of operation of Masonic lodges and the parties they gave rise to. Rojas, *La escritura*, 124–25.

10. Mora, "Que las autoridades eclesiásticas," Mora, *José María Luis Mora*, 33. See also Mora, "Discurso sobre la libertad," Mora, *José María Luis Mora*, 90; Sierra, *Obras completas*, 4:83. Half a century later, José María Gamboa quoted Blackstone's dictum in the same sense: "Reprimir el desenfreno de la prensa equivale a mantener su libertad." Gamboa, "Estudios sobre la legislación de imprenta y derechos de los escritores," EF 23:112 (17 December 1884), 460–61.

11. *Colección de pedimentos*. On religion, José María Luis Mora, "Programa de los principios políticos . . . ," in Mora, *José María Luis Mora*, 311. See also José María Luis Mora, "Libertad de imprenta," first published in *El Observador*, 30 June 1830, in Mora, *José María Luis Mora*, 184. Contrast with Constant's stress on sedition over honor. *Principes de politique* [1815], in Constant, *Œuvres*, 1180. Honor has not been examined as a factor in the political control of the press in early republican times, or it has been seen merely as an excuse for political persecution. Rojas, *La escritura*, 192.

12. Mora, "Libertad de imprenta," Mora, *José María Luis Mora*, 178–79, 184. See "De la liberté des brochures, des pamphlets et des journaux considérée sous le rapport de l'intérêt du gouvernment" in Constant, *Œuvres*, 1236n.

13. For the most systematic study from the point of view of censorship, see Reyna, *La prensa censurada*. On republican traditions before democratic or modern liberalism, see Aguilar and Rojas, *El republicanismo*.

14. See, from 1820, AHDFJ, 2739, 1, 1, 2 and ff. For an analysis of this aspect of the process of republican change after independence based on 1820s pamphlets, see Rojas, *La escritura*.

15. José María Gamboa, "Estudios sobre la legislación de imprenta y derechos de los escritores," EF 23:103 (3 December 1884), 420–21; EF 23:112 (17 December 1884), 452–53.

16. Speech of 25 November 1867 in, Ramírez, *México en pos*, 180.

17. For nineteenth-century legislation as an attempt to replace the structure of censorship formerly provided by the Santo Oficio, see Guibovich, "The Inquisition and Book Censorship," 2, 12.

18. "Reglamento de la libertad de imprenta, publicado en Cádiz," 13 June 1813, in AHDFJ, 2739, 1, 1, 2; Castelán Rueda, *La fuerza*, 54. The decree of 10 November 1810 was one of the first dictated by the Cadiz Cortes and defined political divides that would survive until 1814. Crawley, "French and English Influences." The *Novísima recopilación de las leyes de Indias*, ley 1a., tit. 9, part. 7a, contained the legislation about the press before the decree of 1810. Castelán Rueda, *La fuerza*, 174. The Consitution of 1812 in Tena Ramirez, *Leyes fundamentales*.

19. Rojas, *La escritura*, 48; Reyes Heroles, *El liberalismo*, 1:321n. "Representación al soberano congreso sobre continuar suspensa la libertad de imprenta," 22 October 1813, AHDFJ, 2739, 1, 1, 2; Castelán Rueda, *La fuerza*, 54–55, 78, 88.

20. Delgado Carranco, "Las primeras discusiones," 473, 476–79, 485.

21. Decree of 22 October 1814, art. 40. See Tena Ramirez, *Leyes fundamentales*. José María Gamboa, "Estudios sobre la legislación de imprenta y derechos de los escritores," *EF* 23:112 (17 December 1884), 460–61. See also Miquel i Verges, *La independencia mexicana*; Castelán Rueda, *La fuerza*, 89.

22. Reyes Heroles, *El liberalismo*, 1:70–81; Rojas, *La escritura*, 45, 88.

23. *Gaceta extraordinaria del gobierno de México*, 19 June 1820, in AHDFJ, 1, 1, 2. According to Rafael Rojas, this expansion was central to the process of imagining a modern polis. Rojas, *La escritura*, 45. The evidence below will suggest that the divide between "modern" and "traditional" political practices was not so neat.

24. *Reglamento de libertad de imprenta*, in AHDFJ, 2739, 1, 19. The Cadiz regulation of 22 October 1820 also established a special prosecutor, allowed for appeal of the sentence, and established a "junta de protección de la libertad de imprenta." The law, published in Mexico City in 1821, was more detailed than the decree of 1810. Shubert, "Spain," 182. It was directly inspired in the French law of 17 May 1819 establishing the press jury. *Colección de pedimentos*, 74.

25. *Reglamento adicional para la libertad de imprenta*, 16 December 1821. Both in *Reglamento de libertad de imprenta*. The publication is found in AHDFJ, 2739, 1, 19, 212–329v. On the impact of the same legislation in Buenos Aires, Myers, "Las paradojas de la opinión," 80, 92.

26. "In Spain, at least fifteen major press laws were enacted between 1810 and 1853." In France, there were forty-two laws between 1806 and 1881. Goldstein, *The War for the Public Mind*, 13, 182–84, 223, 225, 138, 142, 144, 150, 154, 49, 51. For a review of the most relevant examples, see José María Gamboa, "Estudios sobre la legislación de imprenta y derechos de los escritores," *EF* 23:104 (4 December 1884), 425; *EF* 23:105 (5 December 1884), 428–29; *EF* 23:111 (16 December 1884), 449; *EF* 23:112 (17 December 1884), 460–61; "La difamación en Inglaterra," *EF* 34:41 (8 March 1890), 678–79; *EF* 34:43 (11 March 1980), 682.

27. Gamboa, "Estudios sobre la legislación de imprenta y derechos de los escritores," *EF* 23:111 (16 December 1884), 449; Shubert, "Spain," 178–79; Goldstein, *The War for the Public Mind*, 14.

28. Shubert, "Spain," 205, 178–86. On the role of private citizens in guaranteeing the success of juries, Constant, *Œeuvres*, 1208.

29. Gamboa, "Estudios sobre la legislación de imprenta y derechos de los escritores," *EF* 23:112 (17 December 1884), 460–61.

30. Donovan, "Magistrates and juries," 380, 219; Laingui and Lebigne, *Histoire du droit pénal*, 11. On the French and Spanish influence on Cadiz, see Crawley, "French and English Influences." On criminal juries, see Speckman, *Crimen y castigo*, 252–66; Padilla Arroyo, "Los jurados populares," 145; Goldstein, *The War for the Public Mind*, 16.

31. Gamboa, "Estudios sobre la legislación de imprenta y derechos de los escritores," *EF* 23:104 (4 December 1884), 425; *EF* 23:105 (5 December 1884), 428–29; Goldstein, *The War for the Public Mind*, 166.

32. See AHDFJ, 2739, 1, 19, 212–329; Decree of 1 May 1875. *EF* 2:53 (13 September 1877), 210. For a French law establishing responsibilities, see *EF* 23:111 (16 December 1884), 449.

33. AHDFJ, 2739, 1, 19, 212–329v; *Reglamento de libertad de imprenta*, articles 50 y 171; Tena Ramirez, *Leyes fundamentales*. On the discussions leading to the Constitution, see Reyes Heroles, *El liberalismo*, 1:328–30.

34. Riva Palacio, *México a través de los siglos*, 11:178; Arrom, "Popular Politics," 74. For the divided opinions regarding candidates' personal attributes and the importance of riots as an expression of new modalities of popular mobilization and cause for subsequent limits to electoral participation, Arrom, "Popular Politics," 82, 87, 90.

35. *Reglamento general*.

36. Decree of 4 September 1829, AHDFJ, 2739, 1, 19. The decree was issued under extraordinary legislative faculties granted by Congress to President Vicente Guerrero on 15 August 1829. In spite of the arrest of several journalists accused of writing subversive articles, some newspapers continued to call for a change in government. Riva Palacio, *México a través de los siglos*, 11:196, 214, 216. For decrees limiting press freedom between 1836 and 1853, see Reyes Heroles, *El liberalismo*, 3:258n.

37. AHDFJ, 2739, 1, 19. Decree of 14 May 1831; Riva Palacio, *México a través de los siglos*, 11:263–65, 288; Rojas, *La escritura*, 194.

38. Decree by José María Tornel, 22 March 1834, AHDFJ, 2739, 1, 19; Mora, *José María Luis Mora*, 310–12. Recent accounts of restrictions do not emphasize the concern about honor. They see the prohibition of voceo as a means of depriving pamphleteers of income or as a resource to prevent the spread of instability. Rojas, *La escritura*, 193; Reyna, *La prensa censurada*, 34–35.

39. Law of 23 May 1835, in Gamboa, "Estudios sobre la legislación de imprenta y derechos de los escritores," *EF* 23:112 (17 December 1884), 460–61; Riva Palacio, *México a través de los siglos*, 12:83. A project of January 1835 by Deputy Parres established a penalty of up to ten years in prison for subversive writers. Riva Palacio, *México a través de los siglos*, 12:51. Rojas sees the mention of vagrants and people without address as evidence of the social marginality of pamphleteers. Most likely, however, it was a way of preventing the editors' ruse. Rojas, *La escritura*, 193.

40. Gamboa, "Estudios sobre la legislación de imprenta y derechos de los escritores," *EF* 23:115 (20 December 1884), 464–65. The decree, which referred in particular to seditious newspapers in Mexico City, was successful in "enmudecer a la prensa" after the unfavorable conclusion of the negotiations with the French fleet blocking Veracruz and demanding payment of the debt. Riva Palacio, *México a través de los siglos*, 12:83, 137.

41. Ibid., 12:143.

42. Ibid., 12:146–47, 149.

43. Decree of 4 June 1842, ibid., 12:185.

44. Decree of 14 June 1843, José María Gamboa, "Estudios sobre la legislación de imprenta y derechos de los escritores," *EF* 23:120 (30 December 1884), 485.

45. Ibid., *EF* 24:7 (13 January 1885), 27; *EF* 24:8 (14 January 1885), 31; AHDFJ, 2740. The law of 1828 established an initial jury of fifteen members and a sentence jury of twelve.

46. Gamboa, "Estudios sobre la legislación de imprenta y derechos de los escritores," EF 24:9 (15 January 1885), 35; AHDFJ, 2740; Mora, *José María Luis Mora*, 310–12.

47. Decree of 21 September 1852, Gamboa, "Estudios sobre la legislación de imprenta y derechos de los escritores," EF 24:9 (15 January 1885), 35; Riva Palacio, *México a través de los siglos*, 13:233. See also decree of 25 April 1853, in Gamboa, "Estudios sobre la legislación de imprenta y derechos de los escritores," EF 24:10 (16 January 1885), 39; Riva Palacio, *México a través de los siglos*, 13:260–61. The conservative government would reestablish the decree in 1858. Rivera, *Tratado breve*, 49.

48. Law of 28 December 1855, ASCJ, 57, 1, 14 (18), 1856; AHDFJ, 2740, 49; Gamboa, "Estudios sobre la legislación de imprenta y derechos de los escritores," EF 24:11 (17 January 1885), 43. On the ambiguities of the law of 1855, see ASCJ, 57, leg. 1, 14 (18), 1856. See also Reyna, *La prensa censurada*, 51–52.

49. Tena Ramírez, *Leyes fundamentales*; Prieto, *Obras completas*, 9:65–67.

50. Gamboa, "Estudios sobre la legislación de imprenta y derechos de los escritores," EF 24:17 (29 January 1885), 67. On the mildness of the Prieto law, see Cosío Villegas, *Imprenta*, 107; Cosío Villegas, *El porfiriato*, 1:728.

51. "Decreto de la Secretaría de Gobernación acerca de la libertad de imprenta" in *Recopilación de leyes*, 9–15.

52. Decree of 28 December 1861, AHDFJ, 2740, 49.

53. Law of 15 June 1864, EF 25:8 (10 July 1885), 31. For a complaint by the public scribe José Arteaga to municipal prefect, 7 December 1864, AHDFJ, 2740, 49; Law of 4 April 1865 in AHDFJ, 2740, 53; José María Gamboa, "Estudios sobre la legislación de imprenta y derechos de los escritores," EF 24:44 (12 March 1885), 174–75; EF 24:45 (13 March 1885), 179.

54. Juárez used extraordinary powers granted by Congress to decree the law. Gamboa, "Estudios sobre la legislación de imprenta y derechos de los escritores," EF 24:11 (17 January 1885), 43; "Decreto de la Secretaría de Gobernación acerca de la libertad de imprenta," particularly articles 6–9, 17, 26, 32, in *Recopilación de leyes*, 9–15; *Legislación mexicana [1687–1902]*, 10:61–64, 228–65. See chapter 5 on the constitutional reform.

55. Recent studies have begun to challenge this view, giving the press a central role in politics, even as an "herramienta indispensable para los levantamientos armados." Barajas Durán, *El país de "el llorón,"* 47. See also Vázquez Mantecón, *La palabra*; Palti, "Los diarios y el sistema político."

56. Gamboa, "Estudios sobre la legislación de imprenta y derechos de los escritores," EF 24:17 (29 January 1885), 67; EF 24:34 (26 February 1885), 135.

57. Cosío Villegas, *La Constitución de 1857*, 38–39; Jacinto Pallares, "Delitos de Imprenta," in *El Publicista: Periódico de Derecho Constitucional, Administrativo e Internacional* 3 (1875), 3–7. A similar perspective in G. Baturoni, "La Libertad de la Prensa," EF 4:72 (21 April 1875), 286–87; EF 4:73 (22 April 1875), 290; EF 4:74 (23 April 1875), 294; EF 4:76 (27 April 1875), 302.

58. I also used evidence from earlier periods and from other sources, mainly the Archivo de la Suprema Corte de Justicia de la Nación and the juridical journal

El Foro, although as a series they are not consistent enough to allow for good comparison. Thus the totals and averages cited below refer only to the 43 cases in Mexico City. For a list of 122 press trials in different archives of Mexico City from 1809 to 1882, not all of them involving juries, see Reyna, *La prensa censurada*, appendix 1.

59. See, e.g., accusations against the government regarding electoral fraud and the sale of certificates of loyalty to traitors, all of them declared not valid for procedural reasons, AHDFJ, 2741, 62; AHDFJ, 2741, 64, both in 1869.

60. On average, complaints were presented 12.7 days after the date of the publication.

61. *Gran jurado nacional*, 20. Waiting too long to respond to a publication undermined a victim's claim. Degollado, *Defensa ante el público*, 9. See, for example, ASCJ, 55, 3, 109, Orizaba, 1870; AHDFJ, 2741, 70. The regulation of February 1868 allowed an interim of twenty-four hours from the presentation of the complaint to the summoning of the first jury. *Legislación mexicana [1687– 1902]*. The average number of days between convening of the first and second juries was 13, but this number is owing to one case in which the absence of one of the parties delayed the conciliation for 144 days. For a case the following year in which the president of the City Council refused to proceed against a text attacking the governor of Chiapas for lack of proper legal representation, see AHDFJ, 2741, 79.

62. AHDFJ, 2743, 2, 1878, for an author complaining about "previa censura" of a play not yet staged. The jury acquitted him later. See also AHDFJ, 2733, 185, 1875, in which G. Gostkowsky complained that juries had been selected in his absence. For appeals granted in spite of political pressures, see a case in Oaxaca in ASCJ, 87, 26, 1878. Charges dropped in AHDFJ, 2740, 40, 1861. For an appeal granted on the grounds that the selection of jurors had not been performed properly, EF 6:9 (15 January 1876), 34. In France also juries tended to acquit journalists. Reddy, *The Invisible Code*, 194, 195. Similar patterns in other European countries in Goldstein, *The War for the Public Mind*. The Mexican rate of guilty sentences from this sample is lower than in most European cases.

63. Complaint against an article criticizing the Supreme Court, 14 April 1849, ASCJ, 6, 6, 157. An accusation against public philanthropies resulting in acquittal in MR, 22 July 1880, 2. *El Monitor Republicano* reasoned in June 1869 that denouncing electoral fraud was not a "deshonra a la nación" but a way to fight "la ignorancia del pueblo" that made despotism possible. MR, 10 June 1869, clipping in AHDFJ, v. 2741, 62.

64. AHDFJ, 2742, 106. See also MR, 29 March 1872.

65. Against Francisco de Cabrera for article "Variedades," published in *Latigo*, 3 January 1863, ASCJ, 1, 86 (255).

66. Ibid.; for a case in 1850 resulting in the archbishop of Mexico banning a calendar published by Baram López, but no jury sentence, AHDFJ, 2740, 34. There were no cases of attacks against morality among the forty-three jury trials; accusation from 1865 in AHDFJ, 2740, 51.

67. "Crónica. El jurado del 'Federalista,'" EF 2:28 (19 August 1877), 110; ibid,

2:32 (24 June 1877), 127. See also Baltazar Tellez Girón denouncing "Noticias de Matamoros," *El Federalista*, no. 1999, AHDFJ, 2742, 126. On the adverse attitudes of jurors and audiences against accusers of the press, see AHDFJ, 2743, 2; Romero Vargas, *Libertad de imprenta*, 7–8. General Mariano Escobedo was one of the heroes of the recent wars. He was not murdered in 1877, but Díaz suspected him of plotting a *lerdista* rebellion from the U.S. border. After the trial, the government used other resources to undermine *El Federalista*, such as preventing circulation through the mail. The paper stopped publication in 1878. Cosío Villegas, *El porfiriato*, 133–34, 152–55.

68. For a jury acquittal of a journalist in Mexico City, see *MR*, 22 July 1880, 2; another case in 1879 against *Le Trait d'Union* in AHDFJ, 2743, 138; five acquittals from 1880 in AHDFJ, 2743, 143; AHDFJ, 2743, 147; another, after a complaint by police officers against *El Monitor Republicano*, in AHDFJ, 2743, 146. For an acquittal in Cuautitlán, Estado de México, in 1880, in a suit brought by a jefe político, AHDFJ, 2743, 143. For two cases in Guadalajara in which district courts protected journalists against a jefe político and a correctional judge, see, respectively, *EF* 1:51 (17 May 1877), 202; *EF* 2:16 (24 July 1877), 61. A similar case in Oaxaca, in 1878, ASCJ, 87, 26, 1878, Oaxaca. In another case, this one in San Luis Potosí, the audience cheered the defendant but the jury found against him, *EF* 19:29 (10 August 1882), 115. For a decision overturning a correctional judge's indictment and imprisonment of a journalist in Tamaulipas in July 1882, *EF* 19:64 (3 October 1882), 257. But see, for a writer found guilty of libel against judicial workers, "Escribientes y juez de juzgados 20 y 30 menor contra *La sombra de Lizardi* por gacetilla en no. 7," AHDFJ, 2743, 136.

69. *EF* 17:111 (8 December 1881), n.; *EF* 2:53 (13 September 1877), 210; for a case in Toluca, *EF* 18:36 (24 February 1882), 141.

70. AHDFJ, 2741, 94, year 1871. See also ASCJ, 169, 20, 20, art. 4, year 1830. For punishment through judicial procedures, see ASCJ, 57, 1, 14 (18); AHDFJ, 2740, 51.

71. AHDFJ, 2740, 42; García Neria, "Las tribulaciones de un editor," 86–88.

72. A favorable sentence for Gostkowsky was overturned on appeal. *EF* 3:45 (22 August 1874), 177. For the large number of pamphlets published between 1830 and 1855 in Mexico City, see Giron Barthe, "El entorno editorial," 52–53.

73. AHDFJ, 2740, 42.

74. The absence of the defendant from the drawing could give place to an appeal, as defendants had the right to reject names from the final list. AHDFJ, 2733, 185; *EF* 5:105 (7 November 1875), 414. On fines AHDFJ, 2740, 41. On last-minute draws, AHDFJ, 2740, 42; AHDFJ, 2740, 54. Mechanisms to compel citizens to attend juries were among the earliest concerns in the legislation. See decree by President Guadalupe Victoria, 14 October 1828, AHDFJ, 2739, 1, 19. See also AHDFJ, 2740, 53. An example for 1880 in AHDFJ, 2743, 139. For the difficulties in bringing together criminal juries, selected since 1869 through similar procedures, see AHDFJ, 2731, 7, 8. On the use of the previous year's list, *Reglamento general*, *EF* 5:105 (7 November 1875), 414.

75. Cosío Villegas, *El porfiriato*, 2:575; Guerra, *México*, 1:416, 380; INEGI, *Estadisticas históricas*, 1:92; Tanck de Estrada, "La educación en la ciudad de México," 131.

76. Toussaint Alcaraz, *Escenario de la prensa*, 69.

77. See, e.g., Bazant, "Lecturas " 237–38; Speckman, "Las posibles lecturas," 66.

78. Ramírez Rancaño, "Estadísticas electorales," 271–99. It is not possible to know how many citizens actually voted. Rodríguez Kuri, *La experiencia olvidada*, 53–54.

79. Ozuna Castañeda and Guzmán Gutiérrez, "Para que todos lean," 276.

80. Mora, *José María Luis Mora*, 185. The practice was common in Europe. Goldstein, *The War for the Public Mind*, 24.

81. See Saborit, *Doblados*; Ruiz Castañeda and Márquez Acevedo, *Diccionario de seudónimos*; Díaz y de Ovando, *Un enigma de Los Ceros*. Anonymity remained a feature of English, French, and German eighteenth-century authors who thought of their audiences as a small, knowledgeable group. Melton, *The Rise*, 124.

82. AHDFJ, 2742, 122, year 1875.

83. Complaint against *La Polémica*, Archivo Histórico del Supremo Tribunal de Justicia de Michoacán (hereafter AHSTJM), 1a. Instancia, Penal, Morelia, 1894, 79, 31 fs.; trial against Cruz Balcazar for libel, ASCJ, 63, 7, 38, art. 278 bis; ASCJ, 63, 7, 38, art. 278 bis; G. Baturoni, "*La Libertad* de la Prensa. Al 'Progreso,'" *EF* 4:78 (29 April 1875), 309.

84. The case was turned over to the Supreme Court before sentencing because the judge didn't appear. ASCJ, 6, 6, 157, Colima, 1849.

85. The editor of *El Imparcial*, from Monterrey, was convicted because he signed an article that others knew had been authored by Antonio Sada. Peña was nevertheless released on appeal because he had not been present at the jury audiences. *EF* 5:35 (12 August 1875), 137–38.

86. *EF* 23:89 (13 November 1884), 365–66.

87. Saborit, *Doblados*. Saborit's fascinating account of the case also illustrates the ambiguity of *Tomochic*'s authorship. See a similar stance in AHDFJ, 2742, 117, 1873; Rabasa, "Moneda falsa," 228.

88. See AHDFJ, 2743, 137. See also *MR*, 27 July 1880, 3; AHDFJ, 2741, 7. For a federal court ordering the Monterrey City Council to seize the copies of a newspaper, *EF* 2:6 (9 January 1874), 22.

89. Sanches was released from the Puebla prison in May 1861, but the case does not contain further information about his trial in Mexico City. AHDFJ, 2740, 44. See also an 1879 case in AHDFJ, 2743, 137, and another in *EF* 2:6 (9 January 1874), 22.

90. AHDFJ, 2741, 64 y 65. See also ASCJ, 55, 3, 109, year 1870.

91. AHDFJ, 2742, 126. The accusation had merits according to the first jury but the file does not contain a sentence.

92. Limantour, *Apuntes*, 159.

93. On the institutional changes, see Rodríguez Kuri, *La experiencia olvidada*;

Davis, *Urban Leviathan*; Warren, "El congreso por su gusto"; Annino, "Cádiz y la revolución territorial."

94. Davis, "El rumbo."

95. Reyna, *La prensa censurada*.

96. ASCJ, 6, 6, 157, 1849, Colima.

97. Decree of 14 October 1828, AHDFJ, 2739, 1, 9. On urban *vecindad* and representation AHDFJ, 2740, 41; Annino, "Ciudadanía versus gobernabilidad"; Annino, "Cádiz y la revolución territorial," 193; Lear, *Workers, Neighbors*. For the oligarchic composition of ayuntamientos, Guerra, *Modernidad e independencias*, 191.

98. AHDFJ, 2739, 1, 9; *Reglamento general*.

99. For François-Xavier Guerra, friendship was a traditional value that permeated all political connections, opposite the modern notion of opinion. The evidence in this and the following chapters suggests there was no incompatibility between the two. Guerra and Lempérière, *Los espacios públicos*. On the importance of these networks in the recruitment of political elites, see chapter 4 below and Camp, *Political Recruitment*. For the category as an egalitarian link between political and social analysis, González Bernaldo, "Sociabilidad," 196, 199.

100. AHDFJ, 2739, 19.

101. Sierra, *Juárez*, 180.

102. Prieto, *Obras completas*, 9:112.

103. Fondo Basave del Castillo Negrete-Centro de Estudios sobre la Universidad, UNAM, (hereafter BCN), 7, 3, 608, s.f. On conservative liberalism, Hale, *Transformation*.

104. AHDFJ, 2742, 107.

105. "El Vaudeville," *La Orquesta*, 6 November 1861, described the drunken and insulting behavior of the representative of France during a ball. The article implied the threat of military intervention and appealed to "dignidad nacional" and denounced that France had sent representatives who were "camorristas y atrabancados," proving that "nos ven como gente sin civilización." The Benito Juárez government saw similar articles as an obstacle in its efforts "por restablecer sus relaciones regulares con la Francia." When the jury met in this case it decided quickly and unanimously that there were no grounds against the publication. AHDFJ, 2740, 47.

106. *EF* 19:29 (10 August 1882), 115.

107. *EF* 5:105 (7 November 1875), 414.

108. AHDFJ, 2740, 41. On the importance and complexity of reading aloud see Ozuna Castañeda and Guzmán Gutiérrez, "Para que todos lean," 278–279.

109. In a similar case, Muiron y Compañía denounced an add of the Casa Christofle in *Le Trait d'Union* that stated that the former "à cessé d'être notre représentation au Mexique," which meant an attack against "la reputación mercantil de nuestra casa" and cause of its "descrédito." AHDFJ, 2743, 138.

110. Decree of 22 March 1834, AHDFJ, 2739, 1, 19. See also Reyna, *La prensa censurada*, 34. On rhetoric and early journalism, Ozuna Castañeda and Guzmán

Gutiérrez, "Para que todos lean," 276–281. Mateos, *Los dramas*, 519–520. See also José María Gamboa, "Estudios sobre la legislación de imprenta y derechos de los escritores," EF 23:115 (20 December 1884), 464–5; Prieto, *Obras completas*, 9:112.

111. ASCJ, 6, 6, 157, year 1849. See also AHDFJ, 2741, 67, year 1869.

112. ASCJ, 55, 3, 109; Reyna, *La prensa censurada*, 39.

113. ASCJ, 63, 7, 38, art. 278 bis.

114. Jacinto Pallares, "Delitos de Imprenta," *El Publicista: Periódico de Derecho Constitucional, Administrativo e Internacional* 3 (1875), 5–7.

115. EF 19:64 (3 October 1882), 257; G. Baturoni, "*La Libertad* de la Prensa," EF 4:72 (21 April 1875), 286–287; EF 4:73 (22 April 1875), 290; EF 4:74 (23 April 1875), 294; EF 4:76, (27 April 1875), 302.

116. EF 19:29 (10 August 1882), 115. Article 7th read: "publicar escritos sobre cualquier materia," which could, with a bit of a stretch, be interpreted not as "on any subject" but also as "on any material."

117. Vidal appealed the arrest but a district court in Toluca upheld the decision EF 18:36 (24 February 1882), 141.

118. "Reglamento de la libertad de imprenta, publicado en Cádiz," 13 June 1813, AHDFJ, 2739, 1, 1, 2; clipping at BCN, fol. 766, probably from MR, 1 December 1884.

119. *Gaceta Extraordinaria del gobierno de México*, 19 June 1820, en AHDFJ, 1, 1, 2; 18 October 1828, AHDFJ, 2739, 1, 19. Similar opinions on criminal judges in Padilla Arroyo, "Los jurados populares," 141. On private behavior, public opinion, and the press since the French Revolution, see Baker, *Inventing the French Revolution*, chap. 8; Ledré, *La Presse*, 11.

120. Journalistic text from 1867 in Ramírez, *México en pos*. For another positive opinion about lynching, in the context of debates about the criminal jury, Moheno, *Sobre la brecha*. Opinions about lynching could be critical: the practice did not exist in Mexico because, according to *La Voz de México*, "Es noble y valiente el pueblo mexicano; y en este punto, muy superior a los yankees." LVM, 22 September 1897, 2. See also *El Imparcial*, 18 September 1897; Palti, "La Sociedad Filarmónica."

121. José María Gamboa, "Estudios sobre la legislación de imprenta y derechos de los escritores." EF 24:17 (29 January 1885), 67. Gamboa condemned these scenes because they often victimized those who dared to press charges against a journalist. EF 24:34 (26 February 1885), 135. Audiences applauding the reading of a denounced text in EF 19:29 (10 August 1882), 115.

2. Representing Public Opinion

1. Rabasa, *El cuarto poder*, 48. Emilio Rabasa (1856–1930) was born in Chiapas and lived in Mexico City. He worked in various minor judicial positions and in journalism and wrote novels before becoming governor of Chiapas, a diplomat,

and a preeminent jurist during the governments of Porfirio Díaz and Victoriano Huerta. Hale, *Emilio Rabasa*.

2. Aurelio Horta, "Los invulnerables" [1888], in Puga y Acal, *Los poetas mexicanos*, 134.

3. See Bourdieu, *Practical Reason*; Bourdieu, *Outline*; Wacquant, "Toward a Reflexive Sociology." On key Bourdieu categories and their links with Habermas's ideas, see Calhoun, "Habitus, Field." Constant's views on the press as a venue to defend and attack reputations in "De la liberté des brochures, des pamphlets et des journaux considérée sous le rapport de l'intérêt du gouvernment" [1814], Constant, *Œuvres*, 1233–34.

4. Bourdieu, *Outline*, 178–80. "The interest at stake in the conduct of honour is one for which economism has no name, and which has to be called symbolic, although it is such as to inspire actions which are very directly material; just as there are professions, like law and medicine, in which those who practise them must be 'above suspicion,' so a family has a vital interest in keeping its capital of honour." Bourdieu, *Outline*, 181. On symbolic capital in capitalist societies, Bourdieu, *Meditaciones*, 186, 254–59. See also Mauss, *The Gift*; Van Young, *The Other Rebellion*, 90. On "the difficulty journalists faced when they sought to protect their honor and to accumulate honors while selling their services to daily newspapers," see Reddy, *The Invisible Code*, 184 and chap. 5.

5. Perry, *Juárez and Díaz*, 184–86; speech by Deputy Fernando Duret on 12 November 1884 in DDCD 1:237.

6. Cosío Villegas, *El porfiriato*, 1:427. Similar accusations in AHDFJ, 2741, 68; a report against Lerdistas and Porfiristas used the same sexual connotations as Vigil: "Ambos partidos se han presentado en el templo de la concordia con la corona de azahar, púdicos y emocionados, pronunciando el deseado, te amo! y se han estrechado las manos." *El Embudo*, 3 December 1871, 3, in AHDFJ, v. 2741, 89, 12 fs. On the distribution of honors, see Cosío Villegas, "Octava llamada particular," in Cosío Villegas, *El porfiriato*, 1:xvi; Macías González, "Mexican Aristocracy," chap. 7. The Porfirio Díaz archive contains numerous examples of the careful distribution of favors, including candidacies to Congress. See Porfirio Díaz to Belio Mejía, 14 June 1881, CPD, 6, 1111. On the Tuxtepecanos' jealousy of rising figures, see Reyes, *De mi vida*, 1:16; Cosío Villegas, *La República Restaurada*, 341; Prida, *De la dictadura*, 82.

7. Vega, *Dos palabras*, 1–2. The author had been accused in a letter to *La Regeneración de Sinaloa* of malfeasance while serving as state fiscal inspector.

8. For the concern about "no tener seguro el honor personal y el de nuestra familia," see "Causa contra Cruz Balcazar por libelos infamatorios," 25 June 1855, ASCJ, 63, 7, 38, art. 278 bis. On the multiple meanings of honor during the Santa Anna era, see Vázquez Mantecón, "El honor y la virtud."

9. On social capital and gender, see Bourdieu, *Dominación*; Bourdieu, *Outline*, 179–80. Specifically on journalists, see Reddy, *The Invisible Code*, 23. For the negotiation of social capital in public life in Buenos Aires, see Gayol, *Sociabilidad en Buenos Aires*, esp. chap. 5. For the importance of the extended family in modern Mexican society, see Lomnitz and Marisol Pérez, *Una familia de la élite*.

See also Guerra, *México*. For a study of early republican lawyers' accumulation of social capital, Uribe Uran, *Honorable Lives*. Heriberto Frías (1870–1925) was born in Querétaro, studied at the Escuela Nacional Preparatoria in Mexico City, and joined the military. His chronicle of the repression of the Tomochic rebellion forced him to leave the army and work in journalism. He was imprisoned for his opposition writings and continued to be active after the revolution. Gamboa (1846–1939) was born in Mexico City and went to school there. After working as a court clerk and journalist he entered the diplomatic service in 1889 and remained there until the end of the Porfiriato. His novel *Santa* (1903) reached large audiences.

10. Warner, *Publics and Counterpublics*, 74–79.

11. Celis de la Cruz, "Vicente García Torres," 147; Giron Barthe, "El entorno editorial," 52–53. On García Torres's prestige after his retirement, see Saborit, *Doblados*, 170.

12. "Dignidad de la Prensa," *La Bala Roja*, 11 June 1869, in AHDFJ, 2741, 61; Celis de la Cruz, "Vicente García Torres," 152–53.

13. Angel Pola, "De mis recuerdos de Reporter: Agonía y muerte de *El Monitor Republicano*," *El Universal*, 16 August 1942, Sunday section, 3, 7. Only *El Siglo Diez y Nueve* survived longer, fifty-two years, from 1841 to 1896. Ochoa Campos, *Reseña histórica*, 108.

14. On the independence of *El Monitor Republicano*, AHDFJ, 2743, 143, 10 January 1880; López Portillo y Rojas, *Elevación y caída*, 219. But see Barajas Durán, *El país de "el llorón."*

15. Data are spotty. See Ochoa Campos, *Reseña histórica*, 119–20, 108; Cosío Villegas, *El porfiriato*, 1:721; Toussaint Alcaraz, *Escenario de la prensa*, 31; Ruiz Castañeda et al., *El periodismo en México*, 232–33. Rafael Reyes Spíndola stated that *El Imparcial* rarely printed more than 60,000 copies. Bravo Ugarte, *Periodistas y Periódicos*, 84; Ochoa Campos, *Reseña histórica*, 125–26, 108; memorandum from Rafael Reyes Spíndola, AL, 2, 14. Estimates of 125,000 copies for 1907 are probably high. Rodríguez Kuri, "El discurso del miedo," 701. According to *La Libertad*, the printings stated by newspapers were fictitious or could be explained only if each citizen of the country subscribed to two or three newspapers. LL, 28 November 1884, 2.

16. Palti, "La Sociedad Filarmónica."

17. Toussaint Alcaraz, *Escenario de la prensa*, 20; Cosío Villegas, *El porfiriato*, 2:575; Guerra, *México*, 1:416, 380; INEGI, *Estadísticas históricas*, 1:92; Tanck de Estrada, "La educación en la ciudad de México," 131.

18. Rabasa, "Moneda falsa," 269. Obvious governmental sponsorship reduced the effect of the *Diario Oficial*'s voice. EA 2:13 (26 April 1875), 1–2; Ochoa Campos, *Reseña histórica*, 119–20, 108. See Rama, *Lettered City*, 52, 88–89.

19. Bonilla, "La imágen política"; EF 21:21 (31 July 1883), 82; Jesus Mercado against *La independencia Medica*, 15 July 1880, AHDFJ, 2743, 147. Newspapers avoided alienating powerful commercial interests. Bulnes, *El verdadero Díaz*, 365–66.

20. *Gaceta de Policía* 1:26 (6 May 1906), 8; ibid. 1:43 (9 September 1906), 3; Co-

sío Villegas, *El porfiriato*, 2:530; Rabasa, *El cuarto poder*; Bonilla, "La imágen política."

21. Othón, *Epistolario*, 87; Rabasa, "Moneda falsa," 302; Rabasa, *El cuarto poder*, 77–78; Frías, *Miserias de México*, 9.

22. Heriberto Barrón to Rafael Chousal, México, RCH, 29, 256, 9. On the centralization of subsidies, Limantour, *Apuntes*, 102; Ochoa Campos, *Reseña histórica*, 125–26. Subsidies reached apolitical publications later. EHA 7:610 (2 January 1898), 6–7; Bonilla, "La imágen política." "El Cuarto poder: Artículo cuasi estadístico," EHA (24 June 1888), quoted in Ruiz Castañeda et al., *El periodismo en México*, 217–18. For the diversity of newspapers and their political affiliations in 1880, see AHDFJ, 2743, 143. See also Bonilla, "La imágen política"; Toussaint Alcaraz, *Escenario de la prensa*.

23. For a formulation of this dilemma and a proposal to read the hidden meanings of journalistic debates as "una suerte de microcosmos en el que se pone en acción una compleja red de rivalidades entre partidos y facciones," see Palti, "La Sociedad Filarmónica."

24. Salado Alvarez, *Memorias*, 219.

25. Palti, "La Sociedad Filarmónica"; Palti, *La invención de una legitimidad*, 397.

26. Rabasa, *El cuarto poder*, 30. On Martínez, *Colección de pedimentos*, 78–79.

27. Rabasa, *El cuarto poder*, 132–33; Ortiz Monasterio, "La literatura como profesión," 329. See also "Dignidad de la Prensa," *La Bala Roja*, 11 June 1869, in AHDFJ, 2741, 61; similar cases in Reddy, *The Invisible Code*.

28. "La prensa mexicana y su porvenir," LL, 29 January 1884, 2; EHA 9:428 (8 July 1893), 6.

29. Frías, *Miserias de México*, 14.

30. Gamboa, *Impresiones* 25.

31. Ibid., 27. According to a writer for *El Monitor Republicano*, "Las tijeras y el engrudo hacen más que la pluma y el tintero." Angel Pola, "De mis recuerdos de Reporter: Agonía y muerte de El Monitor Republicano," *El Universal*, 16 August 1942, Sunday section, 3. On the analysis of other newspapers, Palti, "La Sociedad Filarmónica." See also Rabasa, *El cuarto poder*, 70, 79.

32. "*La Libertad* de la Prensa," G. Baturoni, EF 4:72 (21 April 1875), 286–87.

33. "Quien se mete a periodista / ¡Dios le valga, Dios le asista! / El ha de ser director, / Redactor y corrector, / Regente, editor, cajista, / Censor, colaborador, / Corresponsal y maquinista; / Ha de suplir al prensista / Y a veces . . . hasta al lector." "El Periodista," *El Monitor. Diario del Pueblo*, 31 October 1886, quoted in Lombardo de Ruiz, *De la opinión a la noticia*, 14. I owe this reference to Claudia Agostoni.

34. Francisco W. González in MR, 24 February1886, 1. The term "escritor público" was used by a suspect in a judicial testimony in EF 24:41 (7 March 1885), 162. Used as "journalist" in AHDFJ, 2742, 107; ibid, 2742, 122. More broadly used in *Novísima Recopilación*, law 1, tit. 9, part. 7, cited in Ramírez, *México en pos*, 180. Defined in opposition to "hombres públicos" in *El Fanal de Tampico*, clipping in AHDFJ, 2741, 68.

35. Gutiérrez Nájera also notes that "el carpintero, el sastre o el pintor pueden bastarse a sí mismos, si conocen los principios y reglas de su oficio; pero el periodista tiene que ser, no solamente el homo duplex de que hablaban los latinos, sino el hombre que, como los dioses de Valhalla, puede dividirse en mil pedazos y permanecer entero. . . . no hay ciencia que no tenga la obligación de conocer ni arte con cuyos secretos no deba estar familiarizado. . . . Y todo esto sin tiempo para abrir un libro o consultar un diccionario." Quoted in Bazant, "Lecturas " 214–15.

36. Salado Álvarez, *Memorias*, 139.

37. Rabasa, *El cuarto poder*, 80.

38. Gamboa, *Impresiones* 27. For the value of sincerity in oratory, *Velada fúnebre*, 30–55.

39. Rabasa, *El cuarto poder*, 27–28.

40. Bazant, "Lecturas," 214–15.

41. Green, "Journalists and Dandies." Paper presented at the Centenary of the Famous 41, Sexuality and Social Control in Latin America, 1901, Tulane University, New Orleans, November 2001.

42. Salado Álvarez, *Memorias*, 118–19. See also Campos, *Claudio Oronoz*, 43.

43. Bohemian life was defined as a transitional period of youth associated with poverty, freedom, and certain places in Paris of great prestige for Latin American writers. Seigel, *Bohemian Paris*, 3–7, 40; Easton, *Artists and Writers*, 121–32. In Mexico this did not mean a bourgeois conservatism, as in Gluck, *Popular Bohemia*, 18–19. See, for example, Blanco Fombona, *Rufino Blanco Fombona*; Darío, *Autobiografías*; Gómez Carrillo, *Treinta años*. For romanticism in Latin America as a "civilizing activity" and a literature emerged from "the ego and its circumstances," Anderson Imbert, *Spanish American Literature*, 161.

44. Díaz Mirón, *Prosa*, 91, 109; Puga y Acal, *Los poetas mexicanos*, 16, 28. For a discussion of Díaz Mirón's romanticism, Monterde, *Salvador Díaz Mirón*, 47–54. The aphorism "le style est l'homme même" comes from G.-L. de Buffon [1753], *Discours sur le Style* (Paris, J. Lecoffre, 1872), http://colet.lib.uchicago.edu, accessed January 30, 2004. Buffon's dictum was central to teaching oratory. Elguero, *Lecciones de elocuencia*, 21–23. On metaphor as an expression of superior perception of the poet, see Shelley, *A Defence of Poetry*, 17; Norris, "Deconstructing Genius," 141.

45. Puga y Acal, *Los poetas mexicanos*, 101, 130. Besides Díaz Mirón, Puga y Acal had criticized Manuel Gutiérrez Nájera and Juan de Dios Peza. Puga y Acal, *Los poetas mexicanos*, 141. The book was published in 1888 by Ireneo Paz.

46. "Prólogo a Lirismos de Antaño" [1923], in Puga y Acal, *Los poetas mexicanos*, 151.

47. In the "autumn" of Mexican romanticism, writers lived and died "in the conditions of absolute autonomy that only literature can impose." An example was the poet Manuel Acuña's suicide in 1873 (see chapter 4). Domínguez Michael, *Tiros en el concierto*, 147. For the association of freedom and writing, Rama, *Lettered City*, 43.

48. Quoted in Ortiz Monasterio, "La literatura como profesión," 326.

49. Gamboa, *Impresiones*, 31. Thirty pesos was approximately the same amount earned by low-level policemen or journeymen in 1910. Sesto, *El Mexico*, 134–36; Gamboa, *Impresiones*, 26. See also Frías, *Miserias de México*, 5.

50. Gamboa, *Impresiones*, 31, 27.

51. Frías, *Miserias de México*. See also, on the decadence of bohemian life, this time among students, Frías, *El amor de las sirenas*. See also Rabasa, "Moneda falsa," 397; Rabasa, *El cuarto poder*. Paz published historical novels. Pi-Suñer, "Prólogo," in Paz, *Algunas campañas*. Good journalists, like Manuel Caballero, the man who caused Santiago Sierra's death, could be very poor businessmen, Bazant, "Lecturas," 214–15.

52. Gamboa, *Impresiones*, 47.

53. Campos, *El Bar*, 58, quote on bars on p. 33. See also Rabasa, "Moneda falsa," 231. Gamboa was able to buy good clothes and take his lover to a restaurant once a week. Gamboa, *Impresiones*, 31. Othón's routine in Othón, *Epistolario*, 195. On Frías, Frías, *Miserias de México*, 53. Othón also documented his struggle against alcoholism. Othón, *Epistolario*, 128, 137. The importance of bars in Campos, *El Bar*, 33.

54. Gamboa, *Impresiones*, 27.

55. Caballero boasted that "con los materiales de la noticia diaria logra un periodista sacar material literario que envidiaría un autor de novelas por entregas o un dramaturgo desmelenado." Salado Álvarez, *Memorias*, 219. Gamboa, *Mi diario V*, 97–98. On the contrast between literary "crónica" and simple reporting, according to Manuel Gutiérrez Nájera, see Saborit, *Doblados*, 149. On Puga y Acal against Díaz Mirón, Díaz Mirón, *Prosa*, 91.

56. "En los funerales de Manuel Acuña" [1873], in Sierra, *Obras completas*, 1:346–47. See also Díaz Mirón, *Prosa*, 215; Gamboa, *Mi diario IV*, 148–49; Escudero, *El duelo en México*, 102. On the personal value of literary homage, in salons and newspapers, Othón, *Epistolario*, 89–90. Poverty, disdain, genius in the self-referential bohemian myth examined in Wilson, *Bohemians*; Seigel, *Bohemian Paris*.

57. *EF* 24:103 (12 June 1885), 409.

58. Sierra, *Evolución política*, 295. Francisco W. González, "Boletín," *MR*, 24 February 1886, 1. For an image of a journalist and heroic guerrilla fighter, Frías, *¿Águila o sol?*, 18.

59. *Informes producidos*, 11–12. See also *EF* 34:33 (26 February 1890), 550–51; *El Siglo Diez y Nueve*, in *EF* 34:38 (5 March 1890), 666–67; "La difamación en Inglaterra," in *EF* 34:41 (8 March 1890), 678–79; *EF* 34:43 (11 March 1980), 682. On persecution during the Porfiriato see accusation against *La Polemica*, AHSTJM, 1894, 79, 31 fs; Saborit, *Doblados*.

60. Rabasa, *El cuarto poder*, 48. Similar feminine depictions in France. Bell, "The 'Public Sphere,'" 913.

61. Gamboa, *Impresiones*, 24.

62. *LP*, 7 April 1878, 2.

63. Gamboa, *Impresiones*, 27. Gamboa also enjoyed the power to praise or

criticize "cuanta *prima donna* pasó por México," although his prurient *Diario* did not acknowledge any more intimacy than a furtive glimpse at Luisa Théo's leg in her dressing room. Gamboa, *Impresiones*, 29, 30. See "Dignidad de la Prensa," *La Bala Roja*, 11 June 1869, in AHDFJ, 2741, 61.

64. Infante Vargas, "De lectoras y redactoras." For the success of some feminine editors, see Granillo Vázquez, "De las tertulias al sindicato," 75. See Rabasa, "Moneda falsa," 228. For illuminating analyses of similar patterns in English and Mexican literature, Sedgwick, *Between Men*. See Irwin, *Mexican Masculinities*. On Gamboa and prostitutes, Buffington and Piccato, "Tales of Two Women." For an exceptional elite woman found in a brothel, Lara y Pardo, *La prostitución*, 75–76. For the threat posed by educated women who sought pleasure, Díaz Covarrubias, *Obras completas*, 2:136.

65. Frías, *Miserias de México*, 5.

66. Ibid., 12–23, 28.

67. Gamboa, *Impresiones*, 32. On Mata's decision to confront the government because of the constitutional changes allowing reelection, see Ruiz Castañeda et al., *El periodismo en México*, 213. In 1880 Mata requested an audience with Díaz, 30 July 1880, CPD, 5, 2198. See also Gamboa, *Mi diario IV*, 165. Weeks later, Gamboa saw from his window the humble funeral of Angel de Campo, who was forced to write to sustain his family. Gamboa, *Mi diario IV*, 148–49. A similar banquet, this one fictional, in Frías, *¿Águila o sol?*, 139–41. A similar reasoning presented by Juan de Dios Peza to Porfirio Díaz, 9 August 1877, CPD, 2, 000803: "La prensa no produce jamás lo suficiente para vivir ni quiero consagrarme a la tarea ingrata de los periodistas de oficio. . . . Pedir trabajo cuando se vive pobremente, no es deshonroso y menos, cuando se recurre para solicitarlo a un hombre de corazón."

68. Rabasa, "Moneda falsa," 199.

69. Saborit, *Doblados*, 180. Frías-Mercado suffered bouts of alcoholism and even consumed morphine. For a work intended to please Porfirio Díaz, Frías, *General Félix Díaz*. Bohemia, as a stereotype, also served earlier in France to mark a youthful phase of life. Gluck, *Popular Bohemia*, 18–19. Roumagnac worked for the police and became a well-known criminologist yet was never able to attain economic comfort. See MacGregor Campuzano, "Dos casos"; Piccato, "Interpretations of Sexuality." On his early journalistic career, see LVM, 6 October 1897, 3; Carlos Roumagnac, "Recuerdos de Belem," EN, 5 March 1933, sec. 2, 2; EN 12 March 1933, sec. 2, 2. On Clausell, see Saborit, *Doblados*, 90–95; Frías, *¿Águila o sol?*, 139–40. Villasana, cited above by Gamboa, was later made deputy and customs administrator by Díaz Barajas Durán, *El país de "el llorón,"* 78, 82.

70. Rabasa, "Moneda falsa," 208.

71. Frías, *Miserias de México*, 132, 79–81.

72. Cited in Curiel Defossé, "José (Federico) Francisco," 494. Rabasa acquired his experience in journalism in Chiapas in 1881, and, starting in 1886, in Mexico City. In 1888 he founded *El Universal* with Rafael Reyes Spíndola, later the founder of *El Imparcial*. Serra Rojas and Rabasa, *Antología*, 49, 94, 119.

73. Rodríguez González, "Heriberto Frías," 521. My conclusion in this regard does not fit well with prevalent literary interpretations of Rabasa, Gamboa, and Frías as naturalist writers interested in objective social reality.

74. For his romantic memoirs see, Paz, *Algunas campañas*. See particularly Antonia Pi-Suñer's prologue, 10, 16, 13–14, 23–24. In 1896 Díaz still hoped that Paz would return "al buen camino" after an interview with him. Chousal to Reyes, 24 November 1896, RCH, 14, 168, 32, 33.

75. *MR*, 24 March 1880; *MR*, 25 March 1880; *MR*, 26 March 1880. *La Patria* distinguished its own gacetilla from Caballero's texts, since he also worked for *El Socialista*. *LP*, 25 March 1880, 1–2; *LP*, 28 March 1880, 2, 3; *LP*, 30 March 1880, 2. According to *La Libertad*, it was Zenteno who refused to face Caballero on the field of honor "en virtud. . . . de los informes que por diversos conductos recibió acerca de su contrincante." *LL*, 23 March 1880, 3. Dueling codes prevented a man from fighting a duel if he had been convicted of a crime or cheated on by his wife. Tovar, *Código nacional mexicano*, chap. II, art. 1; Cabriñana, *Código del honor en España*, chap. 13. *La Patria*'s claims of "ánimo sereno" in *LP*, 9 July 1878, 1; *LP*, 31 March 1880, 2. For other examples of duels between journalists, see Bazant, "Lecturas," 211; Escudero, *El duelo en México*.

76. *MR*, 28 March 1880.

77. Leopoldo Zamora, "Editorial. La Prensa," *LP*, 1 April 1880, 1.

78. Hale, *Transformation*.

79. Santiago Sierra hoped to be "declared" an adult in 1869 by the Veracruz legislature in order to become a deputy. Chano (Santiago?) to Justo Sierra, Vera-cruz, 23 January 1869, Colección Justo Sierra Méndez–Centro de Estudios sobre la Universidad, Universidad Nacional Autónoma de México (hereafter JSM), book 1, 16. See also Hale, *Transformation*, 25–27.

80. "Liberales-Conservadores," *LL*, 10 May 1878, in Hale, *Justo Sierra*, 57.

81. Sierra, *Obras completas*, 4:242. See also Cosío Villegas, *El porfiriato*, 1:429.

82. Speaking of Ignacio Vallarta, Jacinto Pallares stated that "el hombre per-fecto en el orden moral, lleva en el fondo íntimo de su conciencia el germen de todas las virtudes. . . . porque en ese hombre todos sus actos son la eclosión espontánea y natural de una organización privilegiada, de un equilibrio divino entre sus deseos, sus sentimientos y sus convicciones." *RLJ*, 1 February 1894 (January–June), 100–101.

83. Sierra, *Obras completas*, 4:83. For an analysis of the philosophical change undergone by Sierra, see Charles A. Hale's introduction in Hale, *Justo Sierra*, 12–13.

84. "Liberales-Conservadores," *LL*, 10 May 1878, in Hale, *Justo Sierra*, 57. On juries, Yáñez, "Don Justo Sierra," 68.

85. Sierra, *Obras completas*, 4:221. Sierra would later justify his support of Díaz, in spite of reelections, in the name of education. Yañez, *Don Justo Sierra*, 179–80.

86. Justo Sierra, "La libertad del crimen" Sierra, *Obras completas*, 4:230. Origi-nally published in *LL*, 13 October 1879.

87. Antonio Guerra y Alarcón, "Importancia del periodismo," *LL*, 26 February 1880, 1–2.

88. From a speech in 1874, Pi Suñer, "Prólogo," 9:296. For visions of the press as an apolitical tool of education, Ignacio Méndez Mora to Porfirio Díaz, 2 July 1885, CPD, 10, 7447–49; Prieto, *Obras completas*, 9:570–71. Prieto began writing for newspapers in 1836 and continued doing so for over sixty years, stopping shortly before his death in 1897. McLean, *Vida y obra*, 42.

89. *LP*, 25 March 1880, 3; Cosío Villegas, *El porfiriato*, 1:548, 556–57. Both newspapers had different candidates in gubernatorial races. *LL*, 6 March 1880, 2; *LL*, 13 March 1880, 2. González subsidized twenty-six newspapers. Cosío Villegas, *El porfiriato*, 1:563.

90. *LP*, 2 April 1880, 3; *LP*, 8 April 1880, 2; *LL*, 20 February 1880, 3; *LL*, 21 February 1880, 3; *LL*, 29 February 1880, 3; *LL*, 9 March 1880, 2; *LL*, 25 March 1880, 2. An earlier exchange of accusations, regarding the execution of Lerdistas in Veracruz, in *LP*, 9 July 1879, 3.

91. *LP*, 21 April 1880, 2; *LP*, 11 April 1880, 3.

92. "¡El director del periódico cadenista (que todo lo que es se lo debe al general Díaz) hablando de ingratitud! Esto es chistoso." *LL*, 2 April 1880, 3; *LL*, 6 April 1880, 3.

93. Paz reproduced the letters and acts signed by his representatives when attempting to arrange a duel. *LP*, 25 April 1880, 1. See also *LP*, 2 April 1880, 2. Cuenca also threatened Paz to "castigar con propia mano, y donde le encuentre." *LL*, 25 April 1880, 3.

94. *LL*, 25 April 1880, 3. See also Sierra, *Obras completas*, 14:14. *LP*, 25 April 1880, 2. There is no mention of the duel in the following days. For earlier accusations of cowardice against *La Libertad*, see *LP*, 18 April 1880, 3.

95. Escudero, *El duelo en México*, 99–102.

96. Sierra, *Obras completas*, 14:14; Urueta, *Jesús Urueta*, 59.

97. Urueta, *Jesús Urueta*, 57, 58, 60. Justo had written about a youthful duel in his novel, *El ángel del porvenir* (1869), dedicated to Santiago. Sierra, *Obras completas*.

98. Urueta, *Jesús Urueta*, 58.

99. *MR*, 1 May 1880, 2, 3; *El Siglo Diez y Nueve*, 29 April 1880, 2.

100. Yañez, *Don Justo Sierra*, 62, 75; *LL*, 29 April 1880, 1. Under other editors *La Libertad* was printed occasionally until 1900, Ruiz Castañeda et al., *El periodismo en México*, 206. Even Justo's poetry seems to have suffered. His complete works do not include any poems between 1881 and 1884. Sierra, *Obras completas*, vol. 1.

101. Sierra, *Obras completas*, 14:70, 62. See also *MR*, 1 May 1880, 3; Escudero, *El duelo en México*, 102.

102. "En los funerales de Ignacio Ramírez" [1879], in Sierra, *Obras completas*, 1:390.

103. *MR*, 2 May 1880, 3.

104. *LL*, 7 May 1880, 2.

105. Clipping without reference, 5 October 1884, BCN, 8, n.p., 654.

106. Sierra, *Obras completas*, 4:129–30. The duel as a possibility was seen as a

moderating influence on journalism. Riva Palacio, *México a través de los siglos*, 11:289.

107. *LL*, 19 January 1884, 2.

108. Camarillo Carbajal, *El sindicato de periodistas*, 33. On journalists' associations and dueling, see Manero, *Apuntes*. In Spain, Cabriñana, *Código del honor en España*, 36–37.

109. *LL*, 5 May 1880, 3. Francisco Cosmes added that journalists who did not abide by the association's decisions would be excluded from the trade. *LL*, 7 May 1880, 2. See initial proposal by *La Constitución* in *MR*, 1 May 1880, 1; *LL*, 1 June 1880, 3.

110. Pi-Suñer, "Prólogo," in Paz, *Algunas campañas*, 10, 16, 13–14, 23–24. Postrevolutionary organizations emphasized mutualist goals and drew closer to other unions. Camarillo Carbajal, *El sindicato de periodistas*, 36, 28–42, 91, 138, 132. See also Manero, *Apuntes*.

111. *MR*, 1 May 1880, 1; Sierra Velenzuela, *Duelos, rieptos y desafíos*, 50.

PART II. *Tumultuous Opinion*

1. Cosío Villegas, *El porfiriato*, 9:760–69, 9:797–98. Carlos Marichal also sees the protests as a consequence of the fight for the presidency. Marichal, "Las estrategias," 47; Marichal, "La deuda externa," 261n. Sierra blamed them on the conservative Catholics attacking public education. Díaz y de Ovando and García Barragán, *La Escuela Nacional Preparatoria*. For Guerra, such riots were symbolic performances of elites' representation of the people. Guerra, *México*, 1:198.

2. Lear, *Workers, Neighbors*; Knight, "The Working Class," 51–79. Both authors see urban riots in the context of working-class participation in the revolution. For broader studies, see Arrom and Ortoll, *Riots*; Taylor, *Drinking, Homicide*. See particularly Rodríguez Kuri, "Desabasto de agua." Useful references are Rudé, *The Crowd*; Thompson, "The Moral Economy"; Bartlett, "An End to Moral Economy"; Cobb, *The Police and the People*. On rhetoric, Palti, *La invención de una legitimidad*; Jaksic, *The Political Power of the Word*. On citizenship, Sábato, "Ciudadanía política y formación," 16; Annino, "Ciudadanía versus gobernabilidad"; Forment, *Democracy in Latin America*; Joseph and Nugent, *Everyday Forms of State Formation*.

3. See Van Young, "Islands in the Storm"; Di Tella, "The Dangerous Classes"; Guedea, "El pueblo de México"; Warren, "El congreso por su gusto."

3. *Eloquence against the Deuda Inglesa*

1. Marichal, "El manejo," 419–44. Noetzlin had been representative in Mexico of the Banque Franco-Egyptienne and since 1881 financial agent of González's government. Castañeda Batres, "Estudio introductorio," 41.

2. Coerver, *The Porfirian Interregnum*, 247–52. See also Quevedo y Zubieta, *El General González*, 129–52; Cosío Villegas, *El porfiriato*, 9:787–98.

3. Marichal, "El manejo," 421, 422.

4. Pérez-Siller, *L'hégémonie des financiers*, 62, 69.

5. Ibid., 9, 87. See also Carmagnani, *Estado y mercado*, 72, 79, 81, 86, 25, 60. On the financial impact of the events, see Téllez, "Préstamos externos," 1:357; Marichal, "El manejo," 429–30, 434–35. The decrease in the value of Mexican bonds in London in *LP*, 23 November 1884, 2; for the reestablishment of diplomatic ties with Great Britain *LL*, 2 November 1884, 2.

6. See, e.g., *DH*, 31 October 1884, 3–4; *DDCD, XII Leg.*, 1:223; Cosío Villegas, *El porfiriato*, 9:793.

7. 15 November 1884, *DDCD, XII Leg.*, 1:322.

8. *MR*, 11 November 1884, 1; *MR*, 23 November 1884, 1.

9. The agreement signed by Rivas on 18 May 1883 added 4,700,000 pounds that had not been authorized by Congress. Casasús, *Historia de la deuda*, 451–52. Rivas was the private secretary of President González, an hacienda owner, and a member of the Jockey Club and in 1884 would be appointed governor of the Federal District.

10. Altamirano to Joaquín D. Casasús, Paris, 5 June 1891, in Altamirano, *Epistolario*, 129–32. On U.S. newspapers' negative view of Mexican events, see Matías Romero to Porfirio Díaz, 12 July 1885, CPD, 10, 7388. For the revolutionary period, see Yankelevich, "En la retaguardia."

11. *MR*, 22 October 1884, 1; *MR*, 25 October 1884, 1. Casasús reviewed criticisms of the Noetzlin agreement published in Mexico and found them justified but causing greater "descrédito de la República en los mercados europeos." Casasús, *Historia de la deuda*, 470–71.

12. *LL*, 27 and 28 November 1884; *LL*, 11 November 1884, 1–2; *LL*, 20 November 1884, 2; *MR*, 7 November 1884, 1. For a list of newspapers that opposed the project, see article reproduced from *Semana Mercantil* in *MR*, 4 November 1884, 3; another list in *LL*, 7 November 1884, 3; Cosío Villegas, *El porfiriato*, 9:791.

13. *LP*, 7 November 1884, 2; *DH*, 19 November 1884, 3; *DH*, 20 November 1884, 4.

14. *LP*, 14 November 1884, 1; *LP*, 18 November 84, 2; *LP*, 19 November 1884, 2; *LP*, 25 November 1884, 3.

15. Mateos, *Los dioses se van*, 7; Cosío Villegas, *La República Restaurada*, 85; Hale, *Justo Sierra*. On Congress, see Guerra, *México*. For the postrevolutionary period, Tannenbaum, *Mexico, the Struggle for Peace*, 83. But see Weldon, "El presidente como legislador"; Piccato, *Congreso y Revolución*.

16. Chano (Santiago?) to Justo Sierra, Veracruz, 23 January 1869, JSM, 1, 16; Rosendo Pineda to Limantour, 9 July 1888, AL, 1, 11. A judgeship could be a consolation for those who failed to reach Congress, F. Bermúdez to Porfirio Díaz, Oaxaca, 30 July 1885, CPD, 10, 7713–14. Control documented in Porfirio Díaz to Belio Mejia, 14 June 1881, CPD, 6, 111; Díaz to Francisco Meijueiro, governor of Oaxaca, 15 June 1881, CPD, 6, 1120. For examples of the coordination of local politics and personal acquiescence of Díaz needed to enter Congress during the early Porfiriato, see Miguel A. Salas to Díaz, Puebla, 3 July 1880, CPD, 5, 2834; Jesús Ma. Margáin to Díaz, Mexico City, 6 July 1880, CPD, 5, 2145; Díaz to Juan

Ocampo, 20 March 1885, CPD, 10, 3012; Apolinar Castillo to Díaz, Chalchi-comula, 30 March 1885, CPD, 10, 3427.

17. For recent studies on the role of eloquence in public life that move beyond formal analysis of speeches into a consideration of institutions and political discourse in general, see *Primer Congreso Internacional*; Cmiel, *Democratic Eloquence*; Seoane Couceiro, *Oratoria y periodismo*; Río, Caballero López, and Albaladejo Mayordomo, *Quintiliano*. On speech and relations of power, Graham, "A Public Sphere?," 720. On rhetoric required by honor, Wyatt-Brown, *The Shaping of Southern Culture*, 301.

18. For the definition of the art, Elguero, *Lecciones de elocuencia*, 9, 14, 32. Eloquence is "persuadir con la dicción" (*persuadere dictione*), as opposed to "la elocuencia artificiosa, que llaman retórica." Cicerón, *De la invención*, 5. On the distinction between "sofistas" or "retóricos" and "filósofos," see Agustín Verdugo, "Tesis sobre la elocuencia," *EF* 21:115 (15 December 1883), 458. On the goodness of the orator, see Quintiliano, *Institución oratoria*; Cicerón, *De la invención*, 1; Davis, "Discourse of Oratory," 27–36.

19. Jacinto Pallares, "La unidad oratoria," *EF* 21:104 (28 November 1883), 413; ibid., *EF* 21:106 (30 November 1883), 420–21; Verdugo, "Tesis sobre la elocuencia," 476–77. Both authors competed for the chair of Literatura y Elocuencia Forense at the Escuela de Jurisprudencia. See also Elguero, *Lecciones de elocuencia*, 9; Cmiel, *Democratic Eloquence*, 25.

20. Elguero, *Lecciones de elocuencia*, 9–11. A useful analysis in Davis, "Discourse of Oratory," chap. 3. The proliferation of rhetoric titles in Spain in Casas, *Obras 2*, 563.

21. Herrejón Peredo, "Sermones y discursos." On the survival of rhetoric in Mexico, see Pérez Martínez, "Hacia una tópica," 359; Salado Álvarez, *Memorias*, 84.

22. *DDCD, XII Leg.*, 214.

23. Pérez Martínez, "Hacia una tópica." Eloquence as a popular art was also construed as a classic legacy, Moliérac, *Iniciación*, 119. For examples see Serra Rojas, *Antología*, 73–79. See examples in Archivo General de la Nación, Fondo Antonio Díaz Soto y Gama (hereafter ADSG), roll 7. On classical rhetoric and civic duties, Guerra, *Modernidad e independencias*, 242.

24. Prieto, *Obras completas*, 9:489.

25. Sierra, "Clichés parlamentarios," in Sierra, *Ensayos y textos*, 27. On the Grito, Yañez, *Don Justo Sierra*, 43–44. For the "alegatas cotidianas del habla popular," see Pérez Martínez, "Hacia una tópica," 360, 366. On the strength of oral modes of expression into the modern era, see Hutton, *History*, 14.

26. Prieto, *Obras completas*, 9:397–99.

27. See Hutton, *History*, 10. On public spaces in Mexico City as commemorations, although without any consideration of their oratorical uses, see Tenorio-Trillo, "1910 Mexico City"; Tenenbaum, "Streetwise History." On civic oratory, Pi Suñer, "Prólogo," in Prieto, *Obras completas*, 9:28–29.

28. Justo Sierra, "La niñez y la escuela," 31 January 1874, in Serra Rojas, *Antología*, 12–16; Prieto, *Obras completas*, 9:19.

29. Justo Sierra, "Discurso pronunciado por el Sr. Lic. D. Justo Sierra en honor del Sr. Lic. D. Manuel de la Peña y Peña, con motivo de la traslación de sus restos a la rotonda de los hombres ilustres," 2 January 1895, in RLJ (January-June 1895), 162, 160, 161. See also Agustín Yáñez, "Introducción" in Sierra, *Juárez*; Cosío Villegas, *El porfiriato*, 2:501; Prieto, *Obras completas*, 9:552; *Velada que a la memoria*. On a "mártir de la Reforma santa," see "En los funerales de F. Castañeda y Nájera" [1876], in Sierra, *Obras completas*, 1:375. On the religious elements of nationalism, Lomnitz, *Deep Mexico*, chap. 2. For other examples of this genre, see Jesús Urueta, "Discurso [Pronunciado en la velada organizada por los estudiantes de Jurisprudencia en honor de Juárez]," 18 July 1901, in Serra Rojas, *Antología*, 17–25; *Velada fúnebre*, 9–12. For the combination of music, poetry, and oratory, see *Velada que a la memoria*. In Argentina the genre was seen simultaneously as ornamental and community building. Palti, "Las polémicas," 179, 181.

30. Jacinto Pallares, "Discurso fúnebre sobre Ignacio Vallarta," 9 January 1894, in RLJ (February 1894), 97.

31. MR, 30 October 1884, 2; MR, 11 November 1884, 1; MR, 14 November 1884, 3. Starting in 1872 the Chamber of Deputies met in the elegant building of the Teatro Iturbide, inaugurated in 1855. Zavala Abascal, *La cámara de diputados*, 89–94.

32. Pasquel, *Díaz Mirón*, 42; Duclós Salinas, *Méjico pacificado*.

33. Díaz Mirón, *Prosa*, 44. See Bertola, "Las oportunidades del poder"; Camp, *Mexican Political Biographies*.

34. Flores Villar, *Los estudiantes*, 17.

35. "Un deber, que estimo sagrado, me ha traido a esta tribuna, en donde verdaderamente me encuentro perplejo ante la magnitud del fin que voy a perseguir y la deficiencia de los medios que para ello están a mi alcance. Y esta perplejidad mía sube de punto ante la consideración de que, bizoño en estas lides parlamentarias, hablo por primera vez, y sin preparación, en el seno de una Asamblea que cuenta entre sus miembros distinguidos oradores y que está acostumbrada a oir elocuentes arengas. Sirva de disculpa a la audacia mía la obligación en que me hallo de decir la palabra de mi conciencia en esta discusion, que es tan grave, que profundamente afecta la honra y el bienestar de México." DDCD, XII Leg., 1:214.

36. DDCD, XII Leg., 1:214. He probably knew, however, that Deputy Fernando Duret was going to follow his speech with another in which he opposed in detail the financial aspects of the project. For Marco Fabio Quintiliano, the exordium was the moment in which the orator earned the benevolence of his audience with humility. Quintiliano, *Institución oratoria*, 178.

37. Díaz Mirón, *Prosa*, 46.

38. MR, 14 November 1884, 3; DDCD, XII Leg., 1:219–20. Other references to Díaz Mirón's "elocuencia varonil" in DDCD, XII Leg., 1:264. For a very similar exordium by the law student Antonio Díaz Soto y Gama in 1898 in San Luis

Potosí, see ADSG, roll 7. On his image, Francisco J. Ariza, "Apuntes para un retrato," *Excélsior*, 3 and 4 May 1946.

39. 14 November 1884, *DDCD, XII Leg.*, 1:290. Prieto was minister of Hacienda on several occasions between 1852 and 1876.

40. Sierra, *Juárez*, 133; McLean, *Vida y obra*, 36. See also "Clichés parlamentarios," in Sierra, *Ensayos y textos*.

41. Justo Sierra's account of the episode, written years after the debate of 1884, suggested that Prieto's eloquence had a great impact on "el corazón del pueblo." Sierra, *Juárez*, 131–32. See Prieto, *Obras completas*, 9:16, 28–29. See also McLean, *Vida y obra*, 20, 136–37.

42. Prieto, *Obras completas*, 9:397–99; McLean, *Vida y obra*, 136. Prieto was "romantic in his negligence of style." Anderson Imbert, *Spanish American Literature*. For oratory and rhetoric "far from fading away during the Romantic period," see Davis, "Discourse of Oratory," 44, 45, and chap. 3.

43. 15 November 1884, *DDCD, XII Leg.*, 1:321.; 14 November 1884, *DDCD, XII Leg.*, 1:290.

44. Elguero, *Lecciones de elocuencia*, 23, 26, 48.

45. Puga y Acal, *Los poetas mexicanos*. "El clasicismo, por otra parte, no es un fenómeno extraño al espíritu romántico . . . en cuanto tiende con nostalgia hacia un fantástico mundo pagano." Praz, *La carne, la muerte*, 48. On the classic/ romantic opposition, see Praz, *La carne, la muerte*, 45. The opposition of reason against authority, and individual against collective, inherited from French romanticism, in Vallejo, *El romanticismo*. On the continuity of romanticism and classicism, see Picard, *Le romantisme social*, 31.

46. Yañez, *Don Justo Sierra*, 31. For romanticism in Mexico as rebellion but also as stress on emotion, Galí i Boadella, *Historias del bello sexo*, 25.

47. Sierra, *Juárez*, 232–33. "En los funerales del general Carlos Pacheco" [1891], in Sierra, *Obras completas*, 1:420. Sierra added, he "era como nosotros, amalgama / de pasión y de error y de conciencia."

48. Monterde, *Salvador Díaz Mirón*, 47–54; Pi Suñer, "Prólogo," 19–20; Saborit, *Doblados*, 176. The influence of Hugo and Byron in Carilla, *El romanticismo*, 1:78, 101; Castelar, *Lord Byron*, 29–31. A critique of the narcissism of that trend in Puga y Acal, *Los poetas mexicanos*, 68–69. On romantic writers' proclivity to dueling, Gamboa, *Mi diario V*, 97–98.

49. Díaz Mirón described his position regarding the Noetzlin agreement as a similarly uphill battle. See Castelar, *Discursos parlamentarios*, 221, 229. Even during the debate about the deuda inglesa Mexican newspapers printed long letters and speeches by Castelar on other themes on page 1. See *LP*, 26 November 1884, 2. Ignacio Manuel Altamirano, for example, befriended Castelar in Telésforo García's house in Paris in 1890. Altamirano to Francisco Sosa, Paris, 26 September 1890, Altamirano, *Epistolario*, 56. His impact in *La Libertad* in Hale, *Justo Sierra*, 51–52. García later bought the house where Castelar died, in Madrid. Yañez, *Don Justo Sierra*, 194. A homage at the Escuela de Derecho after Castelar's death included President Díaz and his ministers. *Velada fúnebre*, quote

on "nuestra raza" in 3–8, 13. Although a republican, in his later years Caste-lar accepted a constitutional monarchy and avoided Jacobin extremes. Castelar, *Autobiografía*.

50. "A Emilio Castelar" [1899], in Sierra, *Obras completas*, 1:357. According to Justo Sierra, in Castelar's writings "el orador hablaba con la pluma, ya que no con la lengua." *Velada fúnebre*, 3–8, 13. *El Foro*, ironically, advertised Cuban cigars called Emilio Castelar. MR, 15 November 1884.

51. Speech delivered on 4 June 1876, Castelar, *Discursos parlamentarios*, 1:221–22. Unity, as predicated by Pallares, was to be achieved by the skillful dissimula-tion of the internal parts of the discourse. Jacinto Pallares, "La unidad oratoria," *EF* 21:106 (30 November 1883), 420–21.

52. "Oratoria Sagrada," *LL*, 24 January 1884, 2; Castelar, *Autobiografía*, lxix–lxx. See school notes for speeches by Antonio Díaz Soto y Gama, detailed in exordio and peroratio, often skipping the rest. ADSG, roll 7. See also Elguero, *Lecciones de elocuencia*, 51. Castelar's first speech was famous for capturing the attention of the audience from the first sentence and ending in a rousing finale. Castelar, *Autobiografía*, xli.

53. *Velada fúnebre*, 33–50, other references to beauty in 17–18. See also Castelar, *Autobiografía*, lxv.

54. *Velada fúnebre*, 28–32. His doctor described him as short, obese, bald, and shortsighted, yet having a beautiful voice. Castelar, *Autobiografía*, lxv–lxvi.

55. *Velada fúnebre*, 35.

56. In famous examples like Berryer, Favre, and Gambetta "los arranques de la pasión, los latidos de la sangre" conveyed by "tribunos," whom Sierra in 1874 contrasted with drier "abogados," were more effective ("ponen la mano sobre el corazón de las multitudes"). Sierra, "Clichés parlamentarios," in Sierra, *Ensayos y textos*, 26–27. On homoerotic desire in Mexican literature, see Irwin, *Mexican Masculinities*.

57. Sierra, *Juárez*, 131–32. For a description of Ignacio Manuel Altamirano's eyes and gesture, and "el movimiento rítmico de sus manos y agitarse su melena hirsuta como la de los leones de Africa," see Joaquín D. Casasús to Angel de Campo in Altamirano, *Epistolario*, 397–98. On Sierra's body, Tablada, *Sombras largas*, 129. Another admiring description, that of José María Lozano, in Díaz Mirón, *Prosa*, 312. After listening to the French counsel, Henri Robert, "el jurado ha quedado seducido por la dulzura del sonido; con frecuencia olvida las pal-abras, pero cuando delibera, recuerda la impresión que la música le ha pro-ducido." Moliérac, *Iniciación*, 169. See Herf, *Reactionary Modernism*, 76–77, for the aesthetic meaning of gestures in politics.

58. Women were still exceptional in oratory contests in the 1920s. González Cárdenas, *Los cien años*, 95–98. For melodrama as a form in which women's voices could emerge in other public settings, see Maza, *Private Lives*; Moheno, *Mis últimos discursos*; Moheno, *Rubin*; Piccato, "The Girl Who Killed a Senator."

59. Castelar, *Autobiografía*, 219. On the importance of authenticity to nineteenth-century politicians, see Sennett, *The Fall of Public Man*, 25–26, a new

association of the public and private in front of large urban audiences "creating thereby a sense of a meaningful public domain in society, human expression is likely to be conceived in terms of gestures and symbols which are real no matter who makes the gesture or uses the symbol," 41. See also Berlin, *Las raíces*, 27, 185.

60. Jacinto Pallares, "La unidad oratoria," EF 21:104 (28 November 1883), 413. On the sincerity of the speaker, see, for example, notes on 15 July 1895, in ADSG, roll 7. An apology of "locura, sí, pero locura necesaria, locura admirable, locura heróica" in ibid. On beauty and sincerity achieved through the art of rhetoric, Elguero, *Lecciones de elocuencia*, 13–14. Postrevolutionary orators like Antonio Díaz Soto y Gama and Aurelio Manrique were accused of madness.

61. 14 November 1884, DDCD, XII Leg., 1: 282, 286. See also his response to the "injurias" published against him by some students. LL, 22 November 1884, 1–2. On reason, Sierra, "Clichés parlamentarios," in Sierra, *Ensayos y textos*, 30–31.

62. 14 November 1884, DDCD, XII Leg., 1: 286. In January 1885, Sierra explained to his constituents from Sinaloa that national and personal honor, not private interests, determined his decision to defend the government's project. He expected "nuevas iras y nuevas injurias en su contra." Justo Sierra to Francisco Cañedo, Governor of Sinaloa, 6 January 1885, in Sierra, *Obras completas*, 14:74–78.

63. Flores Villar, *Los estudiantes*, 18.

64. Moliérac, *Iniciación*, 22, 28; Cicerón, *De la invención*. For the training of passion to make it useful, see Agustín Verdugo, "Tesis sobre la elocuencia," EF 21:114 (14 December 1883), 452–53.

65. Salado Álvarez, *Memorias*, 109. Even the Conservatory had a class on oratory. Gonzalez Navarro, *Historia Moderna* 4:637–38.

66. Mendieta y Nuñez, *Historia de la Facultad*, 128, 132, 133, 137, 166, 150, 211.

67. "Catedra de Oratoria Forense del Instituto Científico y Literario del Estado de San Luis Potosí," ADSG, roll 7; Agustín Verdugo, "Tesis sobre la elocuencia," EF 21:120 (22 December 1893), 476–77.

68. Velázquez Albo, *Origen y desarrollo*, 43, 45, 22–23, 26–27, 30–31. For the decreasing importance of Latin, in spite of Barreda's original plan, Gonzalez Navarro, *Historia Moderna* 4:618, 621; O'Gorman, "Justo Sierra," 152; Hale, *Transformation*, 144.

69. Salado Álvarez, *Memorias*, 57, 155.

70. On contests as an outlet for the "students' irresistible impulse to speak," *El Universal*, 1 June 1930, 2a. sec., 1; González Cárdenas, *Los cien años*, 95–98. On curricula, Universidad Nacional de México, *Plan de estudios*; Bustillo Oro, "Ahí está el detalle." Impatience with long-winded words, "ampulosas y declamatorias" in Congress, in 14 December 1899, DDCD, XIX Leg., III session, 606. On pretentious speeches inspired by Castelar and the value of milder speeches, Mateos, *Los dramas*, 384, 393; Garcia Naranjo, *Recuerdos del Colegio Civil*, 95, 238.

71. MR, 11 November 1884, 3.

72. MR, 19 November 1884, 3. *La Libertad* denied that Bulnes's house had been

attacked by protesters. *LL*, 23 November 1884, 3. Bulnes had also supported the state's view in the debates about nickel coins in 1883. *MR*, 19 November 1884, 3. Federico Gamboa described him as a poor writer and a successful orator: "Sus discursos, escoltados por el merecido prestigio del individuo, el calor de la voz, la seducción convincente del ademán, las modalidades de la mirada y ese magnetismo misterioso que se desprende de las palabras de los hombres de talento." Federico Gamboa, "A guisa de prólogo," in Bulnes, *Los grandes problemas*, xi–xii. Prieto admired his "fecunda vena oratoria," 14 November 1884, *DDCD, XII Leg.*, 1:304. Díaz Mirón recognized his "genio." 15 November 1884, *DDCD, XII Leg.*, 1:337, 342. See also Salado Alvarez, *Memorias*, 164–65.

73. 12 November 1884, *DDCD, XII Leg.*, 1:297, 299, 304, 222. For his later critique of patriotism, see Bulnes, *El verdadero Juárez*.

74. "Dictamen," 375.

75. Bulnes, undated manuscript, Archivo General de la Nación, Fondo Francisco Bulnes (hereafter FB), 14, 10, f. 7. Jacinto Pallares, "La unidad oratoria," *EF* 21:104 (28 November 1883), 413. The same argument, used in a trial, in *Defensa de primera instancia*, 8–9. For a textbook, see Rivera, *Tratado breve*, 48–49. On orators' greater influence over the uneducated, López Portillo y Rojas, *Fuertes y débiles*, 165.

76. Jacinto Pallares, "La unidad oratoria," *EF* 21:113 (12 December 1883), 448. The concern over demagoguery was a traditional theme that even the most expressive romantics echoed. Castelar spoke against it, and even Prieto warned about the dangers of a single-chamber Congress in which an orator could exercise "la seducción omnipotente" of the audience with "la magia de su elocuencia." Speech in defense of the project to establish a Senate, 22 April 1870, in Prieto, *Obras completas*, 9:133–35. See also Irwin, *Plato's Ethics*, 96–97.

77. Joaquín D. Casasús to Angel de Campo Altamirano, *Epistolario*, 397–98. On the prestige of orators as the factor of their success, Le Bon, *Psychologie*, 169.

78. Le Bon, *Psychologie*, 147.

79. See Bulnes's notes on Le Bon in AGN FB, 21, exps. 25, 27. Le Bon, *Psychologie*, 50, 55, 84, 104, cited in *El Universal*, 6 October 1916, 6; Castro Leal, *Díaz Mirón*, 33–34. See also Sodi, *El Jurado en México*, 238–56.

80. Díaz spoke slowly, "con voz ronca y acompasada, sin accionar ni mover las manos, mirando fijamente al interlocutor y sin aire imperativo." Salado Alvarez, *Memorias*, 258. On Díaz's preference for silence, see Garner, *Porfirio Díaz*, 53. On the ambitions of Calero, Salado Alvarez, *Memorias*, 380.

81. *EF* 25:32 (13 August 1885), 128–29; Elguero, *Lecciones de elocuencia*, 27–28, 34.

82. Moliérac, *Iniciación*, 169–71. For negative evaluations of the impact of "la improvisación castelariana" in Mexico, see Francisco J. Hernández, "No es tan fácil ser orador," 27 October 1939, clipping, ADSG, rollo 1.

83. 12 November 1884, *DDCD, XII Leg.*, 1:297, 299, 304, 222.

84. See, for example, Schell, *Integral Outsiders*; Haber, *Industria y subdesarrollo*.

85. 12 November 1884, *DDCD, XII Leg.*, 1:300–301; Bulnes, *Los grandes prob-*

lemas, xi. See also, perhaps also written by Bulnes, "¿Qué cosa es la opinión pública?" *LL*, 28 November 1884, 1.

86. *LP*, 7 November 1884, 2; *MR*, 16 November 1884, 3. Sierra referred later to "el honor—sin el que no hay nacionalidad," Justo Sierra, "Discurso pronunciado por el Sr. Lic. D. Justo Sierra en honor del Sr. Lic. D. Manuel de la Peña y Peña, con motivo de la traslacion de sus restos a la rotonda de los hombres ilustres," 2 January 1895, in *RLJ* (January–June 1895), 172.

87. 12 November 1884, *DDCD, XII Leg.*, 1:216–19.

88. Ibid., 1:224, 284.

89. Sierra, *Juárez*, 556. On honor and sexual morality, Caulfield, *In Defense of Honor*; and the fatherland, through war, see Febre, *Honneur et Patrie*. On health and crime, Buffington, *Criminal and Citizen*.

90. Vega, *Dos palabras*, 1.

91. *Defensa de primera instancia*, 40. For the same reasoning applied in a potential dispute with Guatemala, *Gran jurado nacional*, 238.

92. 12 November 1884, *DDCD, XII Leg.*, 1:219.

93. 13 November 1884, *DDCD, XII Leg.*, 1:260.

94. *DDCD, XII Leg.*, 1:218. Justino Fernández, close to Porfirio Díaz but an enemy of the project, saw further national humiliation in the fact that the Mexican representative was "un negociante extranjero" interested only in profit. 13 November 1884, *DDCD, XII Leg.*, 1:274, 280. Díaz Mirón was a close friend of the customs administrator in Veracruz, Teodoro Dehesa, who became governor in 1892. Flores Villar, *Los estudiantes*, 23.

95. Foreigners owned the money he seized in 1860, and a British consul sued him for defamation in 1855. See Introduction and Degollado, *Defensa ante el público*, 6.

96. Salado Alvarez, *Memorias*, 211. Contrast with Palti, "Las polémicas," 180.

97. *MR*, 22 November 1884, 3

98. "¡Tú, que firme y erguido en la tribuna / como el peñón en donde el faro radia, / sabes cumplir con tu deber de antorcha / sobre este mar en que el honor naufraga!" "Voces interiores," in Díaz Mirón, *Poesía Completa*, 325–28.

99. *LP*, 14 November 1884, 2.

100. *LP*, 15 November 1884, 2.

101. *LP*, 18 November 1884, 2. Even *La Libertad*, which supported the project, devoted a large section of its chronicles to the performance of deputies and the style of their speeches. *LL*, 14 November 1884, 2; *LL*, 16 November 1884, 2–3.

4. Expanding the Public Sphere

1. *DH*, 21 November 1884, 3; *MR*, 14 November 1884, 3; *MR*, 20 November 1884, 1; *MR*, 19 November 1884, 1; *LP*, 19 November 1884, 2; *LP*, 21 November 1884, 2; 16 November 1884, *DDCD, XII Leg.*, 1:344. For a detailed narrative, see Piccato, "El populacho." E. Fuentes y Betancourt, "El congreso y la votación del

sábado," *MR*, 18 November 1884, 1; Francisco Tolentino, governor of Jalisco, to President Manuel González, 27 November 1884, Archivo Manuel González, Universidad Iberoamericana, box 91, f. 106365.

2. *LL*, 19 November 1884, 2.

3. Ibid.; Cosío Villegas, *El porfiriato*, 9:792–93; Flores Villar, *Los estudiantes*, 15, 18, 20, 21; Frías, *El amor de las sirenas*, 118, 252.

4. Flores Villar, *Los estudiantes*, 27–30.

5. This chapter thus builds on Guerra's hypothesis that students were "detrás de la 'plebe' anónima" in nineteenth-century "popular" movements. Guerra, *Modernidad e independencias*, 294.

6. 18 November 1884, *DDCD, XII Leg.*, 1:367.; *MR*, 20 November 1884, 3; Flores Villar, *Los estudiantes*, 34–35; Real Academia, "Diccionario de la lengua 1869." On the multiple meanings of "pueblo," Guerra, "De la política antigua," 139; Guerra, *Modernidad e independencias*, 353; Illades, "La apropiación del 'pueblo,'" paper presented at the Seminario internacional "Identidad, memoria, política y narración," March 2001. For Bulnes, "el populacho" was "una bestia que gasta sangre humana para [teñir?] de púrpura imperial a sus andrajos." Undated manuscript, FB, 14, 10, 4.

7. Flores Villar, *Los estudiantes*, 16–17.

8. *MR*, 19 November 1884, 1; *MR*, 14 November 1884, 3.

9. *MR*, 16 November 1884, 3.

10. *MR*, 23 November 1884, 1. An almost identical description ("Los estudiantes noble generacion que traen sobre su frente el verbo del porvenir") in Multiple signatures to Porfirio Díaz, 29 July 1885, CPD, 10, 6973–9. The political engagement of Mexican Bohemia contrasts with the European archetype of cynicism. Wilson, *Bohemians*, 24. The author does not examine, as part of her exploration of bohemian politics, bohemians' role in riots. Ibid., chap. 13.

11. *MR*, 20 November 1884, 1.

12. Ibid., 2. The students' motto, according to one participant, was "Orden y progreso," and revolution was never their goal. Flores Villar, *Los estudiantes*, 59.

13. BCN, 655; *MR*, 23 November 1884, 1; *LL*, 28 November 1884, 3. For suggestions that students were instigated or paid by others, see *Colección de pedimentos*, 85.

14. BCN, 9, 844; "Biografía de los presos políticos," no date, BCN, 8, fol. 1924; "¿Qué cosa es la opinión pública?" *LL*, 28 November 1884, 1; *Colección de pedimentos*. Joaquín Clausell, later to become an opposition journalist, received a medal. Saborit, *Doblados*, 90–91.

15. *Estadísticas sociales*; Gonzalez Navarro, *Historia Moderna*, 4:627.

16. Vaughan, *State, Education*, 21, 39–41, 70–71.

17. In other words, the Federal District had 2.4 percent of the national population in 1900, but 22.62 percent of the lawyers and 20.03 percent of the physicians. Gonzalez Navarro, *Historia Moderna*, 4:633–34; *Estadísticas sociales*; Gómez-Quiñones, *Porfirio Díaz*, 51.

18. Vaughan, *State, Education*, 67, 71.

19. Camp, *Political Recruitment*, 21, 39, 84, 92, 106–07. Same numbers, and a roster of students who came from other regions of the country and went on to become influential politicians and professionals, in García Naranjo, *Recuerdos del Colegio Civil*, 22–23, 84, 88.

20. "En la muerte del jóven Mariano Olvera," in Sierra, *Obras completas*, 1:246–48. On the Preparatoria, Hale, *Transformation*, 154; Alvarado, "Formación moral del estudiante"; Monsiváis, "Del saber compartido," 103; Palti, *La invención de una legitimidad*, 300, 334, 337.

21. Díaz y de Ovando and García Barragán, *La Escuela Nacional Preparatoria*, 1:131; Gómez-Quiñones, *Porfirio Díaz*, 52. Ironically, some students had fellowships because their fathers had died in combat. See also Lemoine Villicaña, *La Escuela*.

22. Alvarado, "Formación moral del estudiante," 107.

23. Ibid., 110–11, 107. For grants that helped when the family was near poverty, and the gratitude they elicited, Mateos, *Los dioses se van*, 4. Two hundred pesos a year was the cost for a secondary school student at Monterrey's Colegio Civil in 1897. But studying law in Mexico City a few years later required fifty pesos a month. García Naranjo, *Recuerdos del Colegio Civil*, 44, 52.

24. Gonzalez Navarro, *Historia Moderna*, 4:625.

25. For a comprehensive discussion of these debates and their philosophical underpinnings see Hale, *Transformation*, 144–49, 161–62.

26. This includes the philosophers Antonio Caso and José Vasconcelos, products of the Preparatoria and close to Sierra. Gómez-Quiñones, *Porfirio Díaz*, 58–59. Sierra did not introduce any changes in the program while he was director. Díaz y de Ovando and García Barragán, *La Escuela Nacional Preparatoria*, 1:121–23.

27. In response General Vicente Riva Palacio defended "la preciosa teoría del individualismo" against the authoritarian demands of positivism. Ruiz Castaneda, "La universidad libre," 14, 22; Hale, *Transformation*, 195.

28. O'Gorman, "Justo Sierra," 182. See also Díaz y de Ovando and García Barragán, *La Escuela Nacional Preparatoria*, 1:49, 62–63, 85, 89. In the early years, presidents signed the appointment of professors and were involved in the administration of the school. Lemoine Villicaña, *La Escuela*, 45. For the textbook debate, see Hale, *Transformation*; Gonzalez Navarro, *Historia Moderna*, 4:611.

29. Gonzalez Navarro, *Historia Moderna*, 4:608–12; Hale, *Transformation*, 169–71. On funding, Juan N. Mirafuentes, "Enseñanza libre," EA 2:15 (5 May 1875), 2–3; EA 2:17 (10 May 1875), 2. Yet Mirafuentes also pointed to the government's obligation to fund education for the masses. EA 2:18 (12 May 1875), 2–3. Hale, *Transformation*, 165; Mateos, *Los dioses se van*, 4. For the legacy of political conflict inside and around the university, see Garciadiego Dantan, *Rudos contra científicos*.

30. Charles A. Hale argues that doctrinaire positivism was ebbing during the Porfiriato, while the more specific notion of scientific politics gained currency among political elites. O'Gorman sees political discussions about metaphysics as

part of the secular struggle between conservatism and liberalism to define Mexico's identity and entrance into modernity. O'Gorman, "Justo Sierra," 173, 147; Hale, *Transformation*, 171.

31. Alvarado, "Formación moral del estudiante," 101, 118–20. For Pallares, "El espíritu y el corazón tienen como el cuerpo su gimnasia y sometidos a una disciplina moral, alcanzan un desarrollo incalculable." Jacinto Pallares, "La unidad oratoria," *EF* 21:106 (30 November 1883), 420–21. For the lack of moral content of progress as a concern for Porfirian elites, see Piccato, "'El Paso de Venus.'" On introspection, Hale, *Transformation*, 186.

32. Frías, *El amor de las sirenas*, 414–15. For another student bragging that he knew "las mujeres más hermosas designándolas por sus nombres; conocía a las cortesanas y sabía quién las pagaba y quién las gozaba," see Campos, *Claudio Oronoz*, 33. See also Campos, *El Bar*, 73.

33. For the contrast between old, "pendenciero, goloso, descuidado en su traje," and new, more gentlemanly, politically aware students, see *EA* 2:14 (28 April 1875), 1–2; Flores Villar, *Los estudiantes*, 9–10. García Naranjo remembered "la leyenda que envolvía a los estudiantes en la pasada centuria": amusement, adventures, romance, pranks, and protests. Garcia Naranjo, *Recuerdos del Colegio Civil*, 42.

34. Díaz y de Ovando and García Barragán, *La Escuela Nacional Preparatoria*, 30.

35. *EA* 2:15 (3 May 1875), 4–5; Alvarado, "Formación moral del estudiante," 113–15; Díaz y de Ovando and García Barragán, *La Escuela Nacional Preparatoria*, 1:50–51; Ruiz Castaneda, "La universidad libre," 15.

36. *EA* 2:15 (3 May 1875), 4–5; *EA* 2:18 (12 May 1875), 5.

37. "La cuestión de los estudiantes," *EA* 2:15 (5 May 1875), 3. In a play that was critical of the movement the same compromise was nevertheless recognized: students decided to go on strike in spite of parental advice because "es necesario curarse de la ternura; los combates son para las almas fuertes." Mateos, *Los dioses se van*, 6. On the goals of the movement as "libertad para la enseñanza, honor y respeto para la inteligencia, soberanía para la razón," see Juan N. Mirafuentes, "Boletín, Libertad," *EA* 2:15 (3 May 1875), 2–3.

38. Flores Villar, *Los estudiantes*, 11–15. On artistic events, Garcia Naranjo, *La vieja Escuela de Jurisprudencia*, 28–30.

39. Mateos, *Los dioses se van*, 3, 7; Hale, *Transformation*, 166; Sierra, "La novela," 33; Flores Villar, *Los estudiantes*, 33.

40. Flores Villar, *Los estudiantes*, 58; Ruiz Castaneda, "La universidad libre," 14. On the violent practices of German students, see Gay, *The Cultivation of Hatred*; Frevert, *Men of Honour*, chap. 4. For an ironic description of a "lance de honor" among Mexican students, Frías, *El amor de las sirenas*, 79–82.

41. Mateos, *Los dioses se van*, 9. Explaining the title, which probably did not involve a reference to Nietzsche, Anselmo concludes that society is on the brink of revolution: "La virtud se muere, la moral se corrompe, el vicio impera, los Dioses se van." Mateos, *Los dioses se van*, 27. The play, first performed at the

Teatro Nacional on 27 January 1878, was praised by the Catholic *La Voz de México* and criticized by the liberal *La Patria*. Díaz y de Ovando and García Barragán, *La Escuela Nacional Preparatoria*, 1:71. For one attack on positivism from *El Constitucional* in 1875, see Díaz y de Ovando and García Barragán, *La Escuela Nacional Preparatoria*, 1:49.

42. Campos, *Claudio Oronoz*; Frías's novel, dated in Mazatlán, is admittedly autobiographic. Frías, *El amor de las sirenas*, ii. See also Tablada, *Sombras largas*, 60. Contrast with González Rodríguez, *Bajos Fondos*, 38–39. This life of student sin is a precedent of twentieth-century *desmadre*—amply documented by literature in the 1960s. On *desmadre*, see González Rodríguez, *Bajos Fondos*; Ramirez Rodríguez, *Chin-chin*. The best example of the moral meaning and morbid attraction of youth recounted from adulthood is Gamboa, *Impresiones*. For youth as a negative force ("los viejos representan las ideas retrógradas" because they are "cadena opresora, prescribamos el pasado"), see Mateos, *Los dioses se van*, 3. Bohemia was always derivative. Defined in tension and self-referential dramatization of bourgeois identity in Seigel, *Bohemian Paris*, 11.

43. García Naranjo, *La vieja Escuela de Jurisprudencia*, 46. Although clear in the capital, this was also true for other cities like Guadalajara. Azuela, "María Luisa," 707–08.

44. Aragón, "A la República," 237; Alvarado, "Formación moral del estudiante," 101–02, 114. Hale rightly notes that "the confusing positions taken on the issue of the internado suggest that they involved attitudes toward mores and social values rather than formal educational philosophy." Hale, *Transformation*, 162.

45. The preservation of the *internado* raised a discussion at the Chamber of Deputies. In 1877, it was abolished for everyone except students of the Escuela de Agricultura and *preparatorianos* under sixteen. It was reinstated in 1903, in part because of Sierra's change of mind, causing another debate and a personal conflict between the fellow positivists Agustín Aragón and Porfirio Parra. Alvarado, "Formación moral del estudiante," 111, 107–10, 116–17, 130–34. For an exchange between Barreda and an anonymous father who blamed him for failing to prevent the strike, see *EA* 2:15 (3 May 1875), 4. On *f. fuereños* enjoying city life more than locals, see Azuela, "María Luisa," 715.

46. See Mateos, *Los dioses se van*; Sierra, "La novela"; Díaz y de Ovando and García Barragán, *La Escuela Nacional Preparatoria*, 1:65–66; López Portillo y Rojas, *Rosario*, 10. Acuña's death was never clarified, either by a note or by mediums. González Rodríguez, *Bajos Fondos*, 22–23. The characters of the *orgía*, all of them from the interior, also make fun of Sierra and Barreda. Frías, *El amor de las sirenas*, 4, 6, 8. See also Azuela, "María Luisa," 705. For a stylized, less decadent depiction of student life, see Justo Sierra's romantic short story of 1868, "La novela."

47. Frías, *El amor de las sirenas*, 222–23; Parra, *Pacotillas*, 335; García Naranjo, *La vieja Escuela de Jurisprudencia*, 30.

48. Campos, *Claudio Oronoz*, 24; Marsiske, *Movimientos estudiantiles*, 192. On flâneurs, Walkowitz, *City of Dreadful Delight*; Piccato, *City of Suspects*,

chaps. 1, 2; Sarlo, *Una modernidad periférica*. Zarco was one avant la lettre. Quirarte, "Zarco, Poe y Baudelaire," 241.

49. Frías, *El amor de las sirenas*, 83–27, 43, 152; Azuela, "María Luisa," 709, 721.

50. Campos, *Claudio Oronoz*, 125.

51. Sierra, "La novela," 40. For a woman, Rosario Peña, who became the object of the ideal love of several students and poets and inspired Acuña's posthumous "Nocturno a Rosario," see López Portillo y Rojas, *Rosario*; Díaz, *Memorias*, 2:29n. Idealization of a woman, suicide, and "las condiciones de albedrío absoluto que sólo la literatura impone" are connected in Domínguez Michael, *Tiros en el concierto*, 147. Frías, *El amor de las sirenas*, 259. See Gluck, *Popular Bohemia*, 9. For Bohemia as a myth, a complex relationship with an audience, and a construction of the past, Wilson, *Bohemians*, chap. 1.

52. Mateos, *Los dioses se van*, 2.

53. Azuela, "María Luisa," 737–39, 745, 763. In a text signed in 1896, Azuela closes a story of disappointed love, prostitution, alcohol, and death with an anatomy lesson in which a student, who had been a lover of the dead woman, sheds a tear. Azuela, "Impresiones," 728. In *Los dramas de México*, a doctor proceeds with the dissection of the body of his wife, who had abandoned him for a student and was later herself abandoned; the student cannot bear to continue observing the dissection. Mateos, *Los dramas*, 127–29. See also Manuel Acuña, "Ante un cadáver," in Acuña and Martínez, *Obras*. The poem is cited as a "curious example of how Romantic lyricism makes its way through the themes of scientific materialism." Anderson Imbert, *Spanish American Literature*, 205. See also Buffington and Piccato, "Tales of Two Women." For the causal link between alcohol, prostitution, and venereal disease as a common pattern for women, see Ponce, *El alcoholismo*, 76; Sanchez Santos, *El Alcoholismo*, 25; Lara y Pardo, *La prostitución*, 75.

54. Frías, *El amor de las sirenas*, 222; Mateos, *Los dioses se van*, 14–15. For negative views of the consequences of women entering the bureaucracy, see Bulnes, *Toda la verdad*, 36–37.

55. Frías, *El amor de las sirenas*, 78. An indirect, probably inflammatory allusion to the treacherous and lecherous behavior of students while staying in Altamirano's house after the strike of 1875 in Mateos, *Los dioses se van*. See also Mateos, *Los dramas*, 44, 115. On a student's "precocidad generatriz" with prostitutes, Campos, *Claudio Oronoz*, 44.

56. Frías, *El amor de las sirenas*, 27, 374–75. For testimonies from prisoners about the association between sex and disease, see Piccato, "Interpretations of Sexuality"; Gamboa, *Impresiones* 95–97.

57. Mateos, *Los dramas*.

58. Díaz y de Ovando and García Barragán, *La Escuela Nacional Preparatoria*, 1:122, 134. See chapter 2 and clipping without reference, 5 October 1884, BCN, 8, n.d. The first Mexican woman to graduate from a professional school other than the Escuela Normal, for teachers, did so in 1897. Macías González, "El caso de una beldad." Women's exclusion in Cmiel, *Democratic Eloquence*, 29.

59. Campos, *Claudio Oronoz*, 95–96. Contrast with the cynicism of educated courtesans "que especulan con los sentimientos del alma." Díaz Covarrubias, *Obras completas*, 2:136, from *Impresiones y sentimientos* (1859).

60. *Colección de pedimentos*, 69. Letter to *El Tiempo* from several signatories, 23 November 1884, BCN, 8, 661.

61. María C. de Fulcheri and others to Porfirio Díaz, 29 July 1885, CPD, 10, 6973–79.

62. Flores Villar, *Los estudiantes*, 47.

63. MR, 23 November 1884, 1; LL, 22 November 1884, 2–3.

64. MR, 10 November 1884, 1; DH, 19 November 1884, 3. On deaths, MR, 20 November 1884, 1; *La Patria* cited by MR, 21 November 1884, 3; LL, 20 November 1884, 3. On arrests, MR, 20 November 1884, 3; LL, 23 November 1884, 3. Descriptions of street battles in Díaz y de Ovando and García Barragán, *La Escuela Nacional Preparatoria*, 1:124; Flores Villar, *Los estudiantes*, 31, 35–37.

65. The above description based on *El Monitor Republicano, Diario del Hogar, La Patria*. See also clippings in BCN, 8, 657; DH, 19 November 1884, 2; MR, 23 November 1884, 1.

66. DH, 21 November 1884, 3. On the zócalo, Mateos, *Los dramas*, 234.

67. Rodríguez Kuri, *La experiencia olvidada*, chap. 6 and pp. 186, 194, 211. For complaints about the service, including interruptions during a Sunday concert at the zócalo days before the riots, see LP, 12 November 1884, 2. For the impact of this moral economy and actors on another public service, water, see Rodríguez Kuri, "Gobierno local."

68. MR, 23 November 1884, 3. On darkness, MR, 21 November 1884, 2.

69. MR, 23 November 1884, 1; Flores Villar, *Los estudiantes*, 39.

70. LP, 19 November 1884, 2; MR, 21 November 1884, 3; McLean, *Vida y obra*, 39.

71. MR, 23 November 1884, 1. For the dying student, Díaz y de Ovando and García Barragán, *La Escuela Nacional Preparatoria*, 1:125.

72. LL, 22 November 1884, 2; LL, 21 November 1884, 3.

73. Cosío Villegas, *El porfiriato*, 9:792–93; Flores Villar, *Los estudiantes*, 32. After this Batalla had to hide from the police, BCN, 8, 671. Several sympathizers of Díaz were inside the house ready to protect him. Prida, *De la dictadura*, 78. Díaz nevertheless was known to walk from his residence on Humboldt to the National Palace during his first presidency. Gómez-Quiñones, *Porfirio Díaz*, 104.

74. Gonzalez Navarro, *Historia Moderna*, 4:623–25; Yañez, *Don Justo Sierra*, 96; Díaz y de Ovando and García Barragán, *La Escuela Nacional Preparatoria*, 136–37.

75. The statement caused shouts and "violentas manifestaciones de reprobación" among deputies, forcing Díaz Mirón to acknowledge González's heroism. 21 October 1885, DDCD, XII Leg., 2:342.

76. MR, 23 November 1884, 1. González had also attempted to disperse a crowd during the protests of December 1883 against nickel coins, but he had to be rescued by soldiers. Quevedo y Zubieta, *El General González*, 154–56. The episode in Rivas's house in BCN, 8, 681; LL, 27 November 1884, 3.

77. She filed for divorce. Gómez-Quiñones, *Porfirio Díaz*, 96; Flores Villar, *Los estudiantes*, 34–35; García Peña, "El divorcio de Laura Mantecón."

78. Hourcade, *La machicuepa*. See letters from workers at the Amatlán textile factory, the Congreso Nacional Obrero, and several signatories from Apizaco, Puebla, who compared Diódoro Batalla with the French revolutionary Camile Demoulins. Clippings in BCN, 8, docs. 703, 692, 738; but see Bulnes, undated manuscript, FB, 14, 10, 18.

79. "Puede que falten nihilistas, / Mas tenemos estudiantes, / Patriotas brillantes / Juntos con artesanos / encallecidas las manos, / Pero de su patria amantes." Hourcade, *La machicuepa*, 24–26.

80. A student wrote a comedy entitled "La deuda inglesa" that was performed at the famous Teatro Arbeu. Artists painted portraits of opposition deputies and others raised money to reward and support students. Díaz y de Ovando and García Barragán, *La Escuela Nacional Preparatoria*, 1:130–31. Other musical compositions include "La deuda inglesa: Danza para piano," by Juan N. Cordero. The score of this piece is dated 1883, suggesting that the theme was already a matter of conversation before the Noetzlin negotiation. Cordero's polka in BCN, 8, 691. The Carlos Basave archive contains folders with congratulatory letters from Chihuahua, Chihuahua; Aguascalientes, Aguascalientes; Huamantla, Orizaba, and Jalapa, Veracruz; León, Guanajuato; San Luis Potosí, San Luis Potosí; Apizaco and Zacatlán, Puebla; Mérida, Yucatan; Huichapan and Pachuca, Hidalgo; Morelia and Zamora, Michoacán; Toluca, Estado de México. In several of these localities, like Veracruz, Toluca, and Morelia, street demonstrations echoed those of the capital but did not provoke armed confrontations. BCN, 8. This contradicts the common view that the events of November 1884 did not have repercussions outside the capital. Prida, *De la dictadura*, 77.

81. Flores Villar, *Los estudiantes*, 46.

82. "Voces interiores," first published in *El Parnaso Mexicano*, 15 April 1886, in Díaz Mirón, *Poesía Completa*, 325–28.

83. LP, 26 November 1884, 2.

84. 15 November 1884, DDCD, XII Leg., 1:339. See also speech by Duret, 12 November 1884, DDCD, XII Leg., 1:244. In spite of the theoretical inroads of positivism, historical interpretation and debates continued to center on the assessment of personal character throughout the Porfiriato. See Bulnes, *El verdadero Juárez*; Prida, *De la dictadura*; Salado Álvarez, *Memorias*, 185–87.

85. BCN, 8, 690. For a manifesto in similar terms, probably produced by students, proposing exile for the traitors, see MR, 19 November 1884, 4; *Pelado*, literally bald, was used to refer to the urban rabble.

86. Letter signed 22 November 1884, BCN, 8, 672.

87. MR, 25 November 1884, 3; BCN, 8, s. ex, s. doc., folio 1811. Deputy Viñas was also received triumphantly by "autoridades y asociaciones" at the Toluca railroad station. LP, 28 November 1884, 2.

88. *Colección de pedimentos*, 46.

89. For Porfirio's tighter control of Congress, see Cosío Villegas, *La República Restaurada*; Cosío Villegas, *El porfiriato*; Bertola, "Las oportunidades del poder."

See also report from governor of Aguascalientes, Francisco G. Hornedo to Porfirio Díaz, 20 July 1885, CPD, 10, 7099. For policemen and rurales controlling the galleries of the chamber in 1885, see DDCD, XII Leg., 2:333–4. See also Marichal, "El manejo"; Castañeda Batres, "Estudio introductorio." For the approval of the agreement, López Portillo y Rojas, Elevación y caída, 211; Castañeda Batres, "Estudio introductorio," 47. On the repression of other demonstrations, DH, 21 November 1884, 7; LL, 25 November 1884, 3; Rohlfes, "Police and Penal Correction." Evidence of government concern about urban protest is the cancellation in 1885 of a water contract. Rodríguez Kuri, "Gobierno local," 173–77. On the U.S. press, Matías Romero to Porfirio Díaz, 12 July 1885, CPD, 10, 7388. Díaz Mirón engaged in other opposition initiatives in early 1885. Gómez-Quiñones, Porfirio Díaz, 212.

90. The closing of congressional debates on fiscal issues in the name of technocratic specialization would come back to haunt Limantour through Luis Cabrera's denunciation in 1909 of científicos' lack of fiscal transparency and nationalism. Cabrera, Obra política, 1:41–220. See Guerra, México, 1:112; Bertola, "Las oportunidades del poder." Bulnes saw control of Congress as a key to the Porfirian system, lest the Chamber of Deputies take over politics in accord with the dictates of the Constitution and the whims of the "populacho." Undated manuscript, FB, 14, 10, 4; Bulnes, El porvenir de las naciones, 147–48. The argument is central also in Rabasa, La constitución y la dictadura.

5. Honor and the State

1. EF 25:32 (13 August 1885), 127. A later account mentioned only two thousand copies and the press of Francisco Rodríguez. EF 25:65 (1 October 1885), 259 and ff. See also Colección de pedimentos, 57. The students' manifesto in BCN, 8, 838; DDCD, XII Leg., 2: 342; El Partido Liberal, 22 October 1885, 3; EF 25:30 (11 August 1885), 120–21.

2. EF 25:33 (14 August 1885), 132–33. He later added, "Nunca, tampoco, desde hace muchos años, se había usado entre nosotros el vocabulario político que dá el nombre de facciosos a los que invocan un derecho, cuando ese derecho significa libertad." Idem 25:110 (5 December 1885), 440–41. See also EF 25:35 (18 August 1885), 139–40; EF 25:30 (11 August 1885), 120–21; EF 25:63 (29 September 1885), 254; Colección de pedimentos.

3. EF 25:104 (27 November 1885), 416; idem, 25:106 (28 November 1885), 420–21; idem, 25:103 (26 November 1885), 412–13.

4. Colección de pedimentos, 102–03; EF 25:32 (13 August 1885), 128–29. For a critique of journalistic rhetoric in Labastida's initial accusation, see Colección de pedimentos, 70. Viñas accused Montiel y Duarte of betraying the same principles that in 1876 had inspired him to defend freedom of speech and Chávarri himself. EF 25:37 (20 August 1885), 149. See Buffington, Criminal and Citizen.

5. *Colección de pedimentos*, 5, 6, 20, 37, 121, 135; EF 25:38 (21 August 1885), 152–53.

6. EF 25:67 (3 October 1885), 297–98; EF 25:63 (29 September 1885), 253. Chávarri, Adolfo Carrillo, and Trinidad Martínez were sentenced to seven months in prison and a three-hundred-peso fine; Ricardo Ramírez, Enrique M. de los Ríos, Carlos Basave, León Malpica Soler, José R. del Castillo, three months and one hundred pesos; Joaquín Trejo, Lamberto Cabañas, and Arturo Albaradejo were released after being sentenced to penalties which they had already served because they were imprisoned during the trial. EF 25:67 (3 October 1885), 297–98. Later Martínez and Trejo were acquitted and the remaining sentences were reduced after appeal in a higher court and the Supreme Court. EF 25:69 (8 October 1885), 275–6; *Colección de pedimentos*, 135.

7. For a view of the new era as one of arbitrary repression of the press, see "La Libertad de Imprenta" from *Diario del Hogar*, in EF 34:41 (8 March 1890), 678; Saborit, *Doblados*, 181–82. On the liberal critique of the regime as a betrayal, see Guerra, *México*; Cosío Villegas, *El porfiriato*; Beezley, Martin, and French, *Rituals of Rule*. A recent reinterpretation in Barajas Durán, *El país de "el llorón,"* 20.

8. Mem. Rafael Reyes Spíndola, AL, 2, 14. Readership increased thanks to lower prices. Bazant, "Lecturas " 237–38. On the populist style of *El Imparcial*, Salado Alvarez, *Memorias*, 144–45.

9. Camarillo Carbajal, *El sindicato de periodistas*, 21–22; Saborit, *Doblados*, 149; Frías, *Miserias de México*, 34–35; Frías, *¿Águila o sol?*, 127. On Díaz Spíndola's treatment of journalists as employees to be bought, promoted, or discarded, Salado Alvarez, *Memorias*, 149. On the difficulties in the life of independent journalists in the late Porfiriato, Carlos Roumagnac, "Recuerdos de Belem," EN, 14 May 1933, 2. On the social changes among journalists, Juan de Dios Peza to Rafael Chousal, 9 September 1903, RCH, 26, 235, f. 133; Gamboa, *Mi diario IV*, 157; Frías, *Miserias de México*, 24–25. On the effects of lower prices on newspapers, see Francisco Montes de Oca to R. Chousal, Mexico, 7 November 1902, RCH, 24, 226, 22–24. Subsidies were concentrated in *El Imparcial* but also reached other publications, Heriberto Barrón to Rafael Chousal, Mexico, RCH, 29, 256, 9. For the constitutional reform as the main means of repression, Coerver, *The Porfirian Interregnum*, 99.

10. Francisco Montes de Oca to R. Chousal, 30 July 1909, RCH, 32, 312, 32. See also Heriberto Barrón to R. Chousal, 30 July 1903, RCH, 26, 233, f 13. For instructions from Porfirio Díaz to a local ally to terminate a newspaper (*El Proletario*, in San Luis Potosí) see E. Auret to Porfirio Díaz, 28 March 1885, CPD, 10, 3401. See also, on Jalisco, CPD, 11, 4240–42, 4244; EF 26:115 (26 June 1886), 457–58; Bulnes, *El verdadero Díaz*, 338–39. For examples of journalists bought by the regime, see Díaz to Reyes Spíndola, 26 November 1885, CPD, 10, 10710. For a choice between cooptation of a journalist, through a seat in Congress, and a more aggressive course "declarándole guerra fuerte y tenaz, y dándole su merecido castigo," see Gov. of Michoacan, Mariano Jiménez, to Díaz, Morelia, 8 February 1886, CPD, 11, 2075–76, 2083.

11. For the assassination of Luis González, committed in 1885 by a jefe político with the collaboration of a police chief in Morelia, see CPD, 10, 2987; *El Explorador*, 1:30, Morelia, 1 March 1885, pp. 1–4. Francisco Bulnes counted only five journalists murdered during the regime of Díaz, and none of them by order of the president. He does not count González, however. Bulnes, *El verdadero Díaz*, 63–64. See also Gómez-Quiñones, *Porfirio Díaz*, 113–15; López Portillo y Rojas, *Elevación y caída*, 215.

12. *EF* 6:26 (10 February 1876), 103. See also Rodríguez Castillo, "Delitos de injuria," 50. The punishment of *cantar la palinodia* was becoming rare; it was defined by the Real Academia as "Public retraction of something that has been said." Real Academia, *Diccionario de la lengua* 1869.

13. *EF* 7:16 (22 July 1876), 63.

14. Twinam, *Public Lives*, 33.

15. See Cañeque, *The King's Living Image*; Habermas, *Structural Transformation*. As the following chapter will show, the notion of fama pública was still often applied in judicial practice.

16. Vicente Riva Palacio cited in Ruiz Castaneda, "La universidad libre," 22. For the eclectic mix of romantic influences on students, see Garcia Naranjo, *La vieja Escuela de Jurisprudencia*, 71. Individualism as a legal construction that reinforced masculine freedom in García Peña, *El fracaso del amor*. Romanticism, as nationalism, can be linked to a sense of sacrifice that might seem opposed to individualism. Illades, *Nación, sociedad*; Berlin, *Las raíces*. See also Galí i Boadella, *Historias del bello sexo*, 16, 19. The impact of Byron, bohemia, and some aspects of Hugo seems stronger in late Mexican romanticism. Romanticism characterized as "amor, deber, caridad, sacrificios, abnegación" by Rubén M. Campos in Saborit, *Doblados*, 176. By "la hegemonía individual sobre la sociedad," Vallejo, *El romanticismo*, 24. See also Domínguez Michael, *Tiros en el concierto*, 147; Quirarte, "Zarco, Poe y Baudelaire," 242; Puga y Acal, *Los poetas mexicanos*, 32; Monterde, *Salvador Díaz Mirón*, 47–54; Galí i Boadella, *Historias del bello sexo*. For European individualism and romantic attitude, see Warner, *Publics and Counterpublics*, 60; Sennett, *The Fall of Public Man*. For Mexico, García Peña, *El fracaso del amor*.

17. Gamboa, *Mi diario II*, 103. Few Mexican diaries document like Gamboa's the tension between openly defending reputation and turning inward. His aims in the latter direction: "Nunca, lo que se llama nunca," he begins, "me preocupé del público para mis actos o para mis escritos." Gamboa, *Mi diario I*, 3. On the markers of French individualism, see Corbin, "Backstage."

18. Picard, *Le romantisme social*, 65.

19. Contrast with Gay, *Schnitzler's Century*, 258–68. On extended families and patronage, see Lomnitz and Pérez, *Una familia de la élite*. For the prevalence of orality, Ozuna Castañeda and Guzmán Gutiérrez, "Para que todos lean," 279. Individualism as a "radical novedad" associated with the Reforma movement in Guerra, *México*, 1:160.

20. Díaz Mirón, *Prosa*, 109; Almanza, *Sin título*, 8. A recommendation for poets to ignore applause in Puga y Acal, *Los poetas mexicanos*, 104–05, 16. On romantic individualism as an "originary value," Warner, *Publics and Counterpublics*, 60.

21. Decree by Fedinand VII, 12 November 1820, AHDFJ, 2739, 1, 19. On evidence, Rabasa, "La difamación y las personas morales," 28, 30. Honor as universal possession compared in Stewart, *Honor*, 14n, 145–46; Jiménez Huerta, *Derecho penal mexicano*, 51. For the formulation of honor as a natural good, esteemed even by "primitive" peoples, see Carrara, *Programma: Parte speciale*, 5–6.

22. Rivera, *Tratado breve*, 17; Rodríguez Castillo, "Delitos de injuria," 38. Partisanship was more open in graphic form. Even Díaz, upon coming to power, used caricature to counter his Lerdista enemies. Barajas Durán, *El país de "el llorón,"* 125, 311. On intentions as constitutive of crimes, see Ramírez, *México en pos*, 180; Avalos and Calero y Sierra, "Alegato presentado"; Rodríguez Castillo, "Delitos de injuria," 35.

23. Rousseau, *Basic Political Writings*. On domesticity as a foundation of the bourgeois public sphere, Landes, *Women and the Public Sphere*; Maza, *Private Lives*; Habermas, *Structural Transformation*; Habermas, "Further Reflections"; Sennett, *The Fall of Public Man*; Warner, *Letters of the Republic*. On continuities in publicity, Rivera, *Tratado breve*, 16.

24. Guerra, *Modernidad e independencias*, 271; Chambers, *From Subjects to Citizens*; McEvoy, "Seríamos excelentes vasallos."

25. Martínez de Castro, "Exposición de motivos," 95.

26. Martínez de Castro, *Código penal 1871*, arts. 641–43. These definitions are based in the Spanish *Siete Partidas*. Rodríguez Castillo, "Delitos de injuria," 50, 55. Injurias can be translated as "insults," but the equivalence is less precise with difamación (broadly, defamation) and even less for calumnia (for which English "calumny" is a false cognate). Rather than cumbersome and sometimes inappropriate translations, like "false accusations" for calumnia, I have preferred to keep the terms in Spanish when I refer to the judicial context. I owe the insight to Michael Kean.

27. Compare with the *Partidas*, where injuria was "Hecho o dicho contra razón y justicia." Ramírez, *México en pos*, 170. See also Rodríguez Castillo, "Delitos de injuria," 55; Jiménez Huerta, *Derecho penal mexicano*, 51. In Germany only untruthful statements (i.e., when the victim did have honor) were punished. Stewart, *Honor*, 145–46. Penalties in Martínez de Castro, *Código penal 1871*, arts. 645, 646, 656. In 1902 the minimum penalty was increased to two months.

28. Avalos and Calero y Sierra, "Alegato presentado"; Rodríguez Castillo, "Delitos de injuria," 6. The other crimes that required civil action were theft within the family, battery causing minor wounds, betrayal of trust (*abuso de confianza*), statutory rape, abduction, and adultery. Barousse Martínez, "Análisis crítico." I owe this reference to Ira Beltrán. For publishing of sentences, Rivera, *Tratado breve*, 17.

29. Speckman, "Los jueces," 1434.

30. Díaz Infante, "Delitos cometidos," 40–41.

31. Spencer, *Principles of Ethics*, 2:103, 113–15. For his influence, see 14 November 1884, *DDCD, XII Leg.*, 1:309; López Portillo y Rojas, *Fuertes y débiles*, 18; Velázquez Albo, *Origen y desarrollo*, 15–16; García Naranjo, *La vieja Escuela de Jurisprudencia*, 73–74; Bulnes, *Los grandes problemas*, 108.

32. Díaz Infante, "Delitos cometidos," 40–42, 67.

33. Spencer, *Principles of Ethics*, 336–37. Spencer only tangentially examined honor as a moral obligation among "uncivilized races." One reference is found in his examination of the obligations imposed by Christian morals or those faced by duelists—who had no option, according to Spencer's perplexed observation, but to fight each other in defense of their honor. Spencer, *Principles of Ethics*, 326. See Kennedy, *Herbert Spencer*, 62, 65. Honor was not one of the ideas or sentiments listed as being ethical in his *Principles of Ethics*.

34. "The morals of trade" in Spencer, *Essays*, 137, 144, 145–47.

35. Florian, *La teoria psicologica*, viii, ix, 1. The book, published in 1893, was translated and published in Mexico in 1902. Florian, *Teoría psicológica*. References to the author appear in Mexican texts starting in the 1890s. See Rodríguez Castillo, "Delitos de injuria." On the centrality of criminology for social reform, see Buffington, *Criminal and Citizen*; Piccato, "La construcción."

36. Florian, *La teoria psicologica*, 9, 13, 151, 150, 155, 156, 160, 164.

37. Like Guillermo Prieto, Ferri argued that the jury was the best mechanism to interpret actions and determine offenders' motivations—something unnecessary if slanderers were clearly typified, as Florian offered. Florian, *La teoria psicologica*, xi; Martínez de Castro, "Exposición de motivos," 21. Criminal juries only considered serious crimes in the Federal District between 1869 and 1929.

38. *EF* 34:41 (8 March 1890), 678–79; *RLJ* (January–June 1890), 133–46. Penal codes that protect honor include those of Spain, Switzerland, Italy, Argentina, Peru, El Salvador, Cuba, Guatemala, Honduras. Jiménez Huerta, *Derecho penal mexicano*, 23. For a prosecutor and defense attorneys citing in court French legislation regarding libel, see *EF* 41:42 (30 August 1888), 166–67; *Informes producidos*. In Argentina, the state's concern about the penal protection of honor went so far as to deny individuals the right to defend it privately. Gayol, "Honor Moderno," 483. Mexican authorities were ambivalent about this and, as we will see in chapter 7, left a fair amount of leeway for duelists to privately protect their honor. María Luisa González y González, "Libertad de imprenta," *RLJ* (July–December 1902), 260–69. See also *EF* 25:69 (8 October 1885), 275–76; *Colección de pedimentos*. The regime against theft in Vanderwood, *Disorder and Progress*; Piccato, *City of Suspects*, chap. 3.

39. Díaz Infante, "Delitos cometidos," 67, 40; Hale, *Transformation*. See also Ramos, *Los delitos*, 11, 13; Rodríguez Castillo, "Delitos de injuria," 77. For honor defined as the "minimum respect" owed a person, see Jiménez Huerta, *Derecho penal mexicano*, 19.

40. Ramos, *Los delitos*, 16. Ramos referred to Grellet-Dumazeau, *Traité de la*

diffamation, from 1847, a text often cited by Mexican writers on the theme of honor. See Avalos and Calero y Sierra, "Alegato presentado"; *Defensa de primera instancia*. Honor as reputation in Jiménez Huerta, *Derecho penal mexicano*, 21–24; Rodríguez Castillo, "Delitos de injuria," 77.

41. Jiménez Huerta, *Derecho penal mexicano*, 23. For the theory, Rodríguez Castillo, "Delitos de injuria," 29. For the debate between "realistas," who considered honor as the reputation of actual individuals and thus unequally distributed, against "formalistas," who identified honor with reputation and were concerned with attacks against human dignity even if "la persona carezca de honor," Jiménez Huerta, *Derecho penal mexicano*, 19–20.

42. José María Mata added that "private life refers to intimate life, the sanctuary of the domestic home, and it is not possible to confuse it with the public acts of officials." Díaz Infante cited the passages above to illustrate the ambiguity inherited by positivists from 1857. Díaz Infante, "Delitos cometidos," 66.

43. Ramírez, *México en pos*, 179, 181.

44. *EF* 34:41 (8 March 1890), 678–79; *EF* 34:33 (26 February 1890), 550–51; *EF* 34:33 (26 February 1890), 550–51.

45. "La Libertad de Imprenta," by *Diario del Hogar* in *EF* 34:34 (27 February 1890), 651; *EF* 34:33 (26 February 1890), 550–51. See also "La libertad de imprenta," *EF* 34:39 (6 March 1890), 670–71.

46. *EF* 34:41 (8 March 1890), 678–79.

47. See Ireneo Paz, "La sentencia del Sr. Magistrado Horcasitas sobre libertad de la prensa," *EF* 34:43 (12 March 1890), 690–91; *EF* 34:45 (14 March 1890), 694–95; ibid., 34:46 (14 March 1890), 698–99; ibid., 34:47 (18 March 1890), 702.

48. *LL*, 14 October 1882, 2. Jacinto Pallares, "Delitos de Imprenta," in *El Publicista*, 3 (1875), 3–7.

49. The Press Law of 1868 was a federal law whereas penal codes were passed by states—although most emulated the Federal District's. G. Baturoni, "La Libertad de la Prensa," *EF* 4:72 (21 April 1875), 286–87; *EF* 4:73 (22 April 1875), 290; *EF* 4:74 (23 April 1875), 294; *EF* 4:76 (27 April 1875), 302, quotation from 286–87. See Degollado, *Defensa ante el público*, 4, 19.

50. Romero Vargas, *Libertad de imprenta*, 9, 12. Opposed to the reform, Romero Vargas nevertheless refused to be identified with the Jacobins as extreme liberals. Romero Vargas, *Libertad de imprenta*, 40, 49–50. G. Baturoni, "La Libertad de la Prensa," *EF* 4:73 (22 April 1875), 290.

51. G. Baturoni, "La Libertad de la Prensa," *EF* 4:72 (21 April 1875), 286–87. On journalists' fuero, see also Coerver, *The Porfirian Interregnum*, 97.

52. Juzgado de distrito de Jalisco, Guad., 28 June 1877, in *EF* 2:16 (24 July 1877), 61. Article 1110 would be used in 1885 to sentence those who protested against the deuda inglesa.

53. *EF* 17:111 (8 December 1881), n.

54. *LL*, 14 October 1882, 2. An initial project, presented by González, had been shelved in the Chamber of Deputies in 1881, Camarillo Carbajal, "Los periodistas en el siglo XIX," 157.

55. Romero Vargas, *Libertad de imprenta*, 6; Coerver, *The Porfirian Interregnum*, 96–100. See Carlos Rivas, Mexico City, to José G. Carbó, Hermosillo, 25 December 1882, CPD, 7, 1000. On Vallarta's support and continuing debates, see *EF* 25:8 (10 July 1885), 30; *EF* 34:33 (26 February 1890), 550–51. The Supreme Court confirmed that no new legislation was necessary in a decision in 1885. *EF* 25:8 (10 July 1885), 31–32. On support of the press for the reform, Barajas Durán, *El país de "el llorón,"* 302, 306.

56. J. Alberto Salinas y Rivera, "El jurado del general Alonso Flores," *EF* 3:24 (7 February 1878), 95; ibid., 3:25 (8 February 1878), 99; ibid., 3:26 (9 February 1878), 103.

57. Romero Vargas, *Libertad de imprenta*, 6.

58. TSJDF, 11,1897, 116068. See also Barajas Durán, *El país de "el llorón,"* 307.

59. *EF* 25:8 (10 July 1885), 31–32. A similar opinion regarding the framers of the constitution in Díaz Infante, "Delitos cometidos," 67.

60. *EF* 25:69 (8 October 1885), 275–76; *Defensa de primera instancia*. Sentence by district court in the Federal District, 1889, in *EF* 34:22 (8 February 1890), 601–04. See also Díaz Infante, "Delitos cometidos," 62. On the use of the 1868 code and the need to attempt conciliation, see appeal granted by Querétaro District Judge Mariano Torres Aranda, *EF* 23:26 (9 August 1884), 102. See also, for a case in Guadalajara, *EF* 22:49 (13 March 1884), 192–93; another in Nuevo Laredo, *EF* 23:89 (13 November 1884), 365–66. On the distinction between procedure and sentence, see Emilio Velasco's defense of "presos políticos" in 1885. *EF* 25:103 (26 November 1885), 412–13; ibid., 25:104 (27 November 1885), 415–16; Contra Jesús Cárdenas y complices por ultrajes y difamación a funcionario público, AHSTJM, 1894, 118, 47 fs.

61. On the use of the Penal Code outside the capital, Díaz Infante, "Delitos cometidos." On Michoacán, see Coromina, *Recopilación de leyes*. On the beer case, *EF* 21:21 (31 July 1883), 82. The decision was not consequential in terms of freedom of speech because few cases against writers were brought for damages against commercial reputations.

62. Ramos, *Los delitos*, 16.

63. See CP1871, articles 909 to 918. Ultraje meant "Ajamiento, injuria o desprecio de obra o de palabra." Real Academia, *Diccionario de la lengua* 1869. Ultraje also appeared in the Penal Code's articles about "ultrajes to public morality and good customs," (articles 785 to 788). For the need to protect authorities as a reason for the project of constitutional reform, LL, 14 October 1882, 2.

64. "Ataques," by contrast, meant physical violence. Díaz Infante, "Delitos cometidos," 45. This was probably an extrapolation from article 909 of the Penal Code, which punished "el que por escrito, de palabra o de cualquier otro modo injurie en lo privado al Presidente de la República, cuando se halle ejerciendo sus funciones, o con motivo de ellas." On presence as requirement, "Defensa ante la suprema corte por Lic. Emilio Velasco de los acusados de sedición contra decreto del 22 de junio 1885," *EF* 25:103 (26 November 1885), 412. On status, *EF* 33:92 (12 November 1889), 365–66.

65. *Defensa de primera instancia*, 85. Articles 659 and 916 established the same penalties in these cases as those applied in crimes against personal reputations. Article 659 stated that "injuria, la difamación y la calumnia contra el Congreso, contra un tribunal o contra cualquier otro cuerpo colegiado se castigarán como está prevenido para los delitos contra la reputación"; and article 916 specified for this crime the "mismas penas que el ultraje hecho a uno de sus miembros." *EF* 25:103 (26 November 1885), 412–13; *EF* 25:104 (27 November 1885), 415–16. A reform to article 912 from 26 May 1884 established a range of imprisonment for those who inflicted minor physical attacks against officials (two to four years, instead of four years for anyone who attacked the president). A reform of article 659, on injuria, difamación, and calumnia against Congress and other bodies established a minimum punishment of two months and gave the *ministerio público* authority to press charges. Martínez de Castro, *Código penal 1871*, 270, 276–77.

66. *EF* 25:103 (26 November 1885), 412–13; *EF* 25:104 (27 November 1885), 415–17; *EF* 25:106 (29 November 1885), 420–21, 417. See also *EF* 23:36 (26 August 1884), 142. See also Supreme Court resolution of 24 September 1875, in *EF* 5:119 (24 November 875), 474. Velasco also argued defense of the public interest. Article 648 of the Penal Code excused from difamación or injuria "al que manifestare su juicio sobre la capacidad, instrucción, aptitud o conducta de otro; si probare que obró en cumplimiento de un deber, o por interés público."

67. 12 November 1869, AHDFJ, 2741, 70. Manuel López Mesqui denounced his fellow City Council member Vicente García Torres because of an article in *El Siglo Diez y Nueve* on the illegal introduction of lamb meat in the municipal *rastro*. 22 March 1872, AHDFJ, 2742, 106.

68. Romero Vargas, *Libertad de imprenta*, 33–34. See also "Libertad de imprenta," by "profesora normalista Señorita" María Luisa González y González, *RLJ* (July–December 1902), 260–69; *EF* 25:8 (10 July 1885), 29. The accused had complained against an attempt to forcibly recruit them into the Mexican army. See also Díaz Infante, "Delitos cometidos," 67. In 1886, Jalisco's Supreme Court found that the use of article 909 of the Penal Code against the press was unconstitutional and struck down a sentence against a journalist. *EF* 26:115 (26 June 1886), 457–58; "Revisión de Superior Tribunal de Justicia, Guadalajara," 29 July 1886, ibid., 27:32 (13 August 1886), 127–28. For appellate courts and Jacinto Pallares deeming ultrajes unconstitutional, see "Sentencia Juzgado 10. de lo criminal por ultrajes a la autoridad, juez Lic. B. Echauri, contra Silverio Grarcía y Próspero Jiménez," *EF* 26:115 (26 June 1886), 457–58; "Revisión de Superior Tribunal de Justicia, Guadalajara," 29 July 1886, *EF* 27:32 (13 August 1886).

69. Díaz Mirón, *Prosa*, 37.

70. Francisco Nájera, an accountant at the City Council, denounced an article in *La Cuestión Social*. The author of the article, paradoxically, turned out to be a member of the council, Luis Rivera Melo, who quickly published an explanation which settled the issue. 19 March 1861, AHDFJ, 2740, 40. For a successful accusation by postal employees against a publication that revealed deliberate delays in the sale of stamps, 6 March 1879, AHDFJ, 2743, 136. See also AHDFJ, 2740, 51 (11

August 1865). Well into the first years of the Porfiriato, press juries dismissed accusations against public officials because they did not attack private life. Several police officers against *El Monitor Republicano*, 18 April 1880, AHDFJ, 2743, 146. See also case of 8 November 1881, AHDFJ, 151. For a case of an accusation of murder published against a jefe político in Cuautitlán, and decided on the same grounds, AHDFJ, 2743, 143 (12 January 1880).

71. AHDFJ, 2742, 109 (24 August 1872).

72. Filomeno Mata was a frequent object of the new legislation. "La Libertad de Imprenta," *Diario del Hogar*, reproduced in *EF* 34:36 (1 March 1890), 658; *EF* 34:43 (12 March 1980), 687. In a few cases, individuals were punished for uttering offensive opinions outside the earshot of the victim. Inocencio Arriola did just that when, upon making payment of municipal fees, he said that "se los habian de cojer al Gobernador y su secretario." Arriola was sentenced to seventy days in prison. *EF* 21:13 (19 July 1883), 51.

73. *EF* 34:20 (5 February 1889), 293–94. An appeal court struck down the reference to the trade. *EF* 34:20 (5 February 1890), 593–94. The sentence by Judge Andrés Horcasitas was criticized in Ireneo Paz, "La sentencia del Sr. Magistrado Horcasitas sobre libertad de la prensa," *EF* 34:43 (12 March 1890), 690–91; *EF* 34:45 (14 March 1890), 694–95; *EF* 34:46 (15 March 1890), 698–99; *EF* 34:47 (18 March 1890), 702. Horcasitas maintained that the Penal Code corrected the Press Law of 1868 in the leniency of its penalties. *EF* 25:69 (8 October 1885), 275–76. Daniel Cabrera, the editor of *El Hijo del Ahuizote*, for example, met with particularly adverse judges and harsh conditions in the Belem prison during the several trials against him. *EHA* 1:36 (25 April 1886), 2, 6. On dolo and education, see Vega, *Dos palabras*; *EF* 25:8 (10 July 1885), 29; Díaz Infante, "Delitos cometidos," 45; *Defensa de primera instancia*, 36; *EF* 24:103 (12 June 1885), 409; *EF* 33:92 (12 November 1889), 365–66; Contra Jesús Cárdenas y complices por ultrajes y difamación a funcionario público, AHSTJM, 1894, 118.

74. "Chico en cuerpo y en talento / Lástima que ya no exista, / Porque era, según mi cuento / Criminal, criminalista." *LP*, 11 November 1884, 3.

75. Díaz Infante, "Delitos cometidos," 40, 42. For a judge in Tlalpan punishment was necessary because people identify "al representante de la ley, con la ley misma y por esto el menosprecio de la autoridad envuelve como consecuencia forzosa el menosprecio de la ley." The main inspirations for the Penal Code were from Belgian, French, and British legislation. *EF* 33:91 (12 November 1889), 365–66.

76. *Colección de pedimentos*, 74; Díaz Infante, "Delitos cometidos," 45–48.

77. *EF* 25:32 (13 August 1885), 128–29; *EF* 25:36 (19 August 1885), 143–44.

78. *Colección de pedimentos*, 5, 26, 48–49.

79. *EF* 25:39 (22 August 1885), 157–58. See also Carlos Roumagnac, "Recuerdos de Belem," *EN*, 7 May 1933, 2. Lawyers trained in biology would use "doctrinas que tienen por base el método científico." *EF* 50:1 (4 January 1898), 1.

80. *EF* 25:32 (13 August 1885), 128–29.

81. *Colección de pedimentos*, 102–03. See also *LL*, 5 May 1880, 3; *LL*, 1 June

1880, 3. See also *EF* 25:32 (13 August 1885), 128–29; *EF* 25:37 (20 August 1885), 149.

82. Carlos Roumagnac, "Recuerdos de Belem," *EN*, 5 March 1933, 2; *EN*, 7 May 1933, 2. Roumagnac, who suffered from the application of the doctrine in the mid-1890s, attributed it to First District Judge Juan Pérez de León. See also *LVM*, 6 October 1897, 3.

83. *EHA* 4:156 (13 January 1889), 7.

84. *EHA* 4:298 (11 October 1891), 3.

85. Archivo Toribio Esquivel Obregón, Universidad Iberoamericana, box 21, folder 1. For accusation against Daniel Cabrera for difamación based on a caricature, see *EHA* 9:427 (1 July 1894), 7.

86. See Contra Jesús Cárdenas y complices por ultrajes y difamación a funcionario público, AHSTJM, 1894, 118. The best-known case, involving Heriberto Frías, in Saborit, *Doblados.*

87. See, e.g., Sentencia de Juez de Distrito de Tamaulipas, Adalberto Torres, amparando a León A. Obregón, *EF* 19:64 (3 October 1882), 257; "Contra Dionisio Ativia and José Gándara," *EF* 25:8 (10 July 1885), 2, 30. A particularly convoluted case involving drunken journalists, their moralist father, a reluctant madam, an aggressive policeman, a vengeful *prefecto político,* and a judge granting an amparo, in Diligencias [against Daniel Torres and Lauro Castro] practicadas con motivo de un suelto del periódico intitulado *Tranquilino* por contener conceptos calumniosos para la autoridad, AHSTJM, 1894, no. 75. The explanation in *EF* 23:36 (26 August 1884), 142.

88. *EF* 23:89 (13 November 1884), 365–66.

89. *EF* 42:106 (8 June 1889), 421. An article interpreted to contain "apología e instigación del homicidio," *EF* 22:19 (23 January 1884), 72; another, in *Diario del Hogar,* judged libelous because it described students' "desorden" at the Fine Arts School, in TSJDF, 4, several years, 247977, Difamación.

90. Ireneo Paz, "La sentencia del Sr. Magistrado Horcasitas sobre libertad de la prensa," *EF* 34:43 (12 March 1890), 690–91; *EF* 34:45 (14 March 1890), 694–95; *EF* 34:46 (15 March 1890), 698–99; *EF* 34:47 (18 March 1890), 702; *LVM*, 10 August 1897, 3; Carlos Roumagnac, "Recuerdos de Belem," *EN*, 16 April 1933, 2. On repressive judges and the regime, see Saborit, *Doblados,* 97–99. For a case in which the judge also arrested the defense attorney, who had requested that the judge recuse himself from the case, Contra Jesús Cárdenas y complices por ultrajes y difamación a funcionario público, AHSTJM, 1894, 118. For a defense attorney reading fragments of *Don Juan,* by Zorrilla, to expose the judge's bias, *LVM*, 28 October 1897, 2.

91. Carlos Roumagnac, "Recuerdos de Belem," *EN*, 15 November 1933, 2; Ochoa Campos, *Reseña histórica,* 125–26; Campos, *El Bar,* 86.

92. TSJDF, 11, 1897, 116068.

93. *Defensa de primera instancia,* 13.

94. For a similar shift in legal culture that put "private law beyond the sphere of politics," see Adelman, *Republic of Capital,* 249.

6. The Defense of Honor

1. This was very clear for those engaged in commercial activities. Jeremy Adelman has demonstrated the importance of "many small links of obligation" in the development of capitalism and the law in Argentina. Adelman, *Republic of Capital*, 142, see also 160.

2. AHSTJM, 1894, 21; Vega, *Dos palabras*, 4; *Informes producidos*, 22.

3. Ramos, *Los delitos*, 13. For Latin America, see Gayol, "Honor Moderno," 483; Uribe Uran, *Honorable Lives*; Johnson and Lipsett-Rivera, *Faces of Honor*; Caulfield, Chambers, and Putnam, *Honor, Status, and Law*; Twinam, "The Negotiation of Honor"; Lauderdale-Graham, "Making the Private Public."

4. EF 22:49 (13 March 1884), 192–93. María Guillén accused Cayetano Tovar of, among other things, writing a newspaper article in which he accused her of mistreating her son. TSJDF, 4, several years, 116072, Injurias y golpes. A similar accusation prompted by a play in AHDFJ, 2743, 2. An accusation between brothers for a newspaper note in Juliana Garcidueñas y Petra G. de Arista por difamación, AHSTJM, 1898, 33.

5. Stern, *The Secret History*; Twinam, *Public Lives*; Johnson and Lipsett-Rivera, *Faces of Honor*; Seed, *To Love, Honor*; Premo, *Children*.

6. See particularly Herzog, *Upholding Justice*, 3, 8, 97; Stern, *The Secret History*, 9.

7. Illades, *Hacia la república*, 53.

8. TSJDF, 1897, 16/2294, 2514, Difamación; Herzog, *Upholding Justice*, 8, 3, 97.

9. In 1900, for example, of 902 cases of injuria, difamación, and calumnia in the Federal District, 564 were brought before judges by police authorities and 338 by "diverse authorities," probably the Ministerio Público or the victims themselves. All but two of the 902 cases were decided in correctional courts, rather than criminal courts, which usually dealt with more serious offenses. *Cuadros estadísticos e informe 1900*. The 902 cases refer to accusations only; thus the contrast with the number of 177 persons indicted in 1897, i.e., formally charged by a judge, in Mexico City, above. For other authorities, see TSJDF, 3, 1890, 144643, Injurias; TSJDF, 5, 1895, 5/1954, 1136792, Injurias.

10. Peñafiel, *Anuario estadístico 1898*; Estadística, *Estadística del ramo 1871 a 1885*.

11. TSJDF, 3, 1890, 144643, Injurias, 30. Corr. For examples of delays, in this case three months, see TSJDF, 1881, 1428; four years in TSJDF, 4; several years, 247987, Calumnia. Cases sent to archives after several years without movement: TSJDF, 4, several years, 247977, Difamación; TSJDF, 4, several years, 247975, Calumnia; TSJDF, 4, several years, 247975, Injurias y difamacion; TSJDF, 1, several years, 1311363, Injurias; TSJDF, 1, several years, 1311339, Difamación.

12. TSJDF, n.b., 1879, 214, Difamación. Suspects also resented the cost of the trials: Cruz Balcazar was acquitted but was disappointed by the judge's decision not to force the accusers to pay the court costs. Causa contra Cruz Balcazar por

libelos infamatorios, ascj, 63, 7, 38 (278 bis). See also EF 21:21 (31 July 1883), 82; TSJDF, 5, 1895, 5/1954, 1136759, Injurias; TSJDF, 3, 1890, 144643, Injurias.

13. TSJDF, 3, 1890, 144643, Injurias. Other cases of letters denounced in TSJDF, 1, several years, 938776, Injurias; TSJDF, 1, several years, 938776, Injurias. Rivero's case in TSJDF, 4, several years, 116068, Difamación. See also EF 31:42 (30 August 1888), 166–67; TSJDF, 4, 1896, 4, Difamación.

14. TSJDF, 3, 1890, 144643, Injurias. See also TSJDF, 1896, 4/2227, 2109420, Injurias y difamación. On the Chihuahua case, EF 27:42 (27 August 1886), 164. See also Rodríguez Castillo, "Delitos de injuria," 74–75.

15. TSJDF, 3, 1890, 144658, Lesiones e injurias. Other examples in EF 25:103 (26 November 1885), 412–13; EF 25:104 (27 November 1885), 415–41.

16. TSJDF, 1896, 4/2227, 1184295, Injurias.

17. EF 31:118 (21 December 1888), 469. González's case in TSJDF, 1, several years, 889903, Insultos. See also TSJDF, 5, 1895, 5/1954, 1136759, Injurias; TSJDF, 5, 1895, 5/1954, 1136792, Injurias; TSJDF, 3, 1890, 144658, Lesiones e injurias.

18. TSJDF, 3, 1887, 73734, Injurias; TSJDF, 4, several years, 116068, Difamación. Judges also changed the title of the accusation after the indictment. TSJDF, 1, several years, 889973, Injurias.

19. TSJDF, 3, 1887, 83836, Injurias; TSJDF, 1879, 214, Difamación. A cause suspended because there had been no accusation of injurias in EF 22:99 (31 May 1884), 392. The only exception I found was a journalist accused of injuria and difamación sentenced by the judge for ultrajes contra funcionario público. EF 31:82 (26 October 1888), 325–26.

20. Article 651 of the Penal Code stated that the victim "podrá quejarse de injuria, de difamación, o de calumnia, como más le conviniere." See EF 22:50 (11 March 1884), 196–97; CP 1871.

21. TSJDF, 11, 1897, 116068.

22. EF 24:41 (7 March 1885), 162.

23. EF 7:19 (27 June 1876), 74.

24. PC 1871 art. 642, 643.

25. Informes producidos, 10.

26. Carlos Eisenmann, "Incompetencia de los tribunales mexicanos, para conocer de los delitos cometidos en el extranjero por extranjeros," RLJ (January–June 1890), 326–64, 337–38. Communication "es la esencia de la calumnia." Eisenmann, Alegatos presentados, 4. On French jurisdiction, EF 31:42 (30 August 1888), 166–67. On publications in Paris cited as evidence, EF 22:80 (2 May 1884), 315–17, and EF 22:80 (3 May 1884), 315–14.

27. A judge in Veracruz supported the suspect's claim, to no avail. EF 27:65 (1 October 1886), 257–58; "Sentencia Suprema Corte, 14 May 1887," in EF 29:41 (30 August 1887), 163. A similar decision in a case in 1908, this one concerning a letter that was not published but read in Tlalpan, where the judge decided the case should be tried, instead of San Luis Potosí, where the letter was written, TSJDF, 1, several years, 938776, Injurias.

28. *EF* 27:65 (1 October 1886), 257–58; *EF* 29:41 (30 August 1887), 163. Eisenmann refers to the Supreme Court sentence in this case. Eisenmann, *Alegatos presentados*, 7, 9, 37. Enforcement was not consistent, however: in the case of a note published in *Le Petit Gauloir*, in France, authorities agreed that there could be no crime if readers in Mexico were ignorant of the identity of the alleged victim, even if he felt the note alluded to him. *EF* 31:42 (30 August 1888), 166–67.

29. The Mexican legislation was unique in this respect, claimed *EF* 25:103 (26 November 1885), 412. León's case in TSJDF, 1881, 1428, Injurias; see also *EF* 22:99 (31 May 1884), 392. On dolo and knowledge of victim, *EF* 31:27 (8 August 1888), 105. See also *EF* 22:94 (24 May 1884), 372.

30. *Informes producidos*, 28.

31. TSJDF, 4, several years, 247984, Lesiones y difamacion. See also a dispute among women in Belen prison in TSJDF, 1, several years, 889903, Insultos. For one among policemen, TSJDF, 1881, 1428.

32. *EF* 3:32 (24 August 1877), 127. See also J. Alberto Salinas y Rivera, "El jurado del general Alonso Flores," *EF* 3:24 (7 February 1878), 95; *EF* 3:25 (8 February 1878), 99; *EF* 3:26 (9 February 1878), 103. Lawyers also had to respond to accusations that could "empañar la dignidad y decoro de la clase de abogados." AHDFJ, 2740, 59. For military men defending collective honor, see TSJDF, 1897, 16/2294, 229, Injurias.

33. TSJDF, 1897, 16/2994, 974177, Injurias. Other disputes among coworkers in TSJDF, 4, several years, 247994, Calumnia; TSJDF, 1897, 16/2994, 974177, Injurias; TSJDF, 1881, 1428, Injurias.

34. TSJDF, 1, several years, 1311339, Difamación. San Martin explained that he sent the note because his wife and his mother, perhaps trying to prevent violence, would not allow him to leave the house in order to go solve the problem. TSJDF, 1896, 4/2227, 2109420, Injurias y difamación. See also TSJDF, 1896, 4/2227, 2109420, Injurias y difamación; TSJDF, 177, 1911, 175163, Injurias y difamación; TSJDF, 1, 1874, 1068714, Injurias; TSJDF, 1879, 214, Difamación; TSJDF, 3, 1887, 73734, Injurias; TSJDF, 3, 1887, 83836, Injurias; TSJDF, 3, 1890, 144608, Injurias; TSJDF, 3, 1890, 144643, Injurias.

35. See data for the twentieth century in Pablo Piccato, "Estadísticas del crimen en México: Series históricas, 1901–2001," http://www.columbia.edu/~pp143/estadisticascrimen/EstadisticasSigloXX.htm, compiled with the support of the Center for U.S.-Mexican Studies, University of California, San Diego. Comparisons with other societies are difficult because available studies have not focused on crimes against reputation. See Zehr, *Crime*; Johnson, *Urbanization*.

36. AHDFJ, 2740, 49.

37. Alfredo Chavero denuncia un artículo que bajo el rubro de "Una equivocación del Gobernador" publicó *El Monitor Republicano* en su no. 148 correspondiente al 22 del presente junio, AHDFJ, 2741, 94, 16 fs.

38. TSJDF, 1897, 16/2294, 229, Injurias.

39. TSJDF, 5, 1895, 5/1954, 1136759, Injurias.

40. Díaz, *Memorias*, 2:222. Noriega (1806–72) also fought in the war against the United States.

41. J. Alberto Salinas y Rivera, "El jurado del general Alonso Flores," *EF* 3:24 (7 February 1878), 95; *EF* 3:25 (8 February 1878), 99; *EF* 3:26 (9 February 1878), 103.

42. Blood flowing to the heart as a result of moral afflictions could cause death. Díaz Covarrubias, *Obras completas*, 2:120, 356, from *Impresiones y sentimientos* (1859) and *La clase media* (1859). See Harris, *Restraining Rage*.

43. TSJDF, 1, 1874, 1068714, Injurias. *Muina* translated, in a dictionary of the criminal jargon, as "cólera" (rage). Roumagnac, *Los criminales en México*, 126. For a case in which muina, prompted by disagreement with the husband, caused an abortion, see TSJDF-Reclusorio Sur, (1923) 19326. Nursing women in TSJDF, 3, 1890, 144608, Injurias.

44. AHDFJ, 2740, 51. On self-esteem, TSJDF, 5, 1895, 5/1954, 1136759, Injurias; TSJDF, 5, 1895, 1136792, Injurias. For a similar use of "amor propio" exposed to public scorn, see Mateos, *Los dramas*, 301.

45. Soledad Cerón followed Jesús Venegas de Goya down the street for several blocks in Mexico City calling her "puta, cabrona, agachona." TSJDF, 1879, 214, Difamación. In the classroom, see TSJDF, 1897, 16/2294, 229, Injurias. See also ¿Quién habló mal de José Rodríguez Sámano?, AHSTJM, 1894, 11. In the press, cited above, *EF* 22:49 (13 March 1884), 192–93.

46. The violin in TSJDF, 1879, 214, Difamación; TSJDF, 1879, 214, Difamación. For a gesture made to pull a weapon, which in this case was not used and may not have existed, TSJDF, 1896, 4/2227, 1184295, Injurias. The visage in TSJDF, 1897, 16/2994, 974177, Injurias. Letters in TSJDF, 1, several years, 938776, Injurias. The accusation came from Melesio Macías against Jesús R. Esparza, his nephew, who claimed Macías lacked "vergüenza" in accusing him of misusing family moneys.

47. According to Juan N. Mirafuentes, there are "injurias no previstas por la ley penal, que á veces no pueden definirse bien, y que sin embargo, afectan dolorosamente la reputación y el honor. La legislación no ha intentado todavía encontrar los medios de satisfacer esas ofensas rápidas como el rayo, que brotan del fuego de una mirada." Juan N. Mirafuentes, "El duelo," *MR*, 12 January 1869, 1.

48. TSJDF, 1897, 16/2294, 229, Injurias. See also TSJDF, 1897, 16/2294, 2514, Difamación.

49. The original has a certain musicality: "Aquí está esta cabrona tortillera, hija de un chingado, puta desgraciada cara de panza volteada." TSJDF, 4, several years, 247975, Injurias y difamación. Or "puta, cabrona, agachona," cited above. TSJDF, 1879, 214, Difamación. *Tortillera* might have meant "lesbian."

50. Izábal and Izábal, *Algunas observaciones*, 1, 2. Francisco Rodríguez Torales wrote to the Chamber of Deputies asking that Deputy Alonso Mariscal y Piña be stripped of his immunity so he could face the consequences of "los excesos de lenguaje que acostumbra." *Acusacion presentada*, 7.

51. Díaz Infante, "Delitos cometidos." In the same pragmatic spirit but using a different method other jurists suggested that difamación could be defined as

anything containing a reference to a "determined act" rather than general accusations. *EF* 32:56 (23 March 1889), 223; *EF* 32:57 (27 March 1889), 225. The attorney Francisco Llamas Noriega argued that by calling the victims "cobardes, malos liberales y malos caballeros" those protesting against the deuda inglesa were not imputing "un hecho." *Informes producidos*, 28.

52. Mateos, *Los dramas*, 46.

53. If anything, authors like Joaquín Clausell accused Zola of writing about military honor without having direct experience of battle. Saborit, *Doblados*, 83. Mexican jurists followed the trials against *Naná* and other novels accused of obscenity in Europe. *RLJ* (January–June 1890), 133–46.

54. Juan N. Mirafuentes, "El duelo," *MR*, 12 January 1869, 1.

55. *TSJDF*, 1, several years, 889973, Injurias.

56. *Informes producidos*, 15. Irony was part of the resources of celebrated romantic orators, but also a condescending way of addressing ignorant audiences. Moliérac, *Iniciación*, 164–67; Swearingen, *Rhetoric and Irony*, 5–7, 127.

57. The judge could not find fault in the expression, yet also approved of the explanation presented by Trejo. *EF* 23:36 (26 August 1884), 142.

58. Potts, *Testimonio de las diligencias*. On the publication of press and defamation trials in France, see José María Gamboa, "Estudios sobre la legislación de imprenta y derechos de los escritores," *EF* 23:105 (5 December 1884), 428–29; *EF* 23:105 (5 December 1884), 428–29. Deputy Francisco Vasquez could not be tried for abuse of trust because of his parliamentary immunity, but, thought Luis Pliego Perez, his victim, "el referido Sr. Vasques quedará bien castigado con solo el hecho de perder la estimacion de las personas honradas." Luis Pliego Perez to R. Chousal, Mexico City, 18 April 1899, *RCH*, 18, 196, f 65.

59. *TSJDF*, 4, several years, 116072, Injurias y golpes. For a policeman offering to give another, who accused him of calumnia, "una satisfacción particular pública o por los periódicos como mejor la exija" see *ATSJDF*, 1881, 1428.

60. Article 394 of the Code of Penal Procedures of 1880 stated that "the law recognizes as means of proof," among others, "fama pública." Article 407, however, established that fama pública produced only "simple presumption." Distrito Federal, *CPP* 1880. The same wording in Distrito Federal, *CPP* 1894. The code of procedures of 1881 did not contain a reference to fama pública as evidence. For a discussion on the legislation in the State of Mexico, see *EF* 18:99 (30 May 1882), 393–94.

61. *TSJDF*, 1897, 16/2294, 2514, Difamación; *ASCJ*, 6, 6, 157, 1849, Colima. On arrests based on fama pública, see Decree 55, 1 June 1868: fama pública "de plagiario o ladrón está considerada como delito punible con prisión de seis a diez años." But article 384 of the Code of Penal Procedures stated, "En materia criminal, la ley reconoce como medios de prueba. . . . La fama pública." *EF* 18:99 (30 May 1882), 393–94. See also *EF*, 2a. segunda época, 29, 1891.

62. The state's highest court eliminated this part of the sentence. *EF* 7:20 (28 July 1876), 79. For the publication of a sentence, Potts, *Testimonio de las diligencias*, 1. The practice in France in José María Gamboa, "Estudios sobre la legisla-

ción de imprenta y derechos de los escritores," EF 23:105 (5 December 1884), 428–29. "Opinión pública" cited by a judge against a suspect in EF 22:80 (2 May 1884), 315–17.

63. EF 22:80 (2 May 1884), 315–17.

64. Causa contra Cruz Balcazar por libelos infamatorios. ASCJ, 63, 7, 38 (278 bis).

65. ADSG, roll 7.

66. For "genio," see Causa contra Cruz Balcazar por libelos infamatorios. ASCJ, 63, 7, 38 (278 bis); on a suspect "de muy mala conducta, deshonesta y tiene la costumbre de injuriar a las personas," see Tomasa Núñez por Injurias, AHSTJM, 1a. instancia, penal, Morelia, 1898, 50, 6 fs.

67. EF 22:80 (2 May 1884), 315–317, citing Esriche. The same definition of the traits of fama pública cited from the 1852 *Diccionario de Jurisprudencia* in Causa contra Cruz Balcazar por libelos infamatorios. ASCJ, 63, 7, 38 (278 bis).

68. ASCJ, 55, 3, 109, Orizaba; Tomasa Núñez por Injurias, AHSTJM, 1a. instancia, penal, Morelia, 1898, 50, 6 fs; TSJDF, 1, several years, 889964, Difamación.

69. Antonio Quirós to R. Chousal, Mexico City, 17 June 1897, RCH, 15, 174. See also Vega, *Dos palabras*, 12. The same argument in Degollado, *Defensa ante el público*, 3.

70. TSJDF, 1897, 16/2294, 229, Injurias.

71. Carrara, *Programma: Parte speciale*, 9, 15.

72. AHDFJ, 57. Another dispute involving French subjects in EF 31:42 (30 August 1888), 166–67. For a baker, AHDFJ, 2740, 55; for a pulquero, TSJDF, 1, several years, 889964, Difamación. For a doctor accused of defamation for trying to collect his honorarium, Avalos and Calero y Sierra, "Alegato presentado." On personal and political languages, Piccato, "El populacho."

73. TSJDF, 1896, 4/2227, 1076465, Calumnias. The trial for fraud that Andrés Barrón promoted against Lucas A. de Lara dragged through several courts from 1878 to 1886, causing Barrón serious material damages until he decided to counter with an accusation of defamation against de Lara. TSJDF, 4, several years, 247987, Calumnia. Parker H. Sercombe, a banker operating in Mexico, used lawsuits and rumors to further his interests until an accusation of calumnia, accompanied by an arrest warrant, forced him to go back to the United States. Schell, *Integral Outsiders*, 95. See also AHDFJ, 2740, 55; Eugenio de Saint Laurent against Enrique Heuriot for article in *Le Petit Gauloir*, in EF 31:42 (30 August 1888), 166–67; Enrique Biron to City Council, denouncing "Protesta," published in *Diario Oficial*, 26 July 1868, in AHDFJ, 57; Juliana Garcidueñas y Petra G. de Arista por difamación, AHSTJM, 1898, 33; AHDFJ, 2740, 55. Gregorio Velasco was attacking Claudio Miranda's reputation as an "hombre honrado y trabajador" and trying to get him fined by the city because, claimed Miranda, Velasco had a pulquería in the same neighborhood and envied Miranda for the one he owned. TSJDF, 1, several years, 889964, Difamación. Simón León told José M. Malavear that he had been in financial trouble, hoping the information would reach the ears of a relative of Malavear's, and he would cut him some slack on the ten pesos León owed him. TSJDF, 1881, 1428.

74. TSJDF, 5, 1895, 5/1954, 1136788, Difamación.

75. TSJDF, 4, several years, 116068, Difamación. On letters, Carlos Eusenmann, "Incompetencia de los tribunales mexicanos, para conocer de los delitos cometidos en el extranjero por extranjeros," RLJ (January–June 1890), 326–64; Avalos and Calero y Sierra, "Alegato presentado."

76. Avalos and Calero y Sierra, "Alegato presentado"; Juliana Garcidueñas y Petra G. de Arista por difamación, AHSTJM, 1898, 33, 5 fs. See also TSJDF, 4, several years, 247987, Calumnia. For a case between foreign investors, see Eusenmann, "Incompetencia." For a four-hundred-peso case, TSJDF, 1896, 4/2227, 1076465, Calumnias. A small transaction eliciting a dispute between relatives in 1881, TSJDF, 1881, 1428.

77. AHDFJ, 57. See also Carlos Eusenmann, "Incompetencia de los tribunales mexicanos, para conocer de los delitos cometidos en el extranjero por extranjeros," RLJ (January–June 1890), 326–64. See a revealing treatment in Gayol, *Sociabilidad en Buenos Aires*, chap. 3.

78. EF 31:42 (30 August 1888), 166–67. Against an accusation of "quebrado fraudulento," EF 6:26 (10 February 1876), 103.

79. AHDFJ, 2743, 138. Judge José M. Gamboa found that *La Voz de España* was not liable for defamation for writing that a beer tasted bad. EF 21:21 (31 July 1883), 82. Gamboa noted that article 648 of the Penal Code punished difamación against commercial or industrial houses but considered that this contradicted the Constitution's protection of any speech that did not attack private life, morality, and public peace.

80. Rabasa, "La difamación y las personas morales," 31–32. On economic thinking, Weiner, *Race, Nation*, 29, 44.

81. For the social and individual aspects of social capital, see Putnam, *Bowling Alone*, 20. For the reluctance to measure credit and analysis of social capital within families and exchanged as gifts, see Bourdieu, *Practical Reason*, 107, 109; Bourdieu, *Outline*, 179, 181. See also Mauss, *The Gift*.

82. TSJDF, 4, several years, 116068, Difamación. For two French merchants EF 31:42 (30 August 1888), 166–67. For relations, Manuel Córdova accused his neighbor Antonia Moya of calling him "alcahuete de mis hijas," thus implying they were prostitutes. TSJDF, 1897, 16/2294, 2514, Difamación. Benigno Morales accused his estranged wife, María Gordoa, of calling him an "adúltero." EF 32:56 (23 March 1889), 223; EF 32:57 (27 March 1889), 225.

83. Avalos and Calero y Sierra, "Alegato presentado." For two sisters-in-law of apparently little education, see TSJDF, 5, 1895, 5/1954, 1136759, Injurias. A husband summoning witnesses against the wife he was trying to divorce in EF 32:56 (23 March 1889), 223; EF 32:57 (27 March 1889), 225.

84. Several neighbors witnessed the dispute and signed a letter asking the landlord to evict Moya. TSJDF, 1897, 16/2294, 2514, Difamación. On prisons, see the complaint of Enrique Paniagua against Lázaro Reyes for statements detrimental to his masculinity. TSJDF, 4, several years, 247984, Lesiones y difamacion. For another dispute started during visiting hours at the prison, see TSJDF, 1,

several years, 889903, Insultos. For homosexuality and social life in Mexico City prisons, see Piccato, "'Such a Strong Need.'"

85. TSJDF, 3, 1890, 144658, Lesiones e injurias. María Velázquez was accused of defamation by Hermenegilda Peña because "se expresó mal, pero fue encontra de unos perros de la quejosa que le comieron un pedazo de carne que tenía secándose." TSJDF, 1, several years, 889944, Difamación. For a dispute between residents of a former religious building, the antiguo obispado in Morelia, see Injurias, calumnia de María Antonia Avila, AHSTJM, 1886, 6, n. 23.

86. TSJDF, 1, 1874, 1068714, Injurias; TSJDF, 3, 1890, 144608, Injurias; TSJDF, 1897, 16/2294, 2514, Difamación. For a woman accused of mistreating her son, TSJDF, 4, several years, 116072, Injurias y golpes. For a dispute triggered by a fight between children, TSJDF, 177, 1911, 175163, Injurias y difamación. Construction workers mentioned in TSJDF, 3, 1887, 73734, Injurias.

87. TSJDF, 1, several years, 1311339, Difamación.

88. The kinship between the Suarezes and Jiménez is not clear in the statements. TSJDF, 1, several years, 889916, Difamacion. Filandro San Martin was also prevented by his wife and mother from leaving his house to respond to Francisco Espinosa's insults, so he summoned the police. TSJDF, 1896, 4/2227, 2109420, Injurias y difamación. Honor was nevertheless present in testimonies to explain violence. Piccato, *City of Suspects*, chap. 3.

89. TSJDF, 1881, 1428. See also TSJDF, 1, several years, 938776, injurias, 1a instancia Tlalpan. The Morelia case only reached court and was dismissed after it was published in the local newspaper *La Antorcha*. "¿Quién habló mal de José Rodríguez Sámano?" AHSTJM, 1894, 11, 14 fs. The best analysis in a similar case is Gayol, *Sociabilidad en Buenos Aires*. Chance encounters leading to conflict in TSJDF, 5, 1895, 5/1954, 1136759, Injurias; TSJDF, 5, 1895, 5/1954, 1136792, Injurias. On the Paris incident, Altamirano to Joaquín D. Casasús, Paris, 5 June 1891, in Altamirano, *Epistolario*, 129–32.

90. AHDFJ, 2740, 59. Examples of women's agency in TSJDF, 3, 1887, 83836, Injurias; TSJDF, 3, 1890, 144658, Lesiones e injurias. A suspect "aporreada y desgreñada" by the victim in TSJDF, 5, 1895, 5/1954, 1136759, Injurias; see also EF 20:14 (20 January 1883), 54–55; TSJDF, 3, 1887, 73734, Injurias.

91. Ma. Antonia Viveros por Injurias, AHSTJM, 1890, 3. 25, 40 fs. Judge Manuel M. Olaguíbel sentenced Gumersinda Tavera to one year in prison and a two-hundred-peso fine for defamation against Gerónimo Espinosa and María Santos Anzures. Tavera's "haber sido anteriormente . . . de malas costumbres" was a factor in the sentence. EF 20:14 (20 January 1883), 54–55. García Peña, *El fracaso del amor*, 23, 51–52. Women seem to have been less inclined to present themselves as weak victims in cases about honor than in the disputes examined by García Peña. For Latin American women's willingness to defend their honor in court, see Caulfield, Chambers, and Putnam, *Honor, Status, and Law*; Premo, *Children*.

92. TSJDF, 5, 1895, 5/1954, 1136759, Injurias. *Soldaderas* established relationships with soldiers.

93. TSJDF, 5, 1895, 5/1954, 1136759, Injurias. Another accusation against a woman in AHTSJM, Primera Instancia, Morelia, 1886, 6, n.n. and 23. Resisting arrest in TSJDF, 4, several years, 116068, Difamación. See also TSJDF, 4, several years, 247975, Injurias y difamación.

94. Critiques of Mediterranean dichotomies in Wikan, "Shame and Honour"; Fonseca, "Philanderers, Cuckolds."

95. TSJDF, 1879, 214, Difamación. For a victim whose statement was taken at her house, "en atención al sexo y honestidad" in TSJDF, 1897, 16/2294, 2514, Difamación. Wife declaring with husband's authorization in TSJDF, 1879, 214, Difamación; TSJDF, 5, several years, 1136759, Injurias. Husband pressing charges in lieu of wife in TSJDF, 3, 1890, 144608, Injurias. See also TSJDF, 1, several years, 889916, Difamación; Ma. Antonia Viveros por Injurias, AHSTJM, 1890, 3. 25, 40. Women against men in TSJDF, 1, 1874, 1068714, Injurias. Between brothers in Juliana Garcidueñas y Petra G. de Arista por difamación, AHSTJM, 1898, 33. TSJDF, 1, several years, 1311363, Injurias; TSJDF, 1897, 16/2294, 2514, Difamación. Between sisters-in-law in TSJDF, 5, 1895, 5/1954, 1136759, Injurias. Women preventing men from solving a dispute by having a fistfight in TSJDF, 1896, 4/2227, 2109420, Injurias y difamación.

96. F. ex., TSJDF, 3, 1890, 144621, Injurias.

97. Mateos, Los dioses se van, 19. For two husbands defending their wives attacked by a local paper, see Informes producidos.

98. See Informes producidos, 3. A woman bringing charges against a play ("La mujer verdugo y la niña mártir") inspired by a criminal case in which she had been involved in AJA, JJI, 2743, 2. For a case that led to the woman's suicide and to the man's reputation being ruined, see Schell, Integral Outsiders, 21. For a case of defamation involving a French woman and two men in Sonora, see EF 28:56 (25 March 1887), 221–22.

99. Guillen's son testified that was not true. TSJDF, 4, several years, 116072, Injurias y golpes. For another public accusation against a woman abusing children AHDFJ, 2743, 2. See also TSJDF, 1, several years, 889916, Difamación; TSJDF, 3, 1890, 144608, Injurias; TSJDF, 4, several years, 247975, Injurias y difamación. Manuela Lemus called Manuela Franco de Grower "prostituta" because of some missing construction material. TSJDF, 3, 1887, 73734, Injurias; TSJDF, 1, 1874, 1068714, Injurias.

100. TSJDF, 1, several years, 1311363, Injurias. Synonyms of puta in Roumagnac, Los criminales en México, 126.

101. TSJDF, 3, 1890, 144621, Injurias. Such gossip might put her marriage at risk because it causes "deshonra y desprecio, porque deshonrada y despreciada queda la mujer que relaja o mancha el vínculo conyugal," and could destroy "nuestro antes tranquilo y feliz hogar y haciendo caer sobre mis hijos la mancha" of her behavior. Silva's case in TSJDF, 177, 1911, 175147, Injurias y difamación. On honestidad Ramos, Los delitos, 18. Bulnes characterized Mexican popular classes by men's "culto del amasiato." Bulnes, El porvenir de las naciones, 31.

102. I cannot explain the use of "pantera." TSJDF, 3, 1890, 144658, Lesiones e

injurias. Another victim was accused of "alcahueta y que había vendido a su hija." TSJDF, 3, 1887, 83836, Injurias. A man accused of being *alcahuete* of his children in TSJDF, 1897, 16/2294, 2514, Difamación. For a victim that just wanted to stop the meddling, TSJDF, 3, 1890, 144608, Injurias.

103. TSJDF, 5, 1895, 5/1954, 1136759, Injurias. See also TSJDF, 1, several years, 1311408, Lesiones e injurias; Ma. Antonia Viveros por Injurias, AHSTJM, 1890, 3. 25. Violence emerged in another case when the suspect suddenly told the victim, Jesús Venegas de Goya, "que se habia cojido a su marido," leading to a fight between two women. TSJDF, 1879, 214, Difamación. Another fight, leading to a six-month prison sentence, in Ma. Antonia Viveros por Injurias, AHSTJM, 1890, 3. 25. See also See TSJDF, 177, 1911, 175163, Injurias y difamación; TSJDF, 5, 1895, 5/1954, 1136759, Injurias; TSJDF, 1897, 16/2294, 2514, Difamación; TSJDF, 3, 1890, 144658, Lesiones e injurias.

104. Piccato, *City of Suspects*, chap. 4; Piccato, " 'Such a Strong Need.' "

7. The Romero-Verástegui Affair

1. Rocha, *El General Sóstenes Rocha*, 27. This pamphlet was one of the multiple publications related to the case. For details, testimonies, and the speeches of the famous lawyers involved, see "Dictámen," *Gran jurado nacional*. The suspect was accused of dueling, rather than of homicide, as were the other participants in the encounter, including Rocha, the witnesses for the two men, and an attending physician. All were acquitted, except for Romero. *Gran jurado nacional*, 58. A treatment of the case in Speckman, "El último duelo." The jury audiences would long be remembered as one of the most famous in the city. Gamboa, *Mi diario I*, 156; *Excélsior*, 8 October 1929, 2d sec., 1. The case was fit to print in New York since Verastegui was "practically a member of the Cabinet, by reason of his position as chief of the Government stamp department." *New York Times*, 24 September 1894, 5. Contrast with EHA, 12 August 1894, 7.

2. According to Robert Nye, there was an "extraordinary revival of the idea of honour in France in the late nineteenth century and of the skills and ritual practices that sustained it." Nye, "Fencing, the Duel," 366; Nye, *Masculinity and Male Codes*, 172. For the growth of dueling in Germany, see McAleer, *Dueling*, 3. Dueling was in decline in other countries of western Europe by the nineteenth century, but recent studies correct Kiernan's view of the duel as a bourgeois "fantasy" claiming the values of chivalry. Kiernan, *The Duel*, 265. See Spierenburg, *Men and Violence*; Reddy, *The Invisible Code*; Liddle, "State, Masculinities and Law"; Gay, *The Cultivation of Hatred*, chaps. 1, 2; Greenberg, *Honor and Slavery*, xii, 9. See especially Gayol, *Honor y duelo*.

3. Rivera, *Tratado breve*, 8; Vázquez Mantecón, *La palabra*, 59–60. Although concerned with notions of honor, this book does not mention any duels. Unfortunately, for Vicente Riva Palacio, during the early republic the duel "no estaba en uso." Riva Palacio, *México a través de los siglos*, 11:288. In 1894, Francisco

Bulnes claimed that dueling was a recent fad, without strong roots in Mexico. He claimed that his questioning of elder public figures such as Guillermo Prieto and José María Vigil and some research in libraries yielded only three duels in the last forty years. *RLJ* (July–December 1894), 394. For the paucity of duels in the colonial period, see Burkholder, "Honor and Honors," 34. For a similar increase in other countries of Latin America, see Parker, "Law, Honor, and Impunity."

4. Martínez de Castro, "Exposición de motivos," 53, 88.

5. *Estadística del ramo criminal de la República Mexicana.*

6. *RLJ* (July–December 1894), 361. Heriberto Frías mentions "los cadáveres de muchos duelistas" in recent years. Frías, *El último duelo*, 5–6.

7. "La prensa mexicana y su porvenir," *LL*, 29 January 1884, 2. Reports of duels in provincial capitals in *DH*, 23 November 1884, 7; *LP*, 30 March 1880, 3; *LP*, 2 April 1880, 3. Duels were also underrepresented by judicial sources in Germany, Frevert, *Men of Honour*, 6.

8. Tovar, *Código nacional mexicano*, v; *Gran jurado nacional*, 123. Rocha (1831–97) wrote about military duels in his *Enquiridión*.

9. Escudero, a fencing and pistol instructor, was involved in several duels as a witness. His book combined hemerographical research and interviews and sought to remember "those times when honor . . . presided over all acts of life, and its defense was supported by the tip of a sword or the mouth of a gun." Escudero, *El duelo en México*, 277, 242–45. Between 1871 and 1885, for example, there were 48,196 convictions for battery and 533 for homicide in the Federal District. *Estadística del ramo criminal de la República Mexicana.* According to Robert Nye, there were between 200 and 300 duels a year at the turn of the century in France Nye, *Masculinity and Male Codes*, 183–87. Between 1882 and 1912 there were 3,466 convictions related to dueling in Germany. Frevert, "Taming." See also McAleer, *Dueling*, 244n. On Italy, Hughes, "Men of Steel," 68.

10. In Tovar, *Código nacional mexicano*, iv. For a similar ambivalence regarding the duel's historical value in Germany, where it was evidence of educated men's "anti-feudal educational ethos" see Frevert, *Men of Honour*, 137, 3, 7.

11. Manuel Lombardo and Juan Antonio Mateos, respectively, in "Dictamen," 366, 29.

12. Juan N. Mirafuentes, "El Duelo," *MR*, 1 December 1869, 1; Rocha, *El General Sóstenes Rocha*, 64–65; *Gran jurado nacional*, 458.

13. Sierra Velenzuela, *Duelos, rieptos y desafíos*, 52. For the standard narrative, see Sóstenes Rocha in Tovar, *Código nacional mexicano*. The origins of the duel were also debated in Germany and, although ethnic identity was an argument for its Germanic origins, evidence suggests that the practice came to Germany from Spain, Italy, and France. Frevert, *Men of Honour*, 9, 10, 14.

14. Sierra Velenzuela, *Duelos, rieptos y desafíos*, 25. See also *MR*, 1 May 1880, 2.

15. Rodríguez, *El duelo*, 5. The duel "implica un orgullo diabólico, absolutamente contrario a la dulzura y humildad del Evangelio," *El Heraldo, Diario Católico*, 4 January 1890, 1; Federico Peraza Rosado in *Gran jurado nacional*, 387–89; Rodríguez, *El duelo*, 5, 9. More recently, opposing the duel to modern legislation in defense of honor, Jiménez Huerta, *Derecho penal mexicano*, 25. *El*

Heraldo expressed the progressive attitudes of late nineteenth-century Catholic social thought.

16. Tovar, *Código nacional mexicano*, ix. For a similar evolutionist view, also based on a Nordic genealogy, see Juan Antonio Mateos in *Gran jurado nacional*, 26–30. On the French Revolution as origin, Escudero, *El duelo en México*, 27; Rodríguez, *El duelo*, 17. A similar historical account by Deputy Manuel Flores in RLJ (July–December 1894), 381.

17. Larralde and Alfaro, *Código del duelo*, 212. On the international encounters, see Altamirano to Joaquín D. Casasús, Paris, 5 June 1891, in Altamirano, *Epistolario*, 129–32, 137; Escudero, *El duelo en México*. For a scuffle in a Madrid theater that led to a Mexican count killing a Spanish deputy and having to flee to Portugal, see MR, 8 May 1869, 2. In contrast, few cases show American citizens fighting duels against a Mexican. On Porfirian cosmopolitanism, see Beezley, "Porfirian Smart Set"; Tenorio-Trillo, *Mexico*, chap. 2. For a duel between "a wealthy young man from New-York" who had purchased a coffee plantation in Veracruz and a Mexican planter over boundaries, "Verástegui's Death in a Duel," *New York Times*, 24 September 1894, 5; MR, 28 May 1869.

18. Campos, *Claudio Oronoz*, 43. German merchants had several firms in Mexico City, and France and Germany competed during the Porfirian period for the business of the Mexican military. Kelley, "Professionalism," 66; Katz, *La guerra secreta*, 1:81. On famous duels and relevant cases, *L'Echo du Mexique*, 24 June 1892, 3; Escudero, *El duelo en México*, 40; Ramos Pedrueza in *Gran jurado nacional*, 498.

19. *Gran jurado nacional*, 75–76, 582. Against the racial argument, in the same trial, *Gran jurado nacional*, 387.

20. Tovar, *Código nacional mexicano*, 13–15.

21. For a case in 1923 in which a man was acquitted for killing another who had disrespected his wife in a theater, not in a duel but, according to the jury, "in the defense of his honor," see TSJDF, no box, 19321, Homicide.

22. *Gran jurado nacional*, 75. Verástegui sought the discretion of his friends because "a mi edad, en mi posición y teniendo una familia en la cual figuran dos hijos de distinto sexo, ya grandes, se me cae la cara de vergüenza." *Gran jurado nacional*, 281. Yet, according to Ciro B. Ceballos, he was known to engage in scandalous behavior in the cabarets of Betlemitas Street. González Rodríguez, *Bajos Fondos*, 31. See also "A pistol duel," *Los Angeles Times*, 11 August 1894, 2.

23. *Gran jurado nacional*, 471, 381, 402, 333–34, 342, 87, 374. In Heriberto Frías's novelization of the duel the Barajases' house was a site of moral decadence, hypocrisy, and excess, although he suggested that the causes of the duel were political rather than erotic. Frías, *El último duelo*. On the meaning of *intimidad*, see Read Academia, *Diccionario de la lengua 1884*.

24. *Gran jurado nacional*, 437, 445.

25. Sierra Velenzuela, *Duelos, rieptos y desafíos*, 31.

26. The woman's preferences did not always predict the outcome of the dispute. MR, 16 May 1869, 3. See also the mortal fight caused by references to a woman's past in Díaz Covarrubias, *Obras completas*, 127–30. On Barajas's repu-

tation as a cuckold, see Salado Álvarez, *Memorias*, 166. According to Frevert, adultery was not a common cause of duels in Germany, yet the majority of conflicts leading to duels happened in places where "women were in prominent attendance" and men wanted to prove their masculinity. And news of duels reached women. Frevert, *Men of Honour*, 186–87. In debates about dueling, women were often blamed for their role in provoking duels. Frevert, *Men of Honour*, 188. Few men were ever punished in Mexico for adultery, although scandalous behavior justified masculine violence. García Peña, *El fracaso del amor*, 178, 181.

27. Rocha, *El General Sóstenes Rocha*, 59.

28. Martínez de Castro, *Código penal 1871*, 54. That was also the argument in Luis G. de la Sierra, "El duelo y la autoridad pública," *EF* 3:34 (8 August 1874), 133–34.

29. Rocha, *El General Sóstenes Rocha*, 58, 5.

30. Escudero, *El duelo en México*, 231–38; Sierra Velenzuela, *Duelos, rieptos y desafíos*, 25.

31. Sierra Velenzuela, *Duelos, rieptos y desafíos*, 25.

32. *Gran jurado nacional*, 539. Heriberto Barrón, speaking in the name of Rocha, added that for his client the perceptions of society were more important than the legal verdict. *Gran jurado nacional*, 563.

33. Rocha, *El General Sóstenes Rocha*, 76–77. Ramos Pedrueza added that, against the prosecutor's comparison of duelists with gamblers and prostitutes, "hombres de Estado, que sabios ilustres, que literatos distinguidos, que hábiles hombres de negocios recurren al duelo como único elemento que encuentran para resolver esas situaciones tan difíciles como dolorosas." *Gran jurado nacional*, 496. Neither Tovar's nor other codes of dueling cited in Mexico had been legislated by Congress or decreed by any authorities. Tovar, *Código nacional mexicano*, 5, 67.

34. Tovar, *Código nacional mexicano*, 27. The contractual argument in Larralde and Alfaro, *Código del duelo*, 6.

35. Juan N. Mirafuentes, "El Duelo," *MR*, 12 January 1869, 1. For the inconvenience of courts, Tovar, *Código nacional mexicano*, 9, 11–12. For the same attitude in other cases, Nye, *Masculinity and Male Codes*, 176; Parker, "Law, Honor, and Impunity." On jury trials, see Sodi, *El Jurado en México*, 41–44; Vicente García Torres in TSJDF, 11, 1897, 116068. Unlike Cabriñana's code of honor, Tovar's did allow for the celebration of duels for "causas reservadas." Tovar, *Código nacional mexicano*, chap. 2, art. 11; Cabriñana, *Código del honor en España*, art. 6. On lies, *EHA*, 30 September 1894, 2; Speckman, "El último duelo." Romero's attorneys acknowledged that he lied at first but then confessed. *Gran jurado nacional*, 396. A coach driver had contradicted the version that Verástegui had died when he dropped his gun. *EHA*, (18 September 1894), 2. For similar lies in other cases, Escudero, *El duelo en México*, 95–96.

36. Demetrio Salazar, defender of Prida, *Gran jurado nacional*, 20. On the lack of authority of courts of honor, Sierra Velenzuela, *Duelos, rieptos y desafíos*, 50.

But see Lanzilli, *Código del honor*, 45–46. Courts of honor for journalists had no success in Mexico. *LL*, 5 May 1880, 3; *MR*, 1 May 1880, 1.

37. Rocha, "Prólogo" in Tovar, *Código nacional mexicano*, iv–v. Similar ambivalence among modern European states in Frevert, "Taming," 43; Nye, *Masculinity and Male Codes*, 175. For duel as a right, Chatauvillard, *Essai*, 7.

38. CP 1871, arts. 587, 590, 600, 597.

39. Martínez de Castro, *Código penal 1871*, 53–54, 56. He considered that violent crimes could not be punished to the full extent of the law if they occurred "en un combate en que los peligros son iguales para entrambos, en que no hay fraude ni violencia, en que no hay ventaja, en que todo se hace ante testigos imparciales y en virtud de un pacto previo, que es cumplido con lealtad." Martínez de Castro, *Código penal 1871*, 54–55. See also *Código Penal Estado de Veracruz (1868)*, libro 3o, tit. 2o, arts. 558, 559. The Veracruz code was reformed in 1896 and established the same penalties as in the Federal District, *Código penal*. For the importance of distinguishing who was provoked, Sierra Velenzuela, *Duelos, rieptos y desafíos*, 40–41.

40. *RLJ* (July–December 1894), 386–88. A similar argument in *MR*, 13 May 1869, 3; Luis G. de la Sierra, "El duelo y la autoridad pública," *EF* 3:34 (8 August 1874), 134.

41. *RLJ* (July–December 1894), 369. Article 587 of the code, for example, referred to the honorability expected from duelists and instructed authorities to obtain from potential contenders a promise "under their word of honor" not to carry out the duel. See also CP 1871, arts. 600, paragraph 2.

42. Tovar, *Código nacional mexicano*, 8. Science agreed. For Miguel Macedo, "Mexican criminality has the fundamental character of barbaric crime," while the upper classes prefer to use other ways to solve disputes. Macedo, *La criminalidad*, 13, 20. On lower-class fights, see Piccato, *City of Suspects*, chap. 4.

43. De los Reyes, *Orígenes*, 13.

44. Escudero, *El duelo en México*, 122, 158, 111, 177. Compare with Frevert, *Men of Honour*, chap. 2.

45. Escudero, *El duelo en México*, 95–96. Most jurors were merchants, as they had to prove they had an income in excess of one hundred pesos a month, *LVM*, 14 January 1906, 1. For a case of "desafío," judged under colonial laws and ending in dismissal of charges, ASCJ, 24, no leg., 595, 1859.

46. Flores was indeed acquitted. J. Alberto Salinas y Rivera, "El jurado del general Alonso Flores," *EF* 3:24 (7 February 1878), 95; *EF* 3:25 (8 February 1878), 99; *EF* 3:26 (9 February 1878), 103. On article 183, *RLJ* (July–December 1894), 361. Lombardo mentioned six cases, three of which involved generals and one a former governor of the Federal District, in which nobody was punished. "Dictamen," 362. Same argument as Lombardo's in *Gran jurado nacional*, 493, 586. See also Escudero, *El duelo en México*, 231–38. Speckman notes the error in this argument, citing a case in 1874 that was prosecuted. Speckman, "Los jueces," 1437–38.

47. Mateos, *Los dramas*, 266.

48. Láncaster Jones in *Gran jurado nacional*, 572. The refusal to fight could be publicized. *Affair de M. Chatreuil-Boitot*. See also Schell, *Integral Outsiders*, 74. Doing otherwise was "ridículo" and could cost military officers their commisions. Lic. Salazar in *Gran jurado nacional*, 17; Frevert, *Men of Honour*, 144. For a critical perspective on the tragedies thus caused, Frías, *El último duelo*, 151.

49. *Gran jurado nacional*, 565.

50. "Guarda su nombre entre laurel la Gloria / La Amistad entre lágrimas su historia." Díaz, *Memorias*, 2:21, 29n.

51. Juan N. Mirafuentes, "El Duelo," MR, 12 January 1869, 1.

52. Ramos Pedrueza in *Gran jurado nacional*, 494. For Frevert, duels in Germany were associated with a critical stance toward the materialism of modern life—although they could also be useful for social advancement. Frevert, *Men of Honour*, 107. On readiness to die, Mateos, *Los dramas*, 179.

53. Sierra Velenzuela, *Duelos, rieptos y desafíos*, 26. See also Manero, *Apuntes*; Rocha, *El General Sóstenes Rocha*, 27; *Gran jurado nacional*, 522. For an example of a duel between friends, MR, 4 February 1869, 3. The "existential scenario" of duels could create friendship in Germany too. Frevert, *Men of Honour*, 24.

54. He continued: "El martirio solo prueba la fe al grado supremo de exsaltacion a que llega el amor cuando apela al suicidio; la verdad en estos tiemos de incredulidad en los que he nacido, no se prueba ya resistiendo a las torturas, ni venciendo en los torneos; sino con procedimientos lógicos incapaces de producir sensaciones dramáticas ni aspectos pintorescos." AGN FB, 11, 27, 11. He admitted to at least two duels and several violent encounters. Fernando Curiel, "Para leer a Bulnes" in Bulnes, *Las grandes mentiras*, 15.

55. Tovar, *Código nacional mexicano*. Tovar's code followed the lines of the European codes by the count of Chatauvillard and the marquis of Cabriñana. Before that, Mexican military officers used extracts from Chatauvillard's code. Tovar, *Código nacional mexicano*, v. It was translated and published in Mexico, without explicit acknowledgment and even a reference to Chatauvillard as one of the "autores anticuados," in Larralde and Alfaro, *Código del duelo*. For the original Chatauvillard, *Ensayo sobre el duelo*. See also Manero, *Apuntes*; Esteva, *El duelo*; Heraud y Clavijo de Soria, *Manual*. For another translation of Chatauvillard's code, see *Código del duelo*. Other available codes were Cabriñana, *Código del honor en España*; Lanzilli, *Código del honor*. In the late nineteenth century and early twentieth, France saw the emergence of a "very successful" literature of codes of honor. Billacois, *The Duel*, 185.

56. *Gran jurado nacional*, 347, 395.

57. He had to declare that "yo en mi vida militar he intervenido en muchos duelos, como juez de campo, como testigo y como actor, y digo con plena convicción que pocos he visto tan leales, tan caballerosos, nobles y valientes, como los Sres. Verástegui y Romero." Rocha, *El General Sóstenes Rocha*, 28. On rules not followed and Tovar's attendance, *Gran jurado nacional*, 412–19, 558.

58. Tovar, *Código nacional mexicano*, ix. For the critique of the Penal Code of 1871 as "metaphysical," see Almaraz, *Exposición de motivos*, 18, probably in-

spired by Ferri, *Sociologie*, 22. For the same intended effect on dueling regulations in France, see Nye, *Masculinity and Male Codes*, 214.

59. Esteva, *El duelo*, 10–11. One U.S. dollar was worth 1.08 Mexican pesos in 1878. *Estadísticas históricas*, 810. A regular Mauser pistol cost twenty-eight pesos in the gun shop of Korff, Honsberg y Cía. *El Imparcial*, 26 May 1903, 3. Pistols were also favored by Prussian combatants in 77 percent of the recorded cases between 1800 and 1914. In France, by contrast, pistols were used in only 10 percent of the duels of the 1880s. Nye, *Masculinity and Male Codes*, 186; McAleer, *Dueling*, 4. Guns were increasingly frequent during the nineteenth century in Germany, Frevert, *Men of Honour*, 102, 234.

60. Escudero, *El duelo en México*, 241; Tovar, *Código nacional mexicano*, chap. 4, 31; Larralde and Alfaro, *Código del duelo*, 152. By contrast, in Guatemala the use of revolvers in duels was favored by the turn of the century. Lanzilli, *Código del honor*, 54–55. Pistols' inaccuracy as a virtue in *Gran jurado nacional*, 83. According to Ramos Pedrueza, defender of Carrillo, guns had killed only four men in Mexico in duels since 1881. *Gran jurado nacional*, 509.

61. *Gran jurado nacional*, 118, 80.

62. Ibid., 428. Contrast with the description of Mariano Arista's beautiful body in Prieto, *Obras completas*, 9:546. The encounter in Escudero, *El duelo en México*, 233, and a similar one at 185. Only dueling pistols were used at the shooting range of San Felipe Neri, in Mexico City. Escudero, *El duelo en México*, 241.

63. Larralde and Alfaro, *Código del duelo*, 153, 158; *Gran jurado nacional*, 83; McAleer, *Dueling*, 74–75. For a reckless pistol duel in Chihuahua, Salado Alvarez, *Memorias*, 130.

64. *Gran jurado nacional*, 476.

65. Ibid., 280.

66. Ibid., 121, 65, 280. Ireneo Paz described in detail in an editorial in *La Patria* his troubles finding adequate representation in his dispute against the writers of *La Libertad*. LP, 25 April 1880, 1. See also Cabriñana, *Código del honor en España*, 21.

67. Cabriñana, *Código del honor en España*; Larralde and Alfaro, *Código del duelo*, 27, 37. See also Chatauvillard, *Essai*, 97.

68. "Dictámen," 354. On secret causes, *Gran jurado nacional*, 132. See Chatauvillard, *Essai*, 97.

69. *Gran jurado nacional*, 28, 355, 497.

70. Ibid., 476; Chatauvillard, *Essai*, 98.

71. Cabriñana, *Código del honor en España*, 4, chap. 1, art. 2; Tovar, *Código nacional mexicano*, 19, chap. 1, art. 1. For Chatauvillard, "La plus grande difficulté est de classer l'injure, parce qu'elle est telle qu'on la sent, et on la sent de mille manières différentes." Chatauvillard, *Essai*, 94, 11, chap. 1, art. 8.

72. TSJDF, 11,1897, 116068, recurso de casación.

73. Juan N. Mirafuentes, "El Duelo," MR, 12 January 1869, 1; Tovar, *Código nacional mexicano*, 19, 25, 52. For a confrontation caused by "una mirada . . . provocativa" from Salvador Díaz Mirón in Veracruz, see Domingo Bureau to

Porfirio Díaz, Veracruz, 24 August 1887, APD,1. 12, 7094. On slapped editors, Rabasa, "Moneda falsa," 308; Cabriñana, *Código del honor en España*, 5; Chatau-villard, *Essai*, 9.

74. Dated 19 August 1882 and signed A. de Cavera, D'Agostino, F. Bulnes, F. de Lizardi, Jorge Hammeken, and an unreadable signature. FB, 27, 1, 2–3. On the letter, *Gran jurado nacional*, 409.

75. Hobbes, *Leviathan*, 50–53. For an expression of the desire of an autono-mous field, see *L'Echo du Mexique*, 24 June 1892, 3.

76. Frevert notes that, when written down, the code of dueling "forfeits its unimpugned validity" and needs to be stabilized by "external means." Frevert, *Men of Honour*, 81, 138.

77. Escudero, *El duelo en México*, 226. Similar functions in Hughes, "Men of Steel," 65; Frevert, *Men of Honour*, 11, 16. Membership in a Masonic lodge, by contrast, could be an obstacle to a duel, according to Ireneo Paz, who was not a member. LP, 25 April 1880, 1

78. For example, Escudero, *El duelo en México*, 92, 93, 97. See Frevert, "Tam-ing," 41.

79. In fourteen of the seventy-eight duels discussed by Escudero, a civilian confronted an officer of the army. Escudero, *El duelo en México*. See also Hale, *Transformation*, 105; Katz, "The Liberal Republic," 104.

80. Sierra, *Evolución política*, 289.

81. *Gran jurado nacional*, 65, 83, 88; Rocha, *Enquiridión*. See also RLJ (July–December 1894), 394. Escudero describes six duels (of a total of seventy-eight) between military men, including students of the Colegio Militar. Escudero, *El duelo en México*; *Gran jurado nacional*, 561–62; Rocha, *Enquiridión*; McAleer, *Dueling*, chap. 3. Regulations on dueling survived in the military code after they had been stricken from the Federal District's Penal Code. De Pina, *Código penal*, 194–95. On the French and German influence on the reorganization of the Mexican army under Díaz, see Kelley, "Professionalism " 56, 62, 65.

82. *Gran jurado nacional*, 74, 87, 142.

83. Tovar, *Código nacional mexicano*, chap. 1, art. 1; Escudero, *El duelo en México*, 102, 130, 175. Guerra, *México*, 2:11–14; Hughes, "Men of Steel," 68. On the Montes de Oca–Reyes Spíndola encounter, Sobrino F., "José Guadalupe Posada," 75.

84. Guerra, *México*, 1:112.

85. The deputies Nicolás Lemus and Trinidad García engaged in a pistol duel during the years of Benito Juárez's presidency. After García missed, Lemus re-fused to shoot, and there were no wounds or arrests. Escudero, *El duelo en México*, 98. On Congress as a space for civilians early in the República Restau-rada, see Cosío Villegas, *La República Restaurada*, 199–200.

86. *Gran jurado nacional*, 22.

87. "Dictamen," 377.

88. Barajas proposed to Verástegui, for example, that he approach companies that had not been completely honest in their bookkeeping and make them settle with the government by making a lump payment, from which Barajas would take

a percentage. *Gran jurado nacional*, 77, 550, 424–25, 332, 350, 399. See also Speckman, "El último duelo."

89. EHA (20 May 1894), 2–3; Escudero, *El duelo en México*, 238; *Gran jurado nacional*, 292, 355.

90. *Gran jurado nacional*, 525–526.

91. Ibid., 70–71, 63.

92. Ibid., 22.

93. Frías, *El último duelo*, 181, 17; Saborit, *Doblados*, 177.

94. *Los Angeles Times*, 26 August 1895, 1; *Gran jurado nacional*, 613, 640. In his summary of the case, the judge mentioned Romero's relationship with a man accused of falsifying stamps, but the complaint in that case had come from the Ministry of Finance itself, not from Verástegui. *Gran jurado nacional*, 608. Prida, second of Verástegui, gave the name of Minister Limantour to guarantee his freedom on bail. *Gran jurado nacional*, 609. On Romero's political activity under Díaz, see Francisco Romero to Rafael Chousal, Mexico City, 18 November 1904, RCH, 29, 251, 45. He had been involved as a deputy in the debates over the deuda inglesa, but evidence suggests he did not fall from Díaz's grace. LP, 21 November 1884, 2. See also Romero to Porfirio Díaz, requesting an appointment as fencing instructor at the Colegio Militar, 28 January, 1885, CPD, 10, 1914–15. On Rocha, Gamboa, *Mi diario II*, 34; Cosío Villegas, *El porfiriato*. Limantour, *Apuntes*, 15–16, 44.

95. Bulnes, *El verdadero Díaz*, 52. On the amnesty and Romero's release, see *Los Angeles Times*, 10 December 1895, 3; Speckman, "El último duelo."

96. *Gran jurado nacional*, 439, 98, 125.

97. Bulnes, *El verdadero Díaz*, 52

98. *Gran jurado nacional*, 21.

99. "El hombre laborioso que no quiere / Ir al Terreno a que se le ha retado / Para arrostrar allí lo que viniere / Es por blancos y negros criticado, / Cual si un crimen hubiese cometido, / Siendo así que es pacífico y honrado." EHA, 26 August 1894, 6. A sonnet to the same effect entitled "El club de los valientes" (EHA [9 September 1894], 6) reads:

Un grupo de personas muy decentes,
Que andan por esas calles muy campantes,
Tienen yo no sé qué de fulminantes,
Porque son todas ellas . . . muy valientes.
Tienen cincuenta mil duelos pendientes,
Y les basta nomás unos instantes
Para arreglar encuentros arrogantes
En que pierden ¡claro está! los inocentes.
Si un desafío te anuncian, no preguntes
¡Oh, lector! quienes son los mastodontes
Que hacen pleitos al hilo cual pespuntes;
Es el club valeroso, que a los montes,
Ya que es bravo y certero en sus apuntes,
Debía ir a desafiar a los bisontes.

100. An early formulation in Luis G. de la Sierra, "El duelo y la autoridad pública," *EF* 3:34 (8 August 1874), 133–34. See also Moheno, *Honorio Rodríguez*, 50–52; Salado Álvarez, *Memorias*, 215. Bulnes in the trial in "Dictamen," 388, 391–92. See also Bulnes, *El verdadero Díaz*, 96; *Gran jurado nacional*, 512, 513, 519. Comparisons with Frevert, *Men of Honour*, 202; Hughes, "Men of Steel"; Gayol, "Honor Moderno."

101. Díaz Covarrubias, *Obras completas*, 2:381.

102. Juan N. Mirafuentes, "El Duelo," *MR*, 1 December 1869, 1; Rodríguez, *El duelo*, 23. For Manuel Flores, "Today we are *honrados* inasmuch as we are virtuous; today what dishonors us is crime." "Dictámen," 384.

103. Eulogy of Ignacio Vallarta by Jacinto Pallares, *RLJ*, 1 February 1894 (January–June), 101: "Para arriesgar la vida material bastan los impulsos de la vanidad, los estímulos del orgullo o las exigencias de una dignidad bien o mal entendida; y por centenares se cuentan los hombres que por vocación juegan su vida en los combates o que por frívolos motivos la entregan al azar de un duelo." See also Rodríguez, *El duelo*, 23.

104. *Gran jurado nacional*, 390, 394.

105. Ibid., 238.

106. Ibid., 392. For those in the first category, who take a walk on Plateros Street and come away disappointed because they could not find anyone to challenge, see *EHA*, 5 August 1894, 4–5.

107. For a duel avoided in Buenos Aires, see the happiness of Gamboa, *Mi diario I*, 47. Also *EHA*, 5 August 1894, 2–3; Frías, *¿Águila o sol?*, 108. A celebration of a duel that ended only in an injured hand in Tablada, *Sombras largas*, 19–20.

108. *Gran jurado nacional*, 582, 583. Similar arguments, concerning resistance to pain and fatigue, in Frevert, *Men of Honour*, 104–105.

109. *Gran jurado nacional*, 219. Romero claimed he could not have defeated Verástegui in a simple fight because "cuando era una cuarta más grande y otra cuarta más ancho y más corpulento que yo; él si podía haberme arrojado por el balcón." Ibid., 73. See also Altamirano to Joaquín D. Casasús, Paris, 12 June 1891, in Altamirano, *Epistolario*, 139–40. For an example of the extended-arm technique, see the duel between the critic Manuel Puga y Acal and Miguel Miramón, Tablada, *Sombras largas*, 19–20.

110. López Portillo y Rojas, *Fuertes y débiles*, 175–78, 149–51. On the ascendance of boxing in lieu of nobler ways of fighting, see Novo, *Viajes y ensayos*, 33; Escudero, *El duelo en México*, 277; Gamboa, *Mi diario I*, 24.

111. Rodríguez, *El duelo*, 26. On race and hard work, *FB*, 14, 5, 56; Macedo, *La criminalidad*, 14–15; Molina Enriquez, *Los grandes problemas*.

112. Homages to Pacheco's corpse, minus an arm and a leg, in *Velada que a la memoria*. Sierra commented on the paradox: seldom could be seen "un hombre más entero / que ese humilde y glorioso mutilado," "En los funerales del general Carlos Pacheco" [1891], in Sierra, *Obras completas*, 426–30. See also Prieto, *Obras completas*, 9:359.

113. *El Universal*, 5 February 1917, 5; Ramírez Plancarte, *La ciudad de México*, 70. In a list of the belongings of drunkards arrested in the streets in 1917 there were revolvers and automatic pistols of different brands and calibers. Archivo Histórico de la Ciudad de México, Fondo Gobernación, 1110, 43, and 1110, 44. Describing his first impression of Pancho Villa, Martín Guzmán wrote, "Este hombre no existiría si no existiese la pistola. . . . La pistola no es solo su útil de acción: es su instrumento fundamental, el centro de su obra y su juego." Guzmán, *El Aguila*, 1:325–26. For "fiesta de las balas," see Guzmán, *El Aguila*, 1:300–307. On the battle between científicos and Reyistas, see Bulnes, *El verdadero Díaz*, 326–27. On the impact of World War I, Frevert, *Men of Honour*, 196–97, 201. The decadence already observed in Carlos Lessona, "El duelo en los nuevos estudios y en las nuevas ideas," RLJ (July–December 1906), 265–98.

114. Tannenbaum, *Mexico*, 93.

115. 22 December 1921, DDCD, XXIX Legislature, 3:69, 16, 26. Another case in *Excélsior*, 17 December 1921, 4. For examples see Piccato, "Politics and the Technology of Honor." On the survival of the language of honor, see *Nueva Era*, 11 August 1911, 2; *El Universal*, 1 October 1920, 6. On Congress and honor, see Piccato, *El Poder Legislativo*.

116. *Código Penal [1929]*, arts. 1076, 1079, 1065, 1066, 1067; *Código penal [1931]*, arts. 297, 308.

117. Escudero, *El duelo en México*, 242, 90–91. Exiles in Cuba also fought duels. Gamboa, *Mi diario VI*, 422–23.

Conclusion

1. O'Gorman, *México: El trauma de su historia*, 23.
2. *La Jornada*, 17 July 2006.

SOURCES CITED

All periodicals and archives are from Mexico City unless otherwise stated.

Archives

Archivo de la Suprema Corte de Justicia de la Nación
Archivo General de la Nación, Fondo Antonio Díaz Soto y Gama
Archivo General de la Nación, Fondo Francisco Bulnes
Archivo Histórico del Distrito Federal, Fondo Justicia Jurados de Imprenta
Archivo Histórico del Supremo Tribunal de Justicia de Michoacán, Morelia
Archivo J. I. Limantour, Condumex
Archivo Manuel González, Universidad Iberoamericana
Archivo Porfirio Díaz, Universidad Iberoamericana
Archivo Toribio Esquivel Obregón, Universidad Iberoamericana
Archivo del Tribunal Superior de Justicia, Distrito Federal
Fondo Basave del Castillo Negrete, Centro de Estudios sobre la Universidad, Universidad Nacional Autónoma de Mexico
Fondo Rafael Chousal, Centro de Estudios sobre la Universidad, Universidad Nacional Autónoma de Mexico
Santos Degollado Correspondence, Benson Latin American Collection, Austin, Texas

Periodicals

Diario de los Debates de la Cámara de Diputados
Diario del Hogar
El Ahuizote
El Foro

El Heraldo, Diario Católico
El Hijo del Ahuizote
El Imparcial
El Nacional
El Siglo Diez y Nueve
El Universal
Excélsior
Gaceta de Policía
La Jornada
La Libertad
La Patria
La Voz de México
L'Echo du Mexique
Los Angeles Times
Monitor Republicano
New York Times
Nueva Era
Revista de Legislación y Jurisprudencia

Published Sources

Abrams, M. H. *The Mirror and the Lamp: Romantic Theory and the Critical Tradition*. London: Oxford University Press, 1971.

Acuña, Manuel, and José Luis Martínez. *Obras: Poesía y prosa*. Mexico City: Factoría Ediciones, 2000.

Acusación presentada ante la Cámara de Diputados del Congreso de la Unión por el Sr. Francisco Rodríguez Torales contra el Lic. Alonso Mariscal y Piña por los delitos de injurias, difamación y calumnia. Mexico City, 1908.

Adelman, Jeremy. *Republic of Capital: Buenos Aires and the Legal Transformation of the Atlantic World*. Stanford: Stanford University Press, 1999.

Affair de M. Chatreuil-Boitot avec M. Auguste. Paris: Luzé Fils, 1875.

Aguilar, José Antonio, and Rafael Rojas, eds. *El republicanismo en hispanoamérica: Ensayos de historia intelectual y política*. Mexico City: Centro de vestigación y Docencia Económicas; Fondo de Cultura Económica, 2002.

Almanza, Paulino. *Sin título*. [Matehuala]: N.p., 1887.

Almaraz, José. *Exposición de motivos del Código Penal promulgado el 15 de diciembre de 1929*. Mexico City, 1931.

Alonso, Paula, ed. *Construcciones impresas: Panfletos, diarios y revistas en la formación de los estados nacionales en América Latina, 1820–1920*. Buenos Aires: Fondo de Cultura Económica, 2004.

Altamirano, Ignacio Manuel. *Obras completas t. XXII Epistolario (1889–1893)*. Edited by Gloria Sánchez Azcona. Mexico City: Consejo Nacional para la Cultura y las Artes, 1992.

Alvarado, María de Lourdes. "Formación moral del estudiante y centralismo educativo: La polémica en torno al internado (1902–1903)." *Los Estudiantes: Trabajos de historia y sociología*, edited by Lorenzo Luna, 101–38. Mexico City: Universidad Nacional Autónoma de México, 1989.

Anderson Imbert, Enrique. *Spanish American Literature: A History*. Detroit: Wayne State University Press, 1963.

Anderson, Rodney D. *Outcasts in Their Own Land: Mexican Industrial Workers, 1906–1911*. DeKalb: Northern Illinois University Press, 1976.

Annino, Antonio. "Cádiz y la revolución territorial de los pueblos mexicanos, 1812–1821." *Historia de las elecciones en Iberoamérica, siglo XIX: De la formación del espacio político nacional*, edited by Antonio Annino, 177–226. Buenos Aires: Fondo de Cultura Económica, 1995.

——. "Ciudadanía versus gobernabilidad republicana en México: Los orígenes de un dilema." *Ciudadanía política y formación de las naciones: Perspectivas históricas de América Latina*, edited by Hilda Sabato, 62–93. Mexico City: Fondo de Cultura Económica, 1999.

Aragón, Agustín. "A la República Mexicana." *Revista Positiva*, no. 55 (1905), 233–39.

Arrom, Silvia. "Popular Politics in Mexico City: The Parián Riot, 1828." *Riots in the Cities: Popular Politics and the Urban Poor in Latin America, 1765–1910*, edited by Silvia Arrom and Servando Ortoll, 71–96. Wilmington, Del.: Scholarly Resources, 1996.

——. *The Women of Mexico City, 1790–1857*. Stanford: Stanford University Press, 1985.

Arrom, Silvia, and Servando Ortoll. *Riots in the Cities: Popular Politics and the Urban Poor in Latin America, 1765–1910*. Wilmington, Del.: Scholarly Resources, 1996.

Avalos, Miguel V., and Manuel Calero y Sierra. "Alegato presentado por los Sres. Lics. Miguel V. Avalos y Manuel Calero y Sierra ante la Suprema Corte de Justicia, en la revisión del amparo promovido por el Dr. D. Francisco Repetto, contra actos del Juez Menor del Carmen D. Pedro Montejo: Violación de los arts. 14, 16 y 17 Constitucionales, en un proceso seguido por un supuesto delito de difamación." *Revista de Legislación y Jurisprudencia* (1896), 164–87.

Azuela, Mariano. "Impresiones de un estudiante." *Obras completas*. Volume 2: *Novelas*. Mexico City: Fondo de Cultura Económica, 1958.

——. "María Luisa." *Obras Completas*. Volume 2: *Novelas*. Mexico City, 1976.

Baker, Keith Michael. *Inventing the French Revolution: Essays on French Political Culture in the Eighteenth Century*. Cambridge: Cambridge University Press, 1990.

Barajas Durán, Rafael (el Fisgón). *El país de "el llorón de Icamole": Caricatura mexicana de combate y libertad de imprenta durante los gobiernos de Porfirio Díaz y Manuel González (1877–1884)*. Mexico City: Fondo de Cultura Económica, 2007.

Barousse Martínez, Eduardo. "Análisis crítico acerca de los delitos de querella necesaria." N.p., 1946.

Bartlett, Thomas. "An End to Moral Economy: The Irish Militia Disturbances of 1793." *Past and Present* 99 (1983), 41–64.

Bazant, Jan. *Alienation of Church Wealth in Mexico: Social and Economic Aspects of the Liberal Revolution, 1856–1875*. Cambridge: Cambridge University Press, 1970.

Bazant, Mílada. "Lecturas del Porfiriato." *Seminario de Historia de la Educación en México, Historia de la lectura en México*. Mexico City: El Ermitaño–Colegio de México, 1988.

Beezley, William H. "The Porfirian Smart Set Anticipates Thorstein Veblen in Guadalajara." *Rituals of Rule, Rituals of Resistance: Public Celebrations and Popular Culture in Mexico*, edited by William H. Beezley, Cheryl English Martin, and William E. French, 173–90. Wilmington, Del.: Scholarly Resources, 1994.

Beezley, William H., Cheryl English Martin, and William E. French. *Rituals of Rule, Rituals of Resistance*. Wilmington, Del.: Scholarly Resources, 1994.

Bell, David A. "The 'Public Sphere,' the State, and the World of Law in Eighteenth-Century France." *French Historical Studies* 17, no. 4 (1992), 912–34.

Berlin, Isaiah. *Las raíces del romanticismo*. Translated by Silvina Marí. Edited by Henry Hardy. Madrid: Taurus, 2000.

Bertola, Elizabetta. "Las oportunidades del poder: Suplencias e interinatos políticos en la práctica del compromiso y del control electoral en el México porfirista (1876–1911)." *El águila bifronte: Poder y liberalismo en México*, edited by Enrique Montalvo Ortega, 177–95. Mexico City: Instituto Nacional de Antropología e Historia, 1995.

Billacois, François *The Duel: Its Rise and Fall in Early Modern France*. Translated by Trista Selous. New Haven: Yale University Press, 1990.

Blanco Fombona, Rufino. *Rufino Blanco Fombona Íntimo*. Caracas: Monte Avila, 1975.

Bonilla, Laura Edith. "La imágen política de un gobierno: Porfirio Díaz y su relación con la prensa." *Nuestra Historia*, no. 45 (2001), 36–43.

Bourdieu, Pierre. *La dominación masculina*. Translated by Joaquín Jordá. Barcelona: Anagrama, 2000.

——. *Meditaciones Pascalianas*. Translated by Thomas Kauf. Barcelona: Anagrama, 1997.

——. *Outline of a Theory of Practice*. Translated by Richard Nice. New York: Cambridge University Press, 1977.

——. *Practical Reason: On the Theory of Action*. Translated by Randall Johnson. Stanford: Stanford University Press, 1998.

——. "The Sentiment of Honour in Kabyle Society." *Honour and Shame: The Values of Mediterranean Society*, edited by John G. Peristiany, 191–241. Chicago: University of Chicago Press, 1966.

Bravo Ugarte, José. *Periodistas y Periódicos Mexicanos (Hasta 1935, selección)*. Mexico City: Jus, 1966.

Buffington, Robert. *Criminal and Citizen in Modern Mexico*. Lincoln: University of Nebraska Press, 2000.

Buffington, Robert, and Pablo Piccato. "Tales of Two Women: The Narrative Construal of Porfirian Reality." *The Americas* 55, no. 3 (1999), 391–424.

Bulnes, Francisco. *El porvenir de las naciones hispanoamericanas: Once mil leguas sobre el hemisferio norte*. Mexico City: Grijalbo, 1992.

——. *El porvenir de las naciones hispoanoamericanas ante las conquistas recientes de Europa y los Estados Unidos*. Mexico City: Imp. de Nava, 1899.

——. *El verdadero Díaz y la revolución*. Mexico City: Rusebio Gómez de la Puente, 1920.

——. *El verdadero Juárez y la verdad sobre la Intervención y el Imperio*. Mexico City: Nacional, 1972.

——. *Las grandes mentiras de nuestra historia; la nación y el ejército en las guerras extranjeras*. Mexico City: Consejo Nacional para la Cultura y las Artes, 1991.

——. *Los grandes problemas de México*. Mexico City: El Universal, 1927.

——. *Los grandes problemas de México*. Mexico City: Ediciones de El Universal, Imp. Escallada, 1926.

——. *Toda la verdad acerca de la revolución mexicana: La responsabilidad criminal del presidente Wilson en el desastre mexicano*. Translated by Florencio Sánchez Cámara. Mexico City: Editorial los Insurgentes, 1960.

Burkholder, Mark A. "Honor and Honors in Colonial Spanish America." *The Faces of Honor: Sex, Shame, and Violence in Colonial Latin America*, edited by Lyman L. Johnson and Sonya Lipsett-Rivera, 18–44. Albuquerque: University of New Mexico Press, 1998.

Bustillo Oro, Juan. "Ahí está el detalle." Mexico: Grovas-Oro Films, 1940.

Butler, Judith. *Bodies that Matter: On the Discursive Limits of "Sex."* New York: Routledge, 1993.

Buve, Raymond, and Romana Falcón, eds. *Don Porfirio presidente . . . nunca omnipotente. Hallazgos, reflexiones y debates. 1876–1911*. Mexico City: Universidad Iberoamericana, 1998.

Cabrera, Luis. *Obra política de Luis Cabrera*. Edited by Eugenia Meyer. Mexico City: Universidad Nacional Autónoma de México–Coordinación de Humanidades, 1992.

Cabriñana, Marqués de. *Código del honor en España formulado por el Marqués de Cabriñana*. Barcelona: Librería de Feliu y Susanna, 1900.

Calhoun, Craig J. "Habitus, Field, and Capital: The Question of Historical Specificity." *Bourdieu: Critical Perspectives*, edited by Craig J. Calhoun, Edward LiPuma, and Moishe Postone, 61–88. Chicago: University of Chicago Press, 1993.

——. "Introduction: Habermas and the Public Sphere." *Habermas and the Public Sphere*, edited by Craig Calhoun, 1–48. Cambridge, Mass.: MIT Press, 1997.

Camarillo Carbajal, María Teresa. *El sindicato de periodistas, una utopía mexi-*

cana: Las agrupaciones de periodistas en la ciudad de México (1872–1929). Mexico City: Universidad Nacional Autónoma de Mexico, 1988.

———. "Los periodistas en el siglo XIX: Agrupaciones y vivencias." *La república de las letras: Asomos a la cultura escrita del México decimonónico,* edited by Belem Clark de Lara and Elisa Speckman, 153–63. Mexico City: Universidad Nacional Autónoma de México, 2005.

Camp, Roderic Ai. *Mexican Political Biographies, 1884–1935.* Austin: University of Texas Press, 1991.

———. *Political Recruitment Across Two Centuries: Mexico 1884–1991.* Austin: University of Texas Press, 1995.

Camp, Roderic Ai., et al. *Los intelectuales y el poder en México: Intellectuals and Power in Mexico.* Mexico City: Colegio de México–University of California, 1991.

Campos, Rubén M. *Claudio Oronoz.* Mexico City: Premia, 1982.

———. *El bar: La vida literaria de México en 1900.* Mexico City: Universidad Nacional Autónoma de México, Coordinación de Humanidades, Dirección General de Publicaciones, 1996.

Cañeque, Alejandro. *The King's Living Image: The Culture and Politics of Viceregal Power in Colonial Mexico.* New York: Routledge, 2004.

Carilla, Emilio. *El romanticismo en la América hispánica.* 3d ed. Madrid: Editorial Gredos, 1975.

Carmagnani, Marcello. *Estado y mercado: La economía pública del liberalismo mexicano, 1850–1911.* Mexico City: Fondo de Cultura Económica, 1994.

Carmagnani, Marcello, and Alicia Hernández Chávez. "La ciudadanía orgánica mexicana, 1850–1910." *Ciudadanía política y formación de las naciones: Perspectivas históricas de América Latina,* edited by Hilda Sabato. Mexico City: Fondo de Cultura Económica, 1999.

Carrara, Francesco. *Programma del corso di diritto criminale dettato nella R. Università di Pisa: Parte Speciale: Esposizione dei delitti in specie con note per uso della pratica forense.* Volume III. 8th ed. Firenze: Fratelli Cammelli, 1909.

Casas, Bartolomé de las. *Obras completas.* Edited by Paulino Castañeda Delgado. Volume 2. Madrid: Alianza Editorial, 1988.

Casasús, Joaquín D. *Historia de la deuda contraída en Londres, con un apéndice sobre el estado actual de la deuda pública.* Mexico City: Imprenta del Gobierno, 1885.

Castañeda Batres, Oscar. "Estudio introductorio." *La deuda inglesa, Artículos publicados en el "Siglo XIX,"* edited by Francisco Bulnes. Mexico City: Somex, 1990.

Castelán Rueda, Roberto. *La fuerza de la palabra impresa: Carlos María de Bustamante y el discurso de la modernidad, 1805–1827.* Mexico City: Fondo de Cultura Económica—Universidad de Guadalajara, 1997.

Castelar, Emilio. *Autobiografía y algunos discursos inéditos.* Madrid: Angel de San Martín, 1921.

——. *Discursos parlamentarios y políticos de . . . en la Restauración*. Madrid: San Martin, 1885.

——. *Vida de Lord Byron*. Buenos Aires: Poseidon, 1943.

Castro Leal, Antonio. *Díaz Mirón: Su vida y su obra*. Mexico City: Porrúa, 1970.

Castro, Miguel Angel, ed. *Tipos y caracteres: La prensa mexicana (1822–1855); Memoria del coloquio celebrado los días 23, 24 y 25 septiembre de 1998*. Mexico City: Instituto de vestigaciones Bibliográficas, Universidad Nacional Autónoma de México, 2001.

Caulfield, Sueann. *Defense of Honor: Sexual Morality, Modernity, and Nation in Early-Twentieth-Century Brazil*. Durham: Duke University Press, 2000.

Caulfield, Sueann, Sarah C. Chambers, and Lara Putnam, eds. *Honor, Status, and Law in Modern Latin America*. Durham: Duke University Press, 2005.

Celis de la Cruz, Martha. "El empresario Vicente García Torres (1811–1894)." *Tipos y caracteres: La prensa mexicana (1822–1855); Memoria del coloquio celebrado los días 23, 24 y 25 septiembre de 1998*, edited by Miguel Angel Castro, 147–59. Mexico City: Instituto de Investigaciones Bibliográficas, Universidad Nacional Autónoma de México, 2001.

Chambers, Sarah C. *From Subjects to Citizens: Honor, Gender and Politics in Arequipa, Peru, 1780–1854*. University Park: Pennsylvania State University, 1999.

Chandler, James. *England in 1819: The Politics of Literary Culture and the Case of Romantic Historicism*. Chicago: University of Chicago Press, 1998.

Chartier, Roger. *The Cultural Origins of the French Revolution*. Translated by Lydia G. Cochrane. Durham: Duke University Press, 1991.

——. *Espacio público, crítica y desacralización en el siglo XVIII: Los Orígenes Culturales de la Revolución Francesa*. Barcelona: Gedisa, 1995.

——. "Opinion Publique et Propagande." *L'image de la révolution Française*, edited by Michel Vovelle. Paris: Pergamon Press, 1989.

Chatauvillard, Comte de. *Ensayo sobre el duelo, por el conde de Chateauvillard; traducido y arreglado por el C. Eligo Dufoo*. Translated by Eligo Dufoo. Mexico City: Sandoval y Vazquez, 1874.

——. *Essai sur le duel*. Paris: Imprimerie D'Edourad Proux, 1836.

Cicerón, Marco Tulio. *De la invención retórica*. Translated and edited by Bulmaro Reyes Coria. Mexico City: Universidad Nacional Autónoma de México, 1997.

Cmiel, Kenneth. *Democratic Eloquence: The Fight over Popular Speech in Nineteenth-Century America*. New York: Morrow, 1990.

Coatsworth, John H. *Los orígenes del atraso: Nueve ensayos de historia económica de México*. Mexico City: Alianza, 1990.

Cobb, R. C. *The Police and the People: French Popular Protest 1789–1820*. Oxford: Clarendon Press, 1970.

Código del duelo observado en Francia, segun el conde de Chatauvillard. Translated by Aristides Simonpietri. Ponce, Puerto Rico: Tipografía El Comercio, 1887.

Código penal del Estado de Veracruz Llave: Proyecto formado por las Comisiones unidas de la honorable Legislatura y del honorable Tribunal Superior de Justicia, aprobado y mandado observar por la Ley núm. 32 de 15 de agosto de 1896. Xalapa: Oficina. Tip. del Gobierno del Estado, 1896.

Código Penal Estado de Veracruz (1868). Veracruz: Imprenta del Progreso, 1869.

Código Penal para el Distrito y Territorios Federales. Mexico City: Talleres Gráficos de la Nación, 1929.

Código penal para el Distrito y Territorios Federales y para toda la República en Materia de Fuero Federal [1931]. Mexico City: Botas, 1938.

Coerver, Don M. *The Porfirian terregnum: The Presidency of Manuel Gonzalez of Mexico, 1880–1884.* Texas Christian University Monographs in History and Culture, no. 14. Fort Worth: Texas Christian University Press, 1979.

Colección de pedimentos fiscales presentados y de autos y sentencias pronunciados en la causa seguida a algunos periodistas, licenciados y estudiantes, como responsables de conato de sedición, cometido por la prensa. Mexico City: Secretaría de Fomento, 1886.

Connell, R. W. *Masculinities.* Berkeley: University of California Press, 1995.

Constant, Benjamin. *Oeuvres.* Edited by Alfred Roulin. 2d ed. Paris: Gallimard, 1979.

Cook, Alexandra Parma, and Noble David Cook. *Good Faith and Truthful Ignorance: A Case of Transatlantic Bigamy.* Durham: Duke University Press, 1991.

Corbin, Alain. "Backstage." *A History of Private Life IV: From the Fires of Revolution to the Great War,* edited by Michelle Perrot, 451–667. Cambridge, Mass.: Harvard University Press, 1990.

Coromina, Amador. *Recopilación de leyes, decretos, reglamentos y circulares del Estado de Michoacán.* Volume 38. Morelia: Escuela Industrial Militar Porfirio Díaz, 1906.

——. *Recopilación de leyes, decretos, reglamentos y circulares del Estado de Michoacán.* Vol. XXXV. Morelia: Escuela Industrial Militar Porfirio Díaz, 1900.

Cosío Villegas, Daniel. *Historia moderna de México: La república restaurada, vida política.* Mexico City: Hermes, 1959.

——. *Historia moderna de México: El porfiriato, Vida politica interior.* 2 vols. Mexico City: Hermes, 1972.

——. *Imprenta y vida pública.* Mexico City: Fondo de Cultura Económica, 1985.

——. *La Constitución de 1857 y sus críticos.* Mexico City: Hermes, 1957.

Crawley, C. W. "French and English Influences in the Cortes of Cadiz, 1810–1914." *Cambridge Historical Journal* 6, no. 2 (1939), 176–208.

Cuadros estadísticos e informe del Procurador de Justicia concernientes a la criminalidad en el Distrito Federal y territorios 1900. Mexico City: Ministerio Público del Distrito y Territorios Federales, 1903.

Curiel Defossé, Fernando. "José (Federico) Francisco de Paula Demetrio Trinidad (Gamboa) Iglesias." *La república de las letras: Asomos a la cultura escrita del México decimonónico,* edited by Belem Clark de Lara and Elisa Speckman, 491–505. Mexico City: Universidad Nacional Autónoma de México, 2005.

Darío, Rubén. *Autobiografías.* Buenos Aires: Marymar, 1976.

Davidson, James. "Dover, Foucalt and Greek Homosexuality: Penetration and the Truth of Sex." *Past and Present*, no. 170 (2001), 3–51.

Davis, Diane E. "El rumbo de la esfera pública: Influencias locales, nacionales e internacionales en la urbanización del centro de la ciudad de México, 1910–1950." *Actores, espacios y debates en la historia de la esfera pública en la ciudad de México*, edited by Cristina Sacristán and Pablo Piccato, 233–71. Mexico City: Instituto Mora, 2005.

———. *Urban Leviathan: Mexico City in the Twentieth Century*. Philadelphia: Temple University Press, 1994.

Davis, Michael Jonathan. "The Discourse of Oratory: The New Rhetoric and Romantic Writing." Dissertation, University of Texas at Austin, 1996.

Defensa de primera instancia, requisitoria fiscal y sentencia ejecutoria del Tribunal de Circuito de México en la causa instruida a los señores Gral. Manuel Díaz de la Vega y José de las Piedras, por el delito de injurias a la nación. Mexico City: Secretaría de Fomento, 1889.

Degollado, Joaquín M. *Defensa ante el público que hace el que suscribe, de la justicia con que ha sostenido su inmunidad el señor Don Santos Degollado, para impedir que un juez incompetente lo juzgue en el delito de imprenta que le imputa D. Eustaquio Barrón.* Mexico City: Imprenta de Ignacio Cumplido, 1857.

Delgado Carranco, Susana María. "Las primeras discusiones en torno a la libertad de imprenta: *El Diario de México* (1811–1815)." *Empresa y cultura en tinta y papel (1800–1860)*, edited by Miguel Angel Castro, 473–88. Mexico City: Instituto Mora–Universidad Nacional Autónoma de Mexico, 2001.

———. *Libertad de imprenta: Política y educación, su planteamiento y discusión en el Diario de México, 1810–1817.* Mexico City: Instituto Mora, 2006.

de los Reyes, Aurelio. *Los orígenes del cine mexicano: 1896–1900* Mexico City: Fondo de Cultura Económica, 1983.

de Pina, Rafael. *Código penal para el Distrito y territorios federales: Texto al día, concordancias, notas y jurisprudencia.* 5th ed. Mexico City: Porrúa, 1960.

Díaz Covarrubias, Juan. *Obras completas.* Edited by Clementina Diaz y de Ovando. Mexico City: Universidad Nacional Autónoma de Mexico, 1959.

Díaz Infante, Carlos. "Estudios penales: Delitos cometidos por medio de la escritura impresa contra los funcionarios públicos." *Revista de Legislación y Jurisprudencia* (1896), 36–73.

Díaz Mirón, Salvador. *Poesía Completa.* Edited by Manuel Sol. Mexico City: Fondo de Cultura Económica, 1997.

———. *Prosa.* Edited by Leonardo Pasquel. Mexico City: Talleres Gráficos de la Nación, 1953.

Díaz, Porfirio. *Memorias de Porfirio Díaz.* 2 vols. Mexico City: Consejo Nacional para la Cultura y las Artes, 1994.

Díaz y de Ovando, Clementina. *Un enigma de los ceros: Vicente Riva Palacio o Juan de Dios Peza.* Mexico City: Universidad Nacional Autónoma de México, Coordinación de Humanidades Dirección General de Publicaciones, 1994.

Díaz y de Ovando, Clementina, and Elisa García Barragán. *La Escuela Nacional*

Preparatoria. Mexico City: Universidad Nacional Autónoma de México, Instituto de Investigaciones Estéticas, 1972.

Di Bella, Maria Pia. "Name, Blood and Miracles: The Claims to Renown in Traditional Sicily." *Honor and Grace in Anthropology*, edited by John G. Peristiany and Julian Alfred Pitt-Rivers, 151–65. Cambridge: Cambridge University Press, 1992.

"Dictámen de la Sección 2a. del Gran Jurado Nacional." *Revista de Legislación y Jurisprudencia* 7 (1894), 351–409.

Distrito Federal, Mexico. *Código de Procedimientos Penales (1880)*. Mexico City: Ireneo Paz, 1886.

——. *Distrito Federal, Código de Procedimientos Penales (1894)*. Mexico City: Herrero, 1913.

Di Tella, Torcuato. "The Dangerous Classes in Early Nineteenth Century Mexico." *Journal of Latin American Studies* 5 (1973), 79–105.

Domínguez Michael, Christopher. *Tiros en el concierto: Literatura mexicana del siglo V*. Mexico City: ERA, 1997.

Donovan, James M. "Magistrates and Juries in France, 1791–1952." *French Historical Studies* 22, no. 3 (1999), 379–420.

Drescher, Seymour. "Tocqueville's Two Democracies." *Journal of the History of Ideas* 25, no. 2 (1964), 201–16.

Duclós Salinas, Adolfo. *Méjico pacificado, el progreso de Méjico y los hombres que lo gobiernan. Porfirio Díaz-Bernardo Reyes, por . . . (uno de los presos políticos, con motivo de los acontecimientos del "2 de abril de 1903," en Monterrey)*. St. Louis: Imprenta de Hughes y Ca., 1904.

Easton, Malcolm. *Artists and Writers in Paris: The Bohemian Idea, 1803–1867*. London: Edward Arnold, 1964.

Eisenmann, Carlos. *Alegatos presentados al juzgado 20. de Distrito y a la Suprema Corte de Justicia en el juicio de amparo pedido por D. Carlos Eisenmann contra los procedimientos del Juzgado 20. Correccional en las diligencias que comenzó a instruir con motivo de una acusación de calumnia presentada por Ricardo Kent*. Mexico City: Tipografía de la Revista de Legislación y Jurisprudencia, 1890.

El libro secreto de Maximiliano. Mexico City: Universidad Nacional Autónoma de Mexico, 1963.

Eley, Geoff. "Nations, Publics, and Political Cultures: Placing Habermas in the Nineteenth Century." *Culture/Power/History: A Reader in Contemporary Social Theory*, edited by Nicholas B. Dirks, Geoff Eley, and Sherry B. Ortner. Princeton: Princeton University Press, 1994.

Elguero, Francisco. *Lecciones de elocuencia forense dadas en 1914 en la Escuela Nacional de Jurisprudencia de Méjico*. Mexico City: Impr. Manuel León Sánchez, N.d.

Elias, Norbert. *La Sociedad Cortesana*. Translated by Guillermo Hirata. Mexico City: Fondo de Cultura Económica, 1996.

Escalante, Fernando. *Ciudadanos imaginarios: Memorial de los afanes y desven-*

turas de la virtud y apología del vicio triunfante en la República Mexicana: Tratado de Moral Pública. Mexico City: Colegio de México, 1993.

Escudero, Angel. El duelo en México: Recopilación de los desafíos habidos en nuestra República, precedidos de la historia de la esgrima en México y de los duelos mas famosos verificados en el mundo desde los juicios de Dios hasta nuestros días, por el maestro de armas. Mexico City: Mundial, 1936.

Estadística del ramo criminal de la República Mexicana. Mexico City: Secretaría de Fomento, 1890.

Estadísticas históricas de Mexico. 3d ed. Aguascalientes, Ags., Mexico City: Instituto Nacional de Estadística Geografía e Informática, 1994.

Estadísticas sociales del porfiriato, 1877–1910. Mexico City: Dirección General de Estadística, 1956.

Esteva, Gonzalo A. El duelo a espada y a pistola. Mexico City: Tip. de Gonzalo A. Esteva, 1878.

Falcón, Romana, ed. Actores políticos y desajustes sociales. Mexico City: Colegio de México, 1992.

Farge, Arlette. Subversive Words: Public Opinion in Eighteenth-Century France. Translated by Rosemary Morris. University Park: Pennsylvania State University Press, 1994.

Febre, Lucien. Honneur et Patrie. Cher: Perrin, 1996.

Ferri, Henri. La Sociologie Criminelle. Translated by Enrico Ferri. 3d ed. Paris: Arthur Rousseau, 1893.

Fiume, Giovanna. "Introduzione." Onore e storia nelle societá mediterranee, edited by Giovanna Fiume. Palermo: La Luna, 1989.

——. Onore e storia nelle societá mediterranee. Palermo: La Luna, 1989.

Flores Villar, Mariano. Los estudiantes y la conversión de la deuda de Londres: Narración circunstanciada de los sucesos de Noviembre de 1884, relativos a la participación de los estudiantes en el negocio de la conversión de la deuda de Londres por el estudiante de Jurisprudencia, testigo presencial . . . Mexico City: Imprenta en la 2a. de San Lorenzo, 1885.

Florian, Eugenio. La teoria psicologica della diffamazione: Studio sociologico-giuridico. Torino: Fratelli Bocca, 1927.

——. Teoría psicológica de la difamación: Estudio sociológico-jurídico. Translated by P. Herrera de Huerta. Mexico City: Talleres de "La Ciencia Jurídica," 1902.

Fonseca, Claudia. "Philanderers, Cuckolds, and Wily Women: Reexamining Gender Relations in a Brazilian Working-Class Neighborhood." Changing Men and Masculinities in Latin America, edited by Matthew C. Gutmann, 61–83. Durham: Duke University Press, 2003.

Fontana, Biancamaria. Benjamin Constant and the Post-Revolutionary Mind. New Haven: Yale University Press, 1991.

Forment, Carlos A. Democracy in Latin America, 1760–1900. Chicago: University of Chicago Press, 2003.

Foucault, Michel. Discipline and Punish: The Birth of the Prison. Translated by Alan Sheridan. New York: Vintage, 1979.

——. "Governmentality." *The Foucault Effect: Studies in Governmentality: With Two Lectures by and an Interview with Michel Foucault*, edited by Graham Burchell, Colin Gordon, and Peter Miller, 87–104. Chicago: University of Chicago Press, 1991.

Frevert, Ute. *Men of Honour: A Social and Cultural History of the Duel*. Cambridge, Mass.: Polity Press, 1995.

——. "The Taming of the Noble Ruffian: Male Violence and Dueling in Early Modern and Modern Germany." *Men and Violence: Gender, Honor, and Rituals in Modern Europe and America*, edited by Pieter Spierenburg. Columbus: Ohio State University Press, 1998.

Frías, Heriberto. *El amor de las sirenas [Los destripados]*. Mazatlán: Tip. de Valades, 1908.

——. *El último duelo. Novela social de costumbres mexicanas*. Mexico City: Imprenta de la Revista Militar, 1896.

——. *Episodios militares mexicanos: Principales Campañas, jornadas, batallas, combates y actos heroicos, que ilustran la historia del ejército nacional desde la dependencia hasta el triunfo definitivo de la República*. Mexico City: Porrúa, 1987.

——. *General Félix Díaz*. N.p.: N.d., 1901.

——. *Miserias de México*. Mexico City: Botas, n.d.

——. *¿Águila o sol?* Mexico City: Offset, 1984.

Furet, François. *Penser la Révolution française*. Paris: Gallimard, 1978.

Galí i Boadella, Montserrat. *Historias del bello sexo: La introducción del romanticismo en México*. Mexico City: Universidad Nacional Autónoma de México, Instituto de Investigaciones Estéticas, 2002.

Gamboa, Federico. *Impresiones y recuerdos*. Mexico City: Consejo Nacional para la Cultura y las Artes, 1994.

——. *Mi diario I (1892–1896): Mucho de mi vida y algo de la de otros*. Edited by José Emilio Pacheco. Mexico City: Consejo Nacional para la Cultura y las Artes, 1995.

——. *Mi diario II (1897–1900): Mucho de mi vida y algo de la de otros*. Mexico City: Consejo Nacional para la Cultura y las Artes, 1995.

——. *Mi diario III (1901–1904): Mucho de mi vida y algo de la de otros*. Mexico City: Consejo Nacional para la Cultura y las Artes, 1995.

——. *Mi diario IV (1905–1908): Mucho de mi vida y algo de la de otros*. Mexico City: Consejo Nacional para la Cultura y las Artes, 1995.

——. *Mi diario V (1909–1911): Mucho de mi vida y algo de la de otros*. Mexico City: Consejo Nacional para la Cultura y las Artes, 1995.

——. *Mi diario VI (1912–1919): Mucho de mi vida y algo de la de otros*. Mexico City: Consejo Nacional para la Cultura y las Artes, 1995.

García Canclini, Néstor. *Transforming Modernity: Popular Culture in Mexico*. Translated by Lidia Lozano. Austin: University of Texas Press, 1993.

Garciadiego Dantan, Javier. *Rudos contra científicos: La Universidad Nacional durante la Revolución mexicana*. Mexico City: Colegio de México Centro de

Estudios Históricos; Universidad Nacional Autónoma de México Centro de Estudios sobre la Universidad, 1996.

Garcia Naranjo, Nemesio. *Memorias de Nemesio García Naranjo, segundo tomo, Recuerdos del Colegio Civil.* Monterrey: Imprenta "El Porvenir," n.d.

———. *Memorias de Nemesio García Naranjo, tercer tomo, La vieja Escuela de Jurisprudencia.* Monterrey: Imprenta "El Porvenir," n.d.

García Neria, Alejandro. "Las tribulaciones de un editor: Relato, aunque apócrifo, muy bien documentado." *Empresa y cultura en tinta y papel (1800–1860),* edited by Miguel Angel Castro, 79–96. Mexico City: Instituto Mora–Universidad Nacional Autónoma de Mexico, 2001.

García Peña, Ana Lidia. "El divorcio de Laura Mantecón y Manuel González, 1885–1886: La infidelidad masculina y el adulterio femenino." *Cuidado con el Corazón: Los usos amorosos en el México moderno,* edited by José Joaquín Blanco et al., 43–56. Mexico City: Instituto Nacional de Antropología e Historia, 1995.

———. *El fracaso del amor: Género e individualismo en el siglo XIX mexicano.* Mexico City: Colegio de México–Universidad Autónoma del Estado de México, 2006.

Garner, Paul. *Porfirio Díaz, Profiles in Power.* New York: Longman, 2001.

Gay, Peter. *The Cultivation of Hatred: The Bourgeois Experience, Victoria to Freud.* New York: Norton, 1993.

———. *Schnitzler's Century: The Making of Middle-Class Culture, 1815–1914.* New York: Norton, 2001.

Gayol, Sandra. "'Honor Moderno': The Significance of Honor in Fin-de-Siècle Argentina." *Hispanic American Historical Review* 84, no. 3 (2004), 475–98.

———. *Honor y duelo en la Argentina Moderna.* Buenos Aires: Siglo Veintiuno, 2008.

———. *Sociabilidad en Buenos Aires: Hombres, Honor y Cafés, 1862–1910.* Buenos Aires: Signo, 2000.

Geertz, Clifford. *The Interpretation of Cultures: Selected Essays.* New York: Basic Books, 1973.

Gilmore, David, ed. *Honor and Shame and the Unity of the Mediterranean.* Washington: American Anthropological Association, 1987.

———. "Introduction: The Shame of Dishonor." *Honor and Shame and the Unity of the Mediterranean,* edited by David Gilmore. Washington: American Anthropological Association, 1987.

———. *Manhood in the Making: Cultural Concepts of Masculinity.* New Haven: Yale University Press, 1990.

Giron Barthe, Nicole. "El entorno editorial de los grandes empresarios culturales: Impresores chicos y no tan chicos en la ciudad de México." *Empresa y cultura en tinta y papel (1800–1860),* edited by Miguel Angel Castro, 51–64. Mexico City: Instituto Mora–Universidad Nacional Autónoma de Mexico, 2001.

Gluck, Mary. *Popular Bohemia: Modernism and Urban Culture in Nineteenth-Century Paris.* Cambridge, Mass.: Harvard University Press, 2005.

Goldstein, Robert Justin. *The War for the Public Mind: Political Censorship in Nineteenth-Century Europe*. Westport, Conn.: Praeger, 2000.

Gómez Carrillo, Enrique. *Treinta años de mi vida*. Guatemala: José de Pineda Ibarra, 1974.

Gómez-Quiñones, Juan. *Porfirio Díaz, los intelectuales y la Revolución*. Mexico City: Ediciones El Caballito, 1981.

González Bernaldo, Pilar. "Sociabilidad, espacio urbano y politización en la ciudad de Buenos Aires (1820–1852)." *La vida política en la Argentina del siglo XIX : Armas, votos y voces*, edited by Hilda Sábato and Alberto Rodolfo Lettieri, 191–204. Buenos Aires: Fondo de Cultura Económica, 2003.

González Cárdenas, Octavio. *Los cien años de la Escuela Nacional Preparatoria*. Mexico City: Porrúa, 1972.

González de la Rocha, Mercedes. *The Resources of Poverty: Women and Survival in a Mexican City*. Cambridge: Blackwell, 1994.

Gonzalez Navarro, Moisés. *Historia moderna de México*. Volume 4: *El Porfiriato: La vida social*. Mexico City: Hermes, 1957.

González Rodríguez, Sergio. *Los Bajos Fondos*. Mexico City: Cal y Arena, 1990.

González y González, Luis. *La ronda de las generaciones: Los protagonistas de la Reforma y la Revolución Mexicana*. Mexico City: SEP Cultura, 1984.

Goodman, Dena. "Public Sphere and Private Life: Toward a Synthesis of Current Historiographical Approaches to the Old Regime." *History and Theory* 31, no. 1 (1992), 1–20.

Graham, Laura. "A Public Sphere in Amazonia? The Depersonalized Collaborative Construction of Discourse in Xavante." *American Ethnologist* 20, no. 4 (1993), 717–41.

Granados, Luis Fernando. "Calpultin decimonónicos: Aspectos nahuas de la cultura política de la ciudad de México." *Actores, espacios y debates en la historia de la esfera pública en la ciudad de México*, edited by Pablo Piccato and Cristina Sacristán, 41–66. Mexico City: Instituto Mora, 2005.

Granillo Vázquez, Liliana. "De las tertulias al sindicato: Infancia y adolescencia de las editoras mexicanas del siglo XIX." *Empresa y cultura en tinta y papel (1800–1860)*, edited by Miguel Angel Castro, 65–77. Mexico City: Instituto Mora–Universidad Nacional Autónoma de Mexico, 2001.

Gran jurado nacional: A consecuencia de la muerte del Sr. D. José C. Verástegui, y en virtud de los rumores que aseguraban que esa lamentable desgracia había acaecido en un duelo . . . en el cual sucumbió el Sr. Verástegui, y en cuyo suceso habían figurado como autores el occiso, y el Sr. D. Francisco Romero : como testigos del Sr. Verástegui, los Sres. Apolinar Castillo y Ramón Prida . . . Mexico City: Cámara de Diputados, 1895.

Green, James. "Journalists and Dandies: Bohemian Male Sociability in Rio de Janeiro, 1870–1920." Paper presented at the Centenary of the Famous 41, Sexuality and Social Control in Latin America, 1901, Tulane University, New Orleans, November 2001.

Greenberg, James. *Blood Ties: Life and Violence in Rural Mexico*. Tucson: University of Arizona Press, 1989.

Greenberg, Kenneth S. *Honor and Slavery: Lies, Duels, Noses, Masks, Dressing as a Woman, Gifts, Strangers, Death, Humanitarianism, Slave Rebellions, The Pro-Slavery Argument, Baseball, Hunting, and Gambling in the Old South.* Princeton: Princeton University Press, 1996.

Guardino, Peter. "Barbarism or Republican Law?: Guerrero's Peasants and National Politics, 1820–1846." *Hispanic American Historical Review* 75, no. 2 (1995), 185–213.

Guedea, Virginia. "El pueblo de México y la política capitalina, 1808 y 1912." *Mexican Studies/Estudios Mexicanos* 10, no. 1 (1994), 27–61.

Guerra, François-Xavier. "De la política antigua a la política moderna: La revolución de la soberanía." *Los espacios públicos en Iberoamérica: Ambigüedades y problemas, Siglos XVIII–XIX*, edited by Francois-Xavier Guerra and Annick Lempérière. Mexico City: Fondo de Cultura Económica, 1999.

———. *México: Del Antiguo Régimen a la Revolución.* Mexico City: Fondo de Cultura Económica, 1988.

———. *Modernidad e independencias: Ensayos sobre las revoluciones hispánicas.* 3d ed. Colecciones MAPFRE 1492. Mexico City: Editorial MAPFRE; Fondo de Cultura Económica, 2000.

Guerra, François-Xavier, and Annick Lempérière. "Introducción." *Los espacios públicos en Iberoamérica: Ambigüedades y problemas, Siglos XVIII–XIX*, edited by Francois-Xavier Guerra and Annick Lempérière, 5–21. Mexico City: Fondo de Cultura Económica, 1999.

Guerra, François-Xavier, and Annick Lempérière. *Los espacios públicos en Iberoamérica: Ambigüedades y problemas, Siglos XVIII–XIX.* Mexico City: Fondo de Cultura Económica, 1999.

Guibovich, Pedro Manuel. "The Inquisition and Book Censorship in the Peruvian Viceroyalty (1570–1754)." Ph.D. diss., Columbia University, 2001.

Gutiérrez, Ramón A. *When Jesus Came, the Corn Mothers Went Away: Marriage, Sexuality, and Power in New Mexico, 1500–1846.* Stanford: Stanford University Press, 1991.

Gutmann, Matthew. *Changing Men and Masculinities in Latin America.* Durham: Duke University Press, 2003.

———. "Los hijos de Lewis: La sensibilidad antropológica y el caso de los pobres machos." *Alteridades* 4, no. 7 (1994), 9–19.

———. *The Meaning of Macho: Being a Man in Mexico City.* Berkeley: University of California Press, 1996.

Guzmán, Martín Luis. *El Aguila y la Serpiente.* Mexico City: Fondo de Cultura Económica, 1984.

Haber, Stephen. *Industria y Subdesarrollo: La Industrialización de México, 1890–1940.* Mexico City: Alianza Editorial, 1992.

Habermas, Jürgen. "Further Reflections on the Public Sphere." *Habermas and the Public Sphere*, edited by Craig Calhoun, 421–61. Cambridge, Mass.: MIT Press, 1997.

———. "Prefacio a la nueva edición alemana de 1990." *Historia y crítica de la opinión pública: La transformación estructural de la vida pública*, edited by Jürgen Habermas, 1–36. Barcelona: Gustavo Gili, 1994.

———. *The Structural Transformation of the Public Sphere: An Inquiry into a Category of Bourgeois Society*. Cambridge, Mass.: MIT Press, 1991.

———. *The Theory of Communicative Action*. Volume 1: *Reason and the Rationalization of Society*. Translated by Thomas McCarthy. Boston: Beacon Press, 1984.

Hale, Charles A. *Emilio Rabasa and the Survival of Porfirian Liberalism: The Man, His Career, and His Ideas*. Stanford: Stanford University Press, 2008.

———. *Justo Sierra: Un liberal del porfiriato*. Mexico City: Fondo de Cultura Económica, 1997.

———. "The Liberal Impulse: Daniel Cosio Villegas and the Historia moderna de Mexico." *Hispanic American Historical Review* 54, no. 3 (1974), 479–98.

———. *Mexican Liberalism in the Age of Mora*. New Haven: Yale University Press, 1968.

———. *The Transformation of Liberalism in Late Nineteenth-Century Mexico*. Princeton: Princeton University Press, 1989.

Harris, William V. *Restraining Rage: The Ideology of Anger Control in Classical Antiquity*. Cambridge, Mass.: Harvard University Press, 2001.

Heraud y Clavijo de Soria, Antonio. *Manual de Esgrima y duelo*. Mexico City and París: Vda. de Bouret, 1912.

Herf, Jeffrey. *Reactionary Modernism: Technology, Culture and Politics in Weimar and the Third Reich*. New York: Cambridge University Press, 1984.

Hermann, Brigitte. *Con Maximiliano en México: Diario del príncipe*. Mexico City: Fondo de Cultura Económica, 1989.

Herrejón Peredo, Carlos. "Sermones y discursos del primer imperio." *Construcción de la legitimidad política en México*, edited by Carlos Illades, Brian Connaughton, and Sonia Pérez Toledo, 153–67. Zamora: Colegio de Michoacán, 1999.

Herzfeld, Michael. "Honour and Shame: Problems in the Comparative Analysis of Moral Systems." *Man*, n.s. 15, no. 2 (1980), 339–51.

———. *The Poetics of Manhood: Contest and Identity in a Cretan Mountain Village*. Princeton: Princeton University Press, 1985.

Herzog, Tamar. *Upholding Justice: Society, State, and the Penal System in Quito (1650–1750)*. Ann Arbor: University of Michigan Press, 2004.

Hobbes, Thomas. *Leviathan: Authoritative Text: Backgrounds, Interpretations*. Edited by Richard E. Flathman and David Johnston. New York: W. W. Norton, 1997.

Hourcade, Celestino. *La machicuepa de la deuda inglesa y recuerdos de ultratumba por . . . sastre y profesor de corte premiado en Paris y en otras capitales del Viejo y Nuevo mundo; condecorado con medallas de oro y sus correspondientes diplomas honoríficos*. Mexico City: Ireneo Paz, 1884.

Hughes, Steven. "Men of Steel: Dueling, Honor, and Politics in Liberal Italy."

Men and Violence: Gender, Honor, and Rituals in Modern Europe and America, edited by Pieter Spierenburg. Columbus: Ohio State University Press, 1998.

Hurd, Madeleine. *Public Spheres, Public Mores, and Democracy: Hamburg and Stockholm, 1870–1914*. Ann Arbor: University of Michigan Press, 2000.

Hutton, Patrick H. *History as an Art of Memory*. Hanover, N.H.: University Press of New England, 1993.

Illades, Carlos. *Hacia la república del trabajo: La organización artesanal en la ciudad de México, 1853–1876*. Mexico City: Colegio de México–Universidad Autónoma Metropolitana, 1996.

——. "La apropiación del 'pueblo' por el romanticismo social mexicano." Paper presented at the Seminario internacional "Identidad, memoria, política y narración," March 2001.

——. *Nación, sociedad y utopía en el romanticismo mexicano*. Mexico City: Consejo Nacional para la Cultura y las Artes, 2005.

Infante Vargas, Lucrecia. "De lectoras y redactoras: Las publicaciones femeninas en México durante el siglo XIX." *La república de las letras: Asomos a la cultura escrita del México decimonónico*, edited by Belem Clark de Lara and Elisa Speckman, 183–94. Mexico City: Universidad Nacional Autónoma de México, 2005.

Informes producidos ante el Supremo Tribunal de Justicia por los licenciados Manuel Pámanes y Francisco Llamas Noriega defensores de los señores Francisco y José Luis del Hoyo y Enrique Aubert en la apelación interpuesta contra el auto en que se les declaró bien presos por los delitos de injurias y difamación: Pedimento fiscal y sentencia revocatoria del auto apelado. Zacatecas: La Rosa, 1895.

INEGI (Instituto Nacional de Estadística Geografía e Informática), and Instituto Nacional de Antropología e Historia. *Estadisticas históricas de México*. Mexico City: Instituto Nacional de Estadística Geografía e Informática—Instituto Nacional de Antropologia e Historia, 1985.

Irwin, Robert McKee. *Mexican Masculinities*. Minneapolis: University of Minnesota Press, 2003.

Irwin, Robert McKee, Ed McCaughan, and Michelle Nasser. *The Famous 41: Sexuality and Social Control in Mexico, c. 1901*. Basingstoke: Palgrave Macmillan, 2003.

Irwin, Terence. *Plato's Ethics*. Oxford: Oxford University Press, 1995.

Izábal, Antonio T., and Francisco F. Izábal. *Algunas observaciones a la defensa que leyó ante el congreso erigido en gran jurado el Lic. D. Eustaquio Buelna acusado de responsabilidad por. . . .* Culiacan: Tip. de Tomas Ramires, 1881.

Jaksic, Ivan. *The Political Power of the Word: Press and Oratory in Nineteenth-Century Latin America*. London: Institute of Latin American Studies, 2002.

Jiménez Huerta, Mariano. *Derecho penal mexicano: Parte especial, tomo III, La tutela penal del honor y de la libertad*. Mexico City: Antigua Librería de Robredo, 1968.

Johnson, Eric A. *Urbanization and Crime: Germany 1871–1914*. New York: Cambridge University Press, 1995.

Johnson, Lyman L., and Sonya Lipsett-Rivera, eds. *The Faces of Honor, Sex, Shame, and Violence in Colonial Latin America*. Albuquerque: University of New Mexico Press, 1998.

——. "Introduction." *The Faces of Honor, Sex, Shame, and Violence in Colonial Latin America*, edited by Lyman L. Johnson and Sonya Lipsett-Rivera. Albuquerque: University of New Mexico Press, 1998.

Joseph, Gilbert M., and Daniel Nugent, eds. *Everyday Forms of State Formation: Revolution and the Negotiation of Rule in Modern Mexico*. Durham: Duke University Press, 1994.

Kaiser, David Aram. *Romanticism, Aesthetics, and Nationalism*. Cambridge Studies in Romanticism. Cambridge: Cambridge University Press, 1999.

Katz, Friedrich. *La guerra secreta en México*. Translated by Isabel Fraire and José Luis Hoyo. Mexico City: Era, 1985.

——. "The Liberal Republic and the Porfiriato, 1867–1910." *Mexico since Independence*, edited by Leslie Bethell. New York: Cambridge University Press, 1991.

Kelley, James R. "Professionalism in the Porfirian Army Officer Corps." Ph.D. diss., Tulane University, 1970.

Kennedy, James Gettier. *Herbert Spencer*. Boston: Twayne Publishers, 1978.

Kershaw, Ian. *Popular Opinion and Political Dissent in the Third Reich, Bavaria 1933–1945*. Oxford: Oxford University Press, 1983.

Kiernan, V. G. *The Duel in European History: Honour and the Reign of Aristocracy*. Oxford: Oxford University Press, 1988.

Knight, Alan. "Weapons and Arches in the Mexican Revolutionary Landscape." *Everyday Forms of State Formation: Revolution and the Negotiation of Rule in Modern Mexico*, edited by Gilbert Joseph and Daniel Nugent. Durham: Duke University Press, 1994.

——. "The Working Class and the Mexican Revolution, c. 1900–1920." *Journal of Latin American Studies* 16 (1984), 51–79.

Krauze, Enrique. *Porfirio Díaz, místico de la autoridad*. Mexico City: Fondo de Cultura Económica, 1987.

Laingui, André, and Arlette Lebigne. *Histoire du droit pénal, II, La procédure criminelle*. Paris: Cujas, 1979.

Landes, Joan B. *Women and the Public Sphere in the Age of the French Revolution*. Ithaca: Cornell University Press, 1988.

Lanzilli, Pietro. *Código del honor para América Latina*. Guatemala: Tipografía Nacional, 1898.

Lara y Pardo, Luis. *La prostitución en México: Estudios de Higiene Social*. Mexico City: Bouret, 1908.

Larralde, Joaquín, and Anselmo Alfaro. *Código del duelo, traducido, arreglado y anotado por*. Mexico City: Imprenta y Litografía de Ireneo Paz, 1886.

Lauderdale-Graham, Sandra. "Making the Private Public: A Brazilian Perspective." *Journal of Women's History* 15, no. 1 (2003), 28–42.

Lear, John. *Workers, Neighbors, and Citizens: The Revolution in Mexico City.* Lincoln: University of Nebraska Press, 2001.

Le Bon, Gustave. *Psichologie des foules.* 27th ed. Paris: Alcan, 1921.

Ledré, Charles. *La Presse à l'Assaut de la Monarchie, 1815–1848.* Paris: Armand Colin, 1960.

Legislación mexicana; o, colección completa de las disposiciones legislativas expedidas desde la independencia de la república . . . ordenada por los lics. Manuel Dublán y Jose María Lozano . . . [1687–1902]. Edited by Jose María Lozano and Manuel Dublán. Mexico City: Impr. de E. Dublán, 1876–1904.

Lemoine Villicaña, Ernesto. *La Escuela Nacional Preparatoria en el período de Gabino Barreda, 1867–1878: Estudio histórico, documentos.* Mexico City: Universidad Nacional Autónoma de México, 1970.

Lempérière, Annick. "Reflexiones sobre la terminología política del liberalismo." *Construcción de la legitimidad política en México*, edited by Carlos Illades, Brian Connaughton, and Sonia Pérez Toledo, 35–56. Zamora: Colegio de Michoacán, 1999.

Lewis, Oscar. *The Children of Sánchez: Autobiography of a Mexican Family.* New York: Random House, 1961.

Liddle, A. Mark. "State, Masculinities and Law: Some Comments on Gender and English State-Formation." *British Journal of Criminology* 36, no. 3 (1996), 361–80.

Limantour, José Yves. *Apuntes sobre mi vida pública (1982–1911).* Mexico City: Porrúa, 1965.

Lira, Andrés. *Comunidades indígenas frente a la ciudad de México: Tenochtitlan y Tlatelolco, sus pueblos y barrios, 1812–1919.* Mexico City: Colegio de México, 1995.

Lombardo de Ruiz, Irma. *De la opinión a la noticia: El surgimiento de los géneros informativos en México.* Mexico City: Kiosko, 1992.

Lomnitz, Claudio. *Deep Mexico, Silent Mexico: An Anthropology of Nationalism.* Minneapolis: University of Minnesota Press, 2001.

——. "Ritual, Rumor and Corruption in the Constitution of Polity in Modern Mexico." *Journal of Latin American Anthropology* 1, no. 1 (1995), 20–47.

Lomnitz, Larissa. *Networks and Marginality: Life in a Mexican Shantytown.* New York: Academic Press, 1977.

Lomnitz, Larissa A., and Lizaur Marisol Pérez. *Una familia de la élite mexicana: Parentesco, clase y cultura 1820–1980.* Mexico City: Alianza, 1993.

López Portillo y Rojas, José. *Elevación y caída de Porfirio Díaz.* Mexico City: Porrúa, 1975.

——. *Fuertes y débiles.* Mexico City: Porrúa, 1982.

——. *Rosario la de Acuña.* Mexico City: Librería Española, 1920.

Macedo, Miguel. *La criminalidad en México: Medios de combatirla.* Mexico City: Secretaría de Fomento, 1897.

MacGregor Campuzano, Javier. "Dos casos de persecución periodística durante el porfiriato." *Estudios de Historia Moderna y Contemporánea de México* 15 (1993), 65–84.

Macías González, Victor Manuel. "El caso de una beldad asesina: La construcción narrativa, los concursos de belleza y el mito nacional posrevolucionario (1921–1931)." *Historia y Grafía*, no. 13 (1999), 113–54.

——. "The Mexican Aristocracy and Porfirio Díaz." Ph.D. diss., Texas Christian University, 1999.

Mallon, Florencia. *Peasant and Nation: The Making of Postcolonial Mexico and Peru*. Princeton: Princeton University Press, 1995.

Manero, Vicente. *Apuntes sobre el duelo por . . . miembro de la asociación de periodistas*. Mexico City: Tipografía de Benito Nichols, 1884.

Maravall, José Antonio. *Poder, honor y élites en el siglo XVII*. Madrid: Siglo Veintiuno, 1979.

Marichal, Carlos. "El manejo de la deuda pública y la crisis financiera de 1884–1885." *Los negocios y las ganancias de la colonia al México moderno*, edited by Leonor Ludlow and J. Silva R. Mexico City: Instituto Mora, 1993.

——. "La deuda externa: El manejo coactivo de la política financiera mexicana, 1885–1995." *Consenso y coacción: Estado e instrumentos de control político y social en México y América Latina (siglos XIX y XX)*, edited by Riccardo Forte and Guillermo Guajardo. Mexico City: Colegio de México–El Colegio Mexiquense, 2000.

——. "Las estrategias de la deuda durante el porfiriato: La concesión del empréstito de 1888 y el papel de Banamex como banca de gobierno." *Don Porfirio presidente... nunca omnipotente: Hallazgos, reflexiones y debates. 1876–1911*, edited by Raymond Buve and Romana Falcón. Mexico City: Universidad Iberoamericana, 1998.

Marsiske, Renate. *Movimientos estudiantiles en América Latina: Argentina, Perú, Cuba y México, 1918–1929*. Mexico City: Universidad Nacional Autónoma de México, Coordinación de Humanidades, Centro de Estudios sobre la Universidad, 1989.

Martínez de Castro, Antonio. *Código penal para el Distrito Federal y Territorio de la Baja-California sobre delitos del fuero común y para toda la República Mexicana sobre-delitos contra la Federación [1871]. Edición correcta, sacada de la oficial, precedida de la Exposición de motivos dirigida al Supremo Gobierno por el C. Lic. . . . Presidente de la comisión encargada de formar el Código*. Veracruz and Puebla: La Ilustración, 1891.

——. "Exposición de motivos del código penal." *El código penal mexicano y sus reformas*, edited by Ricardo Rodríguez, 19–120. Mexico City: Herrero Hnos., 1902.

Mateos, Juan A. *¡Los dioses se van! Comedia en tres actos y en prosa*. Mexico City, 1877.

——. *Los dramas de México*. Mexico City: Casa Editorial de J. Vicente Villada, 1887.

Mauss, Marcel. *The Gift: The Form and Reason for Exchange in Archaic Societies*. Translated by W. D. Halls. New York: W. W. Norton, 1990.

Maza, Sarah C. *Private Lives and Public Affairs: The Causes Célèbres of Prerevolutionary France*. Berkeley: University of California Press, 1993.

McAleer, Kevin. *Dueling: The Cult of Honor in Fin-de-Siècle Germany*. Princeton: Princeton University Press, 1994.

McEvoy, Carmen. "'Seríamos excelentes vasallos y nunca ciudadanos': Prensa republicana y cambio social en Lima, 1791–1822." *The Political Power of the Word: Press and Oratory in Nineteenth-Century Latin America*, edited by Ivan Jaksic, 34–63. London: Institute of Latin American Studies, 2002.

McGann, Jerome J. *The Romantic Ideology: A Critical Investigation*. Chicago: University of Chicago Press, 1983.

McLean, Malcom D. *Vida y obra de Guillermo Prieto*. Mexico City: Colegio de México, 1960.

Melton, James Van Horn. *The Rise of the Public in Enlightenment Europe*. New York: Cambridge University Press, 2001.

Mendieta y Nuñez, Lucio. *Historia de la Facultad de Derecho*. Mexico City: Universidad Nacional Autónoma de Mexico, 1975.

Miller, Nicola. *In the Shadow of the State: Intellectuals and the Quest for National Identity in Twentieth-Century Spanish America*. London: Verso, 1999.

Miquel i Verges, J. M. *La independencia mexicana y la prensa insurgente*. Mexico City: Colegio de México, 1941.

Moheno, Querido. *Mis últimos discursos: La caravana pasa . . . (Preliminar), Discursos ante el Congreso Jurídico, defensa de la Sra. Jurado, Defensa de la Sra. Alicia Olvera*. Mexico City: Botas, 1923.

——. *Procesos Célebres: Honorio Rodríguez, discurso de defensa*. Mexico City: Botas, 1928.

——. *Procesos Célebres: Rubin, discurso en defensa de la acusada*. Mexico City: Botas, 1925.

——. *Sobre la brecha*. Mexico City: Botas, 1925.

Moliérac, J. *Iniciación a la abogacía*. Translated by Pablo Macedo. 4th ed. Mexico City: Porrúa, 1997.

Molina Enriquez, Andrés. *Los grandes problemas nacionales (1909) (y otros textos, 1911–1919)*. Mexico City: Ediciones ERA, 1983.

Monsiváis, Carlos. "Del saber compartido en la ciudad indiferente: De grupos y ateneos en el siglo XIX." *La república de las letras: Asomos a la cultura escrita del México decimonónico*, edited by Belem Clark de Lara and Elisa Speckman, 89–106. Mexico City: Universidad Nacional Autónoma de México, 2005.

——. *Las herencias ocultas de la Reforma liberal del siglo XIX*. 2d ed. Mexico City: Random House Mondadori, 2006.

Monterde, Francisco. *Salvador Díaz Mirón: Documentos, Estética*. Mexico City: Universidad Nacional Autónoma de México, 1956.

Mora, José María Luis. *Mora legislador*. Edited by Lillián Briseño Senosiain and Laura Suárez de la Torre. Mexico City: Cámara de Diputados, 1994.

Myers, Jorge. "Las paradojas de la opinión: El discurso político rivadaviano y sus dos polos: El 'gobierno de las luces' y 'la opinión pública, reina del mundo.'" *La vida política en la Argentina del siglo XIX: Armas, votos y voces*, edited by Hilda Sábato and Alberto Rodolfo Lettieri, 75–95. Mexico City: Fondo de Cultura Económica, 2003.

Nathans, Benjamin. "The French Revolution in Review: Habermas's 'Public Sphere' in the Era of the French Revolution." *French Historical Studies* 16, no. 3 (1990), 620–44.

Norris, Christopher. "Deconstructing Genius: Paul de Man and the Critique of Romantic Ideology." *Genius: The History of an Idea*, edited by Penelope Murray, 141–65. Oxford: Basil Blackwell, 1989.

Novo, Salvador. *Viajes y ensayos*. Mexico City: Fondo de Cultura Económica, 1996.

Nye, Robert. "Fencing, the Duel and Republican Manhood in the Third Republic." *Journal of Contemporary History* 25 (1990).

——. *Masculinity and Male Codes of Honor in Modern France*. New York: Oxford University Press, 1993.

Ochoa Campos, Moises. *Reseña histórica del periodismo mexicano*. Mexico City: Porrúa, 1968.

O'Gorman, Edmundo. "Justo Sierra y los orígenes de la universidad de México, 1910." *Seis estudios históricos de tema mexicano*, 147–201. Xalapa: Universidad Veracruzana, 1960.

——. *México: El trauma de su historia: Ducit amor patriae*. Mexico City: Consejo Nacional para la Cultura y las Artes, 1977.

Ortiz Monasterio, José. "La literatura como profesión en México en el siglo XIX." *Memoria Coloquio Internacional Manuel Gutiérrez Nájera y la cultura de su tiempo*, edited by Yolanda Bache Cortés et al., 325–33. México: Universidad Nacional Autónoma de México, 1996.

Othón, Manuel José. *Epistolario*. Edited by Rafael Montejano y Aguiñaga. Mexico City: Universidad Nacional Autónoma de México, 1999.

Ozouf, Mona. "Espíritu público." *Diccionario de la Revolución francesa*, edited by François Furet and Mona Ozouf, 567–75. Madrid: Alianza, 1989.

——. "Le concept d'opinion publique au XVIIIème siècle." *L'Homme régénéré: Essais sur la Révolution française*. Paris: Gallimard, 1989.

Ozuna Castañeda, Mariana, and María Esther Guzmán Gutiérrez. "Para que todos lean: *La Sociedad Pública de Lectura* de *El Pensador Mexicano*." *Empresa y cultura en tinta y papel (1800–1860)*, edited by Miguel Angel Castro, 273–84. Mexico City: Instituto Mora–Universidad Nacional Autónoma de México, 2001.

Padilla Arroyo, Antonio. "Los jurados populares en la administración de justicia en México en el siglo XIX." *Secuencia: Revista de historia y ciencias sociales*, no. 47 (2000), 137–70.

Palti, Elías José. "Introducción." *La política del disenso: La "polémica en torno al monarquismo" (México, 1848–1850) . . . y las aporías del liberalismo*, edited by Elías José Palti, 7–58. Mexico City: Fondo de Cultura Económica, 1998.

——. *La invención de una legitimidad: Razón y retórica en el pensamiento mexicano del siglo XIX (Un estudio sobre las formas del discurso político)*. Mexico City: Fondo de Cultura Económica, 2005.

——. "La Sociedad Filarmónica del Pito: Opera, prensa y política en la República Restaurada (México, 1867–1976)." *Historia Mexicana* 52, no. 4 (2003).

——. "La transformación del liberalismo mexicano en el siglo XIX: Del modelo jurídico de la opinión pública al modelo estratégico de la sociedad civil." *Actores, espacios y debates en la historia de la esfera pública en la ciudad de México*, edited by Pablo Piccato and Cristina Sacristán, 67–95. Mexico City: Instituto Mora, 2005.

——. "Las polémicas en el liberalismo argentino: Sobre virtud, republicanismo y lenguaje." *El republicanismo en hispanoamérica: Ensayos de historia intelectual y política*, edited by José Antonio Aguilar and Rafael Rojas, 167–209. Mexico City: Centro de Investigación y Docencia; Fondo de Cultura Económica, 2002.

——. "Los diarios y el sistema político mexicano en tiempos de la República Restaurada (1867–1876)." *Construcciones impresas: Panfletos, diarios y revistas en la formación de los estados nacionales en América Latina, 1820–1920*, edited by Paula Alonso, 167–81. Buenos Aires: Fondo de Cultura Económica, 2004.

——. "Recent Studies on the Emergence of a Public Sphere in Latin America." *Latin American Research Review* 36, no. 2 (2001).

Pani, Erika. *Para mexicanizar el Segundo Imperio: El imaginario político de los imperialistas*. Mexico City: Colegio de México, Centro de Estudios Históricos, Instituto de Investigaciones Dr. José María Luis Mora, 2001.

Pani, Erika, and Alicia Castro de Salmerón, eds. *Conceptualizar lo que se ve: François-Xavier Guerra, historiador: homenaje*. Mexico City: Instituto Mora, 2004.

Parker, Adelaide, and E. Allison Peers. "The Vogue of Victor Hugo in Spain." *Modern Language Review* 27, no. 1 (1932), 36–57.

Parker, David S. "Law, Honor, and Impunity in Spanish America: The Debate over Dueling, 1870–1920." *Law and History Review* 19, no. 2 (2001).

Parra, Porfirio. *Pacotillas, Novela mexicana*. Barcelona: Salvat, 1900.

Pasquel, Leonardo. *Salvador Díaz Mirón*. Xalapa: Universidad Veracruzana, 1984.

Paz, Ireneo. *Algunas campañas*. Mexico: Fondo de Cultura Económica, 1997.

Paz, Octavio. *Generaciones y semblanzas: Dominio mexicano*. Volume 2: *Letras mexicanas*. Mexico City: Fondo de Cultura Económica, 1994.

Peñafiel, Antonio. *Anuario estadístico de la República Mexicana 1898*. Mexico City: Secretaría de Fomento, 1899.

Pérez Martínez, Herón. "Hacia una tópica del discurso político mexicano del siglo XIX." *Construcción de la legitimidad política en México*, edited by Carlos Illades, Brian Connaughton, and Sonia Pérez Toledo, 351–83. Zamora: Colegio de Michoacán, 1999.

Pérez-Siller, Javier. *L'hégémonie des financiers au Mexique sous le Porfiriat: L'autre dictature*. Paris: L'Harmattan–Instituto de Ciencias Sociales y Humanidades, BUAP, 2003.

Peristiany, John G. "Introduction." *Honour and Shame: The Values of Mediterranean Society*, edited by John G. Peristiany, 9–18. Chicago: University of Chicago Press, 1966.

Perrot, Michelle, ed. *A History of Private Life IV: From the Fires of Revolution to the Great War*. Translated by Arthur Goldhammer. Cambridge, Mass.: Harvard University Press, 1990.

Perry, Laurens Ballard. *Juárez and Díaz: Machine Politics in Mexico*. DeKalb: Northern Illinois University Press, 1978.

Picard, Roger. *Le romantisme social*. Paris: Brentanos, 1944.

Piccato, Pablo. *City of Suspects: Crime in Mexico City, 1900–1931*. Durham: Duke University Press, 2001.

———. *Congreso y Revolución: El parlamentarismo en la XXVI Legislatura*. Mexico City: Instituto Nacional de Estudios Históricos de la Revolución Mexicana, 1992.

———. "El parlamentarismo desde la Cámara de Diputados, 1912–1921: Entre la opinión pública y los grupos de choque." *El poder legislativo en las décadas revolucionarias*, edited by Pablo Piccato. Mexico City: Instituto Nacional de Estudios Históricos de la Revolución Mexicana, 1997.

———. "'El Paso de Venus por el disco del Sol': Criminality and Alcoholism in the Late Porfiriato." *Mexican Studies / Estudios Mexicanos* 11, no. 2 (1995), 203–41.

———, ed. *El Poder Legislativo en las décadas revolucionarias, 1908–1934*. Mexico City: Instituto de Investigaciones Legislativas–Cámara de Diputados, 1997.

———. "'El populacho' y la opinión pública: Debates y motines sobre la deuda inglesa en 1884." *Poder y legitimidad en México, Siglo XIX: Instituciones y cultura política*, edited by Brian Connaughton, 531–79. Mexico City: Universidad Autónoma Metropolitana–Miguel Angel Porrúa, 2003.

———. "The Girl Who Killed a Senator: Femininity and the Public Sphere in Post-Revolutionary Mexico." *True Stories of Crime in Modern Mexico*, edited by Robert Buffington and Pablo Piccato. Albuquerque: University of New Mexico Press, 2009.

———. "Interpretations of Sexuality in Mexico City Prisons: A Critical Version of Roumagnac." *The Famous 41: Sexuality and Social Control in Mexico, 1901*, edited by Robert McKee Irwin, Edward J. McCaughan, and Michelle Rocío Nasser, 251–66. New York: Palgrave, 2003.

———. "Jurados de imprenta en México: El honor en la construcción de la esfera pública." *Construcciones impresas: Panfletos, diarios y revistas en la formación de los estados nacionales en América Latina, 1820–1920*, edited by Paula Alonso, 139–65. Buenos Aires: Fondo de Cultura Económica, 2004.

———. "La construcción de una perspectiva científica: Miradas porfirianas a la criminalidad." *Historia Mexicana* 187, no. 1 (1997), 133–81.

———. "Politics and the Technology of Honor: Dueling in Turn-of-the-Century Mexico." *Journal of Social History* 33, no. 2 (1999), 331–54.

———. "Public Sphere in Latin America: A Map of the Historiography." *Social History* (forthcoming).

———. "'Such a Strong Need': Sexuality and Violence in Belem Prison." *Gender, Sexuality, and Power in Latin America since Independence*, edited by Katherine

Elaine Bliss and William E. French, 87–108. Wilmington, Del.: Scholarly Resources, 2006.

Pi Suñer, Antonia. "Prólogo." *Guillermo Prieto, Obras completas.* Mexico City: Consejo Nacional para la Cultura y las Artes, 1994.

Pitt-Rivers, Julian A. "Honour and Social Status." *Honour and Shame: The Values of Mediterranean Society,* edited by Jean Peristiany. London: Weidenfeld and Nicolson, 1965.

Pizarro Suárez, Nicolás. *Obras.* Mexico City: Universidad Nacional Autónoma de México, 2005.

Ponce, Fernando. *El alcoholismo en México.* Mexico City: Antigua Imprenta de Murguía, 1911.

Porter, Roy, and Mikuláš Teich. *Romanticism in National Context.* New York: Cambridge University Press, 1988.

Portes, Alejandro. "Social Capital: Its Origins and Applications in Modern Sociology." *Annual Review of Sociology* 24 (1998), 1–24.

Potts, Juan. *Testimonio de las diligencias practicadas con motivo de la querella que por el delito de difamación, entabló ante el juzgado 10 del ramo criminal de esta ciudad contra el Sr. D. Federico Ferrugia Manly.* Mexico City: Díaz de León, 1875.

Praz, Mario. *La carne, la muerte y el diablo en la literatura romántica.* Translated by Rubén Mettini. Barcelona: El Acantilado, 1999.

Premo, Bianca. *Children of the Father King: Youth, Authority, and Legal Minority in Colonial Lima.* Chapel Hill: University of North Carolina Press, 2005.

Prida, Ramon. *¡De la dictadura a la anarquía! Apuntes para la historia política de México durante los últimos cuarenta y tres años (1871–1913).* 2d ed. Mexico City: Botas, 1958.

Prieto, Guillermo. *Obras completas.* Edited by Boris Rosen Jélomer. Mexico City: Consejo Nacional para la Cultura y las Artes, 1994.

Prieur, Annick. "Domination and Desire: Male Homosexuality and the Construction of Masculinity in Mexico." *Machos, Mistresses, Madonnas: Contesting the Power of Latin American Gender Imagery,* edited by Marit Melhuus and Kristi Anne Stolen, 83–107. London: Verso, 1996.

——. *Mema's House, Mexico City: On Transvestites, Queens, and Machos.* Chicago: University of Chicago Press, 1998.

Primer Congreso Internacional de Retórica en México. Mexico City: Universidad Nacional Autónoma de Mexico, 1998.

Puga y Acal, Manuel. *Los poetas mexicanos contemporáneos (Ensayos críticos de Brummel) Salvador Díaz Mirón, Manuel Gutiérrez Nájera, Juan de Dios Peza.* Mexico City: Universidad Nacional Autónoma de Mexico, 1999.

Putnam, Robert D. *Bowling Alone: The Collapse and Revival of American Community.* New York: Simon and Schuster, 2000.

Quevedo y Zubieta, Salvador. *El General González y su gobierno en México: Anticipo a la historia.* Mexico City: Patoni, 1884.

Quintiliano, Marco Fabio. *Institución oratoria.* Translated by Ignacio Rodríguez and Pedro Sandier. Mexico City: Consejo Nacional para la Cultura y las Artes, 1999.

Quirarte, Vicente. "Zarco, Poe y Baudelaire: La invención del dandy." *Tipos y caracteres: La prensa mexicana (1822–1855), Memoria del coloquio celebrado los días 23, 24 y 25 septiembre de 1998*, edited by Miguel Angel Castro, 238–44. Mexico City: Instituto de Investigaciones Bibliográficas, Seminario de Bibliografía Mexicana del Siglo XIX, Universidad Nacional Autónoma de México, 2001.

Rabasa, Emilio. *El cuarto poder, original de Sancho Polo (seud.)*. Mexico City: O. R. Spíndola, 1888.

——. *La constitución y la dictadura: Estudios sobre la organización política de México*. Mexico City: Tip. de Revista de Revistas, 1912.

——. "La difamación y las personas morales: Opinión del Lic. Emilio Rabasa." *Revista de Legislación y Jurisprudencia* (1895), 25–33.

——. "Moneda falsa." *El cuarto poder y Moneda falsa*, edited by Antonio Acevedo Escobedo, 183–398. Mexico City: Porrúa, 1948.

Rama, Angel. *The Lettered City*. Translated by John Charles Chasteen. Durham: Duke University Press, 1996.

Ramírez, Ignacio. *México en pos de la libertad*. Mexico City: Partido Revolucionario Institucional, 1986.

Ramírez Plancarte, Francisco. *La ciudad de México durante la revolución constitucionalista*. Mexico City: Botas, 1941.

Ramírez Rancaño, Mario. "Estadísticas electorales: Presidenciales." *Revista Mexicana de Sociología* 39, no. 1 (1977).

Ramirez Rodríguez, Armando. *Chin-chin el teporocho*. 8th ed. Mexico City: Organización Editorial Novaro, 1972.

Ramos, Carmen, et al. *Presencia y transparencia: La mujer en la historia de México*. Mexico City: Colegio de México, 1987.

Ramos, Juan Pedro. *Los delitos contra el honor*. Buenos Aires: J. Menéndez, 1939.

Real Academia Española. *Diccionario de la lengua castellana por la Real Academia Española*. 12th ed. Madrid: Imprenta de D. Gregorio Hernando, 1884.

——. *Diccionario de la lengua castellana por la Real Academia Española*. 11th ed. Madrid: Imprenta de Don Manuel Rivadeneyra, 1869.

——. *Diccionario de la lengua castellana, en que se explica el verdadero sentido de las voces, su naturaleza y calidad, con las phrases o modos de hablar, los proverbios o refranes, y otras cosas convenientes al uso de la lengua [. . .]. Tomo quarto*. Madrid: Imprenta de la Real Academia Española, por los herederos de Francisco del Hierro, 1734.

——. *Diccionario de la lengua castellana, en que se explica el verdadero sentido de las voces, su naturaleza y calidad, con las phrases o modos de hablar, los proverbios o refranes, y otras cosas convenientes al uso de la lengua [. . .]. Tomo quinto*. Madrid: Imprenta de la Real Academia Española, por los herederos de Francisco del Hierro, 1737.

Recopilación de leyes, decretos, bandos, reglamentos, circulares y providencias de los supremos poderes y otras autoridades de la República Mexicana. Edited by Basilio José Arrillaga. Mexico City: Imprenta Vicente García Torres, 1861.

Reddy, William M. *The Visible Code: Honor and Sentiment in Postrevolutionary France, 1814–1848.* Berkeley: University of California Press, 1997.

Reglamento de libertad de imprenta de la Republica Mejicana o colección de las leyes vigentes en ella hasta el presente año sobre esta materia. Mexico City: Imprenta de Galván, 1833.

Reglamento general de la libertad de imprenta con sus adiciones y notas. Mexico City: Imp. de Gobierno, 1828.

Reyes Heroles, Jesús. *El liberalismo mexicano.* Mexico City: Universidad Nacional Autónoma de Mexico, 1957.

Reyes, Rodolfo. *De mi vida: Memorias Políticas,* Volume 1 *(1899–1913).* Madrid: Biblioteca Nueva, 1929.

Reyna, María del Carmen. *La prensa censurada durante el siglo XIX.* 2d ed. Colección Divulgación. Mexico City: Instituto Nacional de Antropología e Historia, 1995.

Río, Emilio del, José Antonio Caballero López, and Tomás Albaladejo Mayordomo. *Quintiliano y la formación del orador político.* Logroño, Spain: Gobierno de La Rioja, Instituto de Estudios Riojanos; Calahorra, Spain: Ayuntamiento de Calahorra, 1998.

Riva Palacio, Vicente, et al. *México a través de los siglos: Historia general y completa del desenvolvimiento social, político, religioso, militar, artístico, científico y literario de México desde la antigüedad más remota hasta la época actual.* 16 vols. Mexico City: Editorial Cumbre, 1987.

Rivera, Agustín. *Tratado breve de delitos y penas segun el derecho civil escrito en 1859 por el Dr D. . . . siendo catedrático del mismo derecho en el Seminario Conciliar de Guadalajara.* San Juan de los Lagos: Tip. de José Martín, 1873.

Rocha, Sóstenes. *El General Sóstenes Rocha ante el jurado popular con motivo del duelo verificado entre los señores Verástegui y Romero.* Mexico City: Tipografía Hospicio de Pobres, 1895.

——. *Enquiridión para los sargentos y cabos del ejército mexicano.* Mexico City: Imprenta El Combate, 1887.

Rodríguez Castillo, Rosa María. "Delitos de injuria y difamación." Licenciatura thesis, Universidad Nacional Autónoma de México, 1949.

Rodríguez González, Yliana. "Heriberto Frías." *La república de las letras: Asomos a la cultura escrita del México decimonónico,* edited by Belem Clark de Lara and Elisa Speckman, 521–30. Mexico City: Universidad Nacional Autónoma de México, 2005.

Rodríguez, Juan María. *El duelo: Estudio filosófico moral por . . . Catedrático de la Escuela de Medicina de México; Miembro de la Sociedad Católica, de la Sociedad Médica, de la Sociedad Familiar de Medicina, de la de Historia Natural, Profesor de Química en la E.N. Prepar.* Mexico City: Tipografía Mexicana, 1869.

Rodríguez Kuri, Ariel. "Desabasto de agua y violencia política: El motín del 30 de noviembre de 1922 en la ciudad de México." Unpublished manuscript, 2000.

——. "El discurso del miedo: El Imparcial y Francisco I. Madero." *Historia Mexicana* 40, no. 4 (1991).

——. "Gobierno local y empresas de servicios: La experiencia de la ciudad de México en el porfiriato." *Ferrocarriles y obras públicas*, edited by Sandra Kuntz Ficker and Priscilla Connolly. Mexico City: Instituto Mora, 1999.

——. *La experiencia olvidada: El ayuntamiento de México: política y administración, 1876–1912*. Mexico City: Colegio de México, 1996.

Roeder, Ralph. *Hacia el México moderno: Porfirio Díaz*. Mexico City: Fondo de Cultura Económica, 1996.

——. *Juárez y su México*. Mexico City: Fondo de Cultura Económica, 1972.

Rohlfes, Laurence John. "Police and Penal Correction in Mexico City, 1876–1911: A Study of Order and Progress in Porfirian Mexico." Ph.D. diss., Tulane University, 1983.

Rojas, Rafael. *La escritura de la independencia: El surgimiento de la opinión pública en México*. Mexico City: Taurus–Centro de Investigación y Docencia Económicas, 2003.

Romero Vargas, Ignacio. *Libertad de imprenta: Discursos pronunciados por el senador . . . en las sesiones de los días 24, 25 y 27 de Noviembre de 1882 y voto particular del mismo como miembro de la comisión de puntos constitucionales.* Mexico City: Tipografía de Filomeno Mata, 1882.

Roumagnac, Carlos. *Los criminales en México: Ensayo de psicología criminal; Seguido de dos casos de hermafrodismo observado por los señores doctores Ricardo Egea . . . Ignacio Ocampo.* 2d ed. Mexico City: Tip. El Fénix, 1912.

Rousseau, Jean-Jacques. *The Basic Political Writings*. Translated by Donald A. Cress. Indianapolis: Hackett, 1987.

——. *Lettre à d'Alembert*. Paris: Flammarion, 1967.

Rudé, George. *The Crowd in the French Revolution*. Oxford: Clarendon Press, 1959.

Ruiz Castaneda, Maria del Carmen. "La universidad libre (1875), Antecedente de la Universidad Autónoma." *Deslindes*, no. 110 (1979), 1–35.

Ruiz Castañeda, María del Carmen, and Sergio Márquez Acevedo. *Diccionario de seudónimos, anagramas, iniciales y otros alias*. Mexico City: Universidad Nacional Autónoma de México, 2000.

Ruiz Castañeda, María del Carmen, Luis Reed Torres, Enrique Cordero y Torres, and Salvador Novo. *El periodismo en México: 450 años de historia*. Mexico City: Editorial Tradición, 1974.

Sabato, Hilda. "Introducción." *Ciudadanía política y formación de las naciones: Perspectivas históricas de América Latina*, edited by Hilda Sabato. Mexico City: Fondo de Cultura Económica, 1999.

——. *The Many and the Few: Political Participation in Republican Buenos Aires*. Stanford: Stanford University Press, 2001.

Saborit, Antonio. *Los doblados de Tomóchic*. Mexico City: Cal y Arena, 1994.

Salado Alvarez, Victoriano. *Memorias: Tiempo Viejo, Tiempo Nuevo*. Mexico City: Porrúa, 1985.

Sánchez Santos, Trinidad. *El Alcoholismo en la República Mexicana: Discurso pronunciado en la sesión solemne que celebraron las Sociedades Científicas y Literarias de la Nación, el día 5 de junio de 1896 y en el salón de sesiones de la Cámara de Diputados*. Mexico City: Imprenta del Sagrado Corazón de Jesus, 1897.

Sarlo, Beatriz. *Una modernidad periférica: Buenos Aires 1920–1930*. Buenos Aires: Nueva Visión, 1988.

Schell, William, Jr. *Integral Outsiders: The American Colony in Mexico City, 1876–1911*. Wilmington, Del.: Scholarly Resources, 2001.

Sedgwick, Eve Kosofsky. *Between Men: English Literature and Male Homosocial Desire*. New York: Columbia University Press, 1985.

Seed, Patricia. *To Love, Honor and Obey in Colonial Mexico: Conflicts over Marriage Choice, 1574–1821*. Stanford: Stanford University Press, 1988.

Seigel, Jerrold. *Bohemian Paris: Culture, Politics, and the Boundaries of Bourgeois Life, 1830–1930*. New York: Viking, 1986.

Sennett, Richard. *The Fall of Public Man*. New York: Knopf, 1977.

Seoane Couceiro, María Cruz. *Oratoria y periodismo en la España del siglo XIX*. Madrid: Fundación Juan March, 1977.

Serra Rojas, Andrés. *Antología de la elocuencia mexicana, 1900–1950*. Mexico City: Porrúa, 1950.

Serra Rojas, Andrés, and Emilio Rabasa. *Antología de Emilio Rabasa*. Mexico City: Ediciones Oasis, 1969.

Sesto, Julio. *El Mexico de Porfirio Díaz (hombres y cosas): Estudios sobre el desenvolvimiento general de la República Mexicana después de diez años de permanencia en ella; Observaciones hechas en el terreno oficial y en el particular*. 2d ed. Valencia: Sempere y Compañía, 1910.

Shelley, Percy Bysshe. *A Defence of Poetry*. Indianapolis: Bobbs-Merrill, 1904.

Shubert, Adrizan. "Spain." *The War for the Public Mind: Political Censorship in Nineteenth-Century Europe*, ed. Robert Justin Goldstein, 175–209. Westport, Conn.: Praeger, 2000.

Sierra, Justo. *Ensayos y textos elementales de historia*. Volume 9: *Obras Completas*. Mexico City: Universidad Nacional Autónoma de México, 1977.

——. *Evolución política del pueblo mexicano*. Edited by Edmundo O'Gorman. Mexico City: Universidad Nacional Autónoma de México, 1977.

——. *Juárez: Su obra y su tiempo*. Volume 13: *Obras Completas*. Mexico City: Universidad Nacional Autónoma de México, 1984.

——. "La novela de un colegial." *Cuentos románticos*, 27–83. Mexico City: Factoria Ediciones, 1999.

——. *Obras completas*. Mexico City: Universidad Nacional Autónoma de Mexico, 1948.

Sierra, Justo, and Charles A. Hale. *Justo Sierra, un liberal del Porfiriato*. Vida y pensamiento de Mexico. Mexico City: Fondo de Cultura Económica, 1997.

Sierra Velenzuela, Enrique de. *Duelos, rieptos y desafíos: Ensayo filosófico-jurídico sobre el duelo*. Madrid: Tip. Conde, 1878.

Sobrino F., María de los Angeles. "José Guadalupe Posada y Francisco Montes de Oca: La ilustración al servicio del periodismo independiente, popular y comercial." *Posada y la prensa ilustrada: Signos de modernización y resistencias*, 73–88. Mexico City: Instituto Nacional de Bellas Artes, 1996.

Socolow, Susan Migden. *The Women of Colonial Latin America*. Cambridge: Cambridge University Press, 2000.

Sodi, Demetrio. *El Jurado en México: Estudios sobre el jurado popular*. Mexico City: Imprenta de la Secretaría de Fomento, 1909.

Sommer, Doris. *Foundational Fictions: The National Romances of Latin America*. Berkeley: University of California Press, 1991.

Soto Estrada, Miguel. *La conspiración monárquica en México, 1845–1846*. Mexico City: EOSA, 1988.

Speckman, Elisa. *Crimen y Castigo: Legislación Penal, Interpretaciones de la Criminalidad y Administración de Justicia (Ciudad de México, 1872–1910)*. Mexico: Colegio de México, 2002.

———. "El último duelo: Opiniones y resoluciones en torno al lance Verástegui–Romero (Ciudad de México, 1894)." *Instituciones y formas de control social en América Latina, 1840–1940*, edited by Maria Silvia di Liscia and Ernesto Bohoslavsky, 167–97. Buenos Aires: Pegaso—UNG Sarmiento—Universidad Nacional de la Pampa, 2005.

———. "Las posibles lecturas de La República de las Letras: Escritores, visiones y lectores." *La república de las letras: Asomos a la cultura escrita del México decimonónico*, edited by Belem Clark de Lara and Elisa Speckman, 47–72. Mexico City: Universidad Nacional Autónoma de México, 2005.

———. "Los jueces, el honor y la muerte: Un análisis de la justicia (Ciudad de México, 1871–1931)." *Historia Mexicana* 55, no. 4 (2006), 1411–66.

Spencer, Herbert. *Essays: Moral, Political and Aesthetic*. New York: D. Appleton, 1888.

———. *The Principles of Ethics*. New York: D. Appleton, 1892.

Spierenburg, Pieter, ed. *Men and Violence: Gender, Honor, and Rituals in Modern Europe and America*. Columbus: Ohio State University Press, 1998.

Stern, Steve. *The Secret History of Gender: Women, Men, and Power in Late Colonial Mexico*. Chapel Hill: University of North Carolina Press, 1995.

Stewart, Frank Henderson. *Honor*. Chicago: University of Chicago Press, 1994.

Swearingen, C. Jan. *Rhetoric and Irony: Western Literacy and Western Lies*. New York: Oxford University Press, 1991.

Tablada, José Juan. *Las sombras largas*. Mexico City: Consejo Nacional para la Cultura y las Artes, 1993.

Tanck de Estrada, Dorothy. "La educación en la ciudad de México en la primera mitad del siglo XIX." *Ensayos sobre la Ciudad de México*. Volume 6: *El Corazón de una nación independiente*, edited by Isabel Tovar de Arechederra and Magdalena Mas, 123–36. Mexico City: Universidad Iberoamericana–Consejo Nacional para la Cultura y las Artes, 1994.

Tannenbaum, Frank. *Mexico, the Struggle for Peace and Bread*. Westport, Conn.: Greenwood Press, 1984.

Taussig, Michael T. *Shamanism, Colonialism, and the Wild Man: A Study in Terror and Healing.* Chicago: University of Chicago Press, 1986.

Taylor, William B. *Drinking, Homicide, and Rebellion in Colonial Mexican Villages.* Stanford: Stanford University Press, 1989.

——. *Magistrates of the Sacred: Priests and Parishioners in Eighteenth-Century Mexico.* Stanford: Stanford University Press, 1996.

Téllez, Luis. "Préstamos externos, primas de riesgo y hechos políticos: La experiencia mexicana en el siglo XIX." *Historia económica de México,* edited by Enrique Cárdenas. Mexico City: Fondo de Cultura Económica, 1989.

Tena Ramírez, Felipe. *Leyes fundamentales de México.* 15th ed. Mexico City: Porrúa, 1989.

Tenenbaum, Barbara A. "Streetwise History: The Paseo de la Reforma and the Porfirian State, 1876–1910." *Rituals of Rule, Rituals of Resistance: Public Celebrations and Popular Culture in Mexico,* edited by William H. Beezley et al., 127–50. Wilmington, Del.: Scholarly Resources, 1994.

Tenorio-Trillo, Mauricio. "1910 Mexico City: Space and Nation in the City of the Centenario." *Journal of Latin American Studies* 28 (1996), 75–104.

——. *Mexico at the World's Fairs: Crafting a Modern Nation.* Berkeley: University of California Press, 1996.

Thompson, E. P. "The Moral Economy of the English Crowd in the Eighteenth Century." *Past and Present* 50 (1971), 76–136.

Todorov, Tzvetan. *Benjamin Constant: La passion démocratique.* Paris: Hachette Littératures, 1997.

Toussaint Alcaraz, Florence. *Escenario de la prensa en el Porfiriato.* Mexico City: Fundación Manuel Buendía–Universidad de Colima, 1989.

Tovar, Antonio. *Código nacional mexicano del duelo por el coronel de caballería.* Mexico City: Ireneo Paz, 1891.

Twinam, Ann. "The Negotiation of Honor: Elites, Sexuality, and Illegitimacy in Eighteenth-Century Spanish America." *The Faces of Honor, Sex, Shame, and Violence in Colonial Latin America,* edited by Lyman L. Johnson and Sonya Lipsett-Rivera. Albuquerque: University of New Mexico Press, 1998.

——. *Public Lives, Private Secrets: Gender, Honor, Sexuality, and Illegitimacy in Colonial Spanish America.* Stanford: Stanford University Press, 1999.

Universidad Nacional de México, Facultad de Derecho y Ciencias Sociales. *Plan de estudios, Programas y reglamento de reconocimientos.* Mexico City: Talleres Gráficos de la Nación, 1929.

Uribe Uran, Victor. *Honorable Lives: Lawyers, Family, and Politics in Colombia, 1780–1850.* Pittsburgh: University of Pittsburgh Press, 2000.

Urueta, Margarita. *Jesús Urueta: La historia de un gran desamor. Prol. Baltasar Dromundo.* Mexico City: Stylo, 1964.

Valadés, José C. *El porfirismo: Historia de un Régimen. tomo I, El crecimiento.* Mexico City: Editorial Patria, 1948.

Vallejo, César. *El romanticismo en la poesía castellana.* Lima: J. Mejía Baca y P. L. Villanueva, 1954.

Vanderwood, Paul J. *Disorder and Progress: Bandits, Police, and Mexican Development.* 2d ed. Wilmington, Del.: Scholarly Resources, 1992.

Van Young, Eric. "Islands in the Storm: Quiet Cities and Violent Countrysides in the Mexican Independence Era." *Past and Present,* no. 118 (1988), 130–55.

——. *The Other Rebellion: Popular Violence, Ideology, and the Mexican Struggle for Independence, 1810–1821.* Stanford: Stanford University Press, 2001.

Vaughan, Mary Kay. "Modernizing Patriarchy: State Policies, Rural Households, and Women in Mexico, 1930–1940." *Hidden Histories of Gender and the State in Latin America,* edited by Elizabeth Dore and Maxine Molyneux, 194–215. Durham: Duke University Press, 2000.

——. *The State, Education, and Social Class in Mexico, 1880–1928.* DeKalb: Northern Illinois University Press, 1982.

Vázquez Mantecón, Carmen. *Santa Anna y la encrucijada del Estado: La dictadura (1853–1855).* Mexico City: Fondo de Cultura Económica.

——. "El honor y la virtud en un discurso político del México independiente." *Históricas* 52 (1998), 12–26.

——. *La palabra del poder: Vida pública de José María Tornel, 1795–1853.* Mexico City: Universidad Nacional Autónoma de México, 1997.

Vega, Francisco de P. *Dos palabras en respuesta al autor del libelo infamatorio publicado en esta ciudad bajo el rubro de "Manifestación que hace al público el C. tesorero general del estado Atanasio Aragon, sobre las calumnias que le ha inferido el contador C. . . . ."* Mazatlán: Retes, 1868.

Velada fúnebre organizada por la Escuela N. de Jurisprudencia de Mejico, en honor de Don Emilio Castelar y verificada en la Cámara de Diputados la noche del 17 de junio de 1899, bajo la presidencia del Primer Magistrado de la República. Mexico City: Imp. J. de Elizalde, 1900.

Velada que a la memoria del Sr. Gral. Carlos Pacheco y el primer aniversario de su muerte celebró la sociedad que lleva su nombre en la cámara de diputados la noche del 26 de septiembre de 1892. Discursos y poesías pronunciadas en dicha solemnidad. Mexico City: Tipografía de la Secretaría de Fomento, 1892.

Velázquez Albo, María de Lourdes. *Origen y desarrollo del plan de estudios del bachillerato universitario 1867–1990.* Mexico City: Universidad Nacional Autónoma de Mexico, 1992.

Verdo, Geneviève. "El escándalo de la risa, o las paradojas de la opinión en el período de la emancipación rioplatense." *Los espacios públicos en Iberoamérica: Ambigüedades y problemas, Siglos XVIII–XIX,* edited by François-Xavier Guerra and Annick Lempérière, 225–40. Mexico City: FCE-CEMCA, 1998.

Wacquant, Loic. "Toward a Reflexive Sociology: A Workshop with Pierre Bourdieu." *Sociological Theory* 7, no. 1 (1989), 26–63.

Walkowitz, Judith. *City of Dreadful Delight: Narratives of Sexual Danger in Late-Victorian London.* Chicago: University of Chicago Press, 1992.

Warner, Michael. *The Letters of the Republic: Publication and the Public Sphere in Eighteenth-Century America.* Cambridge, Mass.: Harvard University Press, 1990.

——. *Publics and Counterpublics*. Cambridge, Mass.: MIT Press, 2002.

Warren, Richard. "'El congreso por su gusto hizo de un Justo un ladrón': el cobre, 'la chusma' y el centralismo, 1837." *Instituciones y ciudad: Ocho estudios históricos sobre la ciudad de México*, edited by Carlos Illades and Ariel Rodríguez Kuri, 61–79. Mexico City: FP-SONES-Uníos, 2000.

Weiner, Richard. *Race, Nation, and Market: Economic Culture in Porfirian Mexico*. Tucson: University of Arizona Press, 2004.

Weldon, Jeffrey A. "El presidente como legislador, 1917–1930." *El Poder Legislativo en las décadas revolucionarias, 1908–1934*, edited by Pablo Piccato, 117–46. Mexico City: Instituto de Investigaciones Legislativas–Cámara de Diputados, 1997.

Wikan, Unni. "Shame and Honour: A Contestable Pair." *Man*, n.s., 19, no. 4 (1984), 635–52.

Wilson, Elizabeth. *Bohemians: The Glamorous Outcasts*. London: I. B. Tauris, 2000.

Wyatt-Brown, Bertram. *The Shaping of Southern Culture: Honor, Grace, and War, 1760s–1890s*. Chapel Hill: University of North Carolina Press, 2001.

——. *Southern Honor: Ethics and Behavior in the Old South*. New York: Oxford University Press, 1982.

Yañez, Agustín. *Don Justo Sierra, su vida, sus ideas y su obra*. 2d ed. Mexico City: Universidad Nacional Autónoma de Mexico, 1962.

——. "Don Justo Sierra: Su vida, sus ideas y sus obras." *Obras Completas del Maestro Justo Sierra*, edited by Agustín Yáñez, 7–218. Mexico City: Universidad Nacional Autónoma de México, 1948.

Yankelevich, Pablo. "En la retaguardia de la Revolución Mexicana: Propaganda y propagandistas mexicanos en América Latina, 1914–1920." *Mexican Studies/Estudios Mexicanos* 15, no. 1 (1999).

Zarco, Francisco. *Escritos literarios; selección, prólogo y notas de René Avilés*. 2d ed. Mexico City: Porrúa, 1980.

Zavala Abascal, Antonio. *La cámara de diputados, sus recintos desde la insurgencia hasta nuestros días*. Mexico City: N.p., 1968.

Zedner, Lucia. *Women, Crime, and Custody in Victorian England*. Oxford: Clarendon Press, 1991.

Zehr, Howard. *Crime and the Development of Modern Society: Patterns of Criminality in Nineteenth Century Germany and France*. London: Croom Helm, 1976.

INDEX

Page numbers in italics refer to illustrations.

46; nation identified with, 127; as newspaper readers, 69; offensive language against, 205; oratory of, 116, 146, 295n58; prostitution and, 79, 92, 208, 216, 217, 287n64, 322n82; refusal of, to appear before judicial authorities, 214; reputation of, 190, 192, 193, 200, 206, 226–28, 245, 327–28n26; seclusion of, 265n16; self-restraint of, as victims of insultos and difamación, 202; sexual behavior of, 12, 79, 145–46, 217, 267n29; as students, 146; students' liaisons with, 138, 145–46, 303n53; violent confrontations between, 212, 216–18; visibility of, in public sphere, 14, 15, 18, 79, 214, 225–28, 265n16; as writers, 79–80

Zarco, Francisco, 11, 40, 69, 87, 107, 161, 173
Zempoalteca, Francisco, 164
Zenteno, Cástulo, 84, 288n75
Zola, Émile, 205, 320n53
Zomoza, Miguel, 59
Zuñiga, Eleodoro, 205

PABLO PICCATO is an associate professor in the Department of History at Columbia University. He is the author of various books, including *City of Suspects: Crime in Mexico City, 1900–1931* (Duke, 2001) and, with Ricardo Pérez Montfort and Alberto del Castillo, *Hábitos, normas y escándalo: prensa, criminalidad y drogas durante el porfiriato tardío* (1997).

Made in the USA
Las Vegas, NV
24 January 2024

84804387R00233